Hello! 365 Soy-Free Recipes

(Soy-Free Recipes - Volume 1)

Best Heart Healthy Cookbook Ever For Beginners

Ms. Hanna

Ms. Healthy

Content

Introduction

***

Hi all,

Welcome to MrandMsCooking.com—a website created by a community of cooking enthusiasts with the goal of providing books for novice cooks featuring the best recipes, at the most affordable prices, and valuable gifts.

Hats off to you for believing and trying out "Hello! 365 Soy-Free Recipes". The fact that you are reading this now means that you want to live a higher- quality of living and I am so thrilled for you. Living a high-quality life, both in our mind and in our body, is very beneficial for us. As an introduction, I will share with you my personal journey and the ways I attained my present quality life. Before, I was the healthy consumer I am know, I had many bad habits when it came to my choices. I did not know about the importance of taking care of myself so I ate a lot of junk foods, did not go to bed at a good time, and would sleep in late. Back then, the benefits of being healthy and the harmful effects of my unhealthy lifestyle did not occur to me, thus I remained in my bad habits for quite some time. As a result, I gained a lot of weight and my facial skin was suffering a lot too. That time in my life was very stressful and the more stressful I felt, the more I junk food I would consume. My stress eating was uncontrollable and started gaining a lot of weight. People started commenting on my appearance, and I started researching how to lose weight. Various ways are offered online, and I have learned about many of them. A lot of methods I attempted but I was not able to sustain them due to the lack of comfort they offered. But luckily, I was able to discover something that did fit me. Consuming healthy food and practicing a healthy lifestyle is something that I can do easily and efficiently every day. Until now, even after I attained my desired weight, I continue to consume healthy food because it keeps me beautiful, my body functions better, and I am more positive and have more fun. I know that it is really challenging to those of you who are used to enjoying fried/fatty foods to start consuming healthier ones. But, now is the best time to improve yourself and cleanse your body, mind and spirit. If you can regulate what you eat and what you do, then this will not be hard for you. Sleep on time and rise early in the morning, consume a heavy and healthy breakfast, and you will realize that you will have all the energy and efficiency you need to last the whole day.

Whenever you will hear the words "healthy lifestyle", your initial thought will always be about food. This is correct because as the saying goes, we are what we eat. Just by looking at someone's form and stance, I can already say if he is living a healthy life. To sustain our lives, we consume food. With this, we just need to feed on the freshest and highest quality of food to make our bodies healthy and beautiful. Most of my friends have this notion that healthy foods are not appetizing. They are also not aware that healthy foods and healthy eating are easy to do. Healthy foods are everywhere (eggs, milk, fish, meat, nuts, etc.) and are excellent for our health. Those that were processed, especially in fast food chains, are not good for our health.

So, can we process food and still retain its healthiness? Can we still produce delectable and flavorful food? These articles which I've prepared for you will provide you the answers.

My vision is to impart my knowledge about healthy living on as many people as I can reach. I have written these articles on various subjects for you to be able to select which one fits you best.

- Diabetes Diet
- Clean Eating
- ...

Every subject will contain a different style of eating; however, each one has the common goal of teaching you to eat healthy. There is a variety of styles to meet each individual's personal needs just take a look and pick the that fits you and be on your way to a higher-quality of life. Moreover, I am confident that these compilations of complete recipes will help you practice your chosen style without difficulty.

My overview is already lengthy but I would like to share more things with you later about eating healthy. For this segment, I will not be talking about the negative effects of consuming unhealthy foods because that piece is already vastly available online. Also, my expectation is that since you are reading this piece, I am assuming that you've got all the essential information as to why it is essential to live a healthy lifestyle.

Below is the recipe for a happy and healthy life:

Happy Life = Healthy Mind + Healthy Body

I really appreciate that you have selected "Hello! 365 Soy-Free Recipes" and for reading to the end. I anticipate that this book shall give you the source of strength during the times that you are really exhausted, as well as be your best friend in the comforts of your own home. Make it your model as you head to the kitchen to try one of these new recipes. It would also be great if you can share to me and everyone your personal journey. Send me an e-mail!

List of Abbreviations

C Ms. Mr. King LIST OF ABBREVIATIONS	
tbsp(s).	tablespoon(s)
tsp(s).	teaspoon(s)
c.	cup(s)
oz.	ounce(s)
lb(s).	pound(s)

365 Amazing Soy Free Recipes

***

1. "seder Plate" Salad

"A fresh salad."
Serving: Serves 4–6 | Prep: 20m

Ingredients

- 1/2 cup walnuts
- 1/4 cup neutral vegetable oil, such as grapeseed, divided
- 4 oz. lamb sausage in casing, sliced into 1/4"-thick coins
- 1 tbsp. plus 1 tsp. prepared horseradish
- 2 tbsps. fresh lemon juice
- 2 tsps. honey
- 1/4 tsp. (or more) kosher salt
- 1/8 tsp. (or more) freshly ground black pepper
- 1/2 cup flat-leaf parsley leaves, divided
- 1 romaine heart (about 8 oz.), coarsely chopped
- 1/2 medium apple, such as Honeycrisp, Gala, or Fuji, thinly sliced
- 2 hard-boiled eggs, quartered

Direction

- Preheat an oven to 350°F. On a rimmed baking sheet, toast walnuts till golden brown for 8-10 minutes, tossing once. Cool; chop coarsely.
- Heat 1 tbsp. oil on medium high heat in a medium skillet; cook sausage till brown on both sides for 3-5 minutes, occasionally turning. Put onto a plate. Meanwhile, whisk

1/8 tsp. pepper, 1/4 tsp. salt, honey, lemon juice and horseradish in a medium bowl; in a steady stream, whisk in leftover 3 tbsp. oil slowly. Chop 2 tbsp. parsley coarsely; mix into the dressing. Toss leftover parsley, sausage, apple and romaine in a big serving bowl. Put 2/3 dressing into it; toss till coated. If needed, season with pepper and salt. Top with eggs and walnuts; drizzle leftover dressing. You can make dressing without parsley 3 days ahead, chilled, covered.

Nutrition Information

- Calories: 300
- Total Carbohydrate: 11 g
- Cholesterol: 101 mg
- Total Fat: 25 g
- Fiber: 2 g
- Protein: 9 g
- Sodium: 195 mg
- Saturated Fat: 5 g

2. All-butter Pastry Dough

"A marvelous dish."
Serving: Makes enough for 1 single-crust 9- or 9 1/2-inch tart or pie | Prep: 10m

Ingredients

- 1 1/4 cups all-purpose flour
- 1 stick cold unsalted butter, cut into 1/2-inch cubes
- 1/4 tsp. salt
- 3 to 5 tbsps. ice water

Direction

- With your fingertips/pastry blender or pulse in food processor, blend salt, butter and flour till most of it looks like coarse meal with few roughly pea-sized butter lumps in a bowl.
- Evenly drizzle 3 tbsp. ice water on mixture; pulse/gently mix with a fork till incorporated.

- Squeeze small handful; add 1/2 tbsp. more ice water at a time, pulsing/mixing till incorporated then test if it won't hold together. Don't overwork it; it'll be tough.
- Turn dough onto lightly floured surface; divide to 4 portions. Smear each portion 1-2 times in forward motion to distribute fat with heel of hand. Bring dough together with pastry scraper (optional); press into ball. Flatten to 5-in. disk; chill till firm, wrapped in plastic wrap, for 1 hour.
- You can chill dough for 3 days.

Nutrition Information

- Calories: 1378
- Total Carbohydrate: 119 g
- Cholesterol: 243 mg
- Total Fat: 93 g
- Fiber: 4 g
- Protein: 17 g
- Sodium: 599 mg
- Saturated Fat: 58 g

---

3. Aloo Gobhi Stuffing

"I love this cauliflower and potato recipe!"
Serving: Makes 8 to 10 side-dish servings | Prep: 1h

Ingredients

- 1 stick (1/2 cup) unsalted butter plus additional for buttering pan
- 1 (24-inch) baguette, cut into 3/4-inch cubes (8 cups)
- 3 medium onions, coarsely chopped
- 3 medium carrots, cut into 1/4-inch dice
- 3 celery ribs, cut into 1/4-inch dice
- 1 1/2 lb russet (baking) potatoes, peeled and cut into 1/2-inch dice
- 1 (2-lb) head cauliflower, trimmed and cut into 1/2-inch-wide florets and stem pieces
- 2 1/2 tsps. curry powder (preferably Madras)
- 1 1/2 tsps. sea salt
- 1 tsp. black pepper
- 1 tsp. cumin seeds

- 1/4 tsp. cayenne
- 1 1/2 cups reduced-sodium chicken broth (12 fl oz)
- 1 1/2 cups unsalted roasted cashews (7 oz)

Direction

- In lower and upper oven thirds, put oven racks; preheat the oven to 350°F. Butter the 13x9-in. shallow 3-qt. baking dish.
- Spread bread cubes in 2 big shallow baking pans in 1 layer; bake for 20-25 minutes till dry, switching pan positions halfway through baking oven. Remove from oven.
- Put oven temperature on 450°F.
- Cut 1 stick of butter to pieces; heat till foam subsides in 12-in. deep nonstick skillet on medium heat. Add potatoes, celery, carrots and onions; cook for 8 minutes till veggies are soft, occasionally mixing. Add cauliflower; cook for 8 minutes till cauliflower is crisp tender, mixing. Mix in cayenne, cumin, salt, pepper and curry powder; cook for 2 minutes, mixing. Put into big bowl; toss with bread cubes. Add 1 cup cashews and broth; toss till coated.
- In baking dish, spread stuffing; tightly cover, buttered side down, with buttered foil. Bake in upper oven third for 20 minutes till heated through. Remove foil; sprinkle leftover 1/2 cup cashews. Bake for 10 minutes till top is browned.
- You can assemble, not bake, stuffing 1 day ahead, covered, chilled. Before baking, bring to room temperature.

Nutrition Information

- Calories: 470
- Total Carbohydrate: 55 g
- Cholesterol: 31 mg
- Total Fat: 24 g
- Fiber: 8 g
- Protein: 14 g
- Sodium: 756 mg
- Saturated Fat: 10 g

4. Apricot Caramel Sauce

"You can make this in under 1 hour."
Serving: Makes about 5 cups

Ingredients

- 1 cup sugar
- 4 cups water
- 1 cup firmly packed dried apricots (about 6 oz.)
- 2 tsps. vanilla

Direction

- Cook sugar in a 3-qt. capacity dry heavy saucepan on medium heat, mixing with fork till melted then swirling pan, till sugar gets golden caramel. Take off heat. Add 3 cups water carefully down pan's side; it'll steam and bubble up. Put pan on heat; simmer, mixing, till caramel dissolves.
- Add apricots; simmer, covered, for 10 minutes till soft. Cool it for 10 minutes. Puree with vanilla and leftover 1 cup water till very smooth in a blender. You can make sauce 3 days ahead, covered, chilled; to warm, reheat sauce.

Nutrition Information

- Calories: 121
- Total Carbohydrate: 31 g
- Total Fat: 0 g
- Fiber: 1 g
- Protein: 1 g
- Sodium: 6 mg
- Saturated Fat: 0 g

5. Apricot Pandowdy

""We're leaving the crust whole for a faster and easier version.""
Serving: 6 servings | Prep: 15m

Ingredients

- 1 1/2 lb fresh apricots, quartered lengthwise and pitted
- 1 tbsp. cornstarch
- 1/2 cup plus 1 tbsp. sugar
- 2 tbsps. unsalted butter
- 1 (10-inch) refrigerated pie dough (from a 15-oz package), unrolled
- 1 tbsp. milk

Direction

- Set the oven rack in the middle of the oven. Set the oven to 400°F for preheating.
- Combine the apricots, 1/2 cup of sugar, and cornstarch until well coated.
- Put butter in a 10-inches heavy skillet and heat it over moderate heat until the foam subsides. Mix in the apricot mixture. Bring the mixture to a boil while stirring it often. Spread the mixture immediately into the 9-inches pie plate.
- Fold the pie dough into quarters. Trim 1-inch of the dough from the rounded edge. Unfold the dough, making sure that the trimmed round measures 8-inches in diameter. Top the fruit with the dough. Coat the pastry with milk. Sprinkle it with the remaining tbsp. of sugar.
- Bake it for 20 minutes until the crust is golden and the apricot filling is bubbling. Allow it to cool for 10 minutes before serving.

Nutrition Information

- Calories: 271
- Total Carbohydrate: 52 g
- Cholesterol: 10 mg
- Total Fat: 6 g
- Fiber: 3 g
- Protein: 5 g

- Sodium: 236 mg
- Saturated Fat: 3 g

6. Apricot-blackberry Cobbler

"An easy treat."
Serving: Serves 8

Ingredients

- 2 1/4 to 2 1/2 lbs. apricots (about 18), quartered, pitted
- 2 5- to 6-oz. baskets blackberries
- 1 cup sugar
- 1/4 cup quick-cooking tapioca
- 2 tbsps. (1/4 stick) chilled unsalted butter, diced
- 1 1/2 cups all purpose flour
- 2 tbsps. sugar
- 2 tsps. baking powder
- 1/2 tsp. salt
- 6 tbsps. (3/4 stick) chilled unsalted butter, diced
- 1/2 cup plus 1 tbsp. chilled whipping cream
- Vanilla ice cream or frozen yogurt

Direction

- Fruit: Preheat an oven to 375°F and butter 8x8x2-in. glass baking dish. Gently toss tapioca, sugar, berries and apricots to blend in big bowl; stand, tossing fruit occasionally, for 15 minutes. Put fruit mixture in prepped dish; use butter to dot. Bake for 50 minutes till juices thickly bubble and fruit is tender. Fully cool in dish. You can make it 4 hours ahead; stand in room temperature.
- Biscuit topping: Preheat an oven to 400°F. Whisk salt, baking powder, sugar and flour to blend in medium bowl. Add butter; rub in using fingertips till it looks like coarse meal. Add 1/2 cup cream slowly, mixing with fork till moist clumps form. Gently knead in bowl till dough holds together.
- Roll dough out to 9x6-in. rectangle on lightly floured surface; lengthwise cut dough to 8 3/4-in. wide strips. Put 4 strips in opposing directions, making lattice; firmly press pastry strips ends into fruit. Brush 1 tbsp. cream on dough.
- Bake cobbler for 30 minutes till lattice is golden brown and filling is heated through. Put cobbler into deep bowls and top with ice cream.

Nutrition Information

- Calories: 436
- Total Carbohydrate: 68 g
- Cholesterol: 49 mg
- Total Fat: 18 g
- Fiber: 4 g
- Protein: 5 g
- Sodium: 246 mg
- Saturated Fat: 11 g

7. Apricot-cherry Trifle

"A diet-friendly dessert."
Serving: Makes 4 servings

Ingredients

- 6 ripe apricots, halved and pitted
- 1 tsp. fresh lemon juice
- 2 tbsp. apricot nectar
- 1/2 tsp. vanilla extract
- 1 angel food cake, cut into 1/2-inch slices
- 2 1/2 cups nonfat plain yogurt
- 1 cup bing cherries, halved and pitted

Direction

- In medium saucepan, cook first 4 ingredients on low heat till apricots begin to release juices for 10 minutes. Take off heat; put aside. On waxed paper, lay cake slices; cut 12 cake circles out using standard "rocks" glass. Puree in blender till smooth for 2 minutes when apricots are cool. Cover; refrigerate for 30 minutes. Mix yogurt into apricot mixture. Put few cherry halves on bottom of rock glass. Put 2 tbsp. apricot-yogurt mixture on cherries;

cover with cake slice. Repeat twice. Top with cherries; drizzle yogurt-apricot mixture.

8. Arctic Char Gravlax With White Grapefruit

"To let fish cure, begin this 3 days ahead."
Serving: Makes 8 servings

Ingredients

- 1 2-lb. side of arctic char, skin on, pinbones removed
- 3 tbsps. plus 2 tsps. finely grated white or pink grapefruit zest
- 3 tbsps. kosher salt plus more
- 2 tbsps. muscovado sugar or light brown sugar
- 1 tbsp. granulated sugar
- 1 tbsp. plus 1 tsp. dried whole green peppercorns, crushed
- 1 tbsp. juniper berries, well crushed
- 1/2 cup crème fraîche
- 3 tsps. minced fresh dill, divided
- Crackers or toasts (preferably rye)
- Ingredient info: Juniper berries are sold in the spice section of better supermarkets.

Direction

- Put artic char skin onto big plastic wrap piece, skin side down. In a small bowl, mix crushed juniper berries, 1 tbsp. crushed green peppercorns, both sugars, 3 tbsp. salt and 3 tbsp. grapefruit zest; sprinkle it on fish, evenly spreading, gently pressing so spices adhere. Tightly wrap plastic around fish; wrap with another big plastic sheet. Poke 24 small holes gently through plastic, not the fish, on both fish's sides with tip of sharp knife/thin skewer to let juices escape. On rimmed baking sheet, put fish. Put another rimmed baking sheet over; use 2 15-oz. canned goods to weigh down. Refrigerate, flipping fish after 1 day, for 2 days.

- Remove top baking sheet and canned goods. Unwrap; discard plastic. Keep the cure intact. Rewrap with clean plastic; like before, poke holes in plastic. Put into clean resealable plastic bag and refrigerate with skin side up; chill for 1 day. Scrape off cure gently.
- In a small bowl, whisk leftover 1 tsp. crushed green peppercorns, 2 tsp. dill and crème fraiche; season with salt. On diagonal, slice gravlax thinly; serve on crackers. Put crème fraiche over; garnish with 1 tsp. dill and leftover 2 tsp. grapefruit zest.

9. Ash-roasted Batatas With Lime-cumin Butter

"A tasty recipe."
Serving: Makes 4 servings | Prep: 35m

Ingredients

- 4 medium batatas (about 2 lb total), rinsed and dried
- 1 stick (1/2 cup) unsalted butter, softened
- 1 tbsp. fresh lime juice
- 1 tbsp. chopped fresh flat-leaf parsley
- 2 tsps. cumin seeds, toasted and cooled
- 1/4 tsp. salt
- 1/4 tsp. black pepper
- 12-inch-wide heavy-duty foil; a chimney starter and a charcoal grill (or see cooks' note, below); long metal tongs

Direction

- Tear 4 2-ft. long heavy-duty foil sheets off; stack. Put batatas on top in middle in 1 layer. Fold each foil side over batatas to enclose, working with top foil sheet; flip package quarter turn. Fold over each 2nd foil sheet side to enclose; repeat folding using leftover 2 foil sheets, flipping package quarter turn prior to each layer.
- Open vents on grill's bottom; remove top grill rack and leave the bottom rack in place. In chimney starter, light charcoal; put onto

bottom rack and use tongs to clear space in middle of rack big enough for the foil package. In cleaned space, put package; put lit coals around the package. Don't put coals over or under package.

- Roast batatas, flipping package every 10 minutes, adding charcoal and checking to keep steady heat around package, for 45-50 minutes till an inserted sharp paring knife halfway in batata easily passes through with slight resistance.
- As batatas roast, use a fork to mix pepper, salt, cumin, parsley, lime juice and butter till well combined in small bowl. Carefully unwrap batatas; peel then crosswise cut to 1/2-in. thick slices when cool to handle. Use pepper and salt to season batatas; serve it with lime-cumin butter.
- You can roast batatas instead of grilling, wrapper in 1 foil layer, in center of preheat 400°F oven for 1 1/4-1 1/2 hours.

10. Asparagus And Mushroom Salad With Shaved Parmesan

"Raw asparagus highlights the different flavors in this salad."
Serving: Serves 6

Ingredients

- 1 lb. medium to thick asparagus, trimmed
- 1/2 lb. mushrooms, stems trimmed even with caps
- 4 medium radishes, halved lengthwise and sliced thin crosswise
- 2 tbsps. fresh lemon juice
- 2 tsps. Dijon mustard
- 1/2 tsp. salt, or to taste
- 1/3 cup extra-virgin olive oil
- freshly ground black pepper to taste
- 1 bunch watercress, coarse stems discarded
- a 1/4-lb. piece Parmesan cheese at room temperature

Direction

- Use a sharp knife to diagonally cut the asparagus into very thin slices, transfer into a big bowl. Halve the big mushrooms. Slice mushrooms very thinly and add to the asparagus with radishes. Gently toss the salad.
- Whisk together salt, mustard, and lemon juice in a small bowl. While whisking, add the oil in a stream and whisk until dressing emulsifies. Drizzle dressing over the salad, gently tossing. Grind pepper on top.
- Spread the watercress onto a platter and top with the asparagus salad. Using a vegetable peeler, shave 1/2 - 3/4 of the Parmesan into curls over the salad, reserving leftover Parmesan for another use.

Nutrition Information

- Calories: 209
- Total Carbohydrate: 6 g
- Cholesterol: 13 mg
- Total Fat: 17 g
- Fiber: 2 g
- Protein: 10 g
- Sodium: 397 mg
- Saturated Fat: 5 g

11. Baked Apple, Raisin, And Brown Sugar Dumplings

"A dun dessert dumpling recipe."
Serving: Makes 4 servings | Prep: 30m

Ingredients

- 4 8-oz. Golden Delicious apples, peeled
- 1/2 cup (packed) dark brown sugar
- 1 1/4 tsps. ground cinnamon
- 1/3 cup raisins
- 1 cup chilled heavy whipping cream, divided
- 4 purchased refrigerated uncooked large flaky biscuits (from 16.3-oz. tube), room temperature
- 1 large egg, beaten to blend

Direction

- Preheat an oven to 400°F. Core apples using melon baller; leave bottoms intact. Put in glass pie dish while spacing apart; microwave at 50% power, uncovered, for 10 minutes till tender. To cool, refrigerate for 5 minutes.
- Meanwhile, in small bowl, mix cinnamon and brown sugar. Put 3 tbsp. cinnamon sugar in small saucepan. Add 3 tbsp. heavy cream and raisins; mix till sugar dissolves on low heat. Whisk leftover heavy cream and 3 tbsp. cinnamon sugar to peaks in medium bowl. Refrigerate, covered. On floured surface, roll out every biscuit to thin 8-in. round; brush egg lightly. Put apple in middle of every round; use raisin mixture to fill apples, slightly overfilling. Pull 4 dough sides over apple, from 12, 9, 6 and 3 o'clock positions; twist in middle, creating apple stem shape. Tightly press seams to seal using fingertips. Put dumplings on baking sheet. Brush egg on dumplings; sprinkle leftover cinnamon sugar.
- Bake dumplings for 18 minutes till golden; serve it with cinnamon whipped cream.

Nutrition Information

- Calories: 2113
- Total Carbohydrate: 273 g
- Cholesterol: 142 mg
- Total Fat: 99 g
- Fiber: 13 g
- Protein: 36 g
- Sodium: 2734 mg
- Saturated Fat: 34 g

12. Baked Apples With Cranberries, Raisins, And Apricots

"My favorite!"
Serving: Makes 4 servings | Prep: 25m

Ingredients

- 4 large Golden Delicious apples
- 1/2 cup golden raisins
- 1/2 cup dried cranberries
- 1/3 cup (packed) golden brown sugar
- 1/4 cup chopped dried apricots
- 3/4 tsp. ground allspice, divided
- 1/4 cup (1/2 stick) unsalted butter, melted
- 2 cups sparkling apple-cranberry juice
- 1/4 cup frozen concentrated cranberry juice cocktail, thawed

Direction

- Preheat an oven to 400°F. From apples, remove stems; scoop core of each apple out with melon baller, creating 1-in. wide hollow center yet leaving apple's bottom intact. Around middle of each apple, create 1/8-in. deep cut in skin. Put apples in 8x8x2-in. glass baking dish, hollowed side up.
- In a small bowl, mix 1/2 tsp. allspice, apricots, sugar, cranberries and raisins; pack fruit mixture into the apple's hollows. Sprinkle leftover fruit mixture around the apples in dish. Drizzle butter around apples and in filling in dish. Put cranberry concentrate and sparkling juice in dish; sprinkle dish with leftover 1/4 tsp. allspice. Bake apples, uncovered, basting occasionally with cranberry juice mixture, for 1 hour 10 minutes till tender.
- Put apples in 4 bowls. Put juices from dish in medium saucepan; boil for 4 minutes till thick to coat spoon. Put sauce on apples.

Nutrition Information

- Calories: 453
- Total Carbohydrate: 89 g

- Cholesterol: 31 mg
- Total Fat: 12 g
- Fiber: 9 g
- Protein: 2 g
- Sodium: 16 mg
- Saturated Fat: 7 g

13. Baked Artichokes With Crab And Sourdough Stuffing

"Delightful!"
Serving: Makes 4 servings

Ingredients

- 6 tbsps. (3/4 stick) butter
- 1 cup finely chopped red bell pepper
- 3/4 cup finely chopped onion
- 2 celery stalks, finely chopped
- 8 garlic cloves, minced
- 3 cups fresh breadcrumbs made from crustless sourdough bread
- 8 oz. crabmeat
- 4 large artichokes (each about 1 lb.)

Direction

- Melt butter on medium heat in medium heavy skillet. Add garlic, celery, onion and bell pepper; sauté for 6 minutes till onion is translucent. Put into big bowl; fully cool. Mix in crabmeat and breadcrumbs. Use pepper and salt to season stuffing. You can make it 1 day ahead. Cover; refrigerate.
- Preheat an oven to 375°F. Cut top 1/3 of every artichoke off; discard. Cut stem off. Pull small purple and yellow-tipped leaves off from center. Scoop out fibrous choke using melon baller.
- Pull leaves outward from middle gently till leaves slightly open; pack stuffing between 1st and 2nd center leaf layers and in each artichoke cavity, slightly mounding; put artichokes into 13x9x2-in. baking dish. To reach 3/4-in. up dish's sides, add enough water. Use foil to cover; bake artichokes for 1

hour 15 minutes till outer leaf easily pulls away.

Nutrition Information

- Calories: 632
- Total Carbohydrate: 83 g
- Cholesterol: 101 mg
- Total Fat: 22 g
- Fiber: 14 g
- Protein: 28 g
- Sodium: 1086 mg
- Saturated Fat: 12 g

14. Baked Coconut (cocada De Forno)

"You can prep everything ahead then bake it the day you want to serve it."
Serving: Makes 4 to 6 servings

Ingredients

- 8 tbsps. (1 stick) unsalted butter, at room temperature
- 1/2 cup sugar
- 3 whole eggs
- 1/3 cup coconut milk
- 1/3 cup sweetened condensed milk
- 1 tbsp. Malibu rum
- 1 1/2 cups unsweetened grated coconut
- 2 tbsps. all-purpose flour, sifted
- 1 24-oz. baking dish

Direction

- Preheat an oven to 350°F; use some spray to grease a baking dish lightly.
- Mix sugar and butter for 5 minutes at medium speed till creamy and light in an electric mixer's bowl with paddle attachment. One by one, add eggs; mix. After each addition, scrape bowl's sides.
- Add Malibu, coconut milk and sweetened condensed milk; mix on medium speed for 1 minute till batter is blended well. Add

coconut; mix till all gets incorporated yet looks grainy.

- Use a rubber spatula to fold in flour; spread batter in prepped baking dish. You may keep in, covered with plastic wrap, in the fridge 2 days ahead.
- Bake in oven for 20 minutes till edges set, top looks golden brown and center is slightly jiggly. Remove from oven; rest for 10 minutes.
- Serve this with lemon sorbet scoop.

15. Banana Coconut Muffins

"Moist and easy."
Serving: Makes 8 | Prep: 10m

Ingredients

- 1 1/4 cups all-purpose flour
- 1 tsp. baking powder
- 1/4 tsp. salt
- 2 very ripe bananas, mashed (3/4 cup)
- 1 stick (1/2 cup) unsalted butter, melted
- 2/3 cup sugar
- 1 large egg
- 1/2 tsp. vanilla
- 3/4 cup sweetened flaked coconut
- a muffin tin with 8 (1/2-cup) muffin cups; paper liners

Direction

- Put oven rack in center position; preheat an oven to 375°F. Line liners on muffin cups.
- In a bowl, whisk salt, baking powder and flour. Whisk 1/2 cup coconut, vanilla, egg, sugar, butter and bananas till well combined in a big bowl; fold in flour mixture just till flour is moist.
- Divide batter to lined muffin cups; sprinkle leftover 1/4 cup coconut. Bake for 25 minutes till muffins are golden and puffed. Put muffins onto rack; slightly cool.

Nutrition Information

- Calories: 317

- Total Carbohydrate: 42 g
- Cholesterol: 57 mg
- Total Fat: 15 g
- Fiber: 2 g
- Protein: 4 g
- Sodium: 185 mg
- Saturated Fat: 10 g

16. Banana-stuffed French Toast With Streusel Topping

Serving: Serves 6

Ingredients

- 2 tbsps. plus 1/4 cup (1/2 stick) unsalted butter
- 2 tbsps. plus 1/2 cup sugar
- 2 tbsps. water
- 2 large ripe bananas, peeled, cut into 1/2-inch-thick rounds
- 1 1-lb. unsliced loaf egg bread, ends trimmed, bread cut into 6 slices (each about 1 1/2 inches thick)
- 2 cups milk (do not use low-fat or nonfat)
- 6 large eggs
- 2 1/2 tsps. ground cinnamon
- 1/4 tsp. vanilla extract
- 1 1/2 cups thinly sliced almonds, toasted
- 1/4 cup (packed) golden brown sugar
- 1/4 cup quick-cooking oats
- 2 tbsps. all purpose flour
- Maple syrup

Direction

- Melt 2 tbsp. butter on medium heat in big heavy skillet. Add 2 tbsp. water and 2 tbsp. sugar; mix till sugar dissolves. Keep mixing for 2 minutes till it is foamy. Add bananas; cook, occasionally mixing, for 5 minutes till tender. Put into small bowl; cool. You can make it 4 hours ahead. Cover; chill.
- Preheat an oven to 350°F. Cut 2-in. long slit on 1 side of every bread slice using small sharp

knife, cutting 3/4 way through bread, making pocket that will leave 3 bread sides intact. Evenly divide banana mixture to pockets in bread. Whisk 1/2 cup sugar, 1/2 tsp. cinnamon, vanilla, eggs and milk to blend in a big bowl. Put into big glass baking dish. Put bread in egg mixture; soak, occasionally turning, for 10 minutes.

- In shallow bowl, put almonds. Remove bread carefully from egg mixture; coat both sides in almonds. Put bread on big heavy baking sheet. In medium bowl, mix leftover 2 tsp. cinnamon, flour, oats and brown sugar. Add leftover 1/4 cup butter; rub in with fingertips till moist clumps form. Sprinkle bread with topping.
- Bake French toast for 25 minutes till filling is hot and topping is golden brown. Put toast on plates. Serve with maple syrup while hot.

Nutrition Information

- Calories: 767
- Total Carbohydrate: 93 g
- Cholesterol: 263 mg
- Total Fat: 36 g
- Fiber: 7 g
- Protein: 23 g
- Sodium: 399 mg
- Saturated Fat: 13 g

17. Basic Butter Cookies

"An amazing cookie recipe."
Serving: Makes about 4 dozen cookies

Ingredients

- 2 cups all-purpose flour
- 1/2 tsp. baking powder
- 1/2 tsp. salt
- 1 1/2 sticks (3/4 cup) unsalted butter, softened
- 1 cup sugar
- 1 large egg
- 1/2 tsp. vanilla
- Garnish: coarse or sanding sugar*; or melted chocolate (see cooks' note, below)

Direction

- In a small bowl, whisk salt, baking powder and flour.
- Beat sugar and butter, 6 minutes with handheld mixer, 3 minutes in standing mixer (best with paddle attachment), on medium high speed in an electric mixer's bowl till fluffy and pale; beat in vanilla and egg. Put speed on low. Add flour mixture; mix just till combined.
- Shape dough on plastic wrap sheet to 12-in. 2-in. diameter log. Wrap; roll dough up in plastic wrap. Chill the dough on baking sheet for 4 hours till firm. See note below to roll cookies to balls.
- In lower and upper oven thirds, put oven racks; preheat the oven to 375°F.
- Use a heavy knife to cut enough 1/8-1/4-in. thick slices to fill 2 ungreased big baking sheets, putting slices 1-in. apart; chill leftover log while wrapped in plastic wrap. Sprinkle slices with coarse sugar if garnishing.
- Bake cookies, switching sheets positions halfway through baking, for 12-15 minutes till edges are golden; cool for 3 minutes on sheets. Put onto racks with a metal spatula; fully cool. With leftover dough, make more cookies on the cooled baking sheets.
- You can chill dough log for 5 days or freeze for 1 month, wrapped in double plastic wrap layer. Thaw dough in fridge just till you can slice it if frozen.
- Instead of shaping dough to log then chilling, you may roll dough tbsps. to 1 1/4-in. balls; roll balls in coarse sugar and 1 cup finely chopped nuts. Bake, switching sheets position halfway through baking, for 15 minutes total till bottoms brown.
- Use chocolate to garnish cookies: Melt 3 1/2-oz. chocolate; slightly cool. Put into heavy-duty sealable plastic bag; in 1 corner, snip 1/16-in. opening. Evenly pipe chocolate back and forth on cookies; set chocolate before storing the cookies.

- Cookies keep in airtight container, layered between parchment/wax paper sheets, for 1 week at room temperature.

Nutrition Information

- Calories: 62
- Total Carbohydrate: 8 g
- Cholesterol: 12 mg
- Total Fat: 3 g
- Fiber: 0 g
- Protein: 1 g
- Sodium: 30 mg
- Saturated Fat: 2 g

---

18. BBQ Chicken French Bread Pizzas With Smoked Mozzarella

"Not only is this sweet and smoky pizza is delicious but it also take little time to make it."
Serving: 4 Servings | Prep: 10m

Ingredients

- 2 tsps. vegetable oil
- 1 medium yellow onion, thinly sliced
- 1 (12–14") soft loaf French or Italian bread, split in half lengthwise
- 1 garlic clove, smashed
- 2 cups shredded rotisserie chicken
- 1/2 cup plus 2 tbsps. barbecue sauce, divided
- 3/4 cup coarsely grated smoked mozzarella (about 3 oz.)
- 3 tbsps. coarsely chopped fresh cilantro

Direction

- Preparation: Put rack in the top third of oven then set oven to 425 degrees F to preheat. Pour oil in a medium skillet and heat on low heat. Cook onion for 10 minutes till it becomes tender and translucent, remember to stir once in a while. Set aside.
- Lay bread, in a way that the cut side is up, on a rimmed baking sheet. Put the baking sheet

into the oven and bake for 5 minutes. Get the baking sheet out of oven and use garlic to rub cut sides.
- Toss 1/4 cup barbecue sauce and chicken together in a medium bowl. Use leftover 6 tbsp. of sauce to spread on cut sides of bread. Place reserved onions on sauce in a layer, then place mozzarella and chicken mixture on top in reverse order.
- Put into the oven and bake for 10 minutes till cheese is melted and golden brown. Put cilantro on top.

Nutrition Information

- Calories: 540
- Total Carbohydrate: 61 g
- Cholesterol: 69 mg
- Total Fat: 21 g
- Fiber: 3 g
- Protein: 26 g
- Sodium: 1129 mg
- Saturated Fat: 7 g

---

19. Beef Milanese With Winter Slaw

""This recipe works well with chicken, pork, or veal.""
Serving: Makes 4 servings | Prep: 30m

Ingredients

- 3 tbsps. fresh lemon juice
- 1 tsp. honey
- 1/4 head of red cabbage, cored, thinly sliced (about 2 cups)
- 1 carrot, peeled, cut into matchstick-size pieces (about 1/2 cup)
- 1/4 cup thinly sliced red onion
- 1/4 cup small dill fronds
- Kosher salt, freshly ground pepper
- 4 2-oz. slices beef top round or sirloin, pounded to 1/8" thickness
- 1 cup all-purpose flour
- 2 large eggs, beaten to blend
- 1 cup plain dried breadcrumbs
- Vegetable oil

- Lemon wedges

Direction

- Preparation: In a medium bowl, stir honey and lemon juice. Put in dill, onion, carrot and cabbage; toss to coat. Add pepper and salt to taste.
- Season the beef with pepper and salt. In a shallow dish, put the flour. In another dish, put the eggs and in the third dish, the breadcrumbs.
- Add oil into a large heavy deep skillet to a depth of 1/4-inch. Set over medium-high heat. Place beef in the flour and dredge, working with one slice at a time, shaking off excess. Dunk beef in eggs; letting excess to fall back into the bowl, and put to breadcrumbs; flip and pat to coat. Place beef into the skillet then cook for about 1 minute until golden brown. Gently flip over; cook for 1 more minute. Continue with the rest of the beef. Split up beef among plates; mound slaw over. Serve with lemon wedges.
- Per serving: 29 g carbohydrates, 16 g fat, 340 calories

---

20. Beef Tenderloin With Morels And Tarragon-marsala Sauce

""An amazing yummy dinner for two that comes together in about 30 minutes. Pair with buttery Yukon Gold mashed potatoes to serve.""
Serving: Makes 2 servings | Prep: 30m

Ingredients

- 1 1/2-oz. package dried morels, or 6 oz. fresh morels plus 1/2 cup beef broth
- 2 6-to 8-oz. beef tenderloin steaks
- 2 tbsps. (1/4 stick) butter, divided
- 3/4 cup chopped green onions
- 1/3 cup heavy whipping cream
- 1 tbsp. plus 1 tsp. chopped fresh tarragon
- 1 tbsp. dry Marsala

Direction

- Preparation: Put in a 2-cup measuring cup if using dried morels. Pour hot water enough to reach 1 1/2-cup mark; allow soaking for about 20 minutes until soft. Drain, set 1/2 cup soaking liquid aside. Slice morels in half if large.
- In the meantime, dust steaks with pepper and salt. Put 1 tbsp. butter in a medium nonstick skillet and melt over medium-high heat. Put in steaks and cook to the doneness you want, about 4 minutes each side for medium-rare. Place steaks into plates.
- Put the rest 1 tbsp. butter to the skillet; place in green onions and morels and sauté for 3-4 minutes until softened. Add reserve 1/2 cup morel soaking liquid or beef broth, Marsala, 1 tbsp. tarragon, and cream; simmer for about 5 minutes until thickened to light consistency of a sauce. Add pepper and salt to taste. Place sauce over steaks, dust with the rest 1 tsp. tarragon, then serve.
- Per serving: 35.17g protein, 5.37g net carbohydrates, 1.55g total sugars, 2.35g dietary fiber, 7.73g carbohydrates, 194.94 mg cholesterol, 24.49g saturated fat, 47.08g fat, 69.9% calories from fat, 606.00(kcal) calories

---

21. Beet And Pear Napoleons With Ginger Juice Vinaigrette

"So flavorful."
Serving: Makes 6 servings | Prep: 30m

Ingredients

- 2 trimmed medium red beets (about 3 1/2 inches in diameter; about 1 3/4 lbs.), scrubbed
- 1 (4-inch) piece peeled ginger
- 1/3 cup fresh orange juice
- 1/4 tsp. sugar
- 1 1/2 tbsps. extra-virgin olive oil
- 2 large firm-ripe Anjou pears
- 1 bunch tarragon
- 1 cup mixed baby greens (preferably spicy)

- 1 Granny Smith apple
- Equipment: a 1-inch round cookie cutter
- Garnish: sea salt such as Maldon; poppy seeds

Direction

- Preheat an oven with the rack in the center to 450°F.
- In foil, wrap beets; roast for 1 1/2 hours till tender. Stand till cool enough to handle; crosswise cut to 1/4-in. thick rounds. Fully cool.
- Meanwhile grate the ginger with a Microplane finely above a kitchen towel-lined bowl; gather the towel around the ginger carefully. Squeeze till you get 2 tbsp. ginger juice. Whisk oil, sugar and orange juice in; season with pepper and salt. Evenly divide vinaigrette to 2 small bowls.
- Lengthwise cut pears around core into 1/4-in. thick slices. Cut out 18 rounds from slices out with a cookie cutter; put in 1 vinaigrette bowl.
- Cut 18 rounds out from beef slices; put into other bowl. Toss beets, vinaigrette and pears to coat well.
- Assemble napoleons: On each of the 6 plates, put 1 beet round; top using a tarragon leaf. Put 1 pear round then another tarragon leaf on top; repeat layers twice. Discard the vinaigrette used for the beets.
- Toss some leftover vinaigrette and greens; put around every napoleon. Grate apple and skin into a bowl finely. Put a heaping 1 tsp. apple over the top of every napoleon; sprinkle with poppy seeds and sea salt. If desired, drizzle with extra vinaigrette.
- Use one hand to toss then stack the beets then the other hand to handle the pears to avoid staining the pears red.
- You can roast and slice the beets 3 days ahead, chilled.
- You can make ginger juice vinaigrette 2 days ahead, chilled.

Nutrition Information

- Calories: 129
- Total Carbohydrate: 22 g
- Total Fat: 4 g
- Fiber: 4 g
- Protein: 2 g
- Sodium: 28 mg
- Saturated Fat: 1 g

22. Beet, Chickpea, And Almond Dip With Pita Chips

"So tasty!"
Serving: Makes about 2 cups

Ingredients

- 1 large (8-oz.) beet, peeled, cut into 3/4-inch cubes
- 1 cup drained canned garbanzo beans (chickpeas; from 15 1/2-oz. can)
- 3/4 cup extra-virgin olive oil plus more for chips
- 1/4 cup slivered almonds
- 5 garlic cloves, peeled
- 1 1/2 tbsps. (or more) red wine vinegar
- 6 7-inch-diameter pita breads

Direction

- Cook beet for 12 minutes till tender in medium saucepan with boiling salted water. Drain; put in processor. Add garlic, almonds, 3/4 cup oil and garbanzo beans; blend till smooth. Add 1 1/2 tbsp. red wine vinegar; blend well. Season with extra vinegar (optional), pepper and salt to taste. Put dip in medium bowl. You can make it 1 day ahead. Cover; chill. Before serving, bring to room temperature.
- Preheat an oven to 400°F. Brush oil on both sides of pita breads; lightly sprinkle pepper and salt. Cut each bread to 8 wedges. Put wedges onto rimmed baking sheets; bake for 12 minutes till crisp and lightly brown. Cool chips on the sheets.
- In middle of platter, put dip; surround with chips. Serve.

Nutrition Information

- Calories: 649
- Total Carbohydrate: 51 g
- Total Fat: 47 g
- Fiber: 9 g
- Protein: 11 g
- Sodium: 405 mg
- Saturated Fat: 6 g

23. Bell Pepper And Rice Pilaf

Serving: Serves 8 to 10

Ingredients

- 6 tbsps. (3/4 stick) butter
- 1 large red onion, chopped
- 1 large red bell pepper, seeded, chopped
- 1 large yellow bell pepper, seeded, chopped
- 2 1/3 cups long-grain white rice
- 2 tsps. ground cumin
- 1 tsp. chili powder
- 3 3/4 cups canned low-salt chicken broth
- 1/2 cup chopped fresh cilantro

Direction

- Melt butter on medium heat in big heavy pot. Add bell peppers and onion; sauté for 12 minutes till tender. Add chili powder, cumin and rice; mix for 1 minute. Add broth; boil, occasionally mixing. Cover pot. Lower heat to medium low; simmer for 25 minutes till broth is absorbed and rice is tender. Season pilaf with pepper and salt to taste. Sprinkle cilantro; serve.

Nutrition Information

- Calories: 322
- Total Carbohydrate: 51 g
- Cholesterol: 23 mg
- Total Fat: 10 g
- Fiber: 1 g
- Protein: 7 g
- Sodium: 49 mg

- Saturated Fat: 6 g

24. Berry Scones

"To get light scones, keep diced butter cold. You can cut these to rounds or triangles."
Serving: Makes 8 Scones

Ingredients

- 2 cups all-purpose gluten-free flour
- 1 tsp. xanthan gum
- 1 tbsp. baking powder
- 1/2 tsp. kosher salt
- 2 tbsps. sugar
- 1 cup frozen berries (I love cranberries or blueberries here)
- 5 tbsps. unsalted butter, diced and chilled
- 1 cup milk (low-fat is fine, nonfat is not)

Direction

- Preheat oven to 400°F. Line parchment paper on baking sheets; put aside.
- Mix sugar, salt, baking powder, xanthan gum and flour in a big bowl; put few tbsp. of dry ingredient mixture into small bowl. Add frozen berries; toss till berries are coated. Put small bowl aside.
- Add diced butter to big bowl with dry ingredients; cut it in till butter looks like pea-sized chunks covered with flour. You can use 2 knifes or a pastry cutter to do this then act like you are cutting steak again and again.
- Put milk in butter/dry ingredient mixture; stir to mix. Dough should come together. Add berries to dough when dough comes together; gently fold in till they're distributed evenly throughout. Turn dough onto lightly floured surface, handling as little as you can to avoid melting butter in your hands; pat to 1/2-in. thick rectangle.
- Cut dough to 8 triangles; put triangles on parchment paper-lined baking sheets, few inches apart. Brush bit of milk; if desired, sprinkle a bit of sugar.

- Bake till scones slightly brown around edges and puffed up for 15-20 minutes; immediately serve.

Nutrition Information

- Calories: 216
- Total Carbohydrate: 32 g
- Cholesterol: 22 mg
- Total Fat: 9 g
- Fiber: 4 g
- Protein: 4 g
- Sodium: 226 mg
- Saturated Fat: 5 g

25. Black Cod With Olives And Potatoes In Parchment

"A delicious recipe."
Serving: Makes 8 servings | Prep: 30m

Ingredients

- 1/2 lb. small Yukon Gold potatoes
- 6 tbsps. extra-virgin olive oil, divided
- 1 tbsp. plus 2 tsps. finely chopped oregano, divided
- 2 1/4 tsps. fine sea salt, divided
- 8 (5-oz.) pieces skinless black cod, Pacific cod, or haddock fillet (about 1 inch thick), any bones removed
- 1 lemon, very thinly sliced
- 6 garlic cloves, thinly sliced
- 1/2 cup Kalamata-style black olives, pitted and cut into slivers
- 1/2 cup flat-leaf parsley leaves
- Equipment: an adjustable-blade slicer; 8 (12- to 15-inch) squares of parchment paper; kitchen string

Direction

- Preheat an oven with baking sheet on the bottom rack to 400°F.
- Use slicer to cut potatoes to very thin slices; toss potatoes with 1/4 tsp. sea salt, 1 tsp.

oregano and 2 tbsp. oil. Divide potatoes to parchment squares, putting them in middle, overlapping slightly; put a fish piece over. Sprinkle scant 1/4 tsp. sea salt on each fillet; top each with 1/2 tbsp. oil, 1/2 tsp. oregano, parsley leaves, few olive slivers and garlic slices and a lemon slice.
- Gather up sides of parchment on fish to make a pouch; don't leave openings. Use kitchen string to tie tightly. Put packages onto hot baking sheet; bake for 15-22 minutes till fish just cooks through.
- You can assemble fish in parchment 4 hours in advance, chilled.

Nutrition Information

- Calories: 246
- Total Carbohydrate: 8 g
- Cholesterol: 61 mg
- Total Fat: 12 g
- Fiber: 2 g
- Protein: 26 g
- Sodium: 470 mg
- Saturated Fat: 2 g

26. Blackberry-raspberry Sauce

Serving: Makes about 1 cup

Ingredients

- 2 cups frozen blackberries, thawed
- 1/4 cup black raspberry preserves

Direction

- Mash 1/2 cup blackberries in small bowl with fork; puree leftover berries in processor. Put puree in strainer above bowl, pressing on the solids to release as much liquid as you can. Discard strainer solids. Whisk mashed berries and preserves into puree. You can make it 1 day ahead. Cover; refrigerate.

Nutrition Information

- Calories: 173
- Total Carbohydrate: 41 g
- Total Fat: 1 g
- Fiber: 8 g
- Protein: 2 g
- Sodium: 14 mg
- Saturated Fat: 0 g

27. Blood Orange Tart

"Unique and tasty."
Serving: Serves 8

Ingredients

- 1 refrigerated pie crust (half of 15-oz. package), room temperature
- 2 large blood oranges
- 1 1/4 cups sugar
- 1/4 cup water
- 2 tbsps. fresh lemon juice
- 2 tbsps. cornstarch
- 1/4 cup (1/2 stick) unsalted butter, room temperature
- 1 large egg
- 2 tbsps. Grand Marnier or other orange liqueur
- 6 thin blood orange slices, halved

Direction

- Preheat an oven to 450°F. In 9-in. diameter tart pan that has removable bottom, unfold crust; press crust up sides and on bottom of pan. Fold overhang in; press, making high-standing rim 1/2-in. over pan sides. Use fork to pierce all over. Bake crust for 10 minutes till pale golden and set. Cool in the pan on the rack. Lower oven temperature down to 350°F.
- From 2 oranges, grate peel (orange part only); put in small saucepan. From oranges, cut pith; discard. Cut between membranes above same pan to release the orange segments into the pan. Add lemon juice, 1/4 cup water and 1/4

cup sugar; boil. Lower heat; simmer while stirring often for 22 minutes till segments fall apart and is thick. Cool it to room temperature.
- In medium bowl, mix 1 cup sugar and cornstarch; beat in butter. Add the egg; beat till fluffy. Mix in grand Marnier and orange mixture; it'll look curdled. Put into crust.
- Bake tart for 45 minutes till set; cool on rack. You can make it 1 day ahead, chilled, covered. Use orange slices to garnish; serve at room temperature/cold.

Nutrition Information

- Calories: 355
- Total Carbohydrate: 56 g
- Cholesterol: 39 mg
- Total Fat: 14 g
- Fiber: 2 g
- Protein: 2 g
- Sodium: 128 mg
- Saturated Fat: 7 g

28. Blood-orange And Grapefruit Juice

Serving: Serves 6

Ingredients

- 3 cups fresh pink or red grapefruit juice (from about 4 grapefruit)
- 3 cups fresh blood-orange juice or regular orange juice (from about 11 oranges)
- Garnish: lime slices

Direction

- Mix juices in a pitcher; if desired, add ice.

Nutrition Information

- Calories: 104
- Total Carbohydrate: 24 g
- Total Fat: 0 g
- Fiber: 0 g

- Protein: 1 g
- Sodium: 2 mg
- Saturated Fat: 0 g

29. Blueberry Buckwheat Pancakes

"You can make this in under 1 hour."
Serving: Makes about twenty-four 3-inch pancakes

Ingredients

- 1/2 cup buckwheat flour (available at natural foods stores)
- 1/2 cup all-purpose flour
- 2 tsps. double-acting baking powder
- 2 tsps. sugar
- 1 tsp. salt
- 1/2 stick (1/4 cup) cold unsalted butter, cut into bits
- 2 large eggs
- 1 cup milk
- 1 1/2 cups blueberries, preferably wild, picked over and, if large, halved
- vegetable oil for brushing the griddle
- pure maple syrup as an accompaniment

Direction

- Blend salt, sugar, baking powder and flours in a food processor. Add butter; blend till it looks like fine meal. Whisk milk and eggs in a big bowl. Add flour mixture; whisk batter till well combined. Stand batter for 5 minutes; mix in blueberries.
- Preheat an oven to 200°F. Heat griddle till hot enough that water drops scatter on its surface on medium heat; brush oil. Put batter on griddle to make 3-in. rounds; cook pancakes till golden for 1-2 minutes per side. Put pancakes as cooked onto heatproof platter; in oven, keep warm. Serve syrup with pancakes.

Nutrition Information

- Calories: 69

- Total Carbohydrate: 7 g
- Cholesterol: 26 mg
- Total Fat: 4 g
- Fiber: 1 g
- Protein: 2 g
- Sodium: 90 mg
- Saturated Fat: 2 g

30. Blueberry Cheesecake Bars

Serving: Makes 24 bars

Ingredients

- 16 oz. cream cheese, softened
- 2 large eggs
- 3/4 cup sugar
- 1 tsp. vanilla
- 3/4 cup blueberry or other fruit preserves
- hot shortbread base

Direction

- Preheat an oven to 350°F.
- Whisk cream cheese till smooth in a bowl; whisk in vanilla, sugar and eggs. Spread preserves evenly on hot shortbread; put cream-cheese mixture over. Bake in center of oven for 30 minutes till slightly puffed. Fully cool in pan; cut to 24 bars. They keep for 3 days, chilled and covered.

31. Blueberry Muffin Tops

"A fun recipe!"
Serving: Makes 12

Ingredients

- 3/4 stick (6 tbsps.) unsalted butter
- 1/3 cup whole milk
- 1 whole large egg
- 1 large yolk
- 3/4 tsp. vanilla
- 1 1/2 cups all-purpose flour

- 3/4 cup sugar
- 1 1/2 tsps. baking powder
- 3/4 tsp. salt
- 2 cups fresh blueberries (12 oz)
- 3 tbsps. cold unsalted butter, cut into bits
- 1/2 cup all-purpose flour
- 3 1/2 tbsps. sugar
- 2 muffin-top pans, each with 6 (4- by 1/2-inch) muffin-top cups (1/2-cup capacity)*; or regular muffin pans

Direction

- Batter: In upper oven third, put oven rack; preheat to 375°F. Butter muffin pans generously.
- Melt butter on medium low heat in a small saucepan; take off heat. Whisk in milk; whisk in vanilla, yolk and whole egg till well combined.
- Whisk salt, baking powder, sugar and flour in a bowl. Add milk mixture; mix just till combined. Gently yet thoroughly fold in blueberries.
- Divide batter, evenly spreading, to 12 muffin cups.
- Create topping then bake muffins: With your fingertips, rub all topping ingredients together till crumbly in a bowl; evenly sprinkle on batter in cups.
- Bake for 18-20 minutes till crisp and golden and a diagonally inserted skewer/wooden pick in middle of muffin exits clean.
- Cool for 15 minutes in pan on rack. Run knife around each muffin top's edge; remove from cups carefully. Serve at room temperature/warm.

Nutrition Information

- Calories: 271
- Total Carbohydrate: 41 g
- Cholesterol: 44 mg
- Total Fat: 11 g
- Fiber: 2 g
- Protein: 4 g
- Sodium: 227 mg
- Saturated Fat: 6 g

32. Braised Cauliflower With Curry And Yogurt

"A fun recipe!"
Serving: Serves 4 as a side dish

Ingredients

- 1 1/2 tbsps. extra-virgin olive oil
- 1 medium head cauliflower (about 2 lbs.), trimmed, cored, and cut into florets
- 1 medium onion, halved and sliced thin
- 1 tsp. curry powder
- 1/4 cup plain yogurt mixed with 1/4 cup water
- 2 tbsps. minced fresh cilantro leaves
- Salt
- Freshly ground black pepper

Direction

- Heat oil in a sauté pan/big skillet on medium heat. Add onion and cauliflower; cook, occasionally mixing, for 7 minutes till florets brown lightly. Mix in curry powder; cook for 1 minute till fragrant.
- Add thinner yogurt; cover pan. Lower heat to medium low and simmer for 6 minutes till florets are tender yet hold their shape. Mix in cilantro; season to taste with pepper and salt. If needed, simmer, uncovered, to evaporate leftover liquid in pan; immediately serve.

Nutrition Information

- Calories: 120
- Total Carbohydrate: 14 g
- Cholesterol: 2 mg
- Total Fat: 6 g
- Fiber: 5 g
- Protein: 5 g
- Sodium: 613 mg
- Saturated Fat: 1 g

33. Braised Swiss Chard With Currants And Feta

"The green leaves and red stems of Swiss chard gives a Christmas vibe."
Serving: Makes 4 servings | Prep: 15m

Ingredients

- 1 (1-lb.) bunch Swiss chard
- 1 large garlic clove, finely chopped
- 2 tbsps. olive oil
- 1/2 tsp. salt
- 1/4 tsp. black pepper
- 3 tbsps. dried currants
- 1/3 cup water
- 1 1/2 oz. feta, crumbled (1/3 cup)

Direction

- Slice stems and middle ribs from chard, throwing any hard portion close the base, then slice the ribs and stems widthwise into 3/4-inch-thick pieces. Roughly cut the leaves.
- In a 4-quart heavy pot, cook the garlic in oil for 1 to 2 minutes over moderately-low heat, mixing from time to time, till light golden. Put pepper, salt and chard ribs and stems, and let cook for 4 minutes, mixing from time to time. Put the currants and allow to cook for a minute, mixing, till plump. Put the water and chard leaves and raise the heat to moderate, then let cook with cover for 5 minutes, mixing from time to time, till leaves are soft. Take off heat and mix in feta.

Nutrition Information

- Calories: 136
- Total Carbohydrate: 10 g
- Cholesterol: 11 mg
- Total Fat: 10 g
- Fiber: 2 g
- Protein: 4 g
- Sodium: 373 mg
- Saturated Fat: 3 g

34. Braised Turnips With Poppy-seed Bread Crumbs

"A wonderful turnip recipe! A must try!"
Serving: Makes 4 servings | Prep: 20m

Ingredients

- 3 tbsps. unsalted butter
- 2 lbs. medium turnips (not Japanese), peeled and cut into 1-inch-thick wedges
- 1 1/2 cups water
- 1 tbsp. fresh lemon juice
- 2 tbsps. extra-virgin olive oil
- 1 garlic clove, minced
- 1 cup fine fresh bread crumbs from a baguette
- 1 tbsp. poppy seeds
- 1 tbsp. chopped flat-leaf parsley

Direction

- Braise turnips: in a 12-inch heavy skillet, melt butter on medium heat. Add 1/2 tsp. of salt, lemon juice, water and turnips; boil. Lower heat to low; simmer for 30 minutes, covered. Put heat on medium; mix turnips. Simmer briskly, uncovered, for 20-35 minutes till turnips are just tender and glazed and all liquid evaporates. Should be cooked through yet retain their shape.
- As turnips cook, make breadcrumbs: Heat oil in a big heavy skillet on medium heat till it shimmers. Cook garlic, mixing, for 1 minute till pale golden. Add poppy seeds and breadcrumbs; cook, frequently mixing, for 4-5 minutes till golden. Mix salt to taste and parsley in. Sprinkle breadcrumbs on turnips before serving.
- Drink with Chateau Reynella McLaren Vale Grenache '04.
- You can braise turnips 1 day ahead, uncovered and chilled till cool then cover. Before serving, reheat with a bit of water.
- Breadcrumb mixture can be made 1 day ahead, without parsley, at room temperature in an airtight container. Before using, mix parsley in.

Nutrition Information

- Calories: 320
- Total Carbohydrate: 35 g
- Cholesterol: 23 mg
- Total Fat: 18 g
- Fiber: 6 g
- Protein: 6 g
- Sodium: 356 mg
- Saturated Fat: 7 g

35. Bread Stuffing With Sage And Apricots

"Don't bake this stuffing in a bird."
Serving: Serves 10 to 12

Ingredients

- 1 1-lb. loaf egg bread, cut into 1/2-inch cubes
- 3 cups canned low-salt chicken broth
- 1/2 cup (1 stick) butter
- 2 large onions, chopped
- 2 cups chopped celery
- 2 cups chopped green bell pepper
- 1 cup slivered almonds, toasted
- 1 tbsp. poultry seasoning
- 1 tsp. dried sage
- 1 cup chopped dried apricots (about 6 oz.)
- 6 large eggs, beaten to blend

Direction

- Preheat an oven to 350°F. Butter a 13x9x2-in. glass baking dish. Put bread cubes in a big bowl. Put broth over; stand till bread absorbs most broth.
- Melt butter on medium heat in a big heavy Dutch oven. Add bell pepper, celery and onions; sauté for 15 minutes till veggies are tender yet not brown. Mix in sage, poultry seasoning and almonds; sauté for 5 minutes. Stir in apricots. Put veggie in bread mixture; season with pepper and salt to taste. Cool for 15 minutes. Stir eggs into stuffing; put stuffing in prepped dish.

- Bake stuffing for 1 hour till cooked through and golden on top.

Nutrition Information

- Calories: 392
- Total Carbohydrate: 41 g
- Cholesterol: 159 mg
- Total Fat: 21 g
- Fiber: 5 g
- Protein: 13 g
- Sodium: 258 mg
- Saturated Fat: 8 g

36. Bread With Chocolate And Olive Oil

"So delicious."
Serving: Serves 6

Ingredients

- 6 oz dark chocolate, 60% cocoa
- 6 slices 1-lb white country-style loaf, cut into 8 slices
- 1/4 cup extra-virgin olive oil
- 1/2 tsp sea salt flakes

Direction

- Preheat boiler/oven to 325°F. Grate chocolate coarsely onto plate. Put bread onto heatproof plate or baking sheet. Toast under broiler till both sides are golden. Put grated chocolate on toast, fully covering it. Put olive oil on chocolate; sprinkle salt flakes.

Nutrition Information

- Calories: 1355
- Total Carbohydrate: 237 g
- Total Fat: 28 g
- Fiber: 29 g
- Protein: 54 g
- Sodium: 2310 mg
- Saturated Fat: 7 g

37. Breakfast Burritos With Chorizo And Eggs

Serving: Makes 4 | Prep: 25m

Ingredients

- 12 oz. good quality fresh Mexican chorizo sausages, casings removed
- 4 chopped green onions
- 6 large eggs
- 1 tbsp. olive oil
- 4 9- to 10-inch-diameter flour tortillas
- 2/3 cup (or more) grated Mexican four-cheese blend (3 to 4 oz.)
- 1/2 cup (or more) chopped fresh cilantro
- 1/2 cup purchased tomatillo salsa
- 1 avocado, halved, pitted, peeled, sliced

Direction

- Sauté chorizo in big nonstick skillet on medium high heat, breaking up, for 5-6 minutes till cooked through. Add onions; sauté for 30 seconds. Put into bowl; to keep warm, cover. Wipe out skillet. In medium bowl, whisk eggs; sprinkle pepper and salt. Put oil in same skillet; heat on medium heat. Add eggs and cook till scrambled softly. Take off heat; to keep warm, cover.
- Warm tortillas for 20 seconds per side till pliable in another skillet. Divide chorizo to tortillas. Top with avocado, salsa, cilantro, eggs and cheese. Fold bottom flap up and short sides in; roll tortillas up.

38. Brined Turkey Breast

"If it browns quickly, tent with foil."
Serving: Makes 8 servings

Ingredients

- 16 cups water
- 2 cups sugar
- 2 cups coarse salt
- 5 cloves of garlic, crushed
- 1 tbsp. pickling spices
- 1 fresh turkey breast, 9-11 lbs., deboned
- 6 tbsps. unsalted butter, melted
- Black pepper
- 2 cups chicken broth

Direction

- Boil brine ingredients in a big pot. Lower heat; simmer, covered partially, till salt and sugar dissolve. Cool it to room temperature.
- Rinse turkey breast; discard extra fat. Put, breast-side down, into pot/deep bowl. Put brine on breast; refrigerate overnight, loosely covered.
- Preheat an oven to 350°F. 30 minutes before roasting, remove turkey from brine. Line long heavy-duty aluminum foil pieces on a shallow roasting pan.
- Put turkey in pan. Brush 4 tbsp. melted butter; season using pepper. Loosely gather foil on top; bake for 1 1/2 hours then open foil. Bake, basting with broth and leftover 2 tbsp. butter every 30 minutes, for 2 1/4 hours till an inserted thermometer in thickest part reads 165°F, juices are clear and turkey is golden brown. Put breast onto cutting board; before carving rest for 15 minutes. Keep pan juices for gravy.

39. Broccoflower With Anchovies And Garlic

"A tasty recipe."
Serving: Makes 4 servings

Ingredients

- 1 head broccoflower or cauliflower (1 1/2 lbs.), cut into 2-inch-wide florets
- 1/4 cup olive oil
- 3 garlic cloves, thinly sliced
- 21/2 tsps. chopped canned anchovies, or to taste

- 1/4 tsp. dried hot red pepper flakes
- 1/4 cup pine nuts, toasted
- 1/4 cup golden raisins
- 2 tbsps. chopped fresh parsley

Direction

- In 2 batches, cook broccoflower for 5 minutes till crisp tender in a 5-6-qt. pot with boiling salted water; to stop cooking, put into big bowl of cold water and ice using slotted spoon. Drain florets; pat dry using paper towels.
- Heat oil till hot yet not smoking in a 12-in. nonstick skillet on medium high heat; sauté garlic for 1 minute till golden, mixing. Add red pepper flakes and anchovies; sauté for 1 minute till anchovies melt, mixing. Add florets; toss to coat. Add salt to taste, raisins and pine nuts; sauté for 2 minutes till heated through, mixing. Take off heat; mix in parsley.

Nutrition Information

- Calories: 267
- Total Carbohydrate: 19 g
- Cholesterol: 9 mg
- Total Fat: 19 g
- Fiber: 5 g
- Protein: 8 g
- Sodium: 440 mg
- Saturated Fat: 3 g

40. Broccoli And Brussels Sprouts Slaw

"Such a tasty recipe!"
Serving: 4 servings | Prep: 20m

Ingredients

- 1 small head or 1/2 of a large head of broccoli
- 6 oz. brussels sprouts, trimmed, thinly sliced lengthwise
- 1/2 tsp. kosher salt, plus more
- 2 oil-packed anchovy fillets (optional)
- 1/2 oz. Parmesan, finely grated, plus more, shaved, for serving
- 1/4 cup olive oil
- 3 Tbsp. fresh lemon juice
- Freshly ground black pepper
- 1/2 cup Castelvetrano olives, pitted
- 1/4 cup unsalted roasted almonds, coarsely chopped

Direction

- Trim broccoli stalk; peel. Lengthwise halve head. Thinly slice both halves with stalk starting at crown. Or, slice both brussels sprouts and broccoli in a food processor. Toss 1/2 tsp. salt with brussels sprouts and broccoli in a big bowl; sit to slightly soften for 10 minutes.
- Meanwhile, if using, chop anchovies; mash to paste with side of chef's knife. In a small bowl, mix lemon juice, oil, grated parmesan and anchovies; season with pepper and salt. Drizzle on slaw; toss till coated. Top with shaved parmesan, almonds and olives; serve.
- You can make slaw without almonds 1 day ahead. Cover; chill. Before serving, add almonds.

Nutrition Information

- Calories: 249
- Total Carbohydrate: 15 g
- Total Fat: 20 g
- Fiber: 6 g
- Protein: 7 g
- Sodium: 437 mg
- Saturated Fat: 3 g

41. Broiled Open-faced Crab-meat Sandwiches

"You can make this in under 1 hour."
Serving: Serves 4

Ingredients

- 1/4 cup finely chopped red bell pepper
- 1/4 cup finely chopped green bell pepper
- 1/4 cup finely chopped onion
- 1 garlic clove, minced
- 2 tbsps. unsalted butter
- 1/2 lb. lump crab meat, picked over
- 2 tbsps. fresh lemon juice
- 1 hard-boiled large egg, chopped
- 1 tsp. Worcestershire sauce, or to taste
- 2 tbsps. mayonnaise
- 1 tsp. Dijon-style mustard
- 1/8 tsp. cayenne, or to taste
- 2 English muffins, halved, buttered lightly, and toasted
- 2 tbsps. freshly grated Parmesan

Direction

- Cook garlic, onion and bell peppers in butter in a big skillet on medium low heat, mixing, till veggies are soft. Mix in cayenne, mustard, mayonnaise, Worcestershire sauce, egg, lemon juice and crab meat; divide crab-meat mixture to muffin halves, slightly mounding. Sprinkle parmesan on sandwiches; broil under preheated broil 4-in. from heat till tops are golden for 3-4 minutes.

Nutrition Information

- Calories: 271
- Total Carbohydrate: 16 g
- Cholesterol: 124 mg
- Total Fat: 16 g
- Fiber: 2 g
- Protein: 17 g
- Sodium: 607 mg
- Saturated Fat: 6 g

42. Broiled Plums With Mango Sorbet

Serving: Makes 4 servings | Prep: 15m

Ingredients

- 1/2 lb plums (about 2 medium), pitted and cut into 1/2-inch wedges
- 1 tbsp. sugar
- 1/4 tsp. vanilla
- 1/8 tsp. cinnamon
- 3 tbsps. water
- 2 cups (1 pint) fat-free mango sorbet

Direction

- Preheat the broiler. In a 1 1/2 to 2 quarts 9 to 10 inches circle gratin or different shallow flameproof dish that is not glass, toss the plums along with cinnamon, vanilla and sugar. In dish, allow the plums to sit for 5 minutes to macerate.
- To dish, pour water and let plums broil 6- to 8-inch away from heat for 7 to 10 minutes, slowly mixing one or two times, till fruit has softened. Top fruit and juice from pan with sorbet.
- Note: Plums may be broiled for 2 hours in advance and distribute between serving dishes while warm.

Nutrition Information

- Calories: 177
- Total Carbohydrate: 45 g
- Total Fat: 0 g
- Fiber: 2 g
- Protein: 0 g
- Sodium: 7 mg
- Saturated Fat: 0 g

43. Brown Sugar & Cinnamon Panna Cotta With Apple Cider Gelée

Serving: Makes 10 servings

Ingredients

- 1/4 fresh vanilla bean, split lengthwise
- 8 cups (2 quarts) heavy cream
- 1 cup packed, light brown sugar
- 2 whole cinnamon sticks
- 3 (1/4 oz.) envelopes powdered gelatin (about 3 scant tbsps.)
- 2 1/2 cups apple cider

Direction

- From pod, use small paring knife's tip to scrape vanilla seeds into 5-qt. saucepan. Add cinnamon sticks, brown sugar and cream; simmer on medium heat.
- Take off heat; steep for 20 minutes, uncovered. Remove cinnamon sticks with slotted spoon; cool to room temperature.
- Whisk 2 packages gelatin and 1 cup cream mixture in small saucepan on medium heat for 3 minutes till melted. Whisk it into leftover cooled cream. Put it into 10 wine glasses; over each, leave 3/4-in. space. Chill for 4 hours till firm. You can make it 1 day ahead; refrigerate till needed.
- Meanwhile, heat 1 cup sider till hot yet not boiling in medium saucepan on medium heat; take off heat. Add leftover gelatin package, whisking for 2 minutes till dissolved. Mix leftover 1 1/2 cups cider and cider-gelatin mixture in big bowl; cool it to room temperature.
- In each wine glass, put 4 tbsp. cider mixture when custards are firm; put in fridge. Chill for 1 hour till firm.

Nutrition Information

- Calories: 779
- Total Carbohydrate: 34 g
- Cholesterol: 261 mg
- Total Fat: 71 g
- Fiber: 0 g
- Protein: 6 g
- Sodium: 85 mg
- Saturated Fat: 44 g

44. Brown Sugar Cookies

"Alternate regular sugar with brown one in cookies recipe for an interesting change of flavor!"
Serving: 60 | Prep: 10m | Ready in: 50m

Ingredients

- 2 cups brown sugar
- 1/2 cup unsalted butter, softened
- 2 large eggs
- 1 tsp. vanilla extract
- 2 1/2 cups all-purpose flour
- 3/4 tsp. baking powder
- 1/2 tsp. salt
- 1 cup confectioners' sugar

Direction

- Set oven to 175°C (or 350°F) and begin preheating.
- In a bowl, cream together vanilla extract, eggs, butter and brown sugar with an electric mixer until creamy and smoothened.
- In another bowl, blend salt, baking powder and flour together. Combine flour mixture with butter mixture to fully incorporate the dough.
- Dust a large plate with confectioners' sugar. Drop dough, 1.5 tsps. each cookie, over confectioners' sugar layer and roll until coated. Place dough onto a baking sheet.
- Bake in the prepared oven for 12-14 minutes until lightly browned around the edges. Let cookies cool for 2 minutes on baking pan, then cool thoroughly on a wire rack.

Nutrition Information

- Calories: 62 calories;
- Total Carbohydrate: 10.8 g

- Cholesterol: 10 mg
- Total Fat: 1.8 g
- Protein: 0.8 g
- Sodium: 30 mg

45. Brussels Sprout Slaw With Mustard Dressing And Maple-glazed Pecans

Serving: Makes 8 servings

Ingredients

- Nonstick vegetable oil spray
- 1 cup large pecan halves
- 1/4 cup pure maple syrup
- 1/2 tsp. plus 1 tbsp. coarse kosher salt plus additional for seasoning
- 1/4 tsp. freshly ground black pepper
- 1/4 cup whole grain Dijon mustard
- 2 tbsps. apple cider vinegar
- 2 tbsps. fresh lemon juice
- 1 tbsp. sugar
- 1/4 cup vegetable oil
- 1 1/2 lbs. brussels sprouts, trimmed

Direction

- Heat up the oven to 325 degrees Fahrenheit. Use nonstick spray to spray a big sheet of foil. Place pecans onto a small baking sheet (rimmed). In a small bowl, whisk 1/4 tsp. of pepper, 1/2 tsp. coarse salt, and maple syrup. Add the mixture onto the nuts, tossing to coat, then spread into one layer. Bake for 5 minutes and stir. Continue to bake until glaze bubbles thickly and nuts are toasted, 6 minutes. Move the nuts onto the foil right away and separate them. Completely cool. You can make these 2 days beforehand and store airtight.
- In a small bowl, whisk sugar, lemon juice, vinegar, and mustard, and whisk in the oil, then season with pepper and coarse salt.
- Boil a big pot of water and add in 1 tbsp. of coarse salt, then add in brussels sprouts,

cooking until tender-crisp yet still bright green, 5 minutes. Drain, then rinse using cold water. Cool them on paper towels. Use a processor fitted with a 1/8 to 1/4-inch slicing disk to slice the brussels sprouts, then move into a big bowl. You can make the brussels sprouts and dressing a day before, chilling and covering separately.
- Toss the brussels sprouts with dressing, enough to coat them; let it marinate for 30-60 minutes. Mix in some pecans and place onto a serving bowl. Top with the leftover pecans.
- Get a pure maple syrup that is Grade B since it has a bolder flavor than the delicate Grade A.

46. Burnt Caramel Pudding

"This rich tasting pudding has the perfect balance of sweet and bitter. The secret to this is by starting a cool water bath instead of hot. It gently cooks the pudding to make a glossy and silky structure. It also uses egg yolks to help it set."
Serving: Serves 4

Ingredients

- 2 cups heavy cream
- 1/2 vanilla bean
- 1/2 cup sugar
- 3 large egg yolks, at room temperature
- Fine sea salt
- Whipped cream for serving

Direction

- Preheat the oven to 300 degrees F.
- Put cream in a small pot. Teat the vanilla bean then scruff the seeds with cream; add the scraped pod. Warm the cream gently on low heat.
- Set aside 2 tbsp. of sugar; add the rest of the sugar in a heavy-bottomed pot with 1 1/2 tbsp. of water. Put on medium heat then mix until the sugar dissolves. Turn to high heat and let the liquid bubble for 4 minutes until the mixture is dark amber, swirl the pot from time to time but avoid stirring. Watch the

mixture closely since it happens quickly. Turn to medium heat.

- Moving quickly, remove the vanilla pod from the cream then mix the warm cream with the caramel slowly. Rinse the vanilla pod and reserve for another use. When the cream mixture boils (this will happen quickly), take off the heat then cool the mixture for 10 minutes.
- In a medium bowl, beat a pinch of sea salt, reserved sugar and egg yolks together; mix in a little of the caramel-cream mixture into the egg yolks then slowly mix in the rest until all are blended.
- Filter the mixture to a big measuring cup or a pitcher; transfer to 4, 6oz. ramekins. In a shallow baking pan, put the ramekins then pour cold water in the pan until halfway full. You can add a few grains of sea salt over the pudding if you want the caramel to be slightly salty. Cook for an hour to 1 hour and 15 minutes until the pudding sets.
- Refrigerate the pudding for at least 3 hours or overnight at best. Serve with freshly whipped cream.
- You can use old custard cups that hold 5 oz. but 6oz ramekins should be fine.

Nutrition Information

- Calories: 550
- Total Carbohydrate: 29 g
- Cholesterol: 301 mg
- Total Fat: 47 g
- Protein: 4 g
- Sodium: 366 mg
- Saturated Fat: 29 g

---

47. Butter Croissants

Serving: Makes 24 pastries | Prep: 2h

Ingredients

- 1 recipe croissant dough(2 3/4 lb), chilled

- Special equipment: a ruler, a pastry brush, parchment paper, 2 or 3 garbage bags (unscented), a spray bottle with water

Direction

- Roll dough out and cut: Halve dough; chill 1 half while wrapped in plastic wrap. Roll other half out, dusting with flour as needed, stretching corners to maintain the shape, to 16x12-in. rectangle on lightly floured surface. Use a pastry brush to brush excess flour off; use a sharp knife/pizza wheel to trim edges.
- Put dough with short side nearer you; horizontally halve. Chill 1 half. Vertically cut leftover half to thirds, making 3 rectangles. Diagonally halve every rectangle to create 2 triangles to get 6 triangles in total.
- From croissants: Stretch dough holding short side, the side opposite tip, of a triangle in 1 hand, tugging then sliding with the other hand towards tip to elongate by 50%.
- Put onto work surface with triangle's short side nearer you; roll triangle up toward tip starting with short side; it should overlap thrice with the tip sticking out from bottom; while rolling, you might have to stretch dough.
- Put croissant on parchment-lined big baking sheet, tip side down; if desired, curve ends inward to create crescent shape.
- Use leftover 5 triangles to make more croissants then with leftover rolled-out dough; put onto baking sheet, 2-in. apart. Repeat rolling, cutting then shaping process with chilled dough piece.
- Rise: Slide every baking sheet into garbing bag, using inverted glasses to prop up top of bag to avoid touching croissants; tuck open end under the baking sheet.
- Rise croissants for 2 hours till spongy to touch and slightly puffy.
- Bake: Put oven racks on lower and upper oven thirds; preheat to 425°F.
- Take baking sheets from bags. Generously spritz spray bottle inside oven; close door. Put croissants into oven; spritz before closing

door. Lower temperature to 400°F; bake without opening door for 10 minutes.
- Switch sheets position in oven; rotate sheets 180°. Lower oven temperature to 375°F; bake for 10 minutes till croissants are deep golden.
- Baked then cooled croissants keep for 1 month; freeze on baking sheets, uncovered, till firm. Snugly wrap in foil then put into freezer. Remove foil when ready to serve; bake, unthawed, on baking sheet for 5-10 minutes in 325°F oven.

48.Butter Lettuce With Apples, Walnuts, And Pomegranate Seeds

"For a perfect cold-weather menu, add butter lettuce into your dish. Here's a recipe for a simple salad. You can add any leftover chicken on its top."
Serving: Makes 4 servings

Ingredients

- 2 tbsps. cider vinegar
- 1 tbsp. honey
- 1 tbsp. finely chopped shallot
- 1 1/2 tsps. Dijon mustard
- 1/3 cup vegetable oil
- Kosher salt and freshly ground black pepper
- 2 heads of butter lettuce leaves, gently torn
- 1 1/2 cups store-bought glazed walnuts
- 1 Honeycrisp or Fuji apple, quartered, cored, thinly sliced
- Kosher salt and freshly ground black pepper
- 1 cup pomegranate seeds
- 1/4 cup tarragon leaves
- 1/2 cup crumbled Stilton or Maytag blue cheese (about 2 oz.)

Direction

- For the vinaigrette, mix the first 4 ingredients in a medium bowl. Stir in oil gradually. Season the vinaigrette with salt and pepper according to your taste.
- For the salad, arrange the lettuce in a large bowl. Add the apple, vinaigrette, and walnuts. Toss the mixture well to coat. Season it with salt and pepper. Garnish the salad with cheese, pomegranate seeds, and tarragon.

Nutrition Information

- Calories: 393
- Total Carbohydrate: 26 g
- Cholesterol: 11 mg
- Total Fat: 31 g
- Fiber: 5 g
- Protein: 7 g
- Sodium: 555 mg
- Saturated Fat: 5 g

49.Buttermilk Biscuits

"Amazing buttermilk biscuits that can serve a crowd."
Serving: 60 | Prep: 20m | Ready in: 32m

Ingredients

- 5 lbs. self-rising flour
- 2 tbsps. baking powder
- 1 cup lard, melted
- 2 quarts buttermilk
- 1 cup 2% milk
- 1/4 cup bacon drippings

Direction

- Preheat an oven to 190 °C or 375 °F.
- Mix together the baking powder and self-rising flour in a big bowl. Add in liquified lard and combine till incorporated. Mix in milk and buttermilk just till dough gathers together.
- On a slightly floured area, pat the dough and roll out to 3/4 inch thickness. With a round cookie cutter or biscuit cutter, cut into biscuits. Put on the baking sheets, set about an-inch apart. Glaze tops with the bacon drippings.
- In the prepped oven, let bake for 10 to 12 minutes, till tops and bottoms are browned lightly.

Nutrition Information

- Calories: 189 calories;
- Total Carbohydrate: 29.9 g
- Cholesterol: 6 mg
- Total Fat: 5.1 g
- Protein: 5 g
- Sodium: 552 mg

50. Butternut Squash Soup With Chestnuts

"Such a delicious recipe."
Serving: Makes 6 (first course) servings | Prep: 35m

Ingredients

- 4 large shallots, chopped
- 1 medium carrot, chopped
- 1 celery rib, chopped
- 1 (15-oz.) can diced tomatoes, drained
- 3 large thyme sprigs
- 1 Turkish or 1/2 California bay leaf
- 2 tbsps. extra-virgin olive oil
- 1 1/2 lbs. butternut squash, peeled, seeded, and cut into (1-inch) cubes (about 3 1/2 cups)
- 5 cups water
- 1/4 tsp. grated nutmeg
- 12 bottled cooked chestnuts, chopped (1/2 cup)
- softly whipped cream

Direction

- Cook bay leaf, thyme, tomatoes, celery, carrot and shallots in oil in 4-5-qt. heavy pot on medium low heat, occasionally mixing, for 8 minutes till soft.
- Add 1/4 tsp. pepper, 1 tsp. salt, nutmeg, water and squash; simmer, covered, for 20-25 minutes till squash is very tender. Discard bay leaf and thyme.
- In batches, puree soup till smooth in a blender; be careful, it is hot. If desired, thin soup; season with pepper and salt.
- Put soup on chestnuts in bowls.

- You can make soup 2 days ahead, chilled, covered when cool; if needed, slightly thin with water.

Nutrition Information

- Calories: 203
- Total Carbohydrate: 28 g
- Cholesterol: 18 mg
- Total Fat: 10 g
- Fiber: 5 g
- Protein: 3 g
- Sodium: 43 mg
- Saturated Fat: 4 g

51. Candied Espresso Walnuts

"This is best when served after dinner together with coffee."
Serving: Makes about 4 cups

Ingredients

- Nonstick vegetable oil spray
- 2/3 cup sugar
- 2 tbsps. finely ground espresso coffee beans
- 1 tbsp. instant espresso powder
- 1/2 tsp. ground cinnamon
- 1/4 tsp. coarse kosher salt
- 1 large egg white
- 4 cups walnut halves (about 12 oz.)

Direction

- Set the oven to 325°F for preheating. Use the nonstick spray to coat the large rimmed baking sheet. In a small bowl, mix the sugar and the next 4 ingredients. In a large bowl, beat the egg white until frothy. Add the walnuts and toss them until coated. Sprinkle the walnuts into the espresso mixture. Toss the mixture until coated. Transfer the coated walnuts in a single layer onto the prepared sheet.
- Let it bake for 5 minutes. Loosen the walnuts from the baking sheet by sliding the spatula beneath them. Toss the walnuts, rearranging

them again in a single layer. Bake for 5 more minutes until the walnuts are dry when touched. Loosen again the walnuts from the sheet and let them cool. Note: The candied walnuts can be prepared 2 weeks in advance. Just store them inside the sealed container at room temperature.

Nutrition Information

- Calories: 283
- Total Carbohydrate: 18 g
- Total Fat: 23 g
- Fiber: 2 g
- Protein: 6 g
- Sodium: 54 mg
- Saturated Fat: 2 g

52. Cantaloupe And Pancetta Cream Sauce For Pasta

"A delicious pasta recipe."
Serving: Serves 4 as an appetizer

Ingredients

- 3 tbsps. unsalted butter
- 2 oz. sliced pancetta, diced
- 1/4 cup minced shallot
- 3 cups diced ripe cantaloupe (from 1 medium cantaloupe)
- 1/2 cup heavy cream
- 1/2 tsp. salt
- 1/4 tsp. freshly ground black pepper, plus more for garnish
- 1 tsp. minced fresh marjoram leaves
- 8 oz. spaghetti rigati, linguine, or fettucine
- 1/2 cup freshly grated Parmigiano-Reggiano cheese

Direction

- Boil a bit pot of salted water.
- Heat 1 tbsp. butter on medium high heat in a Dutch oven/big sauté pan. Add pancetta; cook, mixing frequently, for 3-4 minutes till

renders most fat and is crisp. Add shallot; cook, mixing, for 1-2 minutes till soft. Add leftover 2 tbsp. butter; add melon when it melts. Cook, frequently mixing, for 8-10 minutes till melon fully breaks down and makes thick, smooth sauce.
- Add marjoram, pepper, salt and heavy cream; cook for 3 minutes till sauce makes thick, smooth consistency that coats back of spoon and cream reduces by half; take sauce off heat.
- Add pasta to boiling water; mix well. Cook for 10 minutes till al dente. Drain well; put 1/2 cup pasta cooking water aside.
- Put 1/4 cup parmesan and hot pasta in warm sauce; put pan on medium heat. Toss till pasta heats through and is coated with sauce nicely. Add little pasta cooking water to toss pasta and thin sauce if sauce looks very thick.
- Immediately serve pasta, garnished using freshly ground black pepper and leftover parmesan cheese.

Nutrition Information

- Calories: 553
- Total Carbohydrate: 55 g
- Cholesterol: 87 mg
- Total Fat: 31 g
- Fiber: 3 g
- Protein: 15 g
- Sodium: 511 mg
- Saturated Fat: 17 g

53. Caramelized Nectarine-almond Phyllo Cups With Frozen Orange Mousse

"This dessert is created by Dwayne Fortier of the La Reserve located in Houston. It should be prepared well ahead of servings since the mousse requires freezing for at least 6 hours."
Serving: Makes 6

Ingredients

- 6 large egg yolks

- 2/3 cup sugar
- 1/4 cup water
- 1 vanilla bean, split lengthwise
- 2 tsps. grated orange peel
- 2 cups chilled whipping cream
- 1/4 cup Grand Marnier or other orange liqueur
- 1/2 cup (1 stick) unsalted butter, melted
- 4 sheets fresh phyllo pastry or frozen, thawed
- 1 cup apricot preserves
- 3 5-to-6 oz. nectarines, pitted, thinly sliced
- 1/3 cup almond paste (about 4 oz.), crumbled
- 1 large egg yolk
- 1 1/2 tbsps. unsalted butter, room temperature
- 1 1/2 tbsps. all purpose flour
- 1 tsp. vanilla extract

Direction

- To prepare mousse: In a large metal bowl, whisk a cup of water, sugar, and yolks to blend. Set the bowl over a saucepan that has simmering water (be sure that the bottom of the bowl does not touch the water). Whisk the mixture constantly until it thickens and the candy thermometer registers at 170 degrees F, which is about 4 minutes.
- Remove the bowl from the simmering water then scrape the vanilla bean seeds into the egg mixture. Use an electric mixer to beat the mixture for about 5 minutes until it is thick and cool then mix in peel.
- In another large bowl, beat cream until it forms soft peaks. Add in Grand Marnier and beat until the cream mixture forms stiff peaks. Fold into the cooled mousse mixture. Cover and freeze for at least 6 hours or overnight until firm.
- To prepare phyllo cups: Use some melted butter to brush 6 3/4-cup sized custard cups. Place one phyllo sheet on a work surface, covering the remaining phyllo with plastic wrap, then a damp kitchen towel. Brush the sheet with melted butter and top with the second phyllo sheet. Brush again with melted butter and cut the stack of phyllo in to 6 5 1/2 to 6 inch squares. Press one squared stack into

each cup with the butter side down. Repeat the buttering, stacking, and cutting with the remaining two phyllo sheets. Press one square stack on top of the first with the buttered side down in each cup. Position the corners at different angles and extend them over the edges of the cups, then brush the phyllo with butter. These cups can be made 4 hours ahead and let them stand in room temperature.
- Preheat a broiler and using a small saucepan over medium-low heat, stir preserves until they are melted. On a baking sheet, arrange nectarine slices and brush with some of the apricot preserves generously. Broil for about 2 minutes just until the glaze bubbles, moving the baking sheet to make sure they are broiling evenly. Cool the nectarines in a baking sheet. In a processor, combine vanilla, flour, 1 tbsp. of butter, yolk, and almond paste and process until smooth.
- Preheat an oven at 375 degrees F. Divide the almond filling between the phyllo cups in a thin layer. Place the cups on a baking sheet and bake for about 10 minutes until filling is set and the phyllo is golden. Cool for 15 minutes.
- Gently remove phyllo cups from the custard cups and place onto plates then, melt preserves in low heat. Arrange the nectarine slices on top of the almond filling and brush with the preserves. Then, place a scoop of frozen mousse along the side.

Nutrition Information

- Calories: 876
- Total Carbohydrate: 88 g
- Cholesterol: 352 mg
- Total Fat: 55 g
- Fiber: 3 g
- Protein: 9 g
- Sodium: 125 mg
- Saturated Fat: 30 g

54. Caramelized Zucchini With Mint

"You can make this in under 45 minutes."
Serving: Serves 4

Ingredients

- 2 tbsps. olive oil
- 1 lb. zucchini, rinsed and cut into 1/3-inch-thick slices
- 3 tbsps. finely chopped fresh mint leaves
- 1 to 2 tbsps. balsamic vinegar

Direction

- Heat oil till hot yet not smoking in big heavy skillet on medium high heat; in batches, sauté zucchini slices in it with pepper and salt to taste till tender and deep golden for 2 minutes per side; mix in vinegar to taste and mint.

Nutrition Information

- Calories: 86
- Total Carbohydrate: 5 g
- Total Fat: 7 g
- Fiber: 1 g
- Protein: 2 g
- Sodium: 12 mg
- Saturated Fat: 1 g

55. Carne Adobada: Grilled Adobo-marinated Skirt Steak

"Thick cut option: sear in hot pan; finish in preheated 350°F oven."
Serving: Serves 4 | Prep: 30m

Ingredients

- 2 oz. pasilla chiles (6), wiped clean, stemmed, slit open, seeded, and deveined
- 2 oz. guajillo chiles (8), wiped clean, stemmed, slit open, seeded, and deveined
- 1/4 cup distilled white vinegar
- 1/4 cup light Mexican beer
- 1/2 cup chopped white onion
- 4 garlic cloves, peeled
- 1 tsp. fine salt, or 2 tsps. kosher salt
- 1/2 tsp. dried oregano, preferably Mexican
- 1/4 tsp. cumin seeds
- 5 whole cloves
- 2 lbs. skirt steak, cut into four 8- to 9-inch pieces
- 1 tsp. fine salt, or 2 tsps. kosher salt
- 1/2 cup pasilla-guajillo adobo (above)
- About 1 tbsp. mild olive oil or vegetable oil

Direction

- Adobo: Heat a heavy skillet/griddle/comal on medium low heat; 2-3 at a time, toast chiles, flipping over and pressing down with tongs frequently, for 1 minute per batch till chiles are fragrant. Soak chiles with enough cold water to cover for 30 minutes till soft. Drain; discard soaking water.
- Blend chiles, vinegar, beer and leftover adobo ingredients for 3 minutes till smooth, adding little water to puree if needed, in a blender jar. Strain adobo through medium-mesh sieve if you want silky, smooth texture. To marinate steak, put 1/2 cup adobo aside. Keep leftover in airtight container for 5 days, refrigerated, or keep frozen for 1 month.
- Steak: Pat dry steaks; season with salt. Generously coat with adobo; marinate for 1-2 hours in the fridge.
- Heat grill pan/grill on medium high heat; oil grill/grill pan lightly. Cook steaks for 3-5 minutes per side, varies on thickness, for medium-rare. Rest steaks for 5 minutes; serve as whole steaks or slice for taco.

Nutrition Information

- Calories: 593
- Total Carbohydrate: 21 g
- Cholesterol: 147 mg
- Total Fat: 36 g
- Fiber: 9 g
- Protein: 49 g
- Sodium: 727 mg
- Saturated Fat: 12 g

56. Carrot Pancakes With Salted Yogurt

"Gluten-free and vegetarian fritters."
Serving: 4 servings

Ingredients

- 4 large eggs, beaten to blend
- 1 lb. carrots (about 8 medium), peeled, coarsely grated
- 1/3 cup chopped fresh cilantro
- 1/4 cup chickpea flour
- Kosher salt, freshly ground pepper
- 3 tbsps. (or more) olive oil, divided
- 1 cup plain whole yogurt
- 1 cup spicy greens (such as baby mustard greens, watercress, or arugula)
- 1 tbsp. fresh lemon juice
- Flaky sea salt (such as Maldon)

Direction

- In a big bowl, mix chickpea flour, cilantro, carrots and eggs, it'll be loose. Season with pepper and kosher salt.
- In a big skillet, preferably cast iron, heat 2 tbsp. oil on medium high heat. Into skillet, scoop 2 1/2-cupfuls carrot mixture. Press each one to 1/2-in. thick. Cook, occasionally rotating skillet to brown evenly, for 3 minutes per side till pancakes are golden brown. Put onto paper towels; drain. Repeat to create 2 extra pancakes. Put extra oil into skillet if necessary.
- Meanwhile, season the yogurt with pepper and kosher salt. Toss leftover 1 tbsp. oil, lemon juice and greens. Season with pepper and kosher salt.
- Serve the carrot pancakes with salted yogurt and salad, seasoned with extra pepper and sea salt.

Nutrition Information

- Calories: 269
- Total Carbohydrate: 18 g
- Cholesterol: 194 mg
- Total Fat: 18 g
- Fiber: 4 g
- Protein: 11 g
- Sodium: 581 mg
- Saturated Fat: 4 g

57. Cauliflower Soup With Chive Oil And Rye Crostini

"An elegant soup recipe."
Serving: Makes 8 servings

Ingredients

- 2 1-oz. bunches chives
- Kosher salt
- 3/4 cup plus 1 tbsp. olive oil
- 8 thin slices cut from Finnish rye bread (for crostini) or 4 slices pumpernickel bread, cut into 1/3" cubes (for croutons)
- 2 sprigs rosemary
- 1 large head of cauliflower (about 2 lbs.), leaves discarded
- 12 tbsps. (1 1/2 sticks) unsalted butter, softened, divided
- Kosher salt
- 1 large onion, minced
- 1/4 cup heavy cream

Direction

- Crostini and chive oil: In a glass, put a coffee filter; put aside. Blanch chives in medium saucepan with boiling salted water for 10 seconds; to cool, put into medium bowl with ice water. Squeeze dry chives; chop coarsely. Put in blender with 3/4 cup oil; puree till smooth. Through coffee filter; pour; drain at room temperature for 3 hours or refrigerated overnight. Don't press on solids. You can make it 1 week ahead, chilled and covered. Before using, bring to room temperature.
- Preheat an oven to 400°F. Line parchment paper on rimmed baking sheet. Brush 1 tbsp.

olive oil (or toss bread cubes) on bread slices; toss with rosemary sprigs. Put on prepped sheet; bake for 12 minutes till crisp. Fully cool; discard rosemary sprigs. You can make it 1 day ahead; keep at room temperature, airtight.

- Soup: Preheat an oven to 350°F. In a big baking dish, put whole cauliflower head; rub with 4 tbsp. butter. Use salt to season. Put 1/2 cup water in dish; bake, uncovered, for 1 1/2 hours till inserted knife in core meets no resistance; if cauliflower starts to brown, tent with foil. Take cauliflower from oven; cool. Chop coarsely; put aside.
- Melt 2 tbsp. butter on medium low heat in big saucepan. Add onion; cook, occasionally mixing, for 15 minutes till onion is translucent and soft. Add 4 cups water and cauliflower; simmer for 10 minutes till cauliflower is very soft. Slightly cool. Puree in blender in batches till very smooth. You can make it 2 days ahead, chilled, covered.
- Put soup in pot; simmer; if too thick, add more water. Season with salt. Take off heat; whisk in cream and leftover 6 tbsp. butter. In shallow bowls, serve warm. Rest crostini on each bowl's edge or scatter croutons on top; drizzle chive oil.

Nutrition Information

- Calories: 462
- Total Carbohydrate: 18 g
- Cholesterol: 56 mg
- Total Fat: 43 g
- Fiber: 4 g
- Protein: 5 g
- Sodium: 491 mg
- Saturated Fat: 16 g

58. Celery And Jicama Sauté

"A unique side dish."
Serving: Makes 8 to 10 servings | Prep: 25m

Ingredients

- 1 (2 1/2-lb) bunch of celery
- 1 1/4 lb jicama
- 2 tbsps. olive oil
- 2 garlic cloves, smashed
- 1/3 cup coarsely chopped fresh flat-leaf parsley
- 1 tsp. finely grated fresh lemon zest
- 2 tsps. fresh lemon juice
- 1 tsp. salt
- 1/4 tsp. black pepper

Direction

- Use a vegetable peeler to peel strings from celery; on long diagonal, cut celery to 1/4-in. thick slices. Use a sharp knife to peel jicama; cut to 2x1/4-in. matchsticks.
- Heat oil till hot yet not smoking in a 6-8-qt. heavy pot on medium high heat; sauté garlic, flipping, for 2 minutes till golden on all sides. Discard garlic.
- Put celery in oil; sauté, mixing, for 3 minutes till soft. Add jicama; sauté, mixing, for 5 minutes till slightly translucent. Mix in leftover ingredients; take off heat.
- You can cut jicama and celery 1 day ahead; chill in dampened paper towel-lined sealed plastic bag.

Nutrition Information

- Calories: 82
- Total Carbohydrate: 11 g
- Total Fat: 4 g
- Fiber: 6 g
- Protein: 2 g
- Sodium: 409 mg
- Saturated Fat: 1 g

59. Cheddar And Stilton Drop Biscuits

"A great recipe!"
Serving: Makes 12 biscuits

Ingredients

- 2 1/2 cups unbleached all purpose flour
- 2 tbsps. sugar
- 1 tbsp. baking powder
- 3/4 tsp. cream of tartar
- 1/2 tsp. salt
- 7 tbsps. chilled unsalted butter, cut into 1/2-inch pieces
- 1 cup (packed) coarsely grated sharp cheddar cheese, chilled
- 1/2 cup coarsely crumbled Stilton cheese (about 2 oz.), chilled
- 1 1/4 cups chilled buttermilk
- 1 large egg

Direction

- Put 1 rack on top oven third then 1 rack on bottom third; preheat to 400°F. Butter then flour 2 big baking sheets. Whisk initial 5 ingredients to blend well in big bowl. Add butter; rub in with fingertips till it looks like coarse meal. Add both the cheeses; rub in using fingertips till cheeses reduce to small pieces. In small bowl, blend egg and buttermilk. Add to flour mixture, mixing till dough just moistens evenly.
- Drop 6 mounds, using 1/3 cup dough for every biscuit, on each prepped sheet, 2-3-in. apart; bake the biscuits for 10 minutes. Reverse sheets positions. Bake biscuits for 10 minutes till inserted tester in middle exits clean and golden brown. Put biscuits in basket and serve warm.

Nutrition Information

- Calories: 233
- Total Carbohydrate: 24 g
- Cholesterol: 48 mg
- Total Fat: 12 g
- Fiber: 1 g
- Protein: 7 g
- Sodium: 261 mg
- Saturated Fat: 7 g

60. Chicken Breasts Provençal

"A lovely classic French dish."
Serving: Makes 4 servings | Prep: 30m

Ingredients

- 1 lb. ripe plum tomatoes
- 4 (6- to 8-oz.) skinless boneless chicken breasts, tenders reserved for another use
- 1/4 cup all-purpose flour
- 2 tbsps. vegetable oil
- 1 tsp. minced garlic
- 1 flat anchovy fillet, mashed to a paste
- 1/2 cup dry white wine
- 3/4 cup chicken stock or reduced-sodium chicken broth
- 10 pitted brine-cured black olives, thinly sliced lengthwise
- 2 tbsps. unsalted butter, softened
- 1 tbsp. finely shredded basil

Direction

- Core tomatoes; on bottom of each, cut shallow X. Blanch for 10 seconds in medium pot with boiling water. To stop cooking, put into ice bath with slotted spoon. Peel and seed; chop finely.
- Pat dry chicken; sprinkle with 1/2 tsp. each pepper and salt. Dredge in flour; shake excess off.
- Heat oil till it shimmers in 12-in. heavy skillet on medium high heat; cook chicken, flipping once, for 6-8 minutes total till just cooked through and golden. Put onto platter; keep, covered, warm.
- Add anchovy paste and garlic to skillet; cook on medium heat, mixing, for 30 seconds till fragrant. Add wine; boil, scraping brown bits up. Mix in olives, stock and tomatoes; simmer,

uncovered, occasionally mixing, for 8-10 minutes till it thickens into sauce. Whisk in juices from platter and butter.
- Add chicken; simmer for 1 minute till just heated through. Sprinkle basil; serve.

Nutrition Information

- Calories: 430
- Total Carbohydrate: 12 g
- Cholesterol: 161 mg
- Total Fat: 19 g
- Fiber: 2 g
- Protein: 48 g
- Sodium: 296 mg
- Saturated Fat: 5 g

61. Chicken In Lemongrass Sauce

"A Vietnamese dish serve rice with this and it'll be a great meal."
Serving: Makes 4 to 6 servings

Ingredients

- 12 oz. green Chinese long beans or green beans, trimmed, cut into 1 1/2-inch pieces
- 2 tbsps. peanut oil
- 1 1/2 lbs. skinless boneless chicken breast halves, cut crosswise into 1/2-inch-wide strips
- 1 medium onion, sliced
- 4 garlic cloves, minced
- 1/3 cup minced lemongrass*
- 3 tbsps. Thai fish sauce (nam pla)*
- 3 tbsps. sugar
- 2 tsps. ground coriander
- 1 tsp. turmeric
- 1/2 cup chicken stock or canned low-salt chicken broth
- 2 tbsps. spicy oyster sauce*

Direction

- In big saucepan of boiling salted water, cook beans for 2 minutes just till crisp tender. Drain.

- In heavy big skillet, heat oil over high heat. Put in garlic, onion and chicken; stir-fry for 4 minutes till chicken is partly cooked. Put in lemongrass and the following 4 ingredients; mix for 2 minutes. Put in oyster sauce, stock and beans; lower heat and allow to simmer for 4 minutes more, till chicken is cooked through and sauce thickens. Add pepper and salt to taste.

Nutrition Information

- Calories: 373
- Total Carbohydrate: 24 g
- Cholesterol: 125 mg
- Total Fat: 12 g
- Fiber: 3 g
- Protein: 42 g
- Sodium: 1433 mg
- Saturated Fat: 2 g

62. Chickpea And Eggplant Salad

"A simple salad recipe."
Serving: 4 as a side, 2 as a meal

Ingredients

- 1/2 a small red onion, finely sliced
- 1 large eggplant, cut in half lengthwise and sliced into thin half moons
- A good glug of extra virgin olive oil
- Juice and zest of 1 lemon
- 2 (13.5-oz.) cans of chickpeas, drained and rinsed
- 2 large fresh tomatoes
- 1 bunch of fresh parsley, chopped
- 2 tsps. garlic-infused olive oil
- 1 tsp. cayenne pepper
- Slivered almonds, to serve

Direction

- Cover onion in water; put aside for 1/2 hour to reduce harshness of taste.

- Eggplant: Spread half-moon slices out on baking sheet; brush olive oil. Put on high rack under broiler for 5 minutes; remove. Brush mix of lemon juice and olive oil; it's okay to make them very wet. Put under broiler till flesh is soft and slice's edges slightly blacken; put aside in big bowl.
- Spread out chickpeas on same baking sheet; broil till golden. Add to bowl with eggplant.
- Dice tomatoes to small cubes; add to bowl with pepper, salt, zest, leftover lemon juice, cayenne pepper, garlic oil, drained red onion slices and parsley. Stir well. Serve, sprinkled with slivered almonds, warm.

Nutrition Information

- Calories: 1424
- Total Carbohydrate: 241 g
- Total Fat: 31 g
- Fiber: 77 g
- Protein: 66 g
- Sodium: 1712 mg
- Saturated Fat: 3 g

63. Chili Con Carne

"This dish is a little bit complicated but has fantastic flavor."
Serving: Makes 8 servings | Prep: 1h

Ingredients

- 4 tbsps. vegetable oil, divided
- 4 lbs. well-trimmed boneless beef chuck (from about 5 lbs.), cut into 1/2-inch cube
- 2 medium onions, chopped
- 1 head of garlic (about 15 cloves), peeled, chopped
- 1/2 cup ground ancho chiles
- 2 tbsps. ground cumin
- 1/2 tsp. ground allspice
- 1/4 tsp. ground cinnamon
- 1/4 tsp. ground cloves
- 1 12-oz. bottle dark beer
- 1 28-oz. can diced tomatoes in juice

- 2 tsps. dried oregano
- 2 tsps. coarse kosher salt
- 2 tbsps. tomato paste
- 3 tbsps. masa (corn tortilla mix)
- Coarsely grated sharp cheddar cheese
- Chopped green and/or red onion
- Chopped fresh cilantro
- Diced fresh tomatoes (optional)
- Sour cream (optional)
- Ingredient info: Ground ancho chiles are available in the spice section of super markets and at Latin markets. Masa (or masa harina) is sold at super markets and Latin markets.

Direction

- In a big pot, heat 1 tbsp. oil on medium-high heat. Add in 1/3 of the beef, sprinkle salt on top. Cook for around 3 minutes until browned, mixing from time to time. Transfer beef to a big bowl with a slotted spoon. Repeat another 2 times with 2 tbsp. oil and beef.
- Decrease to medium heat. Put in onions and 1 tbsp. oil. Sauté for 8-10 minutes until soft. Add in garlic, mix for 2 minutes. Add cloves, cinnamon, allspice, cumin, and ground anchos; stir for about 1 minute until fragrant. Pour in beer and mix for 1 minute, scraping up brown pieces. Bring juices and beef back to the pot. Add in 2 tsps. coarse salt, oregano, 2 cups water, and tomatoes with juice. Heat chili to a boil. Decrease to low heat, use lid lightly ajar to cover; allow to simmer gently for 1 3/4 -2 hours till the beef is just tender. Cool down for 1 hour; uncover, chill until cold. Cover and chill all night.
- Use a spoon to remove fat from chili. Allow chili to simmer on medium heat. Mix in tomato paste; spread masa on top; mix to combine. Let simmer without cover until beef is very tender and thickened, stirring frequently; if too thick, pour in more water by 1/4 cupfuls, about 30 minutes.
- Distribute chili into bowls. Put garnishes on top then serve.

64. Chinese Plain Rice

"One of the hardest things to do is cooking the rice perfectly the key is if pot is more than half full with rice, change to a bigger one."
Serving: Serves 4

Ingredients

- 2 cups of long grain rice
- 3 cups cold water

Direction

- Rinse the rice in bit of cold water, massaging grains among the palms. Wash in cold water till water is clear. Let drain. In 1 1/2-quart sauce pan, place the rice. Pour in cold water. Boil. Reduce the heat till you can cover the pan without boiling over. Let cook with cover for 15 to 20 minutes, till all the water is soaked in. Fluff rice using fork or chopsticks. Place cover and let sit in warm place till serving time.

Nutrition Information

- Calories: 338
- Total Carbohydrate: 74 g
- Total Fat: 1 g
- Fiber: 1 g
- Protein: 7 g
- Sodium: 12 mg
- Saturated Fat: 0 g

65. Chipotle-glazed Shrimp

"So tasty."
Serving: Serves 6

Ingredients

- 2 tbsps. olive oil
- 1 cup finely chopped onion
- 4 garlic cloves, minced
- 2 tsps. ground cumin
- 1 tsp. dried oregano
- 1 cup water
- 1/4 cup apple cider vinegar
- 2 tbsps. chopped canned chipotle chilies
- 1 1/2 lbs. uncooked jumbo shrimp, peeled, deveined
- 1/4 cup orange juice
- 2 tbsps. golden brown sugar

Direction

- Heat oil on medium heat in medium heavy skillet. Add onion; sauté for 10 minutes till golden brown. Add oregano, cumin and garlic; mix for 1 minute. Put into blender. Put chipotles, vinegar and 1 cup water in blender; puree till smooth. Put 1/2 puree into medium bowl; cool. Put shrimp in bowl; toss till coated. Cover and chill for 2 hours.
- Put leftover puree in medium heavy saucepan. Add brown sugar and orange juice; boil. Lower heat; simmer for 10 minutes till glaze reduces to 1/2 cup and slightly thick. Take off heat; cool.
- Prep barbecue to medium high heat. Take shrimp from marinade; use paper towels to pat dry. Brush some orange juice glaze on shrimp; grill shrimp, occasionally brushing with more glaze, for 2 minutes per side till opaque in center. Put onto platter.

Nutrition Information

- Calories: 156
- Total Carbohydrate: 9 g
- Cholesterol: 143 mg
- Total Fat: 6 g
- Fiber: 1 g
- Protein: 16 g
- Sodium: 703 mg
- Saturated Fat: 1 g

66. Chocolate Caramel Sauce

"You can prep this in less than 45 minutes."
Serving: Makes about 1 1/4 cups

Ingredients

- 1/2 cup sugar
- 3/4 cup heavy cream
- 3 oz. fine-quality bittersweet chocolate (not unsweetened), chopped fine
- 1/8 tsp. salt
- 1/2 tsp. vanilla extract

Direction

- Cook sugar, undisturbed, in dry heavy saucepan on medium heat till it starts to melt; cook, swirling pan, till it is deep golden caramel. Take off heat. Add cream; it'll bubble up then simmer it, mixing, till caramel melts. Add salt and chocolate; cook sauce, whisking, on low heat till sauce is smooth and chocolate is melted. Whisk in vanilla; serve sauce at room temperature/warm on ice cream.

Nutrition Information

- Calories: 567
- Total Carbohydrate: 64 g
- Cholesterol: 98 mg
- Total Fat: 37 g
- Fiber: 2 g
- Protein: 3 g
- Sodium: 148 mg
- Saturated Fat: 22 g

67. Chocolate Mousse

"A low-calorie and low-fat mousse."
Serving: 6 | Ready in: 4h

Ingredients

- 1 tsp. unflavored gelatin
- 2 tbsps. coffee liqueur, rum or strong brewed coffee
- ¾ cup low-fat milk
- 1 large egg
- 1 cup packed light brown sugar
- ⅔ cup unsweetened cocoa powder, preferably Dutch-process
- 2 oz. bittersweet (not unsweetened) chocolate, chopped
- 2 tsps. vanilla extract
- 4 large egg whites
- ½ tsp. cream of tartar
- 3 tbsps. water

Direction

- Sprinkle gelatin on coffee/rum/liqueur in small bowl; let stand for 1 minute till softened.
- Whisk cocoa, 1/4 cup brown sugar, whole egg and milk in medium saucepan till smooth; cook on low heat for 5 minutes till thick, constantly whisking. Take off heat; add softened gelatin mixture, mixing till gelatin melts. Add vanilla and chocolate; mix till chocolate melts. Cool for 30 minutes to room temperature.
- Put 1-in. water to bare simmer in wide saucepan. Mix leftover 3/4 cup brown sugar, water, cream of tartar and egg whites in heatproof bowl big enough to fit above saucepan; put bowl above barely simmering water. Use electric mixer to beat at low speed for 3-5 minutes, constantly moving beaters around, till an instant-read thermometer reads 140°F.
- Put mixer speed on high; beat for 3 1/2 minutes on heat; take bowl off heat. Beat meringue for another 4-5 minutes till cool.
- Whisk 1/4 meringue into chocolate mixture till smooth; fold chocolate mixture back into leftover meringue using rubber spatula till incorporated completely. Put mousse in 6 dessert glasses; chill for 3 hours till set.

Nutrition Information

- Calories: 247 calories;
- Total Carbohydrate: 48 g
- Cholesterol: 34 mg
- Total Fat: 6 g

- Fiber: 4 g
- Protein: 7 g
- Sodium: 67 mg
- Sugar: 40 g
- Saturated Fat: 3 g

68. Chocolate Peanut Butter Torte

Serving: Makes 8 servings

Ingredients

- 1 prebaked pie shell
- 2 large eggs, at room temperature
- 4 large egg yolks, at room temperature
- 1/3 cup sugar
- 1 cup peanut butter
- 7 tbsps. unsalted butter
- 3 oz. bittersweet chocolate
- 1/4 cup lightly salted peanuts, coarsely chopped

Direction

- Preheat oven to 325°F. Set electric mixer on medium-high speed, whisk yolks, eggs, and sugar for 6 minutes until ribbons in a mixing bowl. In a separate microwaveable bowl, combine butter, peanut butter, and chocolate then microwave on high for 1 minute. Mix until mixture is smooth. Set aside to cool.
- Add egg mixture in three additions to chocolate mixture. Into prepped pie shell transfer mixture. Drizzle peanuts on top of the pie and bake for 12 minutes. Pie surface must be soft, and center should be slightly liquidity. Set aside and let it cool for 30 minutes. Serve. Filling will be gooey and overflowing out of the side of the pie slice.

Nutrition Information

- Calories: 565
- Total Carbohydrate: 38 g
- Cholesterol: 165 mg
- Total Fat: 43 g

- Fiber: 3 g
- Protein: 13 g
- Sodium: 166 mg
- Saturated Fat: 16 g

69. Chocolate Puddings With Orange Whipped Cream

Serving: Makes 6 servings | Prep: 25m

Ingredients

- 1/2 cup plus 3 tbsps. sugar, divided
- 2 tbsps. cornstarch
- 2 1/2 cups whole milk, divided
- 2 large egg yolks
- 1 1/2 cups bittersweet chocolate chips (do not exceed 61% cacao) or semisweet chocolate chips
- 2 tbsps. (1/4 stick) unsalted butter
- 1/4 tsp. vanilla extract
- 3/4 cup chilled whipping cream
- 1 tbsp. Grand Marnier or other orange liqueur
- 1/4 tsp. finely grated orange peel
- Test-kitchen tip: If you don't have orange liqueur on hand, skip the orange peel and use another liqueur. Kahlúa or amaretto would work well in this recipe.

Direction

- In a medium saucepan, whip cornstarch, quarter tsp. of salt and half cup plus two tbsps. of sugar to incorporate. Put in egg yolks and half cup of milk; mix till smooth. Mix in the leftover 2 cups of milk. Boil mixture on moderately-high heat, whisk continuously. Boil for a minute, whisk continuously. Take pan off heat; put in butter and chocolate chips. Mix pudding till smooth and melted. Mix in vanilla.
- Evenly distribute pudding between six wineglasses or dessert cups. Put plastic wrap right on the top of each to cover pudding fully. Refrigerate for no less than 3 hours, till cold.

DO AHEAD: may be done up to one day in advance. Keep in refrigerator.

- In a medium bowl, whip leftover 1 tbsp. of sugar, orange peel, Grand Marnier and whipping cream with electric mixer to form peaks. DO AHEAD: may be done 2 hours in advance. Refrigerate with cover.
- Remove puddings cover. Scoop whipped cream dollop on top of each to serve.

Nutrition Information

- Calories: 311
- Total Carbohydrate: 32 g
- Cholesterol: 115 mg
- Total Fat: 18 g
- Fiber: 0 g
- Protein: 5 g
- Sodium: 58 mg
- Saturated Fat: 11 g

70. Chocolate Torte With Calvados-poached Figs

"Cook figs till just soft; intense boiling/overcooking makes then tough."
Serving: Makes 10 servings | Prep: 40m

Ingredients

- 1 cup (2 sticks) unsalted butter, room temperature, plus more for pan
- 1 cup superfine sugar, divided, plus more for pan
- 8 oz. bittersweet chocolate, chopped
- 1 1/2 cups blanched hazelnuts
- 1/2 cup all-purpose flour
- 2 tbsps. unsweetened cocoa powder
- 1 tsp. kosher salt
- 6 large eggs, separated
- 1 tsp. vanilla extract
- 1/2 tsps. cream of tartar
- 2/3 cup Calvados (apple brandy)
- 2/3 cup granulated sugar

- 2 cups dried black Mission figs or pitted prunes (about 8 oz.), halved if large

Direction

- Cake: Put rack in center of oven; preheat it to 375°F. Butter 9-in. diameter cake pan/springform pan; line with parchment round. Butter parchment; sprinkle superfine sugar on pan.
- Melt chocolate in heatproof bowl above saucepan with simmering water without touching water, mixing till smooth; slightly cool.
- Pulse 1/2 cup superfine sugar, salt, cocoa powder, flour and hazelnuts till finely ground in a food processor; through medium-mesh sieve, sift. If needed, pulse any bigger pieces in food processor.
- Beat leftover 3/4 cup superfine sugar and 1 cup butter using electric mixer at high speed for 4 minutes till fluffy and light. One by one, add egg yolks; beat to blend between the additions. Beat in vanilla. Lower speed to low; stir in melted chocolate. Add dry ingredients slowly, mixing till just combined.
- Beat cream of tartar and egg whites with clean beaters on medium high speed till stiff peaks form in medium bowl.
- Fold 1/3 whites to loosen into chocolate batter with rubber spatula; fold leftover whites into batter till just combined. Scrape the batter into prepped pan.
- Bake cake for 20 minutes. Lower oven temperature to 350°F; bake for 30-40 minutes till inserted tester in middle exits clean. Put pan on wire rack; cool cake for 30 minutes. Unmold; fully cool.
- You can bake cake 2 days ahead; tightly wrap and keep at room temperature.
- Figs and assembly: Boil 2/3 cup water, granulated sugar and calvados in a small saucepan, mixing to dissolve sugar. Add figs; lower heat to low. Gently simmer for 20-25 minutes till figs are very soft. Cool.
- Serve cake with syrup and figs.
- You can poach figs 1 week ahead. Cover; chill.

Nutrition Information

- Calories: 683
- Total Carbohydrate: 71 g
- Cholesterol: 160 mg
- Total Fat: 41 g
- Fiber: 5 g
- Protein: 9 g
- Sodium: 237 mg
- Saturated Fat: 18 g

71. Chocolate Truffles

"A super easy recipe."
Serving: Makes 30 to 36 truffles

Ingredients

- 12 oz. good-quality semi-sweet or bittersweet chocolate
- 2/3 cup heavy cream or nondairy whipping cream
- 2 tbsps. Dutch processed cocoa powder
- 2 tbsps. confectioner's sugar
- 3 tbsps. finely chopped unsalted pistachios, almonds, or hazelnuts

Direction

- By hand/food processor fitted with metal blade, chop chocolate finely; put into medium bowl. Put cream into small heavy saucepan; put on rolling boil on medium heat. Put cream on chocolate; mix gently to melt chocolate with a wooden spoon. Don't stir/whisk too strongly or you'll put air in. Cover; chill for 2 hours till firm.
- Line waxed/parchment paper on baking sheet. Drop mixture by rounded teaspoonfuls with small melon baller/ice-cream scoop on prepped sheet. Freeze for 20 minutes till firm.
- Put chopped nuts, confectioner's sugar and cocoa into 3 different shallow bowls.
- Roll 1/3 balls into cocoa mixture, 1/3 in confectioner's sugar and 1/3 in chopped nuts. Roll between your palms quickly to shape

them to perfect round shape. Reroll in sugar/nuts if too much falls off. In 1 layer, put back onto parchment-lined baking sheet/other parchment-lined container. Use plastic to cover; chill till serving time. You can make this 10 days in advance; remain refrigerated.

Nutrition Information

- Calories: 73
- Total Carbohydrate: 8 g
- Cholesterol: 5 mg
- Total Fat: 5 g
- Fiber: 1 g
- Protein: 1 g
- Sodium: 3 mg
- Saturated Fat: 3 g

72. Chocolate-caramel Tartlets With Roasted Bananas And Ginger-citrus Caramel

Serving: Makes 4

Ingredients

- 2/3 cup all purpose flour
- 3 tbsps. unsweetened cocoa powder (preferably Dutch-process)
- 1/2 cup powdered sugar
- 1/4 cup (1/2 stick) unsalted butter, room temperature
- 3 large egg yolks
- 1/2 cup plus 1 tbsp. sugar
- 3 tbsps. water
- 2 tsps. light corn syrup
- 1/4 tsp. fresh lemon juice
- 1/3 cup heavy whipping cream
- 1 tbsp. unsalted butter
- 1 cup heavy whipping cream
- 1 tbsp. light corn syrup
- 3 whole star anise*
- 4 1/2 oz. bittersweet (not unsweetened) or semisweet chocolate, coarsely chopped

- 2 tbsps. (1/4 stick) unsalted butter, room temperature
- 1 oz. bittersweet (not unsweetened) or semisweet chocolate, finely chopped
- 4 tsps. (generous) plus 2 tbsps. chopped lightly salted roasted cashews
- 1/4 cup sugar
- 2 tbsps. water
- 1/2 cup strained orange juice
- 1 2-inch piece peeled fresh ginger, grated, pressed through garlic press to extract 1/2 tsp. juice
- 1/2 vanilla bean, split lengthwise in half
- 3 tbsps. unsalted butter
- 2 tbsps. (packed) golden brown sugar
- 1 large banana, sliced

Direction

- Crust: Into small bowl, sift cocoa and flour. Beat butter and powdered sugar using electric mixer till well blended in medium bowl; beat in flour mixture. One by one, beat in egg yolks. Gather dough to ball; flatten to disk. Chill for 1 hour – 1 day. Slightly soften before rolling out at room temperature.
- Preheat an oven to 375°F. Roll dough out to 1/8-in. thick on floured surface. Cut out rounds using 5-in. diameter bowl/plate as guide. If needed, reroll dough scraps to make 4 5-in. rounds in total. Press each dough round up sides and on bottom of 4 1/4-4 1/2-in. diameter tartlet pan that has removable bottom. Use fork to pierce crusts all over; freeze crusts for 10 minutes. Bake for 15 minutes till starting to pull away from pan's sides and firm to touch; fully cool in pans on the rack.
- Caramel filling: Mix sugar with next 3 ingredients in small heavy saucepan on medium heat till sugar dissolves. Increase heat; boil without mixing, brushing down pan's sides occasionally using wet pastry brush and swirling the pan, for 7 minutes till deep amber color. Take off heat. Add cream; it'll vigorously bubble. Mix on low heat till

caramel is smooth and caramel bits melt. Whisk in butter; put aside.
- Chocolate ganache topping: Boil corn syrup and cream in small heavy saucepan. Add star anise; take off heat. Cover; steep for 15 minutes. Throw star anise away. Boil it; take off heat. Add butter and 4 1/2-oz. coarsely chopped bittersweet chocolate; whisk ganache topping till smooth.
- Mix 1-oz. finely chopped bittersweet chocolate on top of double boiler above simmering water till melted. Brush melted chocolate inside of each crust; sprinkle 1 generous tsp. chopped cashews on each. Put caramel filling, 2 tbsp. for each, on nuts in crusts; chill them for 30 minutes till caramel slightly sets.
- If needed, rewarm chocolate ganache topping till just pourable. Put chocolate ganache on caramel filling; refrigerate for 45 minutes till ganache just sets. Stand tartlets at room temperature. You can make it 1 day ahead. Loosely cover tartlets; stand in room temperature.
- Ginger citrus caramel sauce: Mix 2 tbsp. water and 1/4 cup sugar in small heavy saucepan on low heat till sugar dissolves. Increase heat; boil without mixing, occasionally swirling pan and brushing pan's sides down with wet pastry brush, for 5 minutes till medium amber color (not deep). Take off heat; add 1/2 tsp. ginger juice and orange juice slowly. From vanilla bean, scrape in seeds. Boil, mixing till caramel bits melt. Boil for 4 minutes till sauce reduces to 1/4 cup and is slightly syrupy. You can make it 1 day ahead. Cover; stand in room temperature. Rewarm till just pourable on low heat.
- Preheat an oven to 450°F. In small heavy saucepan, melt butter on low heat. Add the brown sugar; whisk for 1 minute till blended. Add banana slices; toss to coat. Put banana mixture in small baking sheet; bake for 4 minutes till sugar mixture bubbles and bananas start to slightly brown around edges.
- From tartlet pans, remove sides. Put tartlets on plate; around tartlets, drizzle ginger caramel

sauce. Put banana slices alongside; sprinkle leftover 2 tbsp. cashews. Serve.

Nutrition Information

- Calories: 1492
- Total Carbohydrate: 132 g
- Cholesterol: 455 mg
- Total Fat: 110 g
- Fiber: 6 g
- Protein: 14 g
- Sodium: 98 mg
- Saturated Fat: 64 g

73. Chocolate-chestnut Mousse

"Simple and tasty."
Serving: 8–10 servings | Prep: 20m

Ingredients

- 10.5 oz. vacuum-packed or jarred roasted or steamed chestnuts (about 2 cups)
- 2 cups whole milk
- 1/2 cup sugar
- 1 tbsp. vanilla extract
- 1/2 tsp. kosher salt
- 5 oz. best-quality bittersweet chocolate (at least 70% cacao), divided
- 1 1/2 tsps. brandy, divided
- 3 cups heavy cream, divided

Direction

- Boil salt, vanilla, sugar, milk and chestnuts in small saucepan on high heat. Lower heat; simmer. Cook, occasionally mixing, for 15-17 minutes till chestnuts fairly easily smash against pot's side with back of spoon and milk reduces by a quarter.
- Meanwhile, chop 4-oz. chocolate finely. Shave leftover 1-oz. chocolate using peeler; put aside till serving.
- Puree chestnut mixture for 2 minutes till very smooth in blender on high speed. Add 1 tsp. brandy and chopped chocolate; blend on high speed for 30 seconds till chocolate melts.

Scrape into big bowl; cool, occasionally mixing, to room temperature for 15-20 minutes; vigorously mix till smooth if lumps form.

- Use a whisk to whip 2 cups cream till just barely holds soft peaks in another big bowl. Mix 1/3 cream to lighten into chocolate mixture; fold in leftover cream till just incorporated. Put mousse into big serving bowl and cover; chill for 2 hours – 1 day.
- Use a whisk to whip 1/2 tsp. brandy and leftover 1 cup cream to medium peaks in a big bowl. Use reserved chocolate shavings to garnish mousse; serve it with whipped cream next to it.
- You can make mousse 1 day ahead. Cover; chill.
- Try to get 70% bittersweet chocolate, the best quality that you can get.

Nutrition Information

- Calories: 555
- Total Carbohydrate: 45 g
- Cholesterol: 128 mg
- Total Fat: 41 g
- Fiber: 1 g
- Protein: 5 g
- Sodium: 181 mg
- Saturated Fat: 25 g

74. Chocolate-ginger Angel Food Cake

"Mouthwatering chocolate treat with two grams of fiber for each serving. To minimize the spice, you can use candied orange in place of the ginger."
Serving: Makes a 10-inch cake; serves 10

Ingredients

- Parchment paper
- 1 1/3 cups confectioners' sugar
- 1 cup plus 1 tbsp. all-purpose flour
- 1/3 cup unsweetened cocoa powder
- 2/3 tsp. ground ginger

- 9 egg whites
- 1 tbsp. vanilla extract
- 1 tsp. cream of tartar
- 1/4 tsp. salt
- 1 cup plus 2 tbsps. granulated sugar
- 1 cup half-and-half
- 4 oz. semisweet chocolate, chopped
- 3 tbsps. confectioners' sugar
- 1/2 cup candied (crystallized) ginger, chopped

Direction

- Place rack in the middle of the oven then preheat to 350 degrees F. Put parchment paper in a 10-in Bundt or springform pan. In a bowl, sift ground ginger, cocoa, flour and confectioner's sugar together; set aside. Whisk salt, cream of tartar, vanilla and egg whites on medium speed for 1-2mins using a mixer with whisk attachment until the whites turn into soft peaks. Turn to high speed then whisk in 6 tbsp. granulated sugar and whip until combined. Put the remaining 3/4 cup granulated sugar in two additions while whisking for 2mins until whites form into stiff peaks. Mix in the dry ingredients gently into the egg mixture using a spatula; move to the pan. Bake for 35-40mins until the cake bounces back when pressed; take it out of the oven then completely cool. Slide a knife around the edges to loosen then move to a serving platter.
- Prepare the chocolate glaze. On medium-high heat, boil half-and-half in a pot. Lower the heat to a low simmer then whisk in confectioners' sugar and chocolate until the mixture is smooth and the chocolate melts. Spread the glaze over the cake and let it drip down the sides. Add candied ginger on top. Place in a cake saver at room temperature for as long as three days.

75. Chopped Arabic Salad

"A refreshing salad recipe."
Serving: Makes 4 to 6 side-dish servings

Ingredients

- 1 lemon
- 3/4 tsp. salt
- 1/4 tsp. black pepper
- 3 tbsps. olive oil
- 2 (1/2-lb) cucumbers, peeled, halved lengthwise, seeded, and cut into 1/4-inch dice (2 1/3 cups)
- 1 lb tomatoes (3 medium), cut into 1/3-inch dice (2 1/2 cups)
- 1 cup finely chopped red onion (1 small) or 1 cup chopped scallions (about 5)
- 1 cup coarsely chopped purslane (optional)
- 1 cup finely chopped fresh flat-leaf parsley (from 1 large bunch)
- 1/2 cup finely chopped fresh mint (from 1 bunch)

Direction

- From lemon, use a sharp paring knife to cut peel and all white pith; cut segments from 1/2 lemon free from membranes above a bowl. Put segments onto cutting board; squeeze leftover 1/2 lemon and juice from membranes into bowl. Put 2 tbsp. juice into big bowl. Finely chop segments; put into measured juice. Add oil, pepper and salt, whisking to combine; mix in leftover ingredients.

Nutrition Information

- Calories: 143
- Total Carbohydrate: 12 g
- Total Fat: 11 g
- Fiber: 3 g
- Protein: 2 g
- Sodium: 453 mg
- Saturated Fat: 1 g

76. Chopped Salad

"Crunchy vegetables and tangy blue cheese combine in this
simple and delicious salad."
Serving: 4 | Ready in: 15m

Ingredients

- 1 shallot, minced
- 2 tbsps. extra-virgin olive oil
- 2 tbsps. red-wine vinegar
- 4 cups chopped romaine lettuce
- 1 chopped red bell pepper
- 1 cup chopped carrots
- 2 oz. crumbled blue cheese

Direction

- Mix vinegar, oil, and shallot together. Mix carrots, bell pepper, and lettuce together. Toss the vegetables with the dressing and cheese.

Nutrition Information

- Calories: 147 calories;
- Total Carbohydrate: 8 g
- Cholesterol: 11 mg
- Total Fat: 11 g
- Fiber: 3 g
- Protein: 4 g
- Sodium: 190 mg
- Sugar: 4 g
- Saturated Fat: 4 g

77. Cider Mini-doughnuts

Serving: Makes about 36 small doughnuts | Prep: 45m

Ingredients

- 1 cup unfiltered apple cider
- 3 1/2 cups all-purpose flour
- 1 tbsp. baking powder
- 1 1/4 tsps. baking soda
- 1 tsp. salt
- 2 tsps. cinnamon, divided
- 1/2 cup well-shaken buttermilk
- 3/4 stick unsalted butter, melted
- 2 large eggs
- 2 cups sugar, divided
- 3 quart vegetable oil
- Equipment: a 2-inch round cookie cutter; a deep-fat thermometer

Direction

- Boil cider in small heavy saucepan for 12-15 minutes till reduced to 1/3 cup; fully cool.
- Whisk 1 tsp. cinnamon, salt, baking soda, baking powder and flour.
- Whisk 1 cup sugar, eggs, butter, buttermilk and reduced cider in small bowl; mix into flour mixture until it forms a sticky dough.
- Turn dough onto well-floured surface; pat out to 13-in. 1/3-in. thick round with lightly floured hands. Use floured cutter to cut out rounds; put onto floured baking sheet and repeat with scraps; reroll once.
- Heat oil in 5-qt. heavy pot on medium heat to 370°F; into oil, slide 10 doughnuts. Flip when every doughnut floats to surface. Fry, flipping again, for 1 1/2-2 minutes till golden brown. On paper towels, drain. Make extra doughnuts, putting oil to 370°F between the batches. Slightly cool; dredge it in cinnamon sugar made from leftover 1 tsp. cinnamon and leftover 1 cup sugar.

Nutrition Information

- Calories: 773
- Total Carbohydrate: 22 g
- Cholesterol: 16 mg
- Total Fat: 77 g
- Fiber: 0 g
- Protein: 2 g
- Sodium: 150 mg
- Saturated Fat: 6 g

78. Cinnamon Oat Cakes

"Tasty and simple."
Serving: Makes 2 servings

Ingredients

- 2 cups rolled oats
- 4 egg whites
- 1 tsp. cinnamon
- Vegetable oil cooking spray
- 1/2 cup unsweetened applesauce
- 1/2 cup sliced strawberries

Direction

- Mix first 3 ingredients in a bowl; evenly spread in a skillet coated in cooking spray. Cook for 10 minutes, turning once, on medium heat. Enjoy with berries and applesauce on top.

Nutrition Information

- Calories: 395
- Total Carbohydrate: 66 g
- Total Fat: 9 g
- Fiber: 10 g
- Protein: 17 g
- Sodium: 92 mg
- Saturated Fat: 1 g

79. Clementine Sauce

"Searching for a flavorful match for your ice cream, Bomboloni, and fruit? Check this out, Clementine sauce recipe!"
Serving: Makes about 1 1/8 cups | Prep: 10m

Ingredients

- 1 1/4 lbs. clementines (about 8)
- 1 tbsp. sugar
- 1 tbsp. cornstarch
- Pinch of salt
- 2 tbsps. unsalted butter, cut into pieces

Direction

- Measure 1 cup of clementines juice by squeezing it.
- In a small heavy saucepan, mix together, salt, sugar, juice, and cornstarch. Over medium heat, allow mixture to boil while constantly mixing, then simmer briskly, mixing, for 1 minute.
- Take pan out from heat and add in the butter. Stir until the butter melts.
- Transfer into a bowl and use a wax paper or parchment for cover. For about 30 minutes, cool to warm.
- Note: You can make the sauce 3 days ahead. Just chill with cover and reheat over low heat. Serve.

Nutrition Information

- Calories: 244
- Total Carbohydrate: 39 g
- Cholesterol: 27 mg
- Total Fat: 11 g
- Fiber: 4 g
- Protein: 2 g
- Sodium: 133 mg
- Saturated Fat: 6 g

80. Coco Cola

"So tasty."
Serving: Makes 6 (dessert) servings | Prep: 10m

Ingredients

- 1 2/3 cups coconut water
- 1/4 cup coconut-milk powder
- 2 tbsps. sugar
- 1 tsp. xanthan gum
- a soda syphon with 1 seltzer charge and 1 cream charge

Direction

- In a blender, blend xanthan gum, sugar, coconut powder and coconut water. Put into soda syphon; seal well.
- Charge the syphon with seltzer charge and shake syphon several times. Remove empty seltzer charge carefully; charge syphon with the cream charge. Vigorously shake syphon a few times; fill the champagne flutes/other skinny, tall glasses.

Nutrition Information

- Calories: 49
- Total Carbohydrate: 7 g
- Total Fat: 2 g
- Fiber: 1 g
- Protein: 1 g
- Sodium: 97 mg
- Saturated Fat: 2 g

81. Coconut Chicken Curry With Turmeric And Lemongrass

"A lovely curry recipe."
Serving: Serves 4

Ingredients

- 2 lemongrass stalks
- 1 large shallot, chopped
- 4 garlic cloves
- 1 (2-inch) piece ginger, peeled, thinly sliced
- 1 tsp. crushed red pepper flakes
- 1 tsp. ground turmeric
- 1 tbsp. vegetable oil
- 4 chicken legs, drumsticks and thighs separated
- Kosher salt, freshly ground pepper
- 4 kaffir lime leaves (optional)
- 1 (3-inch) cinnamon stick
- 4 cardamom pods, cracked
- 2 star anise pods
- 1 (15-oz.) can unsweetened coconut milk
- 1 tsp. coconut sugar or light brown sugar
- 1/4 cup unsweetened shredded coconut
- Chopped cilantro and chives (for serving)

Direction

- From lemongrass, remove tough outer layers. Grate bottom 1/3 of stalk finely; put aside. Discard leftover stalk. Trim top 1/3 leftover stalk; discard. Whack stalk a few times against cutting board to release essential oils and bruise it. In it, tie a loose knot; put aside.
- Pulse 2 tbsp. water, turmeric, red pepper flakes, ginger, garlic, shallot and reserved grated lemongrass, adding 1-2 splashes water if needed, till paste forms in a food processor.
- Heat oil on medium heat in a big skillet. Season chicken with pepper and salt; cook, skin side down, for 8-10 minutes till skin is crisp and lightly browned. Put onto plate.
- In same skillet, cook spice paste, mixing, for 5 minutes till very fragrant; it'll start to slightly darken as water evaporates and paste starts to fry in leftover fat.
- Put reserved knotted lemongrass, coconut sugar, coconut milk, star anise, cardamom, cinnamon and kaffir lime leaves (optional) in skillet; simmer. Add chicken; cook, occasionally flipping pieces, scraping skillet's bottom often, for 1 1/2 hours till coconut milk breaks (fat separates from liquid and begins to brown other aromatics and chicken) and chicken is fall-apart tender.
- In a small dry skillet, toast shredded coconut, occasionally tossing, on medium heat for 5 minutes till golden brown; cool.
- Put chicken onto platter; put leftover braising liquid over. Put toasted coconut, chives and cilantro over.

82. Collards

"This classic recipe for collard greens is sensational"
Serving: 6 | Prep: 30m | Ready in: 1h30m

Ingredients

- 2 large potatoes, peeled and cubed

- 3 bunches collard greens - rinsed, stemmed and thinly sliced
- 4 slices bacon
- 1/2 onion, diced
- 1/2 cup red wine vinegar

Direction

- In a large pot, cover potatoes with enough water. Bring to a boil over medium heat. Add collards before potatoes are done.
- In a deep skillet placed over medium high heat, arrange bacon. Cook for about 10 minutes until browned on all sides. Remove bacon from skillet and arrange on paper towels to drain off all excess fat; add onion in the same skillet and sauté in bacon fat until softened. Drain fat off the onion, add to the greens. Break bacon into small pieces and sprinkle over green mixture, stir in wine vinegar. Simmer for about 60 minutes over low heat until greens are softened.

Nutrition Information

- Calories: 174 calories;
- Total Carbohydrate: 30.7 g
- Cholesterol: 7 mg
- Total Fat: 3.2 g
- Protein: 7.8 g
- Sodium: 172 mg

83. Common Crackers

"Buttery and crisp."
Serving: Makes about 40

Ingredients

- 4 cups all-purpose flour plus more
- 1 tbsp. salt
- 2 tsps. sugar
- 3/4 tsp. baking powder
- 1/2 cup (1 stick) chilled unsalted butter, cut into 1/2" cubes
- 1 cup heavy cream plus more
- A 1 3/4" biscuit cutter

Direction

- In food processor, pulse 4 cups flour with next 3 ingredients. Add butter; pulse to make coarse meal. Add 1 cup of cream; pulse till stiff dough forms. Bring to ball; flatten to disk. Wrap it in plastic; chill the dough for 30 minutes.
- Preheat an oven to 400°F. Line parchment on baking sheet. Roll dough out to 3/8-in. thick on lightly floured surface. Cut rounds out with biscuit cutter; put on prepped sheet. Gather dough and repeat till you use all dough; brush cream on rounds.
- Bake crackers for 15-17 minutes till golden brown; cool on wire rack. You can make it 1 day ahead; keep at room temperature, airtight.

Nutrition Information

- Calories: 96
- Total Carbohydrate: 11 g
- Cholesterol: 14 mg
- Total Fat: 5 g
- Fiber: 0 g
- Protein: 2 g
- Sodium: 56 mg
- Saturated Fat: 3 g

84. Cornbread-stuffed Cornish Game Hens With Corn Maque Choux

"A fantastic thanksgiving recipe."
Serving: Makes 4 servings

Ingredients

- 3 tbsps. butter
- 1 cup chopped onion
- 1/2 cup chopped celery
- 1 1/2 cups diced peeled cored Granny Smith or Golden Delicious apples
- 2 tsps. chopped fresh sage
- 1/2 tsp. coarse kosher salt
- 1/2 tsp. freshly ground black pepper

- 4 cups 1/2-inch cubes purchased cornbread or corn muffins (about 11 oz.)
- 1 large egg, beaten to blend
- 1/2 cup (packed) coarsely grated sharp cheddar cheese (about 2 oz.)
- 6 tbsps. (about) fresh apple cider or fresh apple juice
- 4 1 1/4- to 1 1/2-lb. Cornish game hens, rinsed, patted dry
- 1 tbsp. chopped fresh sage
- 2 tsps. coarse kosher salt
- 1 tsp. freshly ground black pepper
- 1 tbsp. olive oil
- 4 bacon slices, each halved crosswise
- Corn Maque Choux

Direction

- Stuffing: Melt butter on medium high heat in big heavy skillet. Add celery and onion; sauté for 5 minutes till starting to color. Add apples; sauté for 3 minutes till starting to soften. Mix in 1/2 tsp. pepper, 1/2 tsp. salt and sage; put into big bowl. Stand for 10 minutes till nearly cool.
- Mix cornbread into veggies. Add egg; toss to blend. Stir in cheese then, by tablespoonfuls, enough apple cider to make a moist yet not wet stuffing.
- Game hens: Lightly sprinkle pepper and salt on each hen's cavity; in each, pack 1 cup stuffing. Put leftover stuffing in buttered ramekins and cover using foil. Use toothpicks/turkey lacers to skewer cavities closed. Tuck the wing tips under; to hold shape, tie legs together. In small bowl, mix pepper, coarse salt and sage; sprinkle on hens.
- Preheat an oven to 400°F. Heat oil on medium high heat in big nonstick skillet. In skillet, put 2 hens; sauté, flipping oven with wooden spoon to avoid tearing skin, for 10 minutes till brown. Put, breast side up, on rimmed baking sheet. Repeat with leftover hens. On breast of each hen, put drape 2 bacon strip halves. Tie bacon strips into place using kitchen string. Put ramekins with stuffing onto baking sheet with the hens.
- Put extra stuffing and hens in oven; roast hens for 45 minutes, stuffing for 30 minutes, till juices are clear when you pierce thighs and cooked through. Cut string off hens. Put hens on plates. Put maque choux around hens; serve with extra stuffing.

Nutrition Information

- Calories: 1332
- Total Carbohydrate: 49 g
- Cholesterol: 518 mg
- Total Fat: 89 g
- Fiber: 4 g
- Protein: 80 g
- Sodium: 2073 mg
- Saturated Fat: 29 g

85. Cream Cheese Flan With Quince Compote

"Remove flam from fridge 20 minutes before serving so it reaches room temperature for best flavor."
Serving: Makes 1 (10-inch) flan to serve 8 to 10

Ingredients

- 1/2 cup sugar
- 2 sticks cinnamon
- 3 large quinces (about 1 3/4 lbs.), peeled, cored, and cut into 1/2-inch cubes
- 1 1/2 cups sugar
- 8 oz. cream cheese, softened
- 2 tbsps. vanilla extract
- 1/4 tsp. kosher salt
- 6 large eggs
- 1 1/2 cups heavy cream
- 1 (14-oz.) can sweetened condensed milk
- 10- by 2-inch round cake pan, large roasting pan

Direction

- Compote: Mix cinnamon sticks, sugar and 4 cups water till sugar dissolves in a big saucepan on high heat; boil. Add quince;

lower heat to medium. Simmer, uncovered, occasionally mixing, for 45 minutes till tender. Refrigerate quince in the poaching liquid till cool. You can make compote 3 days ahead, refrigerated.

- Flan: Mix 1/4 cup water and 1 cup sugar in a big heavy saucepan on medium high heat; cook, using rubber spatula/wooden spoon to occasionally gently mix, till caramel is dark amber and sugar melts. Put hot caramel in cake pan immediately, carefully and quickly, tilting to cover halfway up pan's sides and bottom; cool.
- Preheat an oven to 325°F.
- Beat salt, vanilla, leftover 1/2 cup sugar and cream cheese using electric mixer for 3 minutes till very creamy and smooth in a big bowl. Add condensed milk, eggs and cream; beat for 2 minutes till smooth. Put mixture in prepped cake pan.
- Put pan in big roasting pan; to reach halfway up cake pan's sides, use hot water to fill roasting pan. Loosely cover roasting pan with foil; use fork to pierce foil several times.
- Put roasting pan in oven; bake for 1 hour. Remove foil; bake for 1 hour till flan's edge is set yet center slightly jiggles when gently shaken. Remove cake pan from the water; cool flan in the pan on rack. To chill overnight, put into fridge.
- Serve: To loosen flan, run thin knife around pan's inside edge; gently shake pan from side to side. Invert big plate over pan when flan freely moves in pan. Securely hold plate and pan together; invert quickly then turn flan out onto plate. Caramel will go around and over flan. Serve it with quince compote.

Nutrition Information

- Calories: 5622
- Total Carbohydrate: 719 g
- Cholesterol: 1990 mg
- Total Fat: 273 g
- Fiber: 12 g
- Protein: 92 g
- Sodium: 2390 mg

- Saturated Fat: 157 g

86. Creamy Corn And Chestnut Pudding

"Serve this dish as a light supper or for breakfast."
Serving: Makes 10 servings

Ingredients

- 6 tbsps. (3/4 stick) butter
- 1/4 cup all purpose flour
- 3 cups half and half
- 5 cups frozen corn kernels (about 24 oz.), thawed
- 1/4 cup finely chopped shallot
- 1 1/2 tsps. salt
- 1 tsp. cayenne pepper
- 1/2 tsp. ground white pepper
- 1 7.25-to 7.41-oz. jar whole steamed or roasted peeled chestnuts* (about 1 1/2 cups), cut into 1/4-inch pieces
- 1/4 cup chopped fresh chives
- 6 large eggs

Direction

- To prepare: In a big saucepan, melt the butter on medium heat. Add flour and whisk it for a minute. Slowly whisk in half and half, then boil. Lower the heat to medium, then mix it continuously for about 3 minutes, until the mixture becomes a bit thick. Add the succeeding 4 ingredients and the corn and let it simmer for 15 minutes to combine the flavors, mixing frequently. Take it out of the heat, then mix in chives and chestnuts. Move to a big bowl. Do ahead: This can be prepared 1 day in advance. Covered and chilled. Rewarm a bit in the microwave or bring to room temperature prior to continuing.
- Set an oven to preheat to 375 degrees F. Butter a 13x9x2-inch glass baking dish. Whisk the eggs into the corn mixture, one at a time. Move to the prepared baking dish. Let it bake

for around 45 minutes, until it turns golden and puffed. Serve it hot.

Nutrition Information

- Calories: 345
- Total Carbohydrate: 34 g
- Cholesterol: 157 mg
- Total Fat: 19 g
- Fiber: 2 g
- Protein: 9 g
- Sodium: 426 mg
- Saturated Fat: 11 g

87. Creamy Pumpkin And Cashew Curry

"A great vegetarian dish."
Serving: Makes 6 servings

Ingredients

- 2 tbsps. vegetable oil, divided
- 4 1/2 cups 3/4-inch cubes peeled seeded sugar pumpkin or butternut squash (from about one 1 3/4-lb. whole pumpkin)
- 1/2 tsp. black mustard seeds*
- 8 curry leaves**
- 2 small red onions, cut into 1/3-inch wedges
- 2 garlic cloves, chopped
- 1 tbsp. finely grated peeled fresh ginger
- 3 dried chiles de árbol***
- 3/4 cup unsalted roasted cashews
- 1 tsp. ground turmeric
- 1/2 tsp. ground cumin
- 1 1/2 cups canned unsweetened coconut milk****
- 1 cup coconut cream
- 1/2 cup coarsely chopped cilantro plus additional for garnish
- 1 tbsp. fresh lime juice
- Steamed basmati rice

Direction

- Heat 1 tbsp. oil on medium heat in a big skillet. Add pumpkin; cook, occasionally mixing, for 8-10 minutes till golden. Put into bowl.
- Put 1 tbsp. oil in same skillet. Add curry leaves and mustard seeds; cook for 30 seconds till leaves sizzle and seeds pop. Add ginger, garlic and onions; sauté for 4 minutes till onions are golden. Add cumin, turmeric, cashews and chiles; stir-fry for 1 minute. Add coconut cream and coconut milk. Put heat on medium high; boil for 2 minutes till thick. Put pumpkin in pan; lower heat to medium. Simmer for 4 minutes till pumpkin is tender. Mix in lime juice and 1/2 cup cilantro. Put on rice; use extra cilantro to garnish.

88. Crisp Potato-eggplant Tart

""Complete this yummy rich tart with a glass of nicely chilled white wine and a crisp green salad.""
Serving: Makes one 9-inch tart

Ingredients

- 2 1/4 cups finely diced, peeled eggplant
- 1 tsp. coarse salt plus more to taste
- 1/4 cup plus 2 tbsps. safflower oil
- 3 tbsps. minced shallots
- 4 large Idaho potatoes
- Pepper
- 1/4 cup (1/2 stick) unsalted butter

Direction

- In a nonreactive bowl, put the eggplant. Add 1 tsp. salt and toss then let it sit for 20 minutes. Transfer to a clean kitchen towel and twist tightly to press out all moisture. Reserve.
- In a medium sauté pan, put 2 tbsps. of oil and heat over medium heat. Add shallots and eggplant then stir-fry for about 6 minutes, or until very tender. Take away from the heat and reserve.

- Peel the potatoes. Shred potatoes with a mandolin or hand grater into a clean kitchen towel. Twist tightly to press out as much moisture as you can.
- Prepare the oven by preheating to 375 degrees F.
- In a 9-inch ovenproof, nonstick sauté pan over medium heat, put the rest 1/4 cup oil. Add half of the potatoes and press evenly into the pan with a spatula. Add pepper and salt to taste. Place the reserved eggplant atop and spread. Press the rest of potatoes evenly over the eggplant. Add pepper and salt to taste. Cook for about 10 minutes, or until golden on the bottom. Gently flip over and dab bits of butter over the crust. Cook it for about 5 minutes, or until the bottom starts to crisp. Transfer to the preheated oven and bake for 25 minutes, or until tart turns crisp and golden and potatoes are cooked. Take from the oven and let it rest for 5 minutes. Slice into 6 wedges with a sharp serrated knife then serve right away.
- Note: Salting the eggplant helps drain any bitterness. Removing as much of the moisture from both the vegetables is very crucial. For the potatoes, this ensures a crisp and dry crust and a sweet dense flavor for the eggplant. If you shake the pan sometimes as the bottom potato layer browns, it will prevent it from adhering and will make flipping the tart much easier.

Nutrition Information

- Calories: 2347
- Total Carbohydrate: 277 g
- Cholesterol: 122 mg
- Total Fat: 130 g
- Fiber: 40 g
- Protein: 33 g
- Sodium: 1985 mg
- Saturated Fat: 35 g

89. Cured Arctic Char

"This works with other fish. You can use fresh trout or salmon instead of char if you want."
Serving: 8 Servings

Ingredients

- 1 whole large skin-on arctic char, (1-1 1/2 lb.), bones removed
- 1/3 cup kosher salt
- 1/3 cup sugar
- 2 tsps. mustard seeds
- 2 tsps. finely grated orange zest
- 1 tsp. finely grated lemon zest
- 2/3 cup finely chopped fresh dill
- 2 tbsps. aquavit
- 1/4 small red onion, chopped
- 1/4 cup apple cider vinegar
- 2 tsps. sugar
- 1/2 tsps. kosher salt
- Lefse
- Creme fraiche and dill sprigs (for serving)
- Flaky sea salt (such as Maldon)

Direction

- Cured char: under cold running water, rinse char. Use paper towels to pat dry. In a small bowl, mix lemon zest, orange zest, mustard seeds, sugar and salt. Massage into char. Put in a baking dish, skin side down. Put dill on top. Drizzle aquavit on. Use plastic wrap to tightly cover. Directly press onto fish. Chill for 2-4 days (gets firmer and saltier the longer it sits), flipping 2-3 times and pouring any accumulated liquid off every time, till flesh is nearly translucent and very firm. Rinse char thoroughly. Use paper towels to pat dry.
- Do Prior: You can cure and rinse char 1 week in advanced, chilled and covered.
- Pickled onion and assembling: In a small heatproof jar, put onion. In a small saucepan, simmer 2 tbsp. water, kosher salt, sugar and vinegar, mixing to melt. Pour on top of onion. Chill, covered, for at least 8 hours to 2 days till onion is bright pink.

- Slice char thinly. Serve on lefse. Put sea salt, pickled onion, dill and crème fraîche on top.

Nutrition Information

- Calories: 198
- Total Carbohydrate: 10 g
- Cholesterol: 39 mg
- Total Fat: 10 g
- Fiber: 0 g
- Protein: 15 g
- Sodium: 222 mg
- Saturated Fat: 2 g

90. Currant And Molasses Spice Cookies

Serving: Makes about 64 cookies

Ingredients

- 1 1/2 sticks (3/4 cup) unsalted butter, softened
- 1/2 cup sugar
- 1/3 cup unsulfured molasses
- 2 cups all-purpose flour
- 1/2 tsp. baking soda
- 1/2 tsp. salt
- 1 1/2 tsp. ground ginger
- 3/4 tsp. cinnamon
- 1/4 tsp. ground cloves
- 1/2 cup dried currants, soaked in boiling water to cover for 5 minutes, drained, and patted dry

Direction

- Cream the sugar and butter in a bowl using an electric mixer till mixture is fluffy and light and mix in molasses. Sift together the spices, salt, baking soda and flour into the bowl, beat dough till incorporated thoroughly, and mix in currants. Divide the dough in half and shape every half on a sheet of wax paper forming an 8-inch log, with wax paper to support. Refrigerate the logs, covered in wax paper for a minimum of 4 hours or overnight.

- Preheat an oven to 350°F. Using a sharp knife, slice the logs into quarter-inch thick portions and on slightly buttered baking sheets, set the portions 2-inch away. Working in batches, let the cookies bake in the center of oven for 10 to 12 minutes, or till pale golden. To racks, put the cookies and allow to cool.

Nutrition Information

- Calories: 48
- Total Carbohydrate: 7 g
- Cholesterol: 6 mg
- Total Fat: 2 g
- Fiber: 0 g
- Protein: 0 g
- Sodium: 26 mg
- Saturated Fat: 1 g

91. Delicate Bread Pudding

"Tasty puddings with silky custard on the bottom served with orange sauce."
Serving: Serves 6

Ingredients

- 25 oz. brioche, sliced
- 4 cups whole milk, at room temperature
- 3 large eggs, separated
- 1/2 cup sugar
- Pinch of salt
- 1 tsp. vanilla extract
- 1/2 cup sugar, or more to taste
- Grated zest and juice of 1 large orange, or more juice to taste
- 1 cup water
- 1/2 cup dry white wine or cherry or plum eau-de-vie

Direction

- For the puddings, preheat oven to 350 degrees F and butter 6 ten-oz. ramekins. In a pot, mix milk and brioche together; set aside for 10mins.

- On medium-high heat, put the pot and cook until the milk bubbles on the edges. Take off heat.
- Beat sugar and egg yolks together in a bowl until pale and light using a hand mixer or in a mixer with the paddle attachment. Softly whisk the hot brioche mixture with the eggs. Let it disintegrate to chunks without turning it to mash.
- In a big bowl or a mixer bowl, beat salt and egg whites until it forms into soft peaks; stir in vanilla. Mix the whites into the bread mix. Spoon the pudding on ramekins. Fill baking dish with enough boiling water, place the ramekins in the dish. Make sure that the water is halfway to the sides of the ramekins.
- Bake puddings for 25-35mins until an inserted cake tester comes out without residue. Take the puddings out of the water bath.
- Meanwhile, start making the sauce. In a small pot, mix water, sugar, orange juice, and orange zest together; boil. Continue cooking for 5mins. Take off heat and mix in white wine; taste. If desired, adjust sugar and orange juice.
- Turn puddings in shallow bowls and ladle sauce over and around each portion. Serve

Nutrition Information

- Calories: 629
- Total Carbohydrate: 102 g
- Cholesterol: 170 mg
- Total Fat: 15 g
- Fiber: 3 g
- Protein: 20 g
- Sodium: 605 mg
- Saturated Fat: 6 g

92. Dense Chocolate Torte

"Intensely rich chocolate fudge cake."
Serving: Makes 12 to 16 servings | Prep: 25m

Ingredients

- 1 1/2 cups sugar, divided
- 1/2 cup water
- 8 oz. unsweetened chocolate, finely chopped
- 4 oz. semisweet chocolate, finely chopped
- 2 sticks unsalted butter, at room temperature
- 5 large eggs, beaten
- Equipment: a 9-inch springform pan; a large (18-inch) roll of heavy-duty foil
- Accompaniment: whipped cream (optional)

Direction

- Preheat oven to 300°F and place rack in middle. The cake pan and wrap the outside with plastic wrap, then tightly wrap it in a layer of aluminum foil.
- Lightly grease the pan with butter, then sprinkle with sugar, shaking off any excess.
- In a small pot, heat 1/2 cup water and 1 cup sugar. Stir until sugar dissolves then take the pot off the heat to cool.
- Set a big bowl over a pot of barely simmering water, make sure the bottom of the bowl does not touch the water. Put chocolates in the bowl and heat, stirring occasionally, until melted. In a separate bowl, combine remaining 1/2 cup sugar and 2 sticks of butter. Mix until well blended then add the butter mixture into melted chocolate. Pour in sugar syrup; stir. Add in eggs, stirring carefully to avoid making bubbles until combined. Pour mixture into the pan and bake in a hot water bath for about 45-50 minutes until center is almost set and barely wobbles.
- Transfer pan on a rack to cool completely then store in the refrigerator, covered, for at least 8 hours. When it's time to serve, loosen the sides of the pan by running a thin knife around it. Remove side of the pan and serve either slightly chilled or at room temperature.

Nutrition Information

- Calories: 367
- Total Carbohydrate: 31 g
- Cholesterol: 101 mg
- Total Fat: 26 g
- Fiber: 3 g
- Protein: 5 g

- Sodium: 32 mg
- Saturated Fat: 16 g

93. Dilled Pumpernickel-rye Stuffing

"A fun recipe."
Serving: Makes about 14 cups

Ingredients

- 1 (1-lb) loaf unsliced pumpernickel (not black Russian bread)
- 1 (1-lb) loaf unsliced seeded rye bread
- 4 carrots, halved lengthwise and cut into 1/2-inch pieces
- 4 celery ribs, halved lengthwise and cut into 1/2-inch pieces
- 3 medium onions, cut into 1/2-inch pieces
- 2 tbsps. vegetable oil
- 1 stick (1/2 cup) unsalted butter
- 1 lb cremini mushrooms, trimmed and quartered
- 1/4 cup chopped fresh dill
- 1/4 cup chopped fresh flat-leaf parsley
- 1 tbsp. caraway seeds, lightly crushed
- 2 1/2 to 3 cups chicken broth

Direction

- Preheat an oven to 200°F.
- To get 6 cups each, cut enough of both of the breads to 1-in. cubes; spread bread cubes in 2 big shallow baking pans. Bake in lower and upper oven thirds, occasionally mixing, switching pans positions halfway through baking, for 50-60 minutes till bread is dry; cool.
- Put oven temperature on 400°F.
- Meanwhile, cook onions, celery and carrots in butter and oil in 5-qt. heavy pot on medium heat, mixing occasionally, for 10-12 minutes till starting to brown and soft. Add mushrooms; cook, occasionally mixing, for 10 minutes till mushroom release liquid.
- Take off heat; mix in pepper and salt to taste, caraway, parsley, dill and bread. Add broth; toss till bread is moistened evenly. If you want moist stuffing, use 3 cups broth and 2 1/2 cups for dry stuffing.
- Mound stuffing in 4-qt. buttered shallow baking dish; use buttered foil to cover. Bake in center of oven for 30 minutes; uncover. Bake for 15 minutes till stuffing heats through and top is crisp.
- You can dry bread 2 days ahead; keep at room temperature in sealed plastic bag. You can assemble, not bake, stuffing 1 day ahead, covered, chilled. Before baking, bring to room temperature.

Nutrition Information

- Calories: 285
- Total Carbohydrate: 39 g
- Cholesterol: 19 mg
- Total Fat: 11 g
- Fiber: 5 g
- Protein: 8 g
- Sodium: 482 mg
- Saturated Fat: 5 g

94. Diner-style French Toast

"French toast with a dust of powdered sugar."
Serving: Serves 4 | Prep: 20m

Ingredients

- 3 large eggs
- 1 1/4 cups whole milk
- 1 tsp. granulated sugar
- 1 tsp. vanilla extract
- 3/4 tsp. cinnamon
- 1/2 tsp. kosher salt
- 4 tsps. vegetable oil, divided
- 4 tbsps. unsalted butter, softened, divided
- 8 (3/4–inch-thick) slices challah or other rich, dense bread
- Powdered sugar and maple syrup (for serving)

Direction

- In a big bowl, beat salt, cinnamon, vanilla, granulated sugar, milk and eggs.
- Over medium heat, heat a big griddle or 2 nonstick or cast-iron skillets. Grease with thin oil coating, then thin butter coating.
- Dunk every bread slice in batches into the egg mixture. Allow to cook for 2 minutes each side, turning midway through, till golden brown on every side. Redo with the rest of bread, greasing the griddle with leftover oil and butter as necessary. Just prior to serving, dust the French toast with powdered sugar. Serve together with maple syrup on the side.
- Note: In case a griddle or 2 skillets are not available, use a skillet to cook French toast.

Nutrition Information

- Calories: 406
- Total Carbohydrate: 34 g
- Cholesterol: 178 mg
- Total Fat: 24 g
- Fiber: 3 g
- Protein: 13 g
- Sodium: 449 mg
- Saturated Fat: 11 g

95. Double-cherry Streusel Bars

"A flavorful recipe."
Serving: Makes 24

Ingredients

- 1 cup dried Bing (sweet) cherries (about 6 oz.)
- 1 cup tart red cherry preserves (such as Tropical or Smuckers; about 11 oz.)
- 1 tbsp. kirsch (clear cherry brandy)
- Nonstick vegetable oil spray
- 2 cups all purpose flour
- 2/3 cup sugar
- 1/2 tsp. ground cinnamon
- 1/4 tsp. salt
- 3/4 cup (1 1/2 sticks) chilled unsalted butter, cut into 1/2-inch cubes
- 1 3/4 tsps. vanilla extract
- 1/4 tsp. almond extract
- 3 tbsps. whole milk
- 1 cup (packed) sweetened flaked coconut (about 3 oz.)
- 3/4 cup sliced almonds (about 3 oz.)

Direction

- Filling: Blend kirsch, tart cherry preserves and dried cherries to chunky puree in processor. You can make filling 1 day ahead. Put into bowl. Cover; refrigerate.
- Streusel and dough: Preheat an oven to 375°F. Line heavy-duty foil on 13x9x2-in. metal baking pan; leave overhang. Spray nonstick spray on foil. Blend salt, cinnamon, sugar and flour for 5 seconds in processor. Add almond extract, vanilla extract and butter; blend with on/off turns till it looks like coarse meal. Add milk; blend with on/off turns till it comes together with small clumps. Put 1 cup packed mixture into medium bowl; put aside for streusel. Blend leftover mixture till big moist clumps form in processor. Gather dough together in big ball.
- Press dough on bottom of prepped baking pan; use fork to pierce all over. Bake dough for 22 minutes till golden; cool crust for 15 minutes. Maintain the oven temperature.
- To reserved 1 cup of dough, add sliced almonds and sweetened coconut flakes; use fork to mix dough, breaking streusel topping up to small clumps.
- Spread cherry filling on baked crust; sprinkle top with streusel topping. Bake cookie for 30 minutes till streusel topping gets golden brown and cherry filling is bubbling. In pan on rack, cool cookie. Lift cookie from pan using foil overhang for aid. Peel off foil; discard. Lengthwise cut cookie to thirds; crosswise cut to eights making 24 bars in total. You can make bars 2 days ahead; keep bars, refrigerated, in airtight container.

Nutrition Information

- Calories: 199
- Total Carbohydrate: 27 g
- Cholesterol: 15 mg
- Total Fat: 9 g
- Fiber: 1 g
- Protein: 2 g
- Sodium: 40 mg
- Saturated Fat: 5 g

---

96. Double-ginger Sour Cream And Bundt Cake With Ginger-infused Strawberries

"Let's cook a wonderful meal!"
Serving: Makes 12 to 14 servings

Ingredients

- Softened butter (for brushing pan)
- 1/2 cup raw sugar*
- 2 1/4 cups all purpose flour
- 4 tsps. ground ginger
- 2 tsps. baking powder
- 1/2 tsp. salt
- 1 cup (2 sticks) unsalted butter, room temperature
- 2 cups sugar
- 4 large eggs
- 1 large egg yolk
- 2 tsps. vanilla extract
- 1 cup sour cream
- 1 cup chopped crystallized ginger
- 1 2-inch piece fresh ginger, peeled, very thinly sliced
- 2/3 cup water
- 1/2 cup sugar
- 2 tsps. fresh lemon juice
- 2 quarts fresh strawberries, hulled, halved (about 8 cups)
- Sliced fresh mint leaves (optional)

Direction

- To prepare cake: Place the rack in middle of the oven. Start preheating to 350°F. Generously brush all over inside of the 12-cup Bundt pan with softened butter. Sprinkle the butter in pan with raw sugar, coat completely by tilting the pan.
- In a medium bowl, whisk salt, baking powder, ground ginger and flour. In a large bowl, beat one cup of the butter with electric mixer until they become smooth. Put in 2 cups of sugar; then beat on medium-high speed for 2 minutes until blended. Put in eggs, 1 egg at a time, beating well before adding the next. Beat in vanilla and one egg yolk; if needed, stop to scrape down the bowl. Alternately put in flour mixture in 3 times with sour cream in 2 times, beating on low speed until they are just blended after adding the next. Mix in the crystallized ginger. Spread the batter into the pan, avoid dislodging the raw sugar.
- Bake the cake for 55 minutes until tester comes out with some small crumbs attached when inserted near the middle and top turns light brown. Place onto rack and let cool 15 minutes in pan. While rotating the pan, tap the bottom edge of the pan gently on the work surface until the cake has loosened. Position the rack on the top of pan; flip cake onto rack; Discard pan. Let cool completely.
- Make ginger-infused strawberries: In a small saucepan, combine the first four ingredients. Boil over medium-high heat, stirring until the sugar has dissolved. Boil for 4 minutes until the mixture has reduced to scant one cup. Discard from the heat; Allow ginger syrup to cool to room temperature (but don't strain). DO AHEAD: You can make this 2 days in advance. Let chill with a cover.
- In medium bowl, put berries. Strain the ginger syrup. Add over the berries then toss. Let chill for at least 60 minutes with a cover. DO AHEAD: You can make this 120 minutes in advance and keep it chilled. Cut the cake into slices. Arrange on the plates. Add the berries

with the syrup alongside. If desired, sprinkle mint over. Then serve.

Nutrition Information

- Calories: 604
- Total Carbohydrate: 93 g
- Cholesterol: 136 mg
- Total Fat: 25 g
- Fiber: 3 g
- Protein: 6 g
- Sodium: 215 mg
- Saturated Fat: 15 g

97. Dried Tart Cherry And Almond Muffins

"Moist and flavorful."
Serving: Makes 10

Ingredients

- 6 tbsps. orange juice
- 3/4 cup dried tart cherries (about 4 oz.)
- 1 cup plus 2 tbsps. all purpose flour
- 1/2 cup sugar
- 1 1/2 tsps. baking powder
- 1/4 tsp. salt
- 1 7-oz. package almond paste, crumbled
- 6 tbsps. (3/4 stick) unsalted butter, melted, hot
- 3 large eggs
- 1 1/2 tsps. grated orange peel

Direction

- In middle of oven, put rack; preheat it to 375°F. Butter the 10 1/3-cup metal muffin cups. Simmer juice in small saucepan; take off heat. Add cherries; stand for 10 minutes till soft.
- Mix salt, baking powder, sugar and flour in medium bowl. Beat melted butter and almond paste using electric mixer till well blended with some small almond paste pieces in big bowl. One by one, add eggs; beat well after

each. Mix in orange peel and cherry mixture. Add flour mixture; mix till just blended.
- Divide batter to prepped muffin cups; bake for 20 minutes till inserted tester in middle of muffins exits clean yet slightly moist to touch. You can make it 2 days ahead; cool. In foil, wrap muffins; keep in room temperature. Rewarm in the foil for 5 minutes in 350°F oven; serve warm.

Nutrition Information

- Calories: 306
- Total Carbohydrate: 41 g
- Cholesterol: 74 mg
- Total Fat: 14 g
- Fiber: 2 g
- Protein: 5 g
- Sodium: 139 mg
- Saturated Fat: 5 g

98. Drunken Chicken

"Beer and chicken? This drunken chicken recipe will surprise you with its amazing taste!"
Serving: 5 | Prep: 30m | Ready in: 1h30m

Ingredients

- 1 (3 lb.) whole chicken
- salt and pepper to taste
- 1 cup Dijon-style prepared mustard
- 8 fluid oz. beer
- 1/2 cup Italian-style salad dressing

Direction

- Bring an outdoor grill to medium heat.
- Clean the chicken, then pat dry. Add pepper and salt to taste. Cover chicken with mustard.
- Remove 1/2 of the beer amount in the can and add in Italian style dressing. Set beer can on a disposable baking sheet. Place chicken onto the can (can served as a stand), put can into the chicken's cavity.
- Bring chicken and beer on baking sheet to prepared grill. Grill, covered, until no pink

meat remains and juices from the chicken run clear, 60 minutes.

Nutrition Information

- Calories: 724 calories;
- Total Carbohydrate: 14.1 g
- Cholesterol: 204 mg
- Total Fat: 47.7 g
- Protein: 51 g
- Sodium: 1781 mg

---

99. Duck Breast With Sweet Cherry Sauce

Serving: Makes 4 main-course servings | Prep: 1h

Ingredients

- 1 tbsp. extra-virgin olive oil
- 1/2 cup chopped onion (1 small)
- 3 garlic cloves, crushed
- 1 tbsp. finely chopped shallot
- 1 tsp. tomato paste
- 1/2 tsp. black pepper
- 1/2 tsp. ground cumin
- Scant 1/4 tsp. dried hot red pepper flakes
- 3/4 tsp. salt
- 1/2 cup coarsely chopped red bell pepper (1/2 medium)
- 1 plum tomato, coarsely chopped
- 1/4 cup dry red wine
- 1 1/2 to 2 tbsps. cider vinegar
- 2 tbsps. sugar
- 1/2 tsp. Dijon mustard
- 1 1/4 lb dark sweet cherries such as Bing, quartered and pitted (3 cups)
- 2 (3/4-lb) boneless Moulard duck breasts with skin*
- 2 tbsps. water
- 1 tbsp. chopped fresh tarragon or chives
- an instant-read thermometer

Direction

- Heat oil till hot yet not smoking in a 2-3-qt. heavy saucepan on medium heat; cook shallot, garlic and onion, occasionally mixing, for 7 minutes till golden.
- Add 1/4 tsp. salt, hot pepper flakes, cumin, black pepper and tomato paste; cook for 30 seconds, mixing. Add tomato and bell pepper; cook, occasionally mixing, for 5 minutes till soft.
- Mix in sugar, vinegar to taste and wine; simmer for 1 minute. Mix in leftover 1/2 tsp. salt, 1 1/2 cups cherries and mustard; simmer for 1 minute.
- Puree it for 1 minute till very smooth in a blender; be careful, it is hot. Through fine-mesh sieve, force cherry sauce into a bowl; to glaze duck, put 1/4 cup sauce into a small bowl.
- Put oven rack in center position; preheat an oven to 450°F.
- In a crosshatch pattern, score duck skin with a sharp small knife; season duck with pepper and salt all over.
- Heat water till hot in a 12-in. ovenproof heavy skillet on low heat; add duck with skin side down. Cook the duck, uncovered, without flipping, on low heat for 25 minutes till skin is golden brown and most fat is rendered.
- Put duck onto plate; discard all fat from skillet but 1 tbsp. Brush cherry sauce from bowl all over duck; put into skillet with skin side up.
- Roast duck in oven for 8 minutes to get medium rare till thermometer reads 135°F.
- Put duck onto cutting board; put aside skillet. Stand duck for 10 minutes, loosely covered with foil.
- Pour off fat from skillet carefully and immediately after you cover duck; leave brown bits behind. Add leftover cherry sauce, mixing, scraping brown bits up. Add leftover 1 1/2 cups cherries; heat from skillet will warm sauce, cherries will lose the flavor if cooked.
- Cut duck to slices, holding sharp knife at 45° angle; sprinkle chopped herbs. Serve with cherry sauce.

Nutrition Information

- Calories: 330
- Total Carbohydrate: 45 g
- Cholesterol: 71 mg
- Total Fat: 8 g
- Fiber: 4 g
- Protein: 20 g
- Sodium: 516 mg
- Saturated Fat: 2 g

100. Egg And Potato Salad With Green Olives

"Easy and low-fat."
Serving: Makes 6 servings

Ingredients

- 2 lbs. white potatoes, peeled, cut into 1-inch pieces
- 1/4 cup low-fat mayonnaise
- 1/4 cup nonfat milk
- 1 tbsp. Dijon mustard
- 1 tbsp. apple cider vinegar
- 3 large eggs, hard-boiled, peeled, coarsely chopped
- 1 cup thinly sliced celery
- 1/2 cup chopped green onions
- 1/3 cup pimiento-stuffed green olives, chopped
- Paprika

Direction

- On steamer rack in big pot over boiling water, put potatoes; cover. Steam potatoes for 10 minutes till tender; cool.
- Whisk vinegar, mustard, milk and mayonnaise to blend in big bowl. Add olives, green onions, celery, eggs and potatoes; gently toss to blend. Season with pepper and salt. You can make it 6 hours ahead then cover; refrigerate. Put salad in serving bowl. Sprinkle paprika; serve.

101. Endive Cups With Beet, Persimmon And Marinated Feta

"Fantastic appetizer to have on a table. Choose persimmons that are soft, like a ripe tomato."
Serving: Makes 30 to 40 hors d'oeuvres | Prep: 30m

Ingredients

- 1 cup crumbled marinated feta or goat cheese (see Cooks' Note)
- 2 medium golden or red beets
- 3 ripe Fuyu persimmons
- 2 tbsps. Meyer lemon juice (or 1 1/2 tbsps. regular lemon juice)
- 1 tsp. Meyer lemon zest (or regular lemon zest)
- 3 tbsps. extra-virgin olive oil
- Kosher salt and freshly ground black pepper
- Pinch sugar, optional
- 8 heads Belgian endive
- Torn fresh mint, for garnish

Direction

- Make cheese sit in room temperature while you get the rest of the ingredients rest.
- In salted water, boil beets for 20-25 minutes in a small saucepan until fork-tender. Don't overcook, they should be slightly firm. Cool beets then slip skins off using your fingers. Cut beets to half inch cubes then put in a medium bowl.
- Cut bottoms and tops off the persimmons. Slide a knife between the flesh and peel to cut off peel. Cut flesh to half an inch cubes then place in the bowl with beets. Add pepper, salt, oil, lemon zest, and lemon juice. Toss until combined. Let mixture stand for 15 minutes to combine flavors. Adjust seasoning according to your taste but remember cheese will make it saltier. You can add a bit of sugar depending on your lemon's sweetness level.
- As it stands, cut the bottom ends of the endive heads off to separate leaves. Use a sharp knife

to cut a small bit from the curved underside of every leave so it lies flat.

- Put a big tsp. of cheese in every leave to serve. Spoon a little beet-persimmon salad on it. Garnish with torn mint then serve. You can cook the beats 3 days ahead and keep it in the fridge.

Nutrition Information

- Calories: 32
- Total Carbohydrate: 2 g
- Cholesterol: 2 mg
- Total Fat: 2 g
- Fiber: 1 g
- Protein: 1 g
- Sodium: 63 mg
- Saturated Fat: 1 g

---

102. Farfalle With Tuna, Tomatoes And Olives

"A tasty recipe."
Serving: 2 servings; can be doubled

Ingredients

- 6 oz. farfalle (bow-tie) pasta (about 2 1/2 cups)
- 2 tbsps. olive oil
- 2 canned anchovy fillets, 1 tsp. anchovy oil reserved
- 1 14 1/2-oz. can seasoned chunky tomatoes
- 1/2 cup pitted Kalamata olives or other brine-cured black olives (about 12 large), quartered
- 1/2 cup slivered fresh basil
- 1 6-oz. can solid white tuna packed in water, undrained

Direction

- Cook pasta, occasionally mixing, till tender yet firm to chew in big saucepan with boiling salted water.
- Meanwhile, heat 2 tbsp. olive oil on medium high heat in big heavy skillet. Add reserved anchovy oil and anchovies; mash anchovies to

coarse paste with fork in skillet. Add basil, kalamata olives and tomatoes; simmer sauce.

- Thoroughly drain pasta. Mix tuna with its water and pasta into sauce; toss, breaking tuna up to big pieces using fork, for 3 minutes to heat pasta through. Season pasta with pepper and salt; immediately serve.

Nutrition Information

- Calories: 757
- Total Carbohydrate: 107 g
- Cholesterol: 34 mg
- Total Fat: 20 g
- Fiber: 9 g
- Protein: 37 g
- Sodium: 822 mg
- Saturated Fat: 3 g

---

103. Farmhouse Herbed Stuffing

"You can stuff a turkey with this or serve 9 people when you bake it for a side dish; scale recipe up accordingly if making a bigger turkey."
Serving: Makes 8 servings — about 9 cups, or enough to fill a 12-lb. turkey, with extra for baking alongside

Ingredients

- 8 tbsps. (1 stick) unsalted butter
- 2 medium onions, cut into 1/4-inch dice (about 3 cups)
- 6 stalks celery with leaves, cut into 1/4-inch dice (about 2 1/2 cups)
- 1 (14-oz.) package seasoned bread stuffing cubes
- 1/3 cup fresh parsley, chopped
- 1 tsp. celery salt
- 1 tsp. dried sage, crumbled
- 1 tsp. dried rosemary, crushed
- 1/2 tsp. dried thyme, crumbled
- 1/4 tsp. salt
- 1/4 tsp. freshly ground black pepper
- 1 1/4 cups hot Homemade Turkey Stock or canned turkey stock, plus 1/2 cup more if baking all of stuffing outside of turkey

Direction

- Heat butter till hot yet not smoking in 12-in. heavy skillet on medium heat; mix in celery and onion. Cover; cook, occasionally mixing, for 15-20 minutes till soft. You can prep veggies 1 day ahead, refrigerated. Before continuing, reheat; sauté, mixing often, in 12-in. heavy skillet on medium high heat for 5 minutes till heated through.
- Put into big bowl. Add pepper, salt, thyme, rosemary, sage, celery salt, parsley and stuffing cubes; mix in 1 1/4 cups of hot stuck.
- Stuff turkey option: Immediately use to fill cavities; spread leftover in baking dish like in recipe.
- Baking as side dish: Preheat an oven to 350°F; butter 9x13-in. baking dish/3-qt. casserole. Put stuffing in dish; drizzle 1/2 cup hot stock. Use aluminum foil to cover; bake for 30 minutes till heated through. Uncover; bake for 10 minutes till top is golden and slightly crisp. Immediately serve.
- Sage and sausage stuffing option: Sauté 1-lb. bulk pork sausage, breaking pieces up with spoon, in big heavy skillet for 10 minutes till meat isn't pink. Put into big bowl using slotted spoon. Continue with recipe, putting ingredients in bowl with sausage then using 2 tbsp. chopped fresh sage instead of sage and dried rosemary.
- Pecan and dried apricot stuffing: Preheat an oven to 350°F. On rimmed baking sheet, spread 6-oz./1 1/2 cups pecans; toast, occasionally mixing, for 10 minutes till fragrant and browned. Cool. Chop coarsely. Mix hot water to cover and 1 1/2 cusp of diced dried apricots in medium bowl; soak for 30 minutes till apricots plump. Drain well. Continue with recipe, tossing pecans, apricots with other ingredients in big bowl.
- Follow safe procedures; moist stuffing can create bacteria like E. coli or salmonella. Make it right before stuffing so it goes into bird warm to avoid growing bacteria. You can spread stuffing if baking outside of turkey then refrigerate as turkey roasts for a few hours; make same day as you bake it.
- To keep it moist, drizzle extra stock on stuffing baked out of turkey because it won't soak in turkey's juices.

Nutrition Information

- Calories: 222
- Total Carbohydrate: 16 g
- Cholesterol: 32 mg
- Total Fat: 16 g
- Fiber: 3 g
- Protein: 3 g
- Sodium: 376 mg
- Saturated Fat: 8 g

104. Fast White-bean Stew

"This stew is made with baked ham, baby greens, cannellini beans, and tomatoes broth."
Serving: Makes 4 servings | Prep: 10m

Ingredients

- 2 large garlic cloves, chopped
- 1/4 cup plus 1/2 tbsp. extra-virgin olive oil
- 1 (14- to 15-oz.) can stewed tomatoes
- 1 3/4 cups reduced-sodium chicken broth
- 2 (19-oz.) cans cannellini beans, rinsed and drained (3 cups)
- 1 (1/2-lb.) piece baked ham (1/2 to 3/4 inch thick), cut into 1/2-inch cubes
- 1/4 tsp. black pepper
- 1 (5-oz.) bag baby romaine or baby arugula (10 cups loosely packed)
- 8 (3/4-inch-thick) slices baguette

Direction

- In a 3 1/2-4 1/2-qt. heavy pot, cook garlic with 1/4 cup oil over moderately high heat for 1-2 minutes until turning golden, tossing. Use kitchen shears to coarsely cut up tomatoes in a can, and then add (along with juice) to the oil with garlic. Mix in pepper, ham, beans, and broth and boil it. Lower the heat and simmer without a cover for 5 minutes. Mix in greens and cook for 1 minute for arugula and 3 minutes for romaine, until wilted.

- While the stew simmers, turn on the broiler to preheat. On a baking sheet, put bread and drizzle the leftover 1/2 tbsp. oil over. Broil 3-4-in. from the heat source for 1-1 1/2 minutes until turning golden.
- Enjoy the toasts with the stew.

105. Fennel And Potato Hash

*"*Perfect with a fried egg.*"*
Serving: Makes 6 servings

Ingredients

- 2 small fennel bulbs with fronds
- 2 tbsps. olive oil
- 1 1/2 lbs. Yukon Gold potatoes, peeled, cut into 1/2-to 3/4-inch cubes, patted dry
- 1/2 tsp. fine sea salt
- Freshly ground pepper
- 1 garlic clove, chopped
- 1/4 cup coarsely chopped fresh Italian parsley

Direction

- Preparation: Slice fennel into cubes (1/2-inch), you should have about 4 scant cups. Chop fennel fronds finely enough to measure 1/4 cup. Place fennel in boiling salted water and cook for 3 minutes until almost softened. Drain; reserve.
- Put 2 tbsps. oil in a heavy large nonstick skillet and heat over medium heat. Put in potatoes. Cook for 20-25 minutes until crisp and golden, flipping often. Mash potatoes in the skillet with a potato masher. Add pepper, salt, and fennel. Cook for 2-3 minutes, stirring often until fennel turns golden. Put in garlic and cook for 2 minutes. Mix in parsley. Serve hot.
- Per serving: 2.9 g protein, 21.3 g net carbohydrates, 1.0 g total sugars, 4.3 g dietary fiber, 25.5 g carbohydrates, 0 mg cholesterol, 1.0 g saturated fat, 7.3 g fat, 37.8% calories from fat, 173.2 kcal calories

106. Fettuccine With Braised Oxtail

"Pasta with oxtail meat."
Serving: Feeds 4

Ingredients

- 4 oxtails, thawed
- Kosher salt and cracked black pepper
- 4 tbsps. canola oil
- 1 large yellow onion, peeled and chopped
- 3 stalks celery, roughly chopped
- 1 large carrot, peeled, quartered lengthwise, and roughly chopped
- 5 cloves garlic, smashed and peeled
- 2 sprigs fresh rosemary
- 5 sprigs fresh thyme
- 2 cups full-bodied red wine
- 1 quart chicken stock
- 16 oz. uncooked gluten-free fettuccine
- 1 large parsnip, peeled
- 3 tbsps. extra-virgin olive oil
- 2 cups quartered button mushrooms
- 5 large shallots, peeled and quartered
- 2 tsps. finely chopped fresh rosemary
- 1 tbsp. butter
- Parmesan cheese, for serving

Direction

- Preheat oven to 375°F to prepare to braise. Add salt and pepper to the oxtails to season.
- In a large sauté pan to sear the oxtail, heat 2 tbsps. of canola oil over medium-high heat. Cook the oxtails for 5 minutes, until one side is browned. Flip and brown the other side for 5 minutes. Transfer browned oxtails to a Dutch oven.
- To sauté the veggies, drain fat off the sauté pan and add remaining 2 tbsps. of canola oil. Put in garlic, carrot, celery, and onion and cook while stirring occasionally for 10 to 15 minutes, until soft and brown. Toss rosemary sprigs and thyme, cook until fragrant.
- For the braising liquid, pour in wine to deglaze the pan and scrape up the goodness

from the bottom of the pan. Cook for 7 to 8 minutes, until wine reduces by 3/4 of its volume. Add chicken broth and bring to a boil. Lower the heat to low and simmer for 5 minutes. Pour the braising liquid in the Dutch oven, over the oxtails. Sliding into the oven to braise, covered, for 2 to 2 1/2 hours, until meat begins to fall off the bones. Taste the meat to check the flavor.

- Fill a large pot with salted water and bring to a boil to cook the fettucine. Cook in the fettuccine until a little less than al dente in order to hold the shape. If using gluten-free pasta, cook for a shorter period of time, especially when following the directions of manufacturer on the box.
- To make the sauce: Take the oxtails out of the sauce and set aside. Strain sauce to a large saucepan and begin reducing the liquid over medium heat.
- While liquid is reducing, slice the parsnip, starting from the thin end, into small coins. Halfway up the parsnip, slice in half lengthwise, then continue to cut coins from the parsnip in the same size as the first half.
- In a small sauté pan, heat olive oil over medium-high heat to sauté the veggies. Cook and stir mushrooms until wilted and soft. Add the parsnips and cook for 5 to 6 minutes, stirring occasionally, until the parsnips are soft and the mushrooms have browned. Add shallots and cook and stir for 5 minutes, until soft. Add chopped rosemary, cook until fragrant.
- Into the saucepan with the stock, spoon the sauté vegetables. Bring to a boil, reduce to low heat, simmer for 4 to 5 minutes, until the sauce thickens. Stir in butter until incorporated with the sauce.
- Transfer the cooked pasta into the sauce to finish the dish. Pick off the oxtails' meat and place into the sauce. Taste, season with salt and pepper, as needed.
- Serve pasta in large bowls, top with grated over Parmesan cheese.
- You may use veal or venison shanks for osso buco instead of oxtail, or braised chicken legs.

You may also use any hearty pasta can keep its shape of your choice.
- Serve mashed potatoes over the rice. If making the oxtail stock, it would make a hearty soup.

Nutrition Information

- Calories: 959
- Total Carbohydrate: 135 g
- Cholesterol: 15 mg
- Total Fat: 35 g
- Fiber: 15 g
- Protein: 20 g
- Sodium: 1688 mg
- Saturated Fat: 5 g

107. Fingerling Potato Salad

"Let punch up your picnic with the combination of toasted brown mustard seeds and sautéed leeks."
Serving: Makes 8 to 10 servings | Prep: 20m

Ingredients

- 3 1/2 lbs. fingerling potatoes, unpeeled, cut into 3/4"-1" pieces
- 1 tbsp. kosher salt plus more for seasoning
- 9 tbsps. (or more) extra-virgin olive oil, divided
- 2 tbsps. brown mustard seeds
- 3 medium leeks (white and palegreen parts only), halved lengthwise, cut crosswise into ¼" slices (about 5 cups)
- 1 tbsp. (or more) white wine vinegar
- 1 tbsp. Dijon mustard
- Freshly ground black pepper

Direction

- In a big pot, add potatoes. Pour in enough amount of cold water to cover potatoes by 3 inches. Stir in 1 tbsp. of salt and bring to a boil. Lower heat to moderate and simmer for about 10 minutes, until potatoes are softened. Drain potatoes. Move potatoes to a big rimmed baking sheet and allow to somewhat cool.

- In a small skillet, heat 3 tbsp. of oil on moderately high heat. Put into skillet the mustard seeds and cook for about 2 minutes while stirring sometimes, until seeds begin to pop. Transfer oil with seeds into a big bowl.
- In a big skillet, heat 2 tbsp. of oil on moderate heat. Put in leeks and use salt to season and cook for 10 to 12 minutes while stirring sometimes, until just soft.
- Whisk into mustard-seed oil the 1 tbsp. of water, Dijon mustard, vinegar and leftover 4 tbsp. of oil. Put in leeks and potatoes, tossing to coat well. Use pepper and salt to season. Do ahead: You can make this 1 day in advance, chilled with cover. Bring back to room temperature prior to serving, putting more vinegar and oil if dry.

Nutrition Information

- Calories: 319
- Total Carbohydrate: 40 g
- Total Fat: 16 g
- Fiber: 5 g
- Protein: 5 g
- Sodium: 589 mg
- Saturated Fat: 2 g

108. French Fries

"Perfect French fries should be double-fried."
Serving: Makes 4 to 6 servings | Prep: 40m

Ingredients

- About 8 cups vegetable oil
- 2 lbs. medium baking (russet) potatoes, peeled
- Equipment: a deep-fat thermometer; an adjustable-blade slicer fitted with french fry or large (1/4-inch) julienne blade
- Accompaniment: mayonnaise

Direction

- Heat 1 1/2 inches of oil in a 5-quart heavy pot on medium heat to 325 degrees F. As the oil heats, cut potatoes using a slicer to create 1/4 inch sticks.
- In 5 batches, fry potatoes for 1 1/2 minutes for each batch, they will not be golden. Place on paper towels using a slotted spoon to drain. Heat oil back to 325 degrees F between batches.
- Heat oil to 350 degrees F. Fry potatoes again in 5 batches for around 5 minutes for each batch until crisp and golden then place on clean paper towels to let drain. Heat oil back to 325 degrees F between batches.
- Season with salt.

Nutrition Information

- Calories: 4135
- Total Carbohydrate: 40 g
- Total Fat: 448 g
- Fiber: 5 g
- Protein: 5 g
- Sodium: 14 mg
- Saturated Fat: 29 g

109. Fresh Corn Quiche

"A simple dish for brunch."
Serving: 6 servings

Ingredients

- 3 large eggs
- 1/2 small onion, coarsely chopped
- 1 tbsp. all purpose flour
- 1 tbsp. sugar
- 1 tsp. salt
- 1 1/3 cups half and half
- 3 tbsps. butter, melted
- 2 cups fresh corn kernels (cut from about 2 ears) or frozen, thawed
- 1 deep-dish frozen pie crust, thawed

Direction

- Preheat an oven to 375°F. Blend first 5 ingredients till onion is finely chopped in processor. Add butter and half and half; process till just blended. Put into big bowl; mix in corn. Put in crust; bake for 50 minutes till top is golden and filling is slightly puffed. Put onto rack; slightly cool. Serve warm.

Nutrition Information

- Calories: 403
- Total Carbohydrate: 38 g
- Cholesterol: 128 mg
- Total Fat: 25 g
- Fiber: 2 g
- Protein: 8 g
- Sodium: 419 mg
- Saturated Fat: 12 g

110. Fresh Mint Chocolate Chip Ice Cream

Serving: Makes about 1 quart

Ingredients

- 2 cups heavy cream
- 1 cup whole milk
- 2 cups packed fresh mint leaves
- 2 large eggs
- 3/4 cup sugar
- 3 oz. fine-quality bittersweet chocolate (not unsweetened)

Direction

- Blend mint, milk and cream till mint is finely chopped in a blender. Boil cream mixture in a saucepan; cool for 15 minutes. Whisk in sugar and eggs; cook on medium heat, constantly mixing, till thermometer reads 170°F and slightly thick. Don't boil custard; it'll curdle. Through fine sieve, put custard into bowl; chill custard, surface covered in plastic wrap, for 3 hours – 1 day till cold. Chop chocolate. In ice cream maker, freeze custard. Put ice cream into airtight container; mix in chocolate. To harden, put ice cream in freezer.

Nutrition Information

- Calories: 250
- Total Carbohydrate: 20 g
- Cholesterol: 87 mg
- Total Fat: 18 g
- Fiber: 1 g
- Protein: 3 g
- Sodium: 41 mg
- Saturated Fat: 11 g

111. Fresh Mint Iced Tea

"Refreshing low-calorie drink with mint that makes it more flavorful without loading more calories. You can use stevia or honey as sweeteners."
Serving: 8 | Prep: 5m | Ready in: 5h5m

Ingredients

- 5 green tea bags
- 8 cups boiling water
- 10-15 fresh mint springs (1½ cups)
- Honey or stevia (optional)
- Ice cubes

Direction

- In a 2qt heatproof jar with boiling water, soak tea bags for 2-3mins; discard the tea bags. Put in mint springs to the jar. If desired, add stevia or honey to make it sweet; completely cool. Place in the refrigerator for at least four hours. Serve drink with ice.

Nutrition Information

- Calories: 8 calories;
- Total Carbohydrate: 1 g
- Cholesterol: 0 mg
- Total Fat: 0 g
- Fiber: 1 g
- Protein: 1 g
- Sodium: 12 mg
- Sugar: 0 g
- Saturated Fat: 0 g

112. Fried Oysters Rémoulade

Serving: Makes 2 servings

Ingredients

- 2 dozen oysters (such as Belon) on the half shell
- 1/4 cup cornichons or dill pickles
- 1 cup mayonnaise
- 3 tbsps. chopped fresh parsley leaves
- 1 1/2 tbsps. minced shallot
- 1 1/2 tbsps. tomato paste
- 1 tbsp. Tabasco sauce
- 1 tbsp. fresh lemon juice
- 2 quarts vegetable oil for deep-frying
- 1/2 cup cornmeal

Direction

- Put oysters in a bowl, covered and chilled. Clean then dry oyster shells. Line double layer of paper towels on shallow baking pan.
- Remoulade: Chop dill pickles/cornichons finely then whisk with leftover remoulade ingredients in a bowl with salt to taste till well combined. Put remoulade into serving bowl.
- Heat oil in 4-qt. heavy saucepan on medium heat till a deep-fat thermometer reads 375°F.
- Preheat an oven to 200°F.
- Blend cornmeal till powdery for 30 seconds in a blender. Put in bowl; use salt to season cornmeal. In a colander, drain oysters; dip each into cornmeal to coat lightly. Put on plate. In batches of 6, fry the oysters for about 2 minutes till golden. Transfer oysters as they fry with slotted spoon to baking pan; keep warm in oven. Between batches, return oil to 375°F/
- Serve the oysters on shells with the remoulade.

Nutrition Information

- Calories: 2531
- Total Carbohydrate: 66 g
- Cholesterol: 345 mg
- Total Fat: 226 g
- Fiber: 3 g
- Protein: 61 g
- Sodium: 1606 mg
- Saturated Fat: 24 g

113. Frozen Boysenberry And White Chocolate Parfait

"This delicious dessert needed to be prepared 1 day ahead."
Serving: Serves 6

Ingredients

- 1 16-oz. bag frozen boysenberries or blackberries, thawed
- 1/4 cup sugar
- 1 tbsp. crème de
- 1/2 tsp. fresh lemon juice
- 3/4 cup sugar
- 1/4 cup water
- 6 large egg yolks
- 3 oz. imported white chocolate (such as Lindt), chopped, melted
- 2 tsps. vanilla extract
- 1 2/3 cups chilled whipping cream
- 1 16-oz. bag frozen boysenberries or blackberries, thawed
- 1/4 cup sugar
- 2 tbsps. crème de
- Fresh boysenberries, blackberries or strawberries
- Fresh mint sprigs

Direction

- To prepare Parfait: Line plastic wrap on a 9x5-inch loaf pan. In a blender, puree 1/4 cup of sugar and berries till just smooth then strain. Measure 1 1/3 cups puree then put in a heavy small saucepan. Set aside any leftover puree for sauce. Over medium heat, simmer while occasionally stirring 1 1/3 cups puree for 8 minutes till reduced to scant 1 cup. Move to a bowl and let chill for 30 minutes. Add in lemon juice and cassis; stir. Store reduced puree in the fridge till ready to use.

- In a medium metal bowl, combine yolks, water and 3/4 cup sugar. Place bowl over a saucepan of simmering water. Beat yolk mixture by a hand-held electric mixer while occasionally scraping down the bowl's sides for 5 minutes till a candy thermometer reads 140°F. Keep cooking and beating constantly for 3 minutes. Take away from over water. Beat in vanilla extract and melted chocolate till cool. In a separate bowl, beat whipping cream till stiff peaks form. In chocolate mixture, gently mix 1/4 whipped cream then fold in the leftover whipped cream.
- In a medium bowl, place 1 1/3 cups chocolate mixture. Fold in the berry puree that has been reduced. Fill 1/3 of the leftover chocolate mixture in the prepped loaf pan. Add berry-chocolate mixture to cover. Place the leftover chocolate mixture on top. Smooth the top then store the parfait in the freezer overnight. You can prepare this 2 days ahead.
- To prepare sauce: In a processor or a blender, puree crème de cassis, sugar and frozen boysenberries till smooth. Strain. Add in any puree that was set aside from parfait.
- Remove the frozen parfait from the mold. Remove the plastic wrap. Cut into slices with 1/2-in. thick. Sprinkle with sauce. Add fresh mint sprigs and berries to garnish.

114. Frozen Peanut Butter Pie With Candied Bacon

"A luscious pie recipe."
Serving: Makes 8 servings | Prep: 30m

Ingredients

- 7 bacon slices (about 6 oz.)
- 3/4 cup sugar, divided
- 1/8 tsp. ground cinnamon
- About 35 chocolate wafers, finely ground in a blender or food processor (about 2 cups crumbs)
- 3/4 stick unsalted butter, melted
- 1 cup milk
- 1 cup creamy peanut butter (not natural)
- 1/2 tsp. pure vanilla extract
- 1 1/4 cups chilled heavy cream
- 1/3 cup salted roasted peanuts, finely chopped
- a 10-inch pie plate (6-cup capacity)

Direction

- In 2 batches if needed, cook bacon in 12-in. heavy skillet on medium heat, flipping once, for 5-6 minutes total for each batch till lightly browned on edges yet flexible. Put onto paper towels; drain.
- Pour fat from skillet off; put bacon in 1 layer in skillet. Sprinkle cinnamon and 1/4 cup sugar on bacon; cook on low heat, occasionally turning with tongs, for 8-10 minutes till sugar dissolves and caramelizes and coats bacon. Sugar easily burns and melts very slowly; if needed, lower heat when sugar starts to caramelize. Bacon will look lacquered and be dark. Put bacon onto cutting board with tongs; cool. Finely chop 5 slices when bacon is cool; leave leftover 2 slices whole.
- Mix butter and wafer crumbs; press up the side and on bottom of pie plate then chill the pie shell.
- Heat milk and leftover 1/2 cup sugar in a heavy small saucepan on medium heat, mixing till sugar dissolves. Take off heat; whisk in vanilla and peanut butter till well combined. Put into a bowl; fully cool, occasionally mixing, in an ice bath.
- Beat cream using electric mixer till it holds stiff peaks; gently yet thoroughly fold it with chopped bacon and peanuts into peanut butter mixture. Put filling in pie shell; smooth top.
- Cut leftover 2 bacon slices to 2-in. long pieces; put in middle of pie in decorative starburst shape. Freeze pie, uncovered, for 5 hours till

frozen hard. Slightly soften pie in the fridge for 30 minutes before serving.

- You can freeze pie, covered with plastic wrap then foil after 5 hours, for 2 days.

115.Frozen Yogurt With Poached Peaches

""Serve with lightly sweetened Greek yogurt in case you do not have an ice cream maker.""
Serving: 8 servings

Ingredients

- 1 cup heavy cream
- 1 cup plain whole-milk Greek yogurt
- 1 cup whole milk
- 1/2 cup honey
- 2 tbsps. fresh lemon juice
- Pinch of kosher salt
- 4 large ripe peaches (about 2 lbs.)
- 6 fresh lemon verbena leaves
- 1 1/2 cups Cocchi Aperitivo Americano (Italian aperitif wine)
- 1/2 cup sugar
- 1/4 cup chopped unsalted, raw pistachios

Direction

- Preparation: For frozen yogurt: In a large bowl, whisk together salt, lemon juice, honey, milk, yogurt and cream. Following the manufacturer's directions, process in an ice cream maker.
- Remove the frozen yogurt into a shallow baking pan or an airtight container; freeze with a cover for at least 2 hours, till firm.
- Do ahead: You can make frozen yogurt 1 week in advance. Keep frozen.
- For peaches and assembly: Score an "X" in the bottom of each peach with the tip of a paring knife. Cook in boiling water in a large pot for around 1 minute, or till the skins start to peel back where cut. Transfer into ice water in a large bowl with a slotted spoon; allow to cool. Peel the peaches carefully, reserving the skins.

- In a medium saucepan, boil the mixture of 1 1/2 cups of water, the reserved peach skins, sugar, Cocchi Americano and lemon verbena. Lower the heat; simmer for 10-12 minutes, or till the mixture looks syrupy and is slightly thickened.
- Put in the peaches; cover the saucepan; lower the heat; poach the fruit gently for 12-15 minutes, or till the tip of a paring knife easily slices through flesh. (It will take less time to cook when using very ripe fruit.) Transfer the peaches onto a plate with a slotted spoon; allow to cool. Cut into wedges.
- Meanwhile, turn the poaching liquid back to a boil; cook for 15-20 minutes, or till reduced by half. Allow to cool, remove the solids.
- Scoop the frozen yogurt into small bowls or glasses. Top with pistachios, some of the reduced poaching syrup and peaches. Serve.
- Do ahead: You can poach the peaches 3 days in advance. Chill with a cover in the poaching liquid. Just before using, bring the peaches to room temperature; reduce the poaching liquid.

Nutrition Information

- Calories: 380
- Total Carbohydrate: 50 g
- Cholesterol: 49 mg
- Total Fat: 16 g
- Fiber: 3 g
- Protein: 7 g
- Sodium: 60 mg
- Saturated Fat: 9 g

116. Fruit And Seed Bars

Serving: Makes 20 bars | Prep: 5m

Ingredients

- 1 cup old fashioned oats
- 1/2 cup raw pumpkin seeds (also known as pepitas)
- 1/2 cup raw sunflower seeds
- 2 tbsps. flax seeds

- 1 cup dried fruit (blueberries, raisins, currants, cranberries and/or cherries)
- 1/2 cup unsweetened coconut flakes
- 1/3 cup honey
- 1/2 cup sunflower butter

Direction

- Preheat an oven to 325°.
- Pulse initial 6 ingredients till chopped finely (some coarsely chopped pieces are okay) in food processor.
- Add sunflower and honey; pulse to begin mixing.
- Put it into 9x9-in. pan, greased and then lined with parchment; press down into pan till fully even.
- Bake it for 25 minutes.
- Fully cool bars; use a serrated knife to cut to bars.
- Serve.

Nutrition Information

- Calories: 136
- Total Carbohydrate: 14 g
- Cholesterol: 12 mg
- Total Fat: 9 g
- Fiber: 2 g
- Protein: 2 g
- Sodium: 3 mg
- Saturated Fat: 5 g

117. Fruit Salad With Poppy Seed Dressing

Serving: Serves 4

Ingredients

- 1 grapefruit
- 2 oranges
- 2 avocados
- 1/4 cup lemon juice
- Watercress
- 2 heads French endive
- Poppy Seed dressing

Direction

- Halve the oranges and grapefruit and into skinless sections. Peel and cut the avocado and place the slices into lemon juice to avoid being darkened. Place the fruits on watercress and tuck the endive's spears around. Drizzle over the fruit the Poppy Seed Dressing and do not cover the endive, which may use fingers to eat. Serve with the Spiced Cheese Salad mixture balls.

118. Garbanzo And Red Pepper Salad

""A rick and healthy recipe that resembles Indian cooking.""
Serving: Makes 4 servings

Ingredients

- 1/4 cup lowfat plain yogurt
- 1/4 tsp. chili powder
- 1/4 tsp. chat masala
- Sugar
- 1 can (15 oz.) garbanzo beans, drained and rinsed
- 1/2 cup julienned roasted red bell pepper
- 1/2 tsp. ground cumin
- 2 tsp. chopped fresh cilantro
- 2 tsp. chopped fresh mint
- 2 tsp. fresh lime juice
- 1 tsp. minced fresh ginger
- 1 medium head frisée
- 1/2 cucumber, peeled, halved lengthwise and cut into thin half-moons

Direction

- Preparation: In a small bowl, whisk the dressing ingredients together; put in sugar to taste; set aside. In a bowl, gently mix together ginger, lime juice, mint, cilantro, cumin, roasted peppers and garbanzos; set aside. In the center of each of 4 salad bowls, place a bed of frisée. Toss the garbanzo mixture with the dressing to thoroughly coat; put in salt to taste. On top of each pile of frisée, put 1/2 cup of the bean mixture. Divide cucumber slices around the beans.

119. German Apple Pancakes

"A wonderful cake recipe."
Serving: Makes 4 to 6 servings (about 12 pancakes) | Prep: 1h

Ingredients

- 1/4 cup plus 2 tsps. sugar
- 1/2 tsp. cinnamon
- 1 cup all-purpose flour
- 1/2 tsp. salt
- 1 1/2 cups whole milk
- 4 large eggs
- 1 1/2 lb Gala apples (3 or 4)
- 2 tbsps. fresh lemon juice
- 3/4 stick (6 tbsps.) unsalted butter, cut into 12 pieces
- an adjustable-blade slicer

Direction

- Preheat an oven to 200°F.
- Mix cinnamon and 1/4 cup sugar; put aside.
- In a big bowl, whisk leftover 2 tsp. sugar, salt and flour. In slow stream, add milk, whisking. One by one, add eggs; whisk well after each.
- Peel apples; use slicer to cut to 1/8-in. thick slices, rotating around core; throw core away. Cut apple slices to 1/8-in. thick matchsticks; toss in bowl with lemon juice. Fold juice and apples into batter.
- Heat 1/2 tbsp./1 piece butter till foam subsides in 6-in. nonstick skillet on medium heat. Add 1/3 cup batter, evenly spreading to cover bottom; cook, lowering heat if browning very quickly, flipping pancake once with flexible thin heatproof spatula, for 4 minutes total till both sides are golden. Slide pancake onto platter; in oven, keep warm. With

leftover batter and butter, make more pancakes the same way. Sprinkle cinnamon sugar; immediately serve.
- You can make batter with apples 3 days ahead, keep covered, chilled; before using, mix.

Nutrition Information

- Calories: 550
- Total Carbohydrate: 67 g
- Cholesterol: 241 mg
- Total Fat: 26 g
- Fiber: 5 g
- Protein: 13 g
- Sodium: 406 mg
- Saturated Fat: 14 g

120. Ginger Almond Wafers

Serving: Makes about 26

Ingredients

- 1 1/2 cups powdered sugar
- 1 1/4 cups all purpose flour
- 1/2 cup (1 stick) chilled unsalted butter, diced
- 1 tbsp. minced peeled fresh ginger
- 1 tbsp. ground ginger
- 1/2 tsp. ground cinnamon
- 1/2 tsp. salt
- 3/4 cup whole almonds, toasted
- 3 tbsps. whipping cream
- 3 tbsps. chopped crystallized ginger
- Powdered sugar

Direction

- Preheat an oven to 325°F. Line parchment paper on 2 big heavy baking sheets. Blend first 7 ingredients with on/off turns till it looks like coarse meal in processor. Add crystallized ginger, cream and almonds; process till just moist clumps form. Shape dough to 1 1/4-in. diameter balls; put on prepped sheet. Moisten glass's bottom; dip in powder sugar. Press every dough ball to 1/4-in. thick.

- Bake cookies for 28 minutes till brown on edges and bottom. Put cookies on rack; cool. Keep at room temperature, airtight.

Nutrition Information

- Calories: 117
- Total Carbohydrate: 14 g
- Cholesterol: 11 mg
- Total Fat: 6 g
- Fiber: 1 g
- Protein: 2 g
- Sodium: 48 mg
- Saturated Fat: 3 g

121.Ginger And Pink Grapefruit Cheesecake

Serving: Makes 12 servings

Ingredients

- 20 whole graham crackers, coarsely broken
- 6 tbsps. sugar
- 1/2 cup (1 stick) chilled unsalted butter, cut into 1/2-inch cubes
- 3 tbsps. finely chopped crystallized ginger
- 1 1/3 cups heavy whipping cream
- 1 (1-inch-long) piece fresh ginger, peeled, cut into very thin rounds
- 1 cup ginger preserves
- 1 tbsp. water
- 4 (8-oz.) packages cream cheese, room temperature
- 1 1/4 cups sugar
- 1 tbsp. ground ginger
- 2 1/2 tsps. vanilla extract
- 1/4 tsp. salt
- 4 large eggs
- 2 large pink or ruby grapefruits
- Finely chopped crystallized ginger

Direction

- For Crust: Put rack in middle of oven; preheat it to 350°F. Butter the 9-in. springform pan that has 2 3/4-in. high sides.
- Blend sugar and graham crackers to coarse crumbs in processor. Add 1/2 cup butter and blend till crumbs hold together. Press onto sides and on bottom of prepped pan. Bake crust for 15 minutes till starting to color; sprinkle chopped ginger and cool. Lower oven temperature down to 325°F.
- Stack 3 long 18-in. wide foil sheets on work surface; put cake pan in the center. Snugly fold foil up pan sides.
- For Filling: Simmer fresh ginger and cream; remove from heat. Cover. Steep for 30 minutes. Strain the cream. Mix 1 tbsp. water and preserves till preserves melt in small saucepan on medium heat; strain into a small bowl. Discard solids; reserve ginger jelly.
- Beat cream cheese using electric mixer till smooth in big bowl; beat in salt, vanilla, ground ginger and sugar. Add eggs, one at a time; beat well. Add 2 tbsp. ginger jelly; beat till blended. Beat in strained cream slowly; transfer into prepped crust. Put cake pan in big roasting pan; pour enough hot water in roasting pan to reach halfway up cake pan's sides. Put cake in water bath into the oven.
- Bake cake for 2 hours till starting to crack around edges, brown on top and gently set; remove from water. Remove the foil. Put hot cake in fridge, uncovered; chill overnight. You can make it 2 days ahead; keep it chilled. Keep ginger jelly at room temperature.
- For Topping: Line few layers of paper towels on big plate. Cut all pith and peel from the grapefruits; working over bowl, cut between membranes to release segments. Put on paper towels; drain. Use extra paper towels to cover; press to absorb extra liquid. You can prep it 8 hours ahead; chill. As needed, change towels.
- Cut around crust; remove pan sides. On filling, spread 1/4 cup of ginger jelly; arrange grapefruit on top. Brush with ginger jelly.

Sprinkle crystallized ginger. You can make it 1 hour ahead. Chill.

Nutrition Information

- Calories: 859
- Total Carbohydrate: 77 g
- Cholesterol: 245 mg
- Total Fat: 59 g
- Fiber: 2 g
- Protein: 10 g
- Sodium: 487 mg
- Saturated Fat: 33 g

122. Ginger-macadamia Brownies

"Tastes of ginger and macadamia nuts really help the regular brownies stand out. For the end of the festive summer, use strawberries to serve."
Serving: Makes 16

Ingredients

- 3/4 cup (1 1/2 sticks) unsalted butter, cut into pieces
- 4 oz. unsweetened chocolate, chopped
- 1 tsp. instant coffee powder
- 3 large eggs
- 1 1/2 cups (packed) brown sugar
- 2 tsps. vanilla extract
- 1/4 tsp. salt
- 1 cup unbleached all purpose flour
- 1 cup chopped macadamia nuts
- 1/4 cup minced crystallized ginger

Direction

- Set oven at 325°F and start preheating. Use butter to grease an 8x8x2 glass baking dish. In a heavy medium saucepan, combine coffee powder, chocolate and butter. Stir and cook over low heat until smooth. Stir sporadically and let cool.
- Beat eggs in big bowl to blend. Mix in salt, vanilla and sugar. Fold in the chocolate mixture. Combine flour then ginger and nuts into the mixture. Pour the batter into the

greased pan. Let bake for about 40 minutes until moist crumbs stick on the tester inserted in the middle. Allow to cool in pan on rack. Cover and let rest at room temperature overnight. Divide it into 16 squares.

Nutrition Information

- Calories: 315
- Total Carbohydrate: 32 g
- Cholesterol: 58 mg
- Total Fat: 20 g
- Fiber: 2 g
- Protein: 4 g
- Sodium: 62 mg
- Saturated Fat: 9 g

123. Gingerbread Roulade With Caramel And Glaceed Fruits

"So delicious."
Serving: Makes 10 to 12 servings

Ingredients

- 6 large eggs, separated
- 3/4 cup plus 2 tbsps. sugar
- 2 tbsps. (1/4 stick) unsalted butter, melted
- 1 tbsp. mild-flavored (light) molasses
- 1 tsp. vanilla extract
- 3/4 cup all purpose flour
- 1 tsp. baking powder
- 1 1/2 tsps. ground ginger
- 1 1/2 tsps. ground allspice
- 1/4 tsp. salt
- tsp. cream of tartar
- Powdered sugar
- 1/4 cup brandy
- 3/4 cup chilled whipping cream
- 1/4 cup chilled sour cream
- 1/4 cup powdered sugar
- 1 tbsp. brandy
- 3/4 cup (packed) golden brown sugar
- 1/2 cup whipping cream

- 3/4 cup (1 1/2 sticks) unsalted butter, room temperature
- 3 cups powdered sugar
- 3/4 tsp. ground ginger
- 3/4 tsp. ground allspice
- 1/2 cup sugar
- 3 tbsps. water
- 1/2 tbsp. light corn syrup
- Glacséed Fruits

Direction

- Cake: Preheat an oven to 350°F. Butter a 15 1/2x10 1/2x1-in. baking sheet. Use waxed paper to line; butter then flour paper.
- Beat 3/4 cup sugar and yolks using electric mixer for 5 minutes till it falls in heavy ribbon when you lift beaters in a big bowl; beat in vanilla, molasses and melted butter. Sift salt, spices, baking powder and flour on yolk mixture; gently fold in. Beat cream of tartar and whites till soft peaks form using clean dry beaters in another big bowl. Add leftover 2 tbsp. sugar slowly, beating till stiff yet not dry. Fold whites in 3 additions into yolk mixture; evenly spread batter in prepped sheet.
- Bake cake for 15 minutes till inserted tester in middle of cake exits clean. To loosen cake, cut around the baking sheet sides. On work surface, lay kitchen towel; dust using powdered sugar. Turn the cake onto towel; peel paper off. Brush brandy on cake. Roll warm cake up together with towel, starting with 1 long side, jellyroll style; in towel, cool cake.
- Filling: Beat all ingredients till stiff peaks form in medium bowl. Unroll cake; spread filling. Roll cake up only without towel. Put on long platter, seam side down; refrigerate.
- Frosting: Mix cream and brown sugar in small heavy saucepan on medium low heat till it simmers and sugar dissolves. Put in freezer for 15 minutes till cold. Beat spices, powdered sugar and butter till fluffy in medium bowl; beat in the cold brown sugar mixture. Spread the frosting all over the cake; chill for 2 hours

till set. You can make it 2 days ahead, chilled, covered.
- Caramel: Mix corn syrup, water and sugar in small heavy saucepan on low heat, brushing pan sides occasionally with wet pastry brush, till sugar dissolve. Increase heat; boil without mixing, occasionally swirling pan, for 5 minutes till syrup gets deep amber color. Drizzle caramel on cake quickly using tsp.. You can make it 6 hours ahead, chilled.
- If desired, serve cake with fruits.

Nutrition Information

- Calories: 677
- Total Carbohydrate: 97 g
- Cholesterol: 190 mg
- Total Fat: 29 g
- Fiber: 0 g
- Protein: 6 g
- Sodium: 160 mg
- Saturated Fat: 18 g

124. Gingered Apple Slaw

"Simple and fun."
Serving: Makes 4 to 6 servings

Ingredients

- 1/2 cup mayonnaise
- 1 1/2 tsps. finely grated peeled fresh ginger
- 1 tbsp. seasoned rice vinegar
- 2 celery ribs, cut into matchsticks
- 4 apples, of different varieties, cored and cut into matchsticks

Direction

- Mix vinegar, ginger and mayonnaise. Add apples and celery; toss gently to coat.

Nutrition Information

- Calories: 299
- Total Carbohydrate: 26 g
- Cholesterol: 11 mg

- Total Fat: 23 g
- Fiber: 5 g
- Protein: 1 g
- Sodium: 185 mg
- Saturated Fat: 3 g

125. Gluten-free Blueberry Muffins

"Everybody loves this gluten-free blueberry muffin!"
Serving: 12 | Prep: 20m | Ready in: 55m

Ingredients

- 1¾ cups gluten-free all-purpose flour
- 1 tsp. baking powder
- ¼ tsp. baking soda
- ¼ tsp. salt
- 2 large eggs
- ½ cup light brown sugar
- 1 cup buttermilk
- 3 tbsps. canola oil
- 1 tsp. vanilla
- 1½ cups fresh or frozen (not thawed) blueberries
- 1 tbsp. Demerara sugar

Direction

- Preheat the oven to 400 degrees F. Line a twelve-cup muffin pan with paper liners.
- In a medium bowl, mix salt, flour, baking soda, and baking powder together. In a separate medium bowl, beat vanilla, eggs, oil, brown sugar, and buttermilk together until well combined. Form a well in the middle of the dry ingredients then pour the wet ingredients in; mix until it forms into a smooth batter. Add blueberries and stir until incorporated. Split the batter between the muffin cups; add Demerara sugar on top.
- Bake muffins for 20-25mins until golden and an inserted skewer in the middle comes out without residue. Cool for 10mins in the pan then move to a wire rack. Cool for at least 5mins then serve.

Nutrition Information

- Calories: 172 calories;
- Total Carbohydrate: 29 g
- Cholesterol: 32 mg
- Total Fat: 5 g
- Fiber: 3 g
- Protein: 4 g
- Sodium: 169 mg
- Sugar: 13 g
- Saturated Fat: 1 g

126. Grandma Ethel's Brisket With Tzimmes

"The combination of tzimmes and brisket in this recipe is so good since some people don't want to add prunes to it. Feel free to adjust the amount of the ingredients and procedure as listed below. Be sure to achieve a lump of very juicy meat."
Serving: Makes 8 to 10 servings | Prep: 50m

Ingredients

- 1 (6- to 7-lb) first-cut brisket
- 1 3/4 tsps. salt
- 1 tsp. black pepper
- 3 tbsps. olive oil
- 4 cups brown chicken stock or reconstituted brown chicken demi-glace
- 3/4 cup Sherry vinegar
- 2 lb carrots, peeled and cut crosswise into 2-inch-long pieces
- 4 medium sweet potatoes, peeled and cut into 2-inch pieces
- 2 3/4 cups dried pitted prunes

Direction

- Position the oven rack in the oven's center and preheat it at 350°F.
- Pat the brisket to dry and rub 1 tsp. of salt and a half tsp. of pepper all over the meat. Place the 17x11-inch heavy pan for roasting (at least 3 inches deep) on the 2 burners. Warm oil in roasting pan on medium-high heat until the oil

is hot but not yet smoking. Cook the brisket for 5 minutes a side until browned all over, begin with the fat down. Take off the heat and stir in vinegar and stock. Use a heavy-duty foil to tightly cover the pan and braise the brisket inside the oven for 2 hours. Add potatoes and carrots in the pan and braise it covered for 60 minutes. Stir in prunes and continue braising for 30 more minutes until the meat becomes fork-tender. Remove the cover and let it cool at room temperature for 1 hour. Put the cover back on the pan and let it chill for 12 or more hours.

- Position again oven rack in the oven's center and preheat it at 350°F.

- Place the braised brisket on a clean cutting board and slice it 1/4-inch thick across the grain. Discard all the fat found on the surface of sauce and vegetables. Transfer the sliced meat back to the pan and cover it with foil covering. Reheat it for 40 minutes until heated through. Season it with the remaining half tsp. of pepper and 3/4 tsp. of salt. On a big platter, arrange the sliced meat nicely and garnish the dish with sauce and tzimmes.

- Take note that you can chill the brisket for up to 3 days.

Nutrition Information

- Calories: 1326
- Total Carbohydrate: 63 g
- Cholesterol: 346 mg
- Total Fat: 87 g
- Fiber: 9 g
- Protein: 72 g
- Sodium: 1699 mg
- Saturated Fat: 34 g

127. Grass-fed Beef Meatloaf In A Bacon Blanket

"Meatloaf made with grass-fed beef and a bit of pork topped with bacon."
Serving: Makes 4 servings (with generous leftovers) | Prep: 30m

Ingredients

- 1 cup fresh bread crumbs (ground in food processor from 2 slices of bread)
- 1/2 cup milk
- 1 medium onion, finely chopped
- 2 medium carrots, finely chopped
- 1 large celery rib, finely chopped
- 4 large garlic cloves, finely chopped
- 2 tbsps. olive oil
- Salt
- 1 1/2 lbs. ground grass-fed beef (preferably ground once; see Cooks' Notes)
- 1/2 lb. ground pork (preferably shoulder, not lean; and ground once; see Cooks' Notes)
- 1/2 cup ketchup
- 2 large eggs, lightly beaten
- 1 tbsp. Worcestershire sauce
- 2 tsps. smoked paprika (optional; see Cooks' Notes)
- 1/2 tsp. freshly ground black pepper
- 6 bacon slices, halved crosswise
- A large, heavy rimmed sheet pan or flameproof roasting pan (not glass); instant-read thermometer

Direction

- To prepare: Set an oven to preheat to 375 degrees F and place the rack in the middle.
- In the meantime, in a big bowl, mix together the milk and bread crumbs, then put aside.
- In a heavy 12-inch frying pan, cook the garlic, celery, carrot and onion in oil with 1 tsp salt on medium heat for 8-10 minutes with a cover, stirring from time to time, until it becomes tender. Take away from the heat and let cool.
- Mix together the cooked vegetables, 1 tsp salt, pepper, smoked paprika, Worcestershire

sauce, eggs, ketchup, pork and beef with bread crumbs and mix it using your hands, until the mixture becomes cohesive and the vegetables are distributed well.

- Shape the mixture into a 12-inch loaf, approximately 4 1/2 inches wide, in the pan, and lay out the slices of bacon crosswise on top of it.

- Let it roast for 40-45 minutes in the oven, until an instant-read thermometer inserted in the middle reads 160 degrees F.

- If the bacon placed on top did not become crisp, reset the oven to broil and let the meatloaf broil for 2-3 minutes, 4-5 inches from the heat source, until the bacon turns brown and becomes crisp.

- Allow the meatloaf to rest for 10 minutes in the pan prior to moving to a platter.

- Cooks' notes: Smoked paprika coming from Spain is the latest smoky flavor after chipotle chiles. If you can't find it, you may skip this ingredient and you'll still have a tasty meatloaf.

- The meat that was ground once will become coarser and will give a more appealing texture to your meatloaf. You can request your butcher or the supermarket.

- You may also use bison or regular ground chuck for this recipe.

- If you want to make the meatloaf together with scalloped potatoes, you can bake them on the same rack in the oven, side by side. Place the potatoes in the lower third and the meatloaf in the upper third if the pans won't fit side by side. When it comes to broiling, broil each of the ingredients separately to keep control of how much the dish will brown.

- The leftover meatloaf will keep for 4 days, well covered and chilled. It will make a mean sandwich with mayonnaise, tomato and lettuce, or Dijon mustard and caramelized onions.

Nutrition Information

- Calories: 942
- Total Carbohydrate: 39 g
- Cholesterol: 270 mg
- Total Fat: 62 g
- Fiber: 3 g
- Protein: 57 g
- Sodium: 1091 mg
- Saturated Fat: 22 g

---

128. Grass-fed Steaks With Kalamata-olive Chimichurri

"This is best served rare."
Serving: Makes 6 servings

Ingredients

- 3 tbsps. fruity olive oil, divided
- 4 garlic cloves; 2 thinly sliced, 2 pressed
- 1/4 tsp. dried crushed red pepper
- 1 bay leaf, preferably fresh, broken in half
- 1/3 cup finely chopped shallots
- 1/4 cup finely chopped fresh Italian parsley
- 2 tbsps. finely chopped pitted Kalamata olives
- 2 tbsps. red wine vinegar
- 1 to 2 tbsps. water
- 2 14-to 16-oz. 2-inch-thick grass-fed New York strip steaks
- 2 tsps. paprika
- 1 tsp. coarse kosher salt
- 1/4 tsp. cayenne pepper

Direction

- Heat 2 tbsp. oil on medium heat in medium heavy skillet. Add bay leaf, red pepper and sliced garlic; mix for 1 minute till fragrant. Add shallots; sauté for 2 minutes till translucent. Take off heat; mix in vinegar, olives and parsley. Add 1 tbsp. water. By teaspoonfuls, add more water as needed to thin; season chimichurri with pepper and salt. You can make it 2 hours ahead; stand in room temperature.

- Rub pressed garlic and 1 tbsp. oil on steaks; sprinkle generous black pepper amount, cayenne, 1/4 tsp. coarse salt and 1/2 tsp.

paprika on both sides of every steak. Stand for 30 minutes – 2 hours at room temperature.

- Preheat an oven to 400°F. Brush oil on a very big heavy, cast iron is best, ovenproof skillet; heat till nearly smoking on high heat. Add steaks; cook for 5 minutes till browned. Flip steaks; put skillet in oven. Roast for 10 minutes till a horizontally instant-read thermometer in steaks reads 110-115°F for rare.
- Rest steaks for 5 minutes; crosswise slice thinly. Put chimichurri over.

Nutrition Information

- Calories: 315
- Total Carbohydrate: 3 g
- Cholesterol: 82 mg
- Total Fat: 24 g
- Fiber: 1 g
- Protein: 20 g
- Sodium: 309 mg
- Saturated Fat: 8 g

---

129. Gravy-braised Turkey Legs With Cipolline Onions

"So delicious!"
Serving: 6 servings

Ingredients

- 2 whole turkey legs (about 3 1/2 lbs.), drumsticks and thighs separated, patted dry
- Kosher salt, freshly ground pepper
- 2 tbsps. olive oil
- 2 tbsps. unsalted butter
- 1 cup plus 2 tbsps. all-purpose flour
- 1 large yellow onion, chopped
- 1 large leek, white and pale-green parts only, chopped
- 2 celery stalks, chopped
- 4 garlic cloves, chopped
- 1 tsp. black peppercorns
- 1 cup dry white wine
- 1/2 bunch thyme

- 2 dried bay leaves
- 6 cups turkey stock or low-sodium chicken broth, divided
- 1 lb. cipolline or pearl onions
- 1 large egg yolk, room temperature
- 2 tbsps. heavy cream, room temperature
- 1/4 cup chopped fresh parsley

Direction

- Use pepper and salt to season turkey all over generously; sit for 1 hour on big rimmed baking sheet to bring it to room temperature.
- Heat butter and oil on medium heat in a big Dutch oven/other heavy pot. Put 1 cup flour onto plate; dredge turkey in flour, only coating skin. Don't shake excess off. Cook, outer side down, for 5-8 minutes till browned very well. Don't cook on inner side. Put onto plate.
- Add peppercorns, garlic, celery, leek and yellow onion to pot; season using salt. Cook, mixing often, scraping brown bits up from bottom of pot, for 10-12 minutes till starting to brown around edges and veggies are soft.
- Sprinkle in leftover 2 tbsp. flour; cook for 2 minutes, mixing. Add wine; boil, mixing. Cook till pan is nearly dry. Add 3 cups stock, bay leaves and thyme; season with salt. Simmer. Put turkey, browned side up, in pot; as needed, add stock to nearly fully cover without submerging the brown skin to avoid making it soggy. Very gently simmer liquid; cook for 35-45 minutes till turkey cooks through an inserted instant-read thermometer near thigh's bone reads 165°F. Put turkey onto plate.
- Put leftover stock and cipolline in pot; simmer for 20-25 minutes till tender. Put onions on plate with turkey using a slotted spoon; simmer braising liquid for 15-20 minutes till reduced to 3 cups.
- Beat cream and yolk in small bowl; to warm, mix in 1 tbsp. of braising liquid. Add yolk mixture slowly to braising liquid, constantly whisking; take off heat. It'll curdle if you boil gravy after this point. Strain gravy into big bowl and wipe pot out. Put gravy in pot.

Taste; adjust if needed with pepper and salt. Put cilpolline onions and turkey, browned side up, in pot; keep warm on low heat till serving. Top with parsley; serve.

- You can season legs 1 day ahead; keep chilled, uncovered. Before using, bring to room temperature.

Nutrition Information

- Calories: 353
- Total Carbohydrate: 41 g
- Cholesterol: 55 mg
- Total Fat: 14 g
- Fiber: 3 g
- Protein: 11 g
- Sodium: 1032 mg
- Saturated Fat: 5 g

- Bake cakes on griddle for 5 minutes till bottom is deep brown.
- Use a metal spatula to flip; be careful, they tend to stick and are fragile. Fry 2nd side for 1 minute till spotted brown.
- Immediately serve; oil griddle lightly and mix batter between batches.

Nutrition Information

- Calories: 104
- Total Carbohydrate: 12 g
- Cholesterol: 2 mg
- Total Fat: 5 g
- Fiber: 1 g
- Protein: 2 g
- Sodium: 61 mg
- Saturated Fat: 1 g

---

130. Gray's Grist Mill Thin Jonnycakes

"Such a tasty recipe!"
Serving: Makes 20 to 25 small jonnycakes

Ingredients

- 2 cups stone ground cornmeal, preferably jonnycake (flint corn) meal
- 1/2 tsp. salt
- 3/4 cup water, cold
- 1 1/2 cups milk, any kind
- Vegetable oil for frying

Direction

- In a mixing bowl, mix salt and cornmeal. Add cold water; mix till sooth. Mix in milk; if needed, add more to make a pourable, thin batter.
- Oil griddle lightly. Mix batter (it might settle); spoon 1 tbsp. batter out for each cake onto griddle. Should dance out to thin disk. Add 1 tsp. cornmeal to batter if it looks too thin. Thin batter out with a little milk if cake sits too high.

---

131. Greek Yogurt Cheesecake With Pomegranate Syrup

""This light cheesecake recipe has an unexpected tanginess from Greek yogurt.""
Serving: Makes 8 to 10 servings

Ingredients

- Nonstick vegetable oil spray
- 1 1/2 cups fine graham cracker crumbs
- 1/2 cup (1 stick) unsalted butter, melted, cooled slightly
- 1/4 cup sugar
- 2 tsps. powdered gelatin
- 1 1/2 lbs. cream cheese, room temperature
- 1 1/2 cups plain whole-milk Greek yogurt
- 3/4 cup sugar
- 2 tsps. fresh lemon juice
- 1 tsp. vanilla extract
- 1/2 tsp. kosher salt
- 2 cups flash-pasteurized pomegranate juice
- 1/2 cup sugar
- 2 tbsps. light corn syrup
- Pomegranate seeds
- A 9"-diameter springform pan

Direction

- Preparation: For the crust, using nonstick spray, coat the sides and bottom of a pan. Use a parchment paper round to line the bottom. In a medium bowl, combine the remaining ingredients with your fingertips till the mixture holds together when tightly pinched. Pack in an even layer onto the bottom of the pan (the bottom of a flat measuring cup will work well). Chill for at least 1 hour or up to 1 day, till firm.
- For the filling, in a heat-proof bowl, place 1 1/2 tbsps. of cold water and gelatin. Allow to sit for 5-10 minutes, or till softened.
- In a food processor, pulse salt, vanilla, lemon juice, sugar, yogurt and cream cheese together, till completely smooth, scraping down the sides as necessary.
- Place a small skillet on medium heat; put in 1/2-in.-deep water. Place the bowl with the gelatin mixture in the skillet; stir for around 2 minutes, or till the gelatin is dissolved. Take the bowl away from the skillet.
- Drizzle gelatin into the cream cheese mixture with the motor running; stir till well-blended. Transfer into the prepared crust. Firmly tap the pan on the counter to break up any big air bubbles. Smooth the top. Use plastic wrap to tightly cover; before serving, chill for at least 6 hours. Do ahead: You can make the cheesecake 2 days in advance and keep chilled.
- For pomegranate syrup and assembly, place a medium saucepan on medium-low heat, simmer the first 3 ingredients together; simmer while whisking occasionally for 35-40 minutes, or till the syrup measures a generous 1/2 cup, and is shiny and thickened. Allow to cool. Do ahead: You can make the pomegranate syrup 5 days in advance and chill with a cover. Before serving, rewarm slightly.
- Cut the cheesecake into slices; dip a knife into a large glass of warm water; wipe dry between the slices; place on serving plates. Drizzle over with the pomegranate syrup; scatter pomegranate seeds around.

132. Green And Wax Beans With Walnut Gremolata

Serving: Serves 2 generously

Ingredients

- 3/4 lb. green and/or wax beans, trimmed
- 1 tbsp. unsalted butter
- 1/2 tbsp. olive oil
- 2 tbsps. chopped walnuts
- 1 garlic clove, minced
- 1 tbsp. chopped fresh parsley leaves
- 2 tsps. fresh lemon juice
- 1/4 tsp. freshly grated lemon zest

Direction

- On high heat, boil a big saucepan 2/3 full with salted water. Put in beans and simmer till tender-crisp, for 5 minutes. Strain the beans.
- Heat oil and butter in big skillet on medium heat till froth settles and let walnuts cook till golden, mixing from time to time. Mix in and cook garlic for a minute, mixing. Mix in salt to taste, zest, lemon juice, parsley and beans, and heat completely.

Nutrition Information

- Calories: 183
- Total Carbohydrate: 14 g
- Cholesterol: 15 mg
- Total Fat: 14 g
- Fiber: 6 g
- Protein: 4 g
- Sodium: 13 mg
- Saturated Fat: 5 g

133. Green Beans With Blackened Sage And Hazelnuts

"An elegant hazelnut version of swap."
Serving: Makes 8 servings

Ingredients

- 1 tbsp. unsalted butter
- 1 tbsp. olive oil
- 1/2 cup chopped fresh sage
- 3 cloves garlic, finely chopped
- 2 lbs. green beans, trimmed
- 1/2 tsp. salt
- 1/4 cup hazelnuts, chopped

Direction

- Over moderately-high heat, heat a big skillet. Heat oil and butter, then let sage cook for 1 to 2 minutes till it starts to char. Put in the garlic and cook for 2 minutes till golden. Put in the salt and beans; coat by tossing. Cautiously put in a cup of water. Let steam for 3 to 4 minutes till beans are soft enough to easily prick with fork and majority of water has vaporized. Add pepper and salt to season. Scatter hazelnuts over and serve.

134. Griddle Cakes With Marmalade And Clotted Cream

Serving: Makes 4 breakfast or brunch servings | Prep: 25m

Ingredients

- 1/2 cup all-purpose flour
- 1/2 cup quick-cooking oats
- 2 tsps. sugar
- 1 tsp. baking powder
- 1/2 tsp. baking soda
- 1/4 tsp. salt
- 1 cup well-shaken buttermilk
- 1 large egg, lightly beaten
- 5 tbsps. unsalted butter, melted and cooled slightly
- Accompaniments: marmalade or jam; clotted cream or crème fraîche

Direction

- Put oven rack in center position; preheat the oven to 200°F. In oven, warm 4 plates.
- Heat well-seasoned griddle/heavy skillet (cast iron is best) till hot on medium low heat.
- As griddle heats, whisk salt, baking soda, baking powder, sugar, oats and flour; whisk in 3 tbsp. butter, egg and buttermilk till combined.
- Brush some leftover butter on hot griddle. Put 3 tbsp. batter per oatcake on hot griddle; cook for 1-2 minutes till bottoms are golden, edges are set and bubbles form on surface. Use a big spatula to flip cakes; cook for 1-2 minutes till tops spring back when gently pressed. Put as cooked on plates in oven; cover with foil loosely. If needed, brush butter on griddle as needed.
- Brush leftover butter on griddle cakes; immediately serve.

Nutrition Information

- Calories: 311
- Total Carbohydrate: 30 g
- Cholesterol: 87 mg
- Total Fat: 18 g
- Fiber: 2 g
- Protein: 9 g
- Sodium: 385 mg
- Saturated Fat: 10 g

135. Grilled Broccoli Rabe And Radicchio With Pancetta Dressing Topped With A Soft-cooked Egg

"If you can't get broccoli rabe, use kale or escarole."
Serving: Makes 4 servings

Ingredients

- 2 slices day-old country or rustic bread, crusts removed
- Olive oil
- Coarse salt
- 6 slices pancetta (about 1/4 lb.), cut into 14-inch dice
- 1/2 cup white balsamic vinegar
- 1 tbsp. mustard seeds
- 1 tsp. crushed red pepper flakes
- 2 tbsps. sugar
- 1 tsp. fresh thyme leaves, roughly chopped
- 6 tbsps. (3/4 stick) unsalted butter, melted
- 1/4 cup finely chopped red onions (about 1/2 medium onion)
- 1/4 cup finely chopped fennel (about 1/2 bulb)
- 1 lb. young broccoli rabe, washed, dried, and leaves removed (keep for another use)
- 2 heads radicchio, cored and leaves separated
- 2 tbsps. blended olive oil and grape seed oil
- 2 tsps. minced garlic
- 4 large eggs
- 20 shavings Parmigiano-Reggiano

Direction

- Heat an oven to 325°F. Lightly oil then salt day-old bread; bake for 10 minutes till golden brown. Cool then tear to pieces; process till finely ground in food processor. Put aside.
- Heat pancetta in a medium skillet; cook on medium high heat till lightly golden brown for 5 minutes. Drain on paper towel-lined plate. Mix thyme, sugar, red pepper flakes, mustard seeds and vinegar in a medium bowl; whisk in melted butter. Add pancetta, fennel and red onions; put aside pancetta vinaigrette.
- Toss oil, garlic and radicchio leaves with broccoli rabe in a big bowl; to taste, add salt. Heat a grill pan or grill till hot yet not smoking. In batches, put greens on grill, frequently turning till just wilted, for 30 seconds; put into big bowl. Repeat till you grill all radicchio and broccoli rabe; toss with 4 tbsp. pancetta vinaigrette.
- Boil medium pot of water on medium high heat; lower eggs into water using a slotted spoon. To maintain simmer, adjust heat; cook eggs for 5 minutes. Use water and ice to fill medium bowl. Transfer cooked eggs from pan into ice water bath. Gently crack shell all over when eggs are cool to handle then begin to peel; intermittently submerge in ice bath (if too hot) then keep peeling.
- Serve: Portion grilled radicchio and broccoli rabe, mounding in middle of each plate, to 4 serving plates. Over greens, put 5 Parmigiano shavings; put 1 whole soft-cooked egg over. Drizzle leftover vinaigrette over egg then around plate; generously top with breadcrumbs.

Nutrition Information

- Calories: 1230
- Total Carbohydrate: 35 g
- Cholesterol: 347 mg
- Total Fat: 93 g
- Fiber: 6 g
- Protein: 68 g
- Sodium: 2353 mg
- Saturated Fat: 42 g

136. Grilled Chicken Summer Salad

"A fantastic salad recipe."
Serving: Makes 6 servings | Prep: 1.5h

Ingredients

- 5 tbsps. red-wine vinegar
- 1 tbsp. plus 2 tsp. fresh lemon juice
- 1 tbsp. Dijon mustard

- 2 small garlic cloves, minced
- 3/4 tsp. sugar
- 3/4 cup extra-virgin olive oil
- 1/4 cup chopped chives
- 4 cups water
- 1/3 cup kosher salt
- 2 tbsps. sugar
- 4 garlic cloves, smashed
- 1 tsp. black peppercorns
- 1 bunch radishes
- 4 Persian cucumbers or 1 seedless cucumber
- 1/2 cup packed flat-leaf parsley leaves
- 1 (15-to 19-oz.) can chickpeas, rinsed and drained
- 1/4 cup finely chopped red onion
- 1 tbsp. chopped mint
- 1 lb. haricorts verts or other green beans
- 1/2 cup whole almonds with skin, toasted and coarsely chopped
- 3/4 lb. fresh cremini mushrooms, halved
- 3/4 lb. fresh shiitake mushrooms, stems reserved for another use and caps halved
- 2 lbs. skinless boneless chicken thighs
- 1/3 cup basil pesto
- 2 medium tomatoes, cut into 1/2-inch-thick wedges
- 1/4 cup thinly sliced basil
- 4 cups thinly sliced romaine, Bibb, and/or Boston lettuce
- Equipment: a perforated grill sheet

Direction

- Vinaigrette: Whisk all vinaigrette ingredients but chives and oil with 1/4 tsp. pepper and 1/2 tsp. salt. In a slow stream, add oil, whisking till emulsified; whisk in the chives.
- Radish cucumber salad: Boil peppercorns, garlic, sugar, salt and water in 4-qt. pot for 10 minutes, uncovered.
- As brine boils, trim radishes; halve. Lengthwise halve cucumbers; crosswise cut to 1/2-in. thick slices.
- Take brine from heat. Add cucumbers and radishes; stand for 10 minutes, uncovered. Drain in colander; discard peppercorns and garlic. Put cucumbers and radishes in ice bath to halt cooking; drain in colander well.
- Put into big bowl; chill for 20 minutes, uncovered.
- Chickpea salad: Mix pepper and salt to taste, 1/4 cup vinaigrette, onion and chickpeas.
- Green beans: Cook the green beans, uncovered, occasionally mixing, in big pot with well-salted boiling water for 3-6 minutes till just tender; drain. To stop cooking, put into big ice bath. Drain; pat dry.
- Grill chicken and mushrooms: Prep grill above hot charcoal for direct-heat cooking or medium high heat for gas.
- Toss 2 tbsp. vinaigrette with mushrooms; marinate for 10 minutes.
- In 2 batches, grill mushrooms, only covered if using gas grill, frequently mixing, on oiled grill sheet for 5 minutes per batch till golden brown; toss 2 tbsp. vinaigrette with hot mushrooms.
- Use 1/2 tsp. each pepper and salt to season chicken. Oil grill rack; grill chicken on medium hot charcoal or medium heat for gas, only covered for gas grill, occasionally turning chicken, moving as needed to prevent flare-ups, for 8-10 minutes total till just cooked through. Put onto cutting board; rest for 10 minutes.
- Cut to 1/2-in. thick slices; toss in a big bowl with pesto.
- Assemble dish and dress salads: Toss pepper and salt to taste, 3 tbsp. vinaigrette with brined parsley, radishes and cucumber.
- Mix mint into the chickpea salad.
- Toss pepper and salt to taste and 2 tbsp. vinaigrette with beans; sprinkle almonds.
- Toss pepper and salt to taste, basil and 3 tbsp. vinaigrette with tomatoes.
- Toss 1 tbsp. vinaigrette with lettuce.
- Put salads, mushrooms and chicken on a big platter, side by side; serve leftover vinaigrette alongside.
- You can make vinaigrette without chives 1 day ahead, chilled; before serving, add chives.

- You can make radish cucumber salad without parsley 1 day ahead, chilled; before serving, add parsley.
- You can make chickpea salad without mint 1 day ahead, chilled; before serving, add mint.
- You can cook haricot verts 1 day ahead; chill in paper towel-lined sealable bag.
- You can cook chicken and mushrooms in batches in hot oiled 2-burner grill pan on medium high heat.

Nutrition Information

- Calories: 1022
- Total Carbohydrate: 50 g
- Cholesterol: 153 mg
- Total Fat: 76 g
- Fiber: 13 g
- Protein: 42 g
- Sodium: 2240 mg
- Saturated Fat: 14 g

137. Grilled Halibut With Grilled Red Pepper Harissa

"Spicy sauce which has a smoky flavor."
Serving: Makes 4 servings

Ingredients

- 1 red jalapeño chile
- 1 garlic clove, peeled
- 4 5- to 6-oz. halibut or mahi-mahi fillets
- 2 large red bell peppers, quartered lengthwise, seeded
- Olive oil for brushing plus 1/4 cup
- 2 tsps. ground cumin, divided
- 2 tsps. ground coriander, divided
- 1 lemon, halved

Direction

- Prepare the barbecue for medium high heat. On the metal skewer, thread garlic clove and jalapeno. Brush oil on red bell peppers, fish, garlic, and jalapeno; sprinkle with pepper and salt. Sprinkle fish with 1/2 tsp. each of coriander and cumin. Grill garlic, jalapeno, bell peppers, and fish for 8 minutes on each side of vegetables and 4 minutes on each side of fish, until fish is just cooked through and vegetables are charred and tender. Grill lemon for 3 minutes with cut side down, until charred. Remove fish to a plate; tent with foil to keep it warm.
- Peel off charred skins on bell peppers; cut off the stem of jalapeno. Place in a blender, get rid of stem and peel. To the blender, add 1 1/2 tsps. coriander, 1 1/2 tsps. cumin, the remaining 1/4 cup oil and garlic clove. Blend until forming coarse puree. Generously season sauce with pepper and salt to taste.
- On each of four plates, place one fish fillet. Squeeze the grilled lemon over the surface. Use a spoon to spread sauce over fish; serve.

138. Grilled Halloumi With Watercress

"This is what you call 'grilled cheese'. The texture is very squeaky and salty."
Serving: 4 servings

Ingredients

- 1 (8-oz.) package halloumi, sliced 1/4-inch thick
- 1 bunch watercress, tough stems removed
- 2 tbsps. olive oil
- 1 tbsp. fresh lemon juice
- Kosher salt, freshly ground pepper

Direction

- Set the grill over medium-high heat. Grill each side of the halloumi for 2 minutes, until soft and browned. Allow it to cool slightly, and then cut it into large pieces. Toss them in a large bowl.
- Add the oil, watercress, and lemon juice to the cheese. Toss the mixture until combined, and then season it with salt and pepper.

Nutrition Information

- Calories: 213
- Total Carbohydrate: 3 g
- Cholesterol: 50 mg
- Total Fat: 19 g
- Fiber: 0 g
- Protein: 9 g
- Sodium: 530 mg
- Saturated Fat: 9 g

139. Grilled Lamb Kebabs With Turkish Flavors

"Delicious and fun skewers."
Serving: Serves 4

Ingredients

- 2 lbs. boneless lamb leg
- 1/2 cup extra-virgin olive oil, divided
- Kosher salt
- Freshly cracked black pepper
- 1/2 cup dried apricots, cut into medium dice
- 2 tbsps. Maras pepper, or 2 tsps. other dried chili powder mixed with 1 tbsp. paprika
- 1 tsp. minced garlic
- 2 tbsps. roughly chopped fresh mint
- 4 metal skewers

Direction

- In your grill, build a 2 level fire by putting all coals on a single side. When flames die down and coals are medium hot, it should be comfortable to hold your hand 6-in above the grill for about for 3-4 seconds, it's ready to go.
- Trim most of fat lamb off. Cut to approximately 32 even chunks. Mix 1/4 cup olive oil and pepper and salt to taste. Toss it well till coated.
- On skewers, thread lamb chunks, 8 or more for each skewer. Put directly on coals. Cook, flipping, for 8 minutes for medium-rare or till you reach your preference.

- When lamb is done, slide chunks off skewers into a big bowl. Add leftover 1/4 olive oil, mint, garlic, Maras pepper and apricots. Put extra pepper and salt to taste. Vigorously toss. Serve warm.

140. Grilled Peaches With Fresh Raspberry Sauce

"Top with shortbread cookies and vanilla ice cream if wished."
Serving: Makes 6 servings

Ingredients

- 2 1/4 cups (lightly packed) fresh raspberries (about 13 oz.)
- 3 tbsps. water
- 3 tbsps. sugar
- 1 tbsp. fresh lemon juice
- 3 tbsps. unsalted butter
- 1 1/2 tbsps. (packed) dark brown sugar
- 6 medium-size ripe but firm peaches, halved, pitted

Direction

- In a food processor, puree 3 tbsps. water and 2 1/4 cups fresh raspberries until smooth. Use a fine-mesh strainer to strain raspberry puree, pushing on solids to get the maximum amount of liquid; get rid of solids in strainer. Mix in 1 tbsp. fresh lemon juice and 3 tbsps. sugar until blended. Note: Fresh raspberry sauce can be prepared 1 day in advance. Cover and keep in the fridge.
- Prepare the barbecue for medium heat. In a heavy small skillet, melt butter along with brown sugar on medium heat. Take skillet away from heat. Brush melted butter mixture all over peach halves. Grill for 8 minutes, flipping occasionally, until tender. Serve together with sauce.

141. Grilled Pork Loin With Fire-roasted Pineapple Salsa

Serving: Makes 4 servings

Ingredients

- 1 tbsp. tomato paste
- 1 tbsp. mild or hot chili powder (or achiote paste)
- 1/2 cup orange juice
- 3 tbsp. fresh lime juice
- 1 tbsp. olive oil
- 1 lb. pork tenderloin, trimmed
- 1 small golden pineapple (about 1 1/2 lbs.), diced into 1-inch cubes
- 1/2 cup pineapple (or orange) juice
- 1 large red bell pepper, cored, seeded and thinly sliced
- 1/4 small red onion, finely chopped
- 1/4 cup chopped fresh basil
- Vegetable oil cooking spray

Direction

- Combine chili powder and tomato paste. Mix with oil, lime juice, and orange juice in a double resealable plastic bag. Put in the tenderloin and marinate for at least 3 hours. Set a large pan over high heat for 3-4 minutes until smoking. Add pineapple and sear for 4-5 minutes, stirring occasionally. Pour in pineapple juice and mix 1 minute, dragging up brown bits from the pan. Take the pineapple away from the heat. Transfer to a bowl and mix with basil, onion, and pepper. Set a grill pan or grill over high. Use cooking spray to coat. Take the pork from the marinade; put on the grill. (Get rid of the marinade). Lower the heat to medium; cook for 18-20 minutes, flipping occasionally, until internal temperature is 160°F and pork is not pink. Allow the pork to rest for 5 minutes before cutting. Scoop the salsa over the pork.

142. Grilled Skirt Steaks With Parsley Oregano Sauce

"Skirt steak is delicious served plain or with this fantastic sauce."
Serving: Makes 4 servings | Prep: 10m

Ingredients

- 1 (1/2-lb.) skirt steak, cut crosswise into 4 pieces
- 1 cup coarsely chopped flat-leaf parsley
- 2 large garlic cloves
- 2 tsps. dried oregano
- 1/2 tsp. dried hot red-pepper flakes
- 1/4 cup fresh lime juice
- 2/3 cup olive oil
- Equipment: a large (2-burner) ridged grill pan (preferably cast-iron)

Direction

- On moderately-high heat, heat the grill pan till hot, then oil lightly. Blot the steaks dry and scatter a total of quarter tsp. of black pepper and a tsp. of salt all over.
- Let steaks grill, flipping over from time to time, for medium-rare, a total of 2 to 8 minutes, will vary on meat thickness. Turn onto platter and rest for 5 minutes.
- Meanwhile, use blender to purée 3/4 tsp. of salt and the rest of the ingredients till smooth.
- Serve sauce and steaks together.

Nutrition Information

- Calories: 443
- Total Carbohydrate: 4 g
- Cholesterol: 36 mg
- Total Fat: 43 g
- Fiber: 1 g
- Protein: 12 g
- Sodium: 47 mg
- Saturated Fat: 8 g

143. Ham, Artichoke, And Potato Gratin

"Use leftover/good-quality ham for this."
Serving: 10 to 12 servings

Ingredients

- 1/4 cup (1/2 stick) butter
- 4 cups thinly sliced leeks (white and pale green parts only; about 4 large)
- Coarse kosher salt
- 3 lbs. russet potatoes, peeled, thinly sliced (1/8 to 1/4 inch thick)
- 1 1/2 lbs. 1/8-inch-thick ham slices
- 2 8-oz. boxes frozen artichoke hearts, thawed, halved lengthwise
- 2 1/2 cups (packed) coarsely grated Comté cheese (about 10 oz.)
- 1 1/2 cups low-salt chicken broth
- 1/2 cup dry white wine
- 1 1/2 tbsps. all purpose flour
- 1 tsp. coarse kosher salt
- 1 tsp. freshly ground black pepper

Direction

- Preheat the oven to 400°F. Butter a 13x9x2-in. glass baking dish. In a heavy big skillet, melt 1/4 cup butter on medium heat. Put leeks. Sprinkle pepper and coarse salt on. Cook till tender, occasionally mixture for 12 minutes. Put aside.
- Use 1/3 potato slices on bottom of baking dish, overlapping if needed. Put a layer of 1/3 ham on top. Scatter 1/3 leeks on top then 1/3 artichoke hearts. Put aside 3/4 cup cheese. Sprinkle 1/2 leftover cheese on top. Repeat layers once with artichokes, cheese, leeks, ham and potato slices. Use leftover artichoke hearts, leeks, ham and potato slices to cover.
- In small saucepan, whisk broth and following 4 ingredients on medium heat till flour melts. Boil; cook, mixing often for 3 minutes till thick and smooth. Put on gratin. Sprinkle on 3/4 cup cheese. Use foil to cover gratin, tenting the middle to keep cheese from sticking. Bake gratin for 45 minutes. Bake, uncovered, for 50 minutes till juices bubble, top is browned and potatoes are soft. Before serving, let rest for 15 minutes.

144. Haricot Vert And Red-onion Salad With Pistou

"A lively recipe."
Serving: Makes 6 side-dish servings | Prep: 35m

Ingredients

- 2 cups loosely packed fresh basil leaves
- 6 garlic cloves, minced (1 1/2 tbsps.)
- 1/4 cup plus 2 tbsps. extra-virgin olive oil
- 1/2 tsp. fine sea salt
- 1 medium red onion, halved lengthwise, then thinly sliced crosswise
- 1 1/2 lb haricots verts or other thin green beans, trimmed

Direction

- Pistou: In a food processor, puree all pistou ingredients to finely chop basil.
- Salads: Soak onion for 15 minutes in cold water. Drain in colander; pat dry.
- As onion soaks, cook beans, occasionally mixing, uncovered, in 6-8-qt. pot with boiling salted water for 3-6 minutes till just tender. Drain in big colander. To stop cooking, put into big bowl with cold water and ice. Drain; pat dry.
- Toss pistou, onion and beans together; season with pepper and salt.
- You can make pistou 6 hours ahead, put into small bowl, covered, chilled. You can cook beans 1 day ahead; chill in paper towel-lined sealed big plastic bag.

Nutrition Information

- Calories: 167
- Total Carbohydrate: 11 g
- Total Fat: 14 g
- Fiber: 4 g

- Protein: 3 g
- Sodium: 202 mg
- Saturated Fat: 2 g

145. Harvey Wallbanger

Serving: Makes 1 drink

Ingredients

- 1 1/2 oz. vodka
- 4 oz. orange juice
- 1/2 oz. Galliano
- 1 orange slice for garnish

Direction

- Take a highball glass and fill almost with ice cubes. Mix orange juice and vodka and stir well. Then, float Galliano above and garnish with an orange slice.

Nutrition Information

- Calories: 192
- Total Carbohydrate: 16 g
- Total Fat: 0 g
- Fiber: 0 g
- Protein: 1 g
- Sodium: 3 mg
- Saturated Fat: 0 g

146. Herb Roasted Lamb Chops

"So flavorful!"
Serving: Makes 4 servings

Ingredients

- 4 large garlic cloves, pressed
- 1 tbsp. fresh thyme leaves, lightly crushed
- 1 tbsp. fresh rosemary leaves, lightly crushed
- 2 tsps. coarse kosher salt
- 2 tbsps. extra-virgin olive oil, divided
- 6 1 1/4-inch-thick lamb loin chops

Direction

- Mix 1 tbsp. olive oil and initial 4 ingredients in big bowl. Add lamb; flip to coat. Marinate for 30-60 minutes in room temperature.
- Preheat an oven to 400°F. Heat leftover 1 tbsp. olive oil on high heat in big heavy ovenproof skillet. Add lamb; cook for 3 minutes per side till browned. Put skillet in oven; roast lamb chops, 10 minutes to get medium rare, to desired doneness. Put lamb on plater; cover. Rest for 5 minutes.

Nutrition Information

- Calories: 511
- Total Carbohydrate: 2 g
- Cholesterol: 105 mg
- Total Fat: 45 g
- Fiber: 0 g
- Protein: 24 g
- Sodium: 364 mg
- Saturated Fat: 18 g

147. Herbed Rack Of Lamb With Parsley, Mint, And Walnut Sauté

"Ask a butcher to "French" your lamb racks."
Serving: Makes 6 servings

Ingredients

- 3 1 1/4-lb. racks of lamb, frenched
- 5 tbsps. olive oil
- 2 tsps. coarse kosher salt
- 1/2 cup finely chopped fresh Italian parsley
- 1/4 cup finely chopped fresh rosemary
- 1/4 cup finely chopped fresh mint
- 2 tbsps. extra-virgin olive oil
- 1/2 cup finely chopped shallots
- 6 cups (packed) fresh Italian parsley leaves (from 2 large bunches)
- 3/4 cup very coarsely chopped fresh mint leaves
- 1/2 cup water

- 2 tsps. grated lemon peel
- 3/4 cup coarsely chopped toasted walnuts (about 2 1/2 oz.)
- 2 tbsps. walnut oil
- 1 tbsp. fresh lemon juice

Direction

- Lamb: Put lamb racks onto big heavy rimmed baking sheet; brush 1 tbsp. oil on lamb. Sprinkle pepper and 2 tsp. coarse salt. In small bowl, mix all herbs; firmly press to adhere on meat side of lamb. Stand in room temperature for 2 hours. You can make it 6 hours ahead. Cover; refrigerate.
- Preheat an oven to 425°F. Heat leftover 4 tbsp. oil on medium high heat in big heavy nonstick skillet. Add lamb in batches, herb-and-meat side down; cook for 4 minutes till brown. Put racks, herb-and-meat side up, on baking sheet; roast lamb for 13 minutes till inserted meat thermometer in middle reads 125°F for medium rare. Remove from oven; stand for 15 minutes.
- Meanwhile, prep sauté: Heat olive oil on medium heat in big heavy skillet. Add shallots; sauté for 4 minutes till soft. Add parsley; sauté for 2 minutes till wilted. Add lemon peel, 1/2 cup water and mint; cook for 3 minutes till parsley is tender. Mix in lemon juice, walnut oil and walnuts; season with pepper and salt.
- Between bones, cut lamb to individual chops and divide parsley sauté to 6 plates. Put lamb chops over.

Nutrition Information

- Calories: 1067
- Total Carbohydrate: 10 g
- Cholesterol: 157 mg
- Total Fat: 100 g
- Fiber: 4 g
- Protein: 35 g
- Sodium: 786 mg
- Saturated Fat: 35 g

148. Hills Family Sugar Cookie Cutouts

Serving: Makes up to 6 dozen cookies, depending on the size

Ingredients

- 3 1/2 cups unbleached all-purpose flour
- 1 tsp. baking powder
- 3/4 tsp. salt
- 1 cup unsalted butter, at room temperature
- 1 1/2 cups granulated sugar
- 2 large eggs, at room temperature
- 1 1/2 tsps. vanilla
- 1 egg white
- Pinch of salt
- A few drops of vegetable oil
- Up to 1 lb. of confectioners' sugar
- 1 to 3 tbsps. of cream
- If using egg whites: 3 large egg whites at room temperature and 1/2 tsp. cream of tartar
- If using meringue powder: 3 tbsps. meringue powder and 6 tbsps. warm water
- 3 3/4 cups confectioners' sugar
- Optional: 1 to 2 drops of glycerin
- Food coloring

Direction

- Sift salt, baking powder and flour into medium-sized bowl. Cream butter for 1 minute with an electric mixer. Add sugar; beat for 5 minutes at medium speed till light; beat in vanilla and eggs for 2-4 minutes till very light and fluffy. Work flour into creamed mixture slowly with a wooden spoon. Divide dough to 2 portions; wrap in plastic wrap/waxed paper. Refrigerate for a few hours – overnight till firm.
- Heat an oven to 400°. Roll dough out to 1/4-in. thick on floured surface, using extra flour for rolling pin, sprinkled on dough and extra on floured surface to avoid sticking as needed. Use cookie cutters to cut to desired shapes; put onto cookie sheets.

- You can gather and reroll dough; chill for 15 minutes if it is too soft.
- Freeze/refrigerate cut-out cookies on baking sheets to retain firm edges while baking for 10-15 minutes; bake cookies immediately if you lack time. Bake till cookies just barely begin to brown at edges and cookies are puffed for 5-8 minutes. Slightly cool; they're fragile when fresh from the oven. Slightly cool. Transfer onto wire rack; fully cool.
- Glaze then decorate as desired when cool.
- Depending on size, this creates 6 dozen cookies; can easily double or triple this recipe.
- Sugar cookie glaze: Whisk salt and egg white till starting to foam and loosened. Add cream, oil and confectioners' sugar slowly; whisk, adding more cream and sugar till glaze gets spreading consistency to be thin enough to easily spread on cookies to edges without running off of the sides.
- Spread glaze on each cookie using an offset spatula/smooth table knife, filling in shape to edges. You can decorate cookies using colored sprinkles while glaze is wet or leave glaze as it; let dry; with royal icing, add more decoration.
- Royal icing: Be sure all containers and utensils are grease-free and clean before you start. For dividing icing then tinting with different colors (optional), prep few small containers. You have to keep royal icing covered with tight-fitting lid/plastic wrap/damp cloth; it'll dry out if not. Royal icing keeps, covered tightly, for 1 week in the fridge. This recipe makes firmest-textured icing; as mentioned below, adjust texture with extra sugar or water.
- Beat sugar, cream of tartar and egg whites for 6-8 minutes till icing holds billowy peaks and is thick if using egg whites; if desired, add glycerin for more shine.
- Whisk sugar and meringue powder in an electric mixer's bowl if using meringue powder. Add water; beat on low speed till icing holds billowy peaks and is thick for 5 minutes. Don't overbeat; it'll be hard to work with. If desired, add glycerin for more shine.

Adjust icing consistency: Add spoonful of confectioners' sugar at a time, thoroughly whisking till you get desired consistency to thicken. Add few drops of warm water at a time, mixing with a spoon to thin. You need thick icing to pipe details and outlines; flows of color in sections or on a whole cookie can be thinner.
- Cover with container lids/plastic wrap/damp cloth when not using immediately; it hardens very quickly if exposed to air.
- Divide icing to different containers for every color you will use; tint icing with small food coloring amounts till you get desired color.
- Use: You can use a table knife/offset spatula to spread icing onto cookies or pain on with previously unused, small paintbrushes or pipe through tips and pastry bags. Use zipper plastic bag with tiny hole cut from a corner for simple, plain outlines.
- Creates 3 cups of icing.

149. Homemade Corn Tortillas

"The flavor of freshly griddled corn tortillas is supreme! This recipe is easy to make, however, a masa harina is only available in the markets of Latin America and large supermarkets. A masa harina is a dough flour made from dried corn kernels treated with lime then crushed into a fresh dough. The fresh dough is dried again and grounded making it a masa harina."
Serving: 8 | Prep: 40m | Ready in: 1h10m

Ingredients

- 2 cups masa harina
- 1½ cups hot tap water
- ½ tsp. salt

Direction

- In a medium sized bowl, combine masa harina, salt and water until dough forms. Using clean hands, knead dough for 2 minutes, until dough is smooth and easy to shape into a ball. Add enough water if dough is crumbly and dry, 1 tablespoonful at a time.

Otherwise, add enough masa harina. Place a kitchen towel over the bowl to cover and let it rest for 30 minutes.

- Cut dough in 16 equal portions. While working, keep dough covered with kitchen towel. Roll a piece in your palm and shape dough into a ball. Put dough ball in between 2 plastic wraps and press it using your palm. Flatten the dough into a disc, about 5 inches diameter, using rolling pin or your palm. A tortilla press can also work to flatten dough.
- Over medium high heat, warm a small cast-iron skillet. Place tortilla and cook for a minute or two, until bottom has brown spots and edges start to curl. Flip over the other side and cook for half to a full minute until brown spots appear. Lower heat to medium if tortilla is about to get burned. Roll and shape the remaining dough using the same procedure. Simultaneous to cooking tortilla, you can shape the next dough. Pile cooked tortillas and wrap with clean kitchen towel to keep them warm.

Nutrition Information

- Calories: 110 calories;
- Total Carbohydrate: 24 g
- Cholesterol: 0 mg
- Total Fat: 1 g
- Fiber: 3 g
- Protein: 3 g
- Sodium: 148 mg
- Sugar: 0 g
- Saturated Fat: 0 g

150. Honey-orange Madeleines

"Keep these in airtight containers."
Serving: Makes about 18

Ingredients

- Melted butter
- 2 large eggs
- 1/3 cup honey
- 1/4 cup sugar
- 1 1/2 tsps. grated orange peel
- 1/2 tsp. orange flower water
- 1/2 tsp. vanilla extract
- 1 cup all purpose flour
- 3/4 cup (1 1/2 sticks) unsalted butter, melted, room temperature
- Sugar

Direction

- Preheat an oven to 400°F. Brush melted butter on madeleine mold; dust flour. Mix grated orange peel, 1/4 cup sugar, honey, and eggs in an electric mixer's bowl; put above saucepan with simmering water. Don't let bowl touch water. Mix for 2 minutes till just lukewarm; take from above water. Beat using electric mixer for 12 minutes till tripled in volume and pale yellow. Add vanilla extract and orange flower water. Mix in flour slowly on low speed, occasionally scraping bowl. Put 1/3 batter in medium bowl. Fold 3/4 cup of melted butter slowly into batter in the medium bowl; don't fold in water on bottom of butter. Fold mixture gently into leftover batter; it'll slightly thicken.
- Put batter in madeleine mold, filling nearly to top; bake for 10 minutes, turning the pan halfway through cooking, till cookies are springy to the touch. Onto rack, invert pan, then use the tip of knife to pry out cookies lightly. Sprinkle sugar on cookies. Wipe molds out; brush melted butter. Dust flour; repeat using leftover batter. Fully cool on rack. You can make it 1 day ahead; keep in room temperature in airtight containers.

Nutrition Information

- Calories: 133
- Total Carbohydrate: 14 g
- Cholesterol: 41 mg
- Total Fat: 8 g
- Fiber: 0 g
- Protein: 2 g
- Sodium: 9 mg
- Saturated Fat: 5 g

151. Horseradish-crusted Beef Tenderloin

"For well done, add 5-10 minutes to roasting time."
Serving: 8 | Ready in: 1h10m

Ingredients

- 2 tbsps. prepared horseradish
- 1 tbsp. extra-virgin olive oil
- 1 tsp. Dijon mustard
- 2 lbs. trimmed beef tenderloin, preferably center-cut (see Note)
- 1 tsp. kosher salt
- 2 tsps. freshly ground pepper
- Creamy Horseradish Sauce (recipe follows)

Direction

- Preheat an oven to 400°F.
- Mix mustard, oil and horseradish in small bowl. Rub pepper and salt on tenderloin; coat in horseradish mixture. Use kitchen string to tie in 3 places. Put into small roasting pan.
- Roast for 35-45 minutes till an inserted thermometer in the thickest part of tenderloin registers 140°F to get medium-rare. Put on cutting board; rest for 5 minutes. Discard string. Slice. Serve alongside creamy horseradish sauce.

Nutrition Information

- Calories: 211 calories;
- Total Carbohydrate: 2 g
- Cholesterol: 79 mg
- Total Fat: 11 g
- Fiber: 0 g
- Protein: 26 g
- Sodium: 299 mg
- Sugar: 1 g
- Saturated Fat: 4 g

152. Hot Cocoa With Ancho Chiles And Spice

"The Product is Earthy-fruity spice powder with a mild kick. The Payoff is hot chocolate with the combination of complex, subtle flavor and an intriguing, gentle spiciness."
Serving: Makes 4 servings | Prep: 15m

Ingredients

- 3 cups low-fat milk
- 3/4 cup bittersweet chocolate chips
- 2 tbsps. sugar
- 1 tbsp. natural unsweetened cocoa powder
- 3/4 tsp. ground ancho chiles
- 1/4 tsp. freshly grated nutmeg
- 1/4 tsp. plus 1/8 tsp. ground allspice
- 3 cinnamon sticks, broken in half

Direction

- In a medium saucepan, add a pinch of salt and first 7 ingredients then bring to a simmer while stirring frequently. Put in cinnamon sticks. Cover and take away from heat, allow to soak about 5 minutes. Bring to a simmer while whisking then get rid of cinnamon.

153. Iceberg And Cabbage Slaw

"A glorious recipe."
Serving: 12 Servings

Ingredients

- 1/4 cup buttermilk
- 2 tbsps. fresh lemon juice
- 1 tbsp. mayonnaise
- 3 tbsps. olive oil
- Kosher salt, freshly ground pepper
- 1 head of iceberg lettuce, outer leaves removed, thinly sliced
- 1/2 head of small green cabbage, outer leaves removed, thinly sliced
- 4 scallions, thinly sliced
- 3 tbsps. chopped fresh chives
- 1 tsp. celery seeds

Direction

- Whisk mayonnaise, lemon juice and buttermilk in a big bowl; whisk in oil. Use pepper and salt to season dressing.
- Add celery seeds, chives, scallions, cabbage and lettuce to dressing; toss till well coated. Taste; season with pepper and salt.
- You can slice chives, scallions, cabbage and iceberg 2 hours ahead; chill, covered with damp paper towel, in a big bowl.

Nutrition Information

- Calories: 57
- Total Carbohydrate: 4 g
- Cholesterol: 1 mg
- Total Fat: 5 g
- Fiber: 1 g
- Protein: 1 g
- Sodium: 213 mg
- Saturated Fat: 1 g

154. Iced Almond Latte

"Preparing coffee with almond syrup."
Serving: Serves 6

Ingredients

- 2 cups plus 1 tsp. finely ground espresso coffee beans
- 3 cups water
- 3 tbsps. golden brown sugar
- 1 1/2 cups whole milk
- 5 tsps. almond syrup (such as Torani)
- Ice cubes
- Espresso Whipped Cream

Direction

- Fill a cup of brown espresso beans on the basket of coffeemaker or coffee filter. Pour 1 1/2 cups of water into the coffeemaker and brew, then pour the coffee into the bowl. Redo the process with the leftover 1 1/2 cups water and 1 cup ground espresso beans to make two

cups of coffee in total. Stir in sugar, followed by the milk and almond syrup. Let the mixture chill in the fridge for a minimum of 2 hours or overnight until it becomes cold.
- Put in ice to fill the six glasses. Split the coffee mixture among the glasses, then put whipped cream on top of each. Sprinkle the leftover 1 tsp of ground espresso beans on top.

155. Individual Chocolate Raspberry Baked Alaskas

Serving: Makes 6 servings | Prep: 1.25h

Ingredients

- 4 oz fine-quality bittersweet chocolate (not unsweetened), chopped
- 1 stick (1/2 cup) unsalted butter, cut into tbsp. pieces
- 2 1/4 cups sugar
- 3 whole large eggs
- 1/8 tsp. salt
- 1/2 cup unsweetened cocoa powder
- Raspberry ice cream , slightly softened
- 8 large egg whites
- Special equipment: 6 (8-oz) shallow ceramic or glass gratin dishes

Direction

- Cake: Preheat an oven to 375°F. Butter 8-in. square baking pan. Line wax paper on bottom; butter paper.
- Melt butter and chocolate in metal bowl above saucepan with barely simmering water, mixing, till smooth. Take bowl from pan. Whisk 3/4 cup sugar into the chocolate mixture; whisk in salt and whole eggs. Sift cocoa over; whisk just till combined.
- Put batter in baking pan, evenly spreading; bake in center of oven for 20-25 minutes till a tester exits with few crumbs adhering. Cool cake for 5 minutes in pan on rack. Invert onto rack; fully cool.

- Cut cake to 6 even pieces; in each gratin dish, put 1 piece, trimming to fit. Put a big 1/2 cup ice cream scoop over each cake piece; freeze, covered, for 25 minutes till ice cream is just hard. Unless making ahead, don't let ice cream get rock hard.
- Before serving, make meringue: Preheat an oven to 450°F.
- Beat pinch of salt and egg whites till just holds soft peaks with an electric mixer. Little by little, add leftover 1 1/2 cups sugar, beating on high speed; beat for 5 minutes in standing mixer, 12 minutes with handheld, till whites hold glossy and stiff peaks.
- Take gratin dishes from freezer; mound meringue over cake and ice cream, spreading to gratin dish's edge. Bake on baking sheet in center of oven for 6 minutes till golden brown; immediately serve.
- You can freeze cake and ice cream in gratin dishes for 1 day, covered. Soften for 15 minutes at room temperature before covering in meringue.
- Be aware the egg whites here aren't cooked fully; it might be a problem if salmonella is common where you live.

156. Irish Hot Chocolate

Serving: Makes about 4 1/2 cups, serving 4 to 6.

Ingredients

- 1/2 cup unsweetened cocoa powder
- 1/3 cup sugar
- 1 tsp. vanilla
- 1/2 cup cold water
- 2 1/4 cups milk
- 3/4 cup half-and-half
- 1/2 cup Baileys Original Irish Cream liqueur, or to taste
- Whipped cream and shaved bittersweet chocolate for garnish

Direction

- Heat pinch of salt, water, vanilla, sugar and cocoa powder in a big heavy saucepan on low heat, whisking, till it is a smooth paste and cocoa powder dissolve. Add half and half and milk, both scalded, slowly; simmer hot chocolate for 2 minutes, whisking. Mix in Baileys. Blend hot chocolate in batches in a blender for frothier results. Divide hot chocolate to mugs; top with whipped cream and chocolate.

Nutrition Information

- Calories: 352
- Total Carbohydrate: 48 g
- Cholesterol: 31 mg
- Total Fat: 11 g
- Fiber: 4 g
- Protein: 8 g
- Sodium: 84 mg
- Saturated Fat: 7 g

157. Jam-filled Crepes

"Such a delicious recipe."
Serving: Makes 8 servings | Prep: 25m

Ingredients

- 1 cup plus 2 tbsps. whole milk
- 2 large eggs
- 1 cup all-purpose flour
- 2 tbsps. granulated sugar
- 3 tbsps. plus 1 tsp. unsalted butter, melted and cooled slightly
- 1/4 tsp. salt
- About 2/3 cup apricot or strawberry jam (from a 10- to 12-oz jar)
- 1 tbsp. brandy
- Confectioners sugar (preferably vanilla sugar) for dusting (see cooks' note)
- a 10-inch nonstick skillet

Direction

- In a blender, blend salt, 2 tbsp. butter, granulated sugar, flour, eggs and milk, scraping side down 1-2 times, for 1 minute till batter is smooth; stand batter for 1 hour at room temperature to avoid tough crepes. Mix brandy and jam in small bowl.
- Preheat an oven to 250°F.
- Put 1/2 tsp. butter in skillet; brush to coat bottom then heat till hot for 30 seconds on medium heat. Put 1/4 cup batter in skillet, tilting to evenly coat bottom; cook for 1 1/2-2 minutes till bottom is pale golden. To loosen crepe, jerk skillet; use spatula to flip skillet. Cook for 30-60 seconds till bottom is pale golden. Put crepe onto work surface with a spatula, flipping so first cooked side is facedown. Spread 1 tbsp. jam all over crepe; roll up like a jellyroll. Put onto heatproof platter; keep warm in oven. In same manner, make 7 more crepes, putting into oven; you can put rolled crepes stacked like logs or side by side. Generously dust using vanilla sugar.
- Vanilla sugar: In an airtight container, mix 1 lengthwise halved then chopped vanilla bean and 2 cups confectioners' sugar; stand for 24 hours, covered. To remove vanilla bean, sift before using; keeps indefinitely in airtight container in room temperature. You can make crepes without jam 1 day ahead kept chilled in airtight container, separated between wax paper layers. In batches, reheat crepes in middle of 350°F oven on a big baking sheet for 1 minute till hot. Spread jam; roll up. On baking sheet in the oven, heat all rolled crepes for 1-2 minutes till hot; dust with vanilla sugar.

Nutrition Information

- Calories: 233
- Total Carbohydrate: 36 g
- Cholesterol: 63 mg
- Total Fat: 7 g
- Fiber: 1 g
- Protein: 4 g
- Sodium: 115 mg

- Saturated Fat: 4 g

158. Kale With Garlic And Bacon

"Bright and tasty."
Serving: Makes 8 servings | Prep: 50m

Ingredients

- 2 1/2 lbs. kale (about 4 bunches), tough stems and center ribs cut off and discarded
- 10 bacon slices (1/2 lbs.), cut into 1/2-inch pieces
- 4 garlic cloves, finely chopped
- 2 cups water

Direction

- Stack several kale leaves; lengthwise roll to cigar shape. Use a sharp knife to crosswise cut to 1/4-in. wide strips; repeat with leftover leaves.
- Cook bacon, occasionally mixing, till crisp in a wide 6-8-qt. heavy pot on medium heat; put onto paper towels with a slotted spoon. Drain. Pour off all fat from pot but 3 tbsp.; discard. Cook garlic in leftover fat, mixing, on medium low heat for 30 seconds till pale golden. Add kale; pot will get full. Cook, turning with tongs, for 1 minute till bright green and wilted. Add water; simmer, partially covered, for 6-10 minutes till just tender. Toss with pepper and salt to taste and bacon.
- Big kale leaves are easy to cut for this recipe; coarsely chop if you can only get small leaves.

Nutrition Information

- Calories: 513
- Total Carbohydrate: 1 g
- Cholesterol: 132 mg
- Total Fat: 44 g
- Fiber: 0 g
- Protein: 26 g
- Sodium: 305 mg
- Saturated Fat: 14 g

159. Key Lime Pie

"This drink tastes like pie"
Serving: 2 | Prep: 5m | Ready in: 5m

Ingredients

- 1/2 lime, cut into wedges
- 4 fluid oz. vodka
- 1 1/2 fluid oz. frozen limeade concentrate, thawed
- 1 tsp. vanilla extract
- 2 twists lime zest, garnish

Direction

- In a mixing glass, place lime wedges in the bottom and muddle properly. Add ice to cover, pour in vanilla, lime juice and vodka. Shake properly, then stain mixture into stemmed cocktail glasses. Decorate with a twist of lime.

160. Kielbasa And Cabbage Soup

"It is good to make a hearty soup with the Polish pair."
Serving: Serves 4 to 6

Ingredients

- 3 large red potatoes
- Salt
- 2 medium onions, chopped
- 2 tbsps. rendered bacon fat, lard, or butter
- 3 large garlic cloves, finely chopped
- 3 1/2 cups beef stock or low-sodium broth
- 14 oz. smoked kielbasa, halved lengthwise and cut into 3/4" pieces
- 1 lb. savoy cabbage (about 1/2 medium), chopped
- 3 medium carrots, halved lengthwise and cut into 1/2" pieces
- 2 celery stalks, halved lengthwise and cut into 1/2" pieces
- Sour cream
- Chopped dill

Direction

- In a big saucepan, add potatoes and generously cover with water, then use salt to season well. Cover the pan partly and bring water to a boil, then lower heat to simmer for 30 to 40 minutes, until soft. Drain and allow to cool until warm, then peel potatoes. Keep warm with a cover.
- In a heavy 5- to 6-qt. pot, cook onions in fat together with 1/4 tsp. of salt on moderately low heat, covered, until starting to brown while stirring sometimes. Put in garlic and cook for 1 minute while stirring.
- Put in celery, carrots, cabbage, kielbasa, 1 1/2 cups of water and stock, then simmer for 15 to 20 minutes, partly covered, until vegetables are softened.
- Cut potatoes in half or quarters, then place into each bowl with 1-2 pieces. Ladle over potato the soup and put a dollop of sour cream together with some dill on top.

161. Lamb And Eggplant Moussaka

"You can make it in 2 smaller casserole dishes. You can use other ground meats like pork, veal or turkey."
Serving: Makes 12 to 14 servings

Ingredients

- 3 lb eggplant (2 large or 3 medium)
- 2 large russet potatoes
- Salt as needed
- 1/3 cup olive oil, or as needed
- 2 cups diced onion
- 1 1/4 lb ground lamb (or substitute beef, turkey, pork, or combination)
- 2 cups chopped plum tomatoes
- 2 tsp minced garlic
- 2 cloves
- Small piece cinnamon stick (or 1/4 tsp ground cinnamon)

- 1 bay leaf
- Pinch ground allspice
- Freshly ground black pepper, as needed
- 1/2 cup water
- 2 tbsp tomato paste
- 1/4 cup dry red wine
- 1/4 cup plain bread crumbs
- 2 cups Cheese Sauce

Direction

- If desired, peel, salt then rinse eggplant.
- Cover potatoes in enough water in a pot; boil on medium high heat. Lightly boil for 5 minutes then cool. Cut to 1/8-in. slices; put aside.
- Heat 1 tbsp. olive oil till it shimmers in a skillet on medium high heat. Few slices at 1 time, put eggplant in hot oil; sauté eggplant slices, flipping as needed, for 2-3 minutes per side till lightly colored and tender. Put onto rack to drain while sautéing leftover eggplant, putting more oil in skillet as needed.
- Meat sauce: In a skillet, heat 1 tbsp. olive oil. Add onion; cook on medium high heat, frequently mixing, for 10-12 minutes till tender. Add ground meat; cook on medium heat, frequently mixing, for 5 minutes till meat loses raw appearance. Add 1/2 cup water, pepper, salt, allspice, bay leaf, cinnamon, cloves, garlic and tomatoes; simmer for 30 minutes till flavorful and thick. Add red wine and tomato paste; simmer for 10 minutes till wine gets sweet aroma.
- Preheat oven to 350°F.
- Assemble moussaka: Scatter breadcrumbs in a rectangular, deep baking dish. Put layer of 1/2 eggplant slices on breadcrumbs. Add meat sauce; spread to even layer. Put even sliced potato layers on sauce. In an even layer, put leftover eggplant on meat sauce; put cheese sauce on eggplant. Bake, uncovered, for 45 minutes till eggplant is very tender and cheese sauce is golden brown and thick. Rest moussaka before cutting and serving for 20 minutes.

- Prep eggplant to cook: You can salt the eggplant before cooking it to draw out bitterness.
- If desired, peel eggplant; slice eggplant to required thickness. Put slices into colander then put colander into big bowl. Liberally sprinkle kosher salt on slices; rest for 20 minutes till salt draws moisture to surface. Thoroughly rinse eggplant; drain. Blot dry.

Nutrition Information

- Calories: 296
- Total Carbohydrate: 24 g
- Cholesterol: 34 mg
- Total Fat: 18 g
- Fiber: 6 g
- Protein: 11 g
- Sodium: 696 mg
- Saturated Fat: 6 g

162. Lamb Tagine With Tomatoes And Caramelized Sweet Onions

Serving: Makes 6 to 8 servings

Ingredients

- 9 cups chopped sweet onions (such as Vidalia or Maui; about 3 lbs.), divided
- 3 lbs. boneless lamb stew meat, cut into 3/4- to 1-inch pieces
- 2 cups water
- 2 cinnamon sticks
- 1 tsp. ground cinnamon
- 1 tsp. salt
- 1 tsp. coarsely ground black pepper
- 1 tsp. ground ginger
- 1/8 tsp. crumbled saffron threads
- 4 cups chopped plum tomatoes (about 1 1/2 lbs.)
- 4 tbsps. chopped fresh Italian parsley, divided
- 1/4 cup olive oil

Direction

- Boil saffron, ginger, pepper, salt, ground cinnamon, cinnamon sticks, 2 cups water, lamb and 3 cups chopped onions in a big heavy pot on medium high heat. Partially cover; lower heat to medium low. Gently simmer for 1 1/2 hours. Add 2 tbsp. parsley and tomatoes; simmer, partially covered, for 30 minutes till juices thicken and lamb is tender. Season with pepper and salt to taste. Discard cinnamon sticks.
- Meanwhile, heat oil on high heat in big heavy skillet. Add leftover 6 cups of chopped onions; sauté for 10 minutes till starting to brown. Lower heat to medium; sauté, mixing often, for 45 minutes till onions are deep brown. You can make onions and stew 1 day ahead. Cool then cover; separately chill. Rewarm each on low heat before proceeding.
- Put lamb stew in big shallow bowl; scatter leftover 2 tbsp. parsley and caramelized onions over.

Nutrition Information

- Calories: 822
- Total Carbohydrate: 24 g
- Cholesterol: 166 mg
- Total Fat: 63 g
- Fiber: 4 g
- Protein: 41 g
- Sodium: 551 mg
- Saturated Fat: 24 g

163. Lamb With Preserved Lemons

"A hearty entrée."
Serving: Makes 8 to 10 servings

Ingredients

- 5 lbs. boneless well-trimmed lamb shoulder, cut into 2 1/2- to 3-inch cubes
- Coarse kosher salt
- 2 medium onions, halved, sliced
- 2 preserved lemons,* quartered
- 1 large head of garlic, cloves separated and peeled (about 21)
- 3 tbsps. chopped fresh cilantro plus additional for garnish
- 1 tbsp. cumin seeds, coarsely ground in spice mill
- 2/3 cup water
- 1/2 cup (1 stick) chilled butter, diced

Direction

- Preheat an oven to 300°F. Sprinkle pepper and coarse salt all over lamb; put in 13x9x2-in. glass baking dish in 1 layer. Blend cumin seeds, 3 tbsp. cilantro, garlic, lemons and onions to smooth puree in processor. Add 2/3 cup water; blend. Evenly put puree on lamb; briefly mix to coat lamb in puree. Evenly scatter butter on top.
- Bake lamb, uncovered, for 4-4 1/2 hours till very tender. Put lamb into bowl using slotted spoon. Tilt baking dish; spoon fat off sauce's surface. Put lamb in sauce; mix to blend. Season stew with pepper and salt to taste. You can make it 2 days ahead, chill stew till cold, uncovered then cover; keep refrigerated. Rewarm in 350°F oven, covered, for 30 minutes.
- Sprinkle extra chopped cilantro on lamb; serve.

Nutrition Information

- Calories: 880
- Total Carbohydrate: 7 g
- Cholesterol: 235 mg
- Total Fat: 73 g
- Fiber: 1 g
- Protein: 48 g
- Sodium: 856 mg
- Saturated Fat: 34 g

164. Lasagna Bolognese

"Fit for a special occasion recipe because of its time-consuming preparation but the long wait is always worth the effort and time. The cinnamon and wine give it distinct taste. Try using a nice dry wine like a Cabernet Sauvignon or Zinfandel. Serve with green salad and crispy bread."

Serving: 12 | Prep: 30m | Ready in: 2h30m

Ingredients

- 1 lb. dry lasagna noodles
- 1 1/2 tbsps. olive oil, divided
- 1 (28 oz.) can Italian whole peeled tomatoes (such as La Valle®)
- 1 onion, coarsely chopped
- 2 carrots, coarsely chopped
- 2 stalks celery, coarsely chopped
- 3 cloves garlic, coarsely chopped
- 1 tbsp. fresh sage
- 1 tbsp. fresh rosemary
- 2 tbsps. olive oil
- 1 lb. ground beef
- 1 lb. sweet Italian sausage links, removed from casing and crumbled
- 2 tbsps. all-purpose flour
- 1 cup dry red wine
- 1/4 cup heavy cream
- 1/2 cup grated Parmesan cheese
- 1 pinch ground cinnamon
- 1 (16 oz.) container ricotta cheese, broken apart with a fork
- 3 eggs, lightly beaten
- 1 lb. shredded mozzarella cheese, divided
- kosher salt to taste
- freshly ground black pepper to taste

Direction

- Boil a big saucepan filled with slightly salted water on high heat. Add in one tbsp. olive oil. When the water is boiling, add in lasagna pasta and bring to a boil again. Cook pasta without the lid, stir every now and then until the pasta is cooked through yet firm to bite, 8 minutes. Drain pasta using a colander in the sink. Sprinkle 1 1/2 tsp. olive oil over cooked noodles to keep them from sticking together.
- Put tomatoes (flesh, juice, seeds) in bowl of food processor, pulse one minute until pureed. Reserve the tomatoes. Put the celery, onion, garlic, carrots, rosemary and sage in food processor, pulse until the vegies are chopped.
- Warm two tbsp. of olive oil on high heat in a big pot until very hot and smoking; put the chopped veggies in. Turn the heat down to medium and stir veggies until tender and starting to brown, 10 minutes. Add the Italian sausage and ground beef; crumble the meat while cooking for 10 minutes. Add in the flour when the meat is not pink and stir for two minutes longer. Pour the red wine in and let it simmer for 15 minutes, stirring every now and then, until the wine has lessened. Put the cream, pureed tomatoes, cinnamon and parmesan cheese in meat sauce and boil on medium heat; reduce heat so it simmers and close the pot with its lid. Stir the sauce from time to time, 20 minutes. Reserve the sauce.
- Combine the 3/4 lb. grated mozzarella cheese, ricotta cheese, kosher salt, pepper and eggs in a big bowl. Set aside fourth lb. of the mozzarella for garnishing.
- Turn the oven to 175°C (350°F). Use olive oil to grease a 9x 13-in. baking pan.
- To assemble the lasagna, arrange four pasta noodles lengthwise, in the base of prepared baking pan, and overlap them slightly to cover the base thoroughly. On top of the pasta, place a third of ricotta cheese mixture and fourth of meat sauce. Arrange another layer of pasta going widthwise, pour a third of ricotta cheese mixture and fourth of meat sauce like before; place the third layer of pasta, the remaining ricotta mixture, and fourth of the meat sauce. Finish with the last layer of pasta topped with the remaining fourth of meat sauce. Drizzle the reserved mozzarella all over the lasagna.
- Bake in the oven 45-55 minutes until the cheese is melted and slightly browned and lasagna is bubbly. Before serving, let it sit 5 minutes.

Nutrition Information

- Calories: 568 calories;

- Total Carbohydrate: 38.3 g
- Cholesterol: 130 mg
- Total Fat: 29.5 g
- Protein: 33.8 g
- Sodium: 858 mg

165. Lemon Buttermilk Pie With Saffron

"A fun pie recipe."
Serving: Makes 8 servings

Ingredients

- 1 1/4 cups all-purpose flour
- 1 tbsp. sugar
- 1/2 tsp. kosher salt
- 1/2 cup (1 stick) chilled unsalted butter, cut into pieces
- 1/4 cup buttermilk
- 2 tbsps. all-purpose flour, plus more
- 6 large egg yolks
- 3 large eggs
- 1 1/4 cups buttermilk
- 1 1/4 cups sugar
- 1 tbsp. finely grated lemon zest
- 1/3 cup fresh lemon juice
- 1/4 tsps. kosher salt
- Pinch of saffron threads
- 2 tbsps. unsalted butter, melted, cooled slightly
- Whipped cream (for serving)

Direction

- Buttermilk pie dough: Pulse salt, sugar and flour to mix in a food processor. Add butter; pulse till it looks like coarse meal with few pea-sized butter pieces left.
- Put into big bowl. Add buttermilk; mix with fork, adding tbsps. buttermilk at a time if needed, till just shaggy dough comes together; very lightly knead till there are no dry spots. Into disk, pat; wrap in plastic. Chill for 4 hours.

- You can make dough 2 days ahead. Chill.
- Assembly and filling: Preheat an oven to 325°F. Roll pie dough out to 14-in. round on lightly floured surface. Put in 9-in. pie dish; let dough slump down into the dish. Trim dough; leave 1-in. overhang. Fold the overhang under; crimp edge. Use a fork to prick bottom all over; freeze for 15 minutes.
- Line foil/parchment paper on crust; leave overhang. Fill with dried beans/pie weights. Put pie dish on rimmed baking sheet; bake for 20-25 minutes till crust is dry around edge. Remove weights and parchment; bake for 10-12 minutes till surface looks dry.
- Meanwhile, blend saffron, salt, lemon juice, lemon zest, sugar, buttermilk, eggs and egg yolks till smooth in a blender. Add 2 tbsp. flour then butter as motor runs. Tap blender jar against the countertop to remove air bubbles in filling; put into the warm crust.
- Bake pie, rotating it halfway through, covering edges using foil if they brown a lot before filling finishes, for 55-65 minutes till filling sets around edge yet center slightly jiggles. Put pie dish onto wire rack; cool pie. Serve whipped cream with pie.
- You can bake pie 2 days ahead. Keep for 6 hours at room temperature or cover then chill for longer.

Nutrition Information

- Calories: 421
- Total Carbohydrate: 53 g
- Cholesterol: 248 mg
- Total Fat: 20 g
- Fiber: 1 g
- Protein: 8 g
- Sodium: 299 mg
- Saturated Fat: 11 g

166. Lemon Cream Cheese Icing

Serving: Makes 1 cup

Ingredients

- 3/4 cup powdered sugar
- 1 3-oz. package cream cheese
- 1 tbsp. fresh lemon juice
- 1 tsp. finely grated lemon peel
- 1 tsp. vanilla extract
- 1/4 cup (or more) whipping cream

Direction

- Great on lb. cake. Blend vanilla, lemon peel, lemon juice, cream cheese and sugar with on/off turns in processor; blend in enough cream to make thick yet pourable icing.

Nutrition Information

- Calories: 208
- Total Carbohydrate: 24 g
- Cholesterol: 40 mg
- Total Fat: 12 g
- Fiber: 0 g
- Protein: 2 g
- Sodium: 83 mg
- Saturated Fat: 7 g

167. Lemon Curd

"Creamy and rich."
Serving: 10 | Prep: 10m | Ready in: 4h20m

Ingredients

- 3 eggs
- 1 cup white sugar
- 1/3 cup lemon juice
- 1/4 cup butter
- 2 tsps. lemon zest

Direction

- Whisk lemon juice, sugar and eggs till well mixed in a double boiler above simmering water; keep mixing for 7-10 minutes till thick.
- Through a mesh sieve, drain to remove lumps; fold in butter till incorporated well. Stir in lemon zest and cover curd; chill for around 4 hours till thick in the fridge.

Nutrition Information

- Calories: 142 calories;
- Total Carbohydrate: 20.9 g
- Cholesterol: 68 mg
- Total Fat: 6.1 g
- Protein: 2 g
- Sodium: 22 mg

168. Lemon Mousse With Boysenberry Purée

"Be sure plastic wrap touches surface when covering curd to avoid forming a skin on top."
Serving: Makes 6 servings

Ingredients

- 3/4 cup plus 6 tbsps. sugar
- 4 large eggs
- 4 large egg yolks
- 1 cup fresh lemon juice
- 1/2 cup plus 2 tbsps. (1 1/4 sticks) unsalted butter
- 3/4 cup frozen boysenberries, thawed, drained
- 1 3/4 cups chilled whipping cream
- Fresh boysenberries (optional)

Direction

- Whisk yolks, eggs and 3/4 cup and 2 tbsp. sugar to blend in medium stainless-steel bowl. Boil butter and lemon juice in small heavy saucepan; whisk hot lemon mixture slowly into egg mixture. Put bowl above saucepan with simmering water without touching water; mix for 4 minutes till an inserted thermometer in mixture reads 160°F and starts to thicken. Put curd in small bowl. On surface of curd, press plastic wrap; refrigerate till cold.

- Puree 4 tbsp. sugar and thawed boysenberries in blender. To remove seeds, strain into medium bowl; discard seeds. You can make puree and curd 1 day ahead. Cover the puree; chill puree and curd.
- Beat cream using electric mixer till soft peaks form in big bowl. Put 3/4 cup whipped cream in small bowl; put aside. Fold 1 cup of curd to make mousse into whipped cream; put leftover curd aside. Put mousse in a pastry bag with big plain tip.
- On bottom of each of the 6 6-8-oz. wineglasses/Champagne flutes, put 1 tbsp. berry puree; pipe 3/4-in. thick mousse layer on puree. Top with generous 1 tbsp. reserved curd. Repeat layers with curd and mousse. Put reserved whipped cream over. You can make it 8 hours ahead. Cover; refrigerate. If desired, garnish with fresh boysenberries.

Nutrition Information

- Calories: 620
- Total Carbohydrate: 45 g
- Cholesterol: 375 mg
- Total Fat: 47 g
- Fiber: 1 g
- Protein: 8 g
- Sodium: 80 mg
- Saturated Fat: 28 g

169. Lemon Sauce

"A lovely recipe!"
Serving: Makes 1 1/4 cups

Ingredients

- 1/3 cup sugar
- 1 tbsp. cornstarch
- 3/4 cup water
- 1/4 cup fresh lemon juice
- 4 thin lemon slices
- 1 tsp. grated lemon peel

Direction

- Whisk cornstarch and sugar to blend in small saucepan. Add 3/4 cup water and whisk on medium high heat for 2 minutes till it boils and thickens. Mix in grated lemon peel, lemon slices and lemon juice; cool. You can make it 1 day ahead. Cover; chill. Before serving, bring to room temperature.

Nutrition Information

- Calories: 134
- Total Carbohydrate: 36 g
- Total Fat: 0 g
- Fiber: 1 g
- Protein: 1 g
- Sodium: 5 mg
- Saturated Fat: 0 g

170. Lemon-chicken Drumsticks

"Satisfying and easy."
Serving: Makes 6 servings

Ingredients

- 12 chicken drumsticks (about 3 lbs.)
- Finely grated zest and juice of 2 lemons
- 2 tbsps. chopped fresh thyme leaves
- 2 tbsps. extra-virgin olive oil
- Salt and freshly ground black pepper, to taste
- Favorite orzo or rice, for serving (if desired)
- 2 tbsps. chopped parsley, for garnish

Direction

- Rinse chicken; pat dry.
- In a big bowl, mix pepper, salt, olive oil, thyme and lemon juice and zest. Add drumsticks; toss till coated. Cover; refrigerate for 2-4 hours – overnight.
- Preheat an oven to 375°F.
- Put drumsticks into shallow roasting dish that'll fit; to avoid crowding, use 2 dishes. Put

marinade on chicken; bake, occasionally basting, for 1 1/4 hours till drumsticks are golden brown and cooked through.

- Put under broiler 4-in. from heat source till browned, carefully watching, for 2-3 minutes per side if they don't brown enough.
- Put rice/orzo onto platter; put drumsticks over. Put chicken pan juices into small saucepan; cook till thick on medium high heat. Put on chicken; sprinkle parsley. Immediately serve.

171. Lemon-lattice White Chocolate Cake

"So yummy!"
Serving: Serves 12

Ingredients

- 3/4 cup fresh lemon juice
- 2 tbsps. cornstarch
- 1 cup plus 2 tbsps. sugar
- 3 large eggs
- 6 large egg yolks
- 1/2 cup plus 1 tbsp. unsalted butter, cut into small pieces
- 2 tbsps. grated lemon peel
- 2 1/4 cups whipping cream
- 4 1/2 oz. imported white chocolate (such as Lindt), chopped
- 3/4 tsp. vanilla extract
- 2 3/4 cups sifted all purpose flour
- 1 tsp. baking powder
- 3/4 tsp. salt
- 4 oz. imported white chocolate (such as Lindt), chopped
- 1 cup whipping cream
- 1/2 cup plus 2 tbsps. milk
- 1 tsp. vanilla extract
- 1/2 cup (1 stick) unsalted butter, room temperature
- 2 cups sugar
- 4 large eggs, separated

Direction

- Lemon curd: Mix cornstarch and lemon juice in medium heavy saucepan, mixing till cornstarch is dissolved. Whisk in leftover ingredients; cook on medium heat for 7 minutes till it starts to boil, smooth and thick, constantly mixing. Put in medium bowl; to avoid forming a skin, directly put plastic wrap on curd's surface. Refrigerate for 6 hours till chilled. You can prep it days ahead.
- Frosting: Mix chocolate and 1/2 cup cream in small heavy saucepan on low heat till it is smooth and chocolate melts; put into big bowl. Whisk in vanilla and leftover 1 3/4 cups cream; refrigerate for 6 hours till well chilled. You can prep it 1 day ahead.
- Cake: Put rack in middle of oven; preheat it to 350°F. Butter the 3 9-in. diameter cake pans that have 1 1/2-in. high sides; line waxed paper on bottoms. Butter paper. Use flour to dust pans; tap excess out. Sift salt, baking powder and flour into medium bowl then repeat sifting.
- Mix 1/2 cup cream and chocolate till it is smooth and chocolate melts in a medium heavy saucepan on low heat; mix in vanilla, milk and leftover 1/2 cup cream.
- Beat 1 cup sugar and butter using electric mixer till fluffy in big bowl; beat in yolks. Mix dry ingredients, alternately with the white chocolate mixture, into butter mixture, starting then ending with dry ingredients. Beat egg whites with electric mixer with clean dry beaters to soft peaks in medium bowl. Beat in leftover 1 cup sugar slowly; beat till stiff yet not dry. In 2 additions, fold whites into the cake batter. Divide batter to prepped cake pans; bake for 24 minutes till cakes start to pull away from pan's sides and inserted tester in middle exits clean. Cool cakes for 10 minutes in pans on racks. Turn out cakes on racks; peel waxed paper off. Fully cool. You can prep it 4 hours ahead; cover. Stand in room temperature.
- Beat frosting using electric mixer till stiff peaks form in another big bowl. On platter, put 1

cake layer; evenly spread 2/3 cup of lemon curd on cake layer. Spread 3/4 cup of frosting on curd; put 2nd cake layer over. Spread 2/3 cup curd on cake then 3/4 cup frosting; put 3rd cake layer over. Evenly frost sides and tops of cake using 3 cups frosting.

- Put leftover lemon curd into pastry bag with no. 2 star tip; around cake's top, pipe circle of curd, 1/2-in. from edge. Pipe diagonal lines inside circle, making lattice pattern, evenly spaced; keep leftover curd for another time. Put leftover frosting in a clean pastry bag with no. 2 star tip then pipe ruffled border around bottom and top cake edges. You can prep it maximum of 6 hours ahead, refrigerated. 30 minutes before serving, stand in room temperature.

Nutrition Information

- Calories: 835
- Total Carbohydrate: 91 g
- Cholesterol: 321 mg
- Total Fat: 49 g
- Fiber: 1 g
- Protein: 11 g
- Sodium: 270 mg
- Saturated Fat: 29 g

172. Lemon-lime Pound Cake

"A delightful dessert recipe with sweet soda pop."
Serving: Makes 12 servings

Ingredients

- Nonstick vegetable oil spray
- 3 cups all purpose flour
- 1/2 tsp. salt
- 1 1/2 cups (3 sticks) unsalted butter, room temperature
- 3 cups sugar
- 5 large eggs
- 1 1/2 tsps. grated lemon peel
- 1 1/2 tsps. grated lime peel

- 3/4 cup plus 2 tbsps. (about) lemon-lime soda (such as 7UP)
- 1 1/4 cups powdered sugar

Direction

- Set an oven to 325°F and start preheating. Coat 12-cup Bundt pan using non-stick spray over. In a bowl, beat salt and flour to combine. In a large bowl, whisk butter with an electric mixer until fluffy. Whisk in sugar gradually. Whisk in eggs, 1 each time; then whisk in a tsp. each of lime peel and lemon peel. Whisk in the flour mixture in 4 additions alternating with 3/4 cup of the lemon-lime soda in 3 additions. Add the batter into the sprayed pan.
- Bake the cake for an hour plus 15 minutes until the top turns golden and a tester comes out clean after inserted near the center. Cool cake for 5 minutes in pan. Transfer the cake on the rack to cool entirely. In a bowl, mix the remaining 1/2 tsp. each of lime peel and lemon peel with powdered sugar. Beat in enough of the remaining 2 tbsps. soda to have a thick smooth icing. Sprinkle cake with icing.

Nutrition Information

- Calories: 631
- Total Carbohydrate: 91 g
- Cholesterol: 139 mg
- Total Fat: 28 g
- Fiber: 1 g
- Protein: 6 g
- Sodium: 135 mg
- Saturated Fat: 15 g

173. Lemon-poppy Seed Waffles With Blueberry Sauce

"Have these waffles every day with or without syrup! It will surely bring you different happiness each day."
Serving: Makes 4 servings

Ingredients

- 1 lb. frozen blueberries, thawed, undrained
- 1/2 cup plus 2 tbsps. apple juice
- 1/2 cup sugar
- 1 tbsp. cornstarch
- 1 tbsp. fresh lemon juice
- 1 1/2 cups all purpose flour
- 6 tbsps. sugar
- 2 tbsps. poppy seeds
- 1 1/2 tsps. baking powder
- 1 tsp. baking soda
- 1/4 tsp. salt
- 3 large eggs
- 1 1/4 cups buttermilk
- 1/4 cup (1/2 stick) unsalted butter, melted
- 1 tbsp. grated lemon peel

Direction

- Prepare blueberry sauce: In a heavy medium saucepan, boil 1/2 cup apple juice, blueberries, and sugar. On medium heat, let mixture simmer for about 15 minutes until volume is reduced to 2 cups. Add 1 tbsp. of cornstarch on the leftover 2 tbsp. of apple juice; mix until cornstarch dissolves. Pour cornstarch mixture into blueberry mixture and add in the lemon juice. Allow mixture to boil while constantly stirring. Let it simmer for around 1 minute until thickened. Let slightly cool. (This can be done 2 days ahead. Refrigerate with cover and reheat before serving on medium-low heat.)
- Preparation for lemon-poppy seed waffles: In a big bowl, combine the first 6 ingredients; mix to blend. In a small bowl, add buttermilk, melted butter, lemon peel and eggs; beat until blended. Pour all of the buttermilk mixture at once into the flour mixture. Stir until just incorporated. Put side for 15 minutes.

- Follow manufacturer's instruction to preheat the waffle iron. Scoop batter onto the waffle iron then cover. For around 7 minutes, cook until golden and heated through (depending on the waffle iron, cooking time varies). Do it again with the rest of the batter. Quickly serve with the warm blueberry sauce.

Nutrition Information

- Calories: 642
- Total Carbohydrate: 108 g
- Cholesterol: 173 mg
- Total Fat: 18 g
- Fiber: 5 g
- Protein: 14 g
- Sodium: 802 mg
- Saturated Fat: 9 g

174. Lemon-ricotta Pancakes

"A fun pancake recipe."
Serving: Makes 4 servings

Ingredients

- 2 cups ricotta
- 2 cups mixed fresh berries
- 1/3 cup plus 4 tbsps. sugar, divided
- 2 tbsps. fresh lemon juice
- 1 1/2 cups all-purpose flour
- 1/2 cup chestnut flour
- 2 tbsps. baking powder
- 1/2 tsp. kosher salt
- 4 large eggs, separated
- 2 tbsps. finely grated lemon zest
- 1 1/2 cups whole milk
- Melted unsalted butter for brushing
- **Ingredient info:**Chestnut flour can be found at specialty foods stores.

Direction

- Line cheesecloth on fine-mesh strainer; put above small bowl. Put ricotta in strainer; drain for 15 minutes. Put aside.

- Gently mix lemon juice, 1/3 cup sugar and berries in a medium bowl; macerate, occasionally tossing, for 15 minutes till juices release and sugar dissolves.
- Whisk salt, baking powder and both flours in a big bowl. Beat egg whites till frothy in a medium bowl using electric mixer. Beat in 2 tbsp. sugar slowly, beating till stiff peaks. Whisk zest, leftover 2 tbsp. sugar and egg yolks to blend in another medium bowl; whisk in milk. Put yolk mixture in dry ingredients; whisk to just blend. Add 1/2 egg white mixture; fold to just blend. Fold in ricotta; fold in leftover egg white mixture.
- Heat griddle/big heavy nonstick skillet on medium low heat; brush melted butter. Put batter in batches, using scant 1/2 cup batter for every pancake, onto griddle; cook for 1 1/2 minutes till bubbles appear on top of pancake, edges are dry and bottom is golden brown. Flip pancakes; cook for 1 minute till just cooked through and browned. Put pancakes on plates; serve it with berries and the juices.

175. Lemon-rosemary Chicken Skewers

Serving: Makes 24 servings

Ingredients

- 8 skinless boneless chicken breast halves (each about 7 oz.)
- 48 8-inch bamboo skewers, soaked in water 30 minutes, drained
- 1 1-pint basket grape tomatoes or small cherry tomatoes
- 1 cup olive oil
- 1 cup fresh lemon juice
- 6 bay leaves, broken into small pieces
- 3 tbsps. chopped fresh rosemary
- 4 large garlic cloves, pressed
- 2 tsps. salt
- 2 tsps. hot pepper sauce
- 1 cup light mayonnaise

Direction

- Lengthwise cut every chicken breast half to 6 thin strips; fully thread each strip on 1 skewer; at 1 end, leave 1/2-in. skewer exposed. Onto end of skewer, press 1 grape tomato; divide skewers to 2 15x10x2-in. glass baking dishes; if needed, stack skewers.
- Into bowl, put oil; whisk in the next 6 ingredients. Put marinade on chicken; marinate at room temperature, flipping often, or 1 hour or cover then chilled overnight.
- Preheat an oven to 425°F. Take skewers from marinade. Put on 2 big rimmed baking sheets; put marinade aside. Bake chicken for 8 minutes till just cooked through; put onto platter.
- Put reserved marinade in medium saucepan; boil for 1 minute on medium high heat. Cool marinade for 15 minutes. Strain. Put 1/2 cup marinade in medium bowl and whisk in mayonnaise; use pepper and salt to season sauce to taste. Put leftover marinade on chicken to moisten then serve sauce with chicken.

Nutrition Information

- Calories: 153
- Total Carbohydrate: 2 g
- Cholesterol: 21 mg
- Total Fat: 13 g
- Fiber: 0 g
- Protein: 7 g
- Sodium: 172 mg
- Saturated Fat: 2 g

176. Lentils With Bitter Greens

"Simple and yummy."
Serving: Serves 2

Ingredients

- 1/2 cup dried lentils, picked over and rinsed
- 1 1/2 cups low-salt chicken broth

- 1/2 cup water
- 1 1/2 tbsps. extra-virgin olive oil
- 1 tbsp. red-wine vinegar
- 2 tsps. fresh lemon juice
- 1 small bunch arugula, coarse stems discarded, the rest washed and spun dry
- 1/2 head radicchio
- 1 medium Belgian endive
- 2 oz. crumbled feta cheese (about 1/3 cup)

Direction

- Simmer lentils in water and broth in a saucepan till tender for 20 minutes, covered; drain. Toss lemon juice, vinegar, oil and lentils; cool nearly to room temperature.
- Chop endive, radicchio and arugula to 1/4-in. pieces; put into lentils. Add salt and feta with, to taste, coarsely ground black pepper, tossing well.

177. Lime Snowballs

"So tasty!"
Serving: Makes about 30

Ingredients

- 1 1/2 cups all purpose flour
- 1/2 cup cornstarch
- 1 cup (2 sticks) unsalted butter, room temperature
- 1/2 cup powdered sugar
- 2 tbsps. fresh lime juice
- 1 tsp. (packed) finely grated lime peel
- 1/2 tsp. lime oil*
- Additional powdered sugar

Direction

- Preheat an oven to 350°F. Line parchment paper on 2 baking sheets. Whisk cornstarch and flour to blend in medium bowl. Beat 1/2 cup powdered sugar and butter using electric mixer till fluffy and light in big bowl; mix in lime oil, lime peel and lime juice. Beat in flour

mixture till smooth; refrigerate dough for 45 minutes till just firm.
- Shape dough, using scant 1 tbsp. for each, to balls; put on prepped sheets, 1-in. apart.
- Bake cookies for 23 minutes till browned on bottom and pale golden on top. Put baking sheets on racks; sift generous powdered sugar amount on cookies immediately. Fully cool cookies on baking sheets. You can make ahead; keep at room temperature airtight for 5 days or freeze for 2 weeks. Before serving, dust with extra powdered sugar.

Nutrition Information

- Calories: 95
- Total Carbohydrate: 9 g
- Cholesterol: 16 mg
- Total Fat: 6 g
- Fiber: 0 g
- Protein: 1 g
- Sodium: 1 mg
- Saturated Fat: 4 g

178. Linguine With Mussels And Fresh Herbs

"A tasty pasta recipe!"
Serving: Makes 6 servings | Prep: 20m

Ingredients

- 1/4 cup extra-virgin olive oil
- 2 tbsps. unsalted butter
- 4 large garlic cloves, sliced
- 1 tsp. fennel seeds
- 1/4 tsp. hot red pepper flakes
- 1 cup dry white wine
- 2 lbs. cultivated mussels, scrubbed
- 1 lb. thin linguine
- 1/2 cup grated Parmigiano-Reggiano
- 1 1/2 cups chopped herbs such as basil, dill, flat-leaf parsley, and oregano

Direction

- Heat butter and oil till foam subsides in a 5-6-qt. heavy pot on medium heat; cook red pepper flakes, 1/4 tsp. each of pepper and salt, fennel seeds and garlic, mixing, for 3-4 minutes till garlic is soft. Add wine; boil for 4-5 minutes till reduced by half. Add mussels; cook, covered, occasionally shaking pan, for 5-8 minutes till mussels open wide. Discard unopened clams after 8 minutes. Take off heat; keep warm.
- Meanwhile, cook linguine till al dente in pasta pot with well-salted boiling water. Put 1/2 cup cooking water aside; drain linguine.
- Toss herbs, cheese and linguine with liquid and mussels from pot; if desired, thin using reserved cooking water.

179. Linguine With Pancetta, Peas, And Zucchini

"To lengthwise peel zucchini to thin ribbons, use a vegetable peeler, stopping when you reach very center when it is all seeds. You can use this for carrots or use 1/2 zucchini and 1/2 carrots."
Serving: Serves 6

Ingredients

- 2 tbsps. extra-virgin olive oil
- 3 oz. pancetta, diced
- 1 cup chopped scallions
- 2 garlic cloves, thinly sliced
- 1 lb. linguine
- 1 cup frozen peas
- 2 medium zucchini, peeled into ribbons (see headnote)
- Kosher salt
- Crushed red pepper flakes
- 1/2 cup fresh basil leaves, chopped
- 1/2 cup fresh Italian parsley leaves, chopped
- 1/2 cup freshly grated Grana Padano

Direction

- For pasta, boil a big pot of salted water. Add olive oil to a big skillet on medium heat. Add pancetta when oil is hot; cook for 4 minutes till fat is rendered. Add garlic and scallions; cook for 3 minutes till scallions are wilted.
- Put linguine in boiling water. Add zucchini and peas to skillet when pasta is cooking; season with red pepper flakes and salt. Toss for 2 minutes till zucchini starts to wilt. Add 1 cup pasta water; simmer, as pasta cooks, reduce by half.
- Use a small strainer/spider to remove when pasta is al dente; add with parsley and basil directly to sauce, reserving pasta water. Toss to coat pasta in sauce; if pasta looks dry, add splash of pasta water. Take off heat; sprinkle grated Grana Padano and toss. Serve.

180. Liptauer With Rye Toast And Pickled Red Onions

"For this typical Austro-Hungarian cheese spread, the piquant pickled red onions are the perfect topping."
Serving: Makes 2 cups

Ingredients

- 1/2 small garlic clove, pressed
- 1/2 tsp. (or more) coarse kosher salt
- 3/4 cup (1 1/2 sticks) butter, room temperature
- 1 cup (8 oz.) whole-milk quark* or Greek-style yogurt
- 2 tbsps. finely chopped cornichons** or sour pickles
- 2 tbsps. chopped fresh chives
- 1 tbsp. grated onion
- 1 tbsp. Hungarian sweet paprika
- 1 1/2 tsps. (or more) white wine vinegar or juice from pickles
- 1/4 tsp. Hungarian hot paprika
- Lightly toasted sliced rye bread
- Pickled Red Onions

Direction

- Using the back of the spoon, mash the garlic with 1/2 tsp. of coarse salt in a small bowl until it forms a paste. Beat the butter in a medium bowl using the electric mixer until creamy and smooth. Add the quark, garlic paste, and the next 6 ingredients. Fold the mixture until well-combined. Season the mixture with salt and if desired, more vinegar. This can be prepared a day ahead. Just keep it covered and chilled. Allow it to stand at room temperature for 1 hour, making sure to stir it before using it.
- Serve the mixture with drained Pickled Red Onions and rye toast.
- The slightly tangy and soft unripened cow's milk cheese is available at some specialty stores, natural food stores, or supermarkets.
- The tiny brine-packed French pickles are available at some specialty foods stores and supermarkets.

181. Little Gem Lettuce With Green Goddess Dressing

"Use other small and crunchy greens like romaine hearts for Little Gem if you can't find it."
Serving: Serves 4

Ingredients

- 2 oil-packed anchovy fillets, chopped
- 1 garlic clove, finely grated
- 1/2 cup mayonnaise
- 1/2 cup sour cream
- 1/2 cup (loosely packed) basil leaves
- 2 tbsps. parsley leaves with tender stems
- 2 tbsps. tarragon leaves
- 2 tbsps. plus 1 tsp. fresh lemon juice
- 4 1/2 tsps. olive oil, plus more
- Kosher salt
- 6 heads of Little Gem lettuce, cores removed, leaves separated
- 2 small watermelon radishes, trimmed, thinly sliced

Direction

- Blend 4 1/2 tsp. oil, 1 tbsp. lemon juice, tarragon, parsley, basil, sour cream, mayonnaise, garlic and anchovies till smooth with only a few green flecks in a blender; season dressing using salt.
- Mix together the leftover 1 tbsp. plus 1 tsp. lemon juice, radishes and lettuce in a big bowl. Drizzle oil; season with salt then toss to mix.
- Put a few spoonful of dressing on salad; keep the leftover dressing for another time.
- You can make dressing 1 day ahead, chilled, covered.

182. Low-fat Orange And Almond Cream Cheese Pie

"An indulgent dessert that's low-fat!"
Serving: Serves 10

Ingredients

- Nonstick vegetable oil spray
- 1 3/4 cups low-fat granola
- 1/2 cup blanched slivered almonds (about 2 oz.)
- 1/4 cup plus 1 tbsp. orange juice
- 1 tbsp. honey
- 1/2 cup orange juice
- 1 envelope unflavored gelatin
- 1 16-oz. container nonfat cottage cheese
- 4 oz. nonfat cream cheese, room temperature
- 1/4 cup canned evaporated skim milk
- 3 tbsps. sugar
- 2 tbsps. honey
- 1/2 tsp. almond extract
- 4 oranges
- 1/4 cup apricot preserves
- 1 tbsp. sliced almonds, toasted

Direction

- Crust: Preheat an oven to 400°F. Spray nonstick vegetable oil spray on 9-in. diameter springform pan. Coarsely grind blanched slivered almonds and granola in processor; put into medium bowl. Mix in honey and orange juice. Press it on bottom of prepped springform pan; bake for 10 minutes till crust starts to color and is set. Put springform pan on rack; fully cool crust.

- Filling: Mix gelatin and orange juice in small heavy saucepan on low heat for 3 minutes till gelatin dissolves; take off heat. Puree almond extract, honey, sugar, evaporated milk, cream cheese and cottage cheese till very smooth in blender; put into big bowl. Mix in gelatin mixture; put filling in crust. Cover; refrigerate overnight. You can make cheese pie 1 day ahead, kept refrigerated.

- From oranges, cut white pith and peel; crosswise cut oranges to 1/4-in. thick rounds. Halve each round. Drain orange pieces on few paper towel layers. Decoratively put oranges on cheese pie. Mix apricot preserves in small heavy saucepan on low heat till melted. Brush apricot glaze on oranges. Sprinkle almonds on pie; serve.

183. Mango Sauce

"The quick but delicious fruit sauces."
Serving: 8 | Ready in: 10m

Ingredients

- 1 large ripe mango, peeled and cubed (see Tip)
- 2 tbsps. sugar, or more to taste
- 1 tbsp. lime juice

Direction

- In a blender, puree lime juice, mango and sugar. (Pass the mango through a fine sieve set over bowl, if it is fibrous.)

Nutrition Information

- Calories: 38 calories;
- Total Carbohydrate: 10 g
- Cholesterol: 0 mg
- Total Fat: 0 g
- Fiber: 1 g
- Protein: 0 g
- Sodium: 0 mg
- Sugar: 9 g
- Saturated Fat: 0 g

184. Maple-glazed Sour Cream Doughnuts With Sugared-walnut Streusel

"Gently fold in the dry ingredients by hand to get these cake doughnuts to have the tender texture."
Serving: Makes about 24 doughnuts and 24 doughnut holes

Ingredients

- 1 large egg white
- 1/4 cup sugar
- 1 tsp. ground cinnamon
- 1 1/2 cups chopped walnuts (about 6 oz.)
- 3 1/2 cups all purpose flour
- 1 tbsp. baking powder
- 1 tsp. ground cinnamon
- 1 tsp. salt
- 1/2 tsp. baking soda
- 1 cup sugar
- 2 large eggs
- 2 tsps. (packed) finely grated orange peel
- 1/2 tsp. vanilla extract
- 1/3 cup melted unsalted butter, cooled briefly
- 1 cup sour cream
- 2 cups powdered sugar
- 1/4 tsp. maple extract
- 5 tbsps. (about) heavy whipping cream
- Canola oil (for deep-frying)

Direction

- To make streusel: Set oven to 300°F to preheat. Use parchment paper to line rimmed baking sheet. In a bowl, whisk egg white for about 1 minute until frothy. Whisk in cinnamon and sugar. Fold in the nuts. Spread the mixture on the prepared sheet. Bake for about 12 minutes until starting to dry. Stir with metal spatula to break up the nuts. Keep baking for about 10 minutes until coating and nuts are golden brown and dry; let cool on sheet. Move the streusel to work surface. Chop nuts to get small (rice-size) bits. Move into shallow bowl.

- To make doughnuts: in medium bowl, whisk the first 5 ingredients to blend. Beat eggs and sugar using electric mixer in large bowl for about 3 minutes until very thick. Beat in vanilla and orange peel. Beat in butter gradually; beat in the sour cream in 2 increments. Fold in dry ingredients gently in 4 increments (dough will become lightly sticky). Put aside for 1 hour with a cover.
- To make glaze: In medium bowl, combine maple extract and powdered sugar. Put in 4 tbsps. cream; and whisk until it gets smooth. Whisk in extra cream, 1 tsp. each time, to form a medium-thick glaze. Allow to stand with a cover for up to 3 hours.
- Slightly sprinkle flour over 2 rimmed baking sheets. On slightly floured surface, press out 1/3 of dough to get the thickness of 1/2- to 2/3-inch. Cut out dough rounds using round cutter 2 1/2-inch in diameter. Place on the floured sheets. Repeat the process with the rest of dough in 2 more batches. Collect all the dough scraps. Press out the dough; cut more dough rounds until no scraps left.
- Cut out middle of each dough round using round cutter measuring 1-inch-diameter to make doughnut holes and doughnuts.
- Line several layers of paper towels to 2 baking sheets. In large deep skillet, add oil to depth of 1 1/2 inches. Insert deep-fry thermometer and heat oil to reach 365°F to 370°F. Fry doughnut holes for about 2 minutes in 2 batches, turning once, until golden brown. Transfer to paper towels using slotted spoon. Fry doughnuts, 3 or 4 pieces each time, for about 1 minute per side, until golden brown. Move doughnuts to paper towels using slotted spoon. Let doughnut holes and doughnuts cool completely.
- Spread 1 side of doughnut with glaze, one by one, then dip the glazed side into streusel.

Place doughnuts on rack with streusel side up. Allow glaze to set for minimum of 30 minutes. Use the same glaze to coat doughnut holes and dip them into streusel.

Nutrition Information

- Calories: 261
- Total Carbohydrate: 36 g
- Cholesterol: 32 mg
- Total Fat: 12 g
- Fiber: 1 g
- Protein: 4 g
- Sodium: 161 mg
- Saturated Fat: 4 g

185. Maple-glazed Turkey With Gravy

"Maple syrup caramelizes the skin of the turkey to make a super-thin coating. Since black peppercorns are steeped in the syrup, it added a floral note to it with some heat."
Serving: Makes 8 servings (with leftovers) | Prep: 30m

Ingredients

- 1 (14-lb.) turkey at room temperature 1 hour, any feathers and quills removed with tweezers or needlenose pliers, and neck and giblets removed and reserved for another use if desired
- 2 to 2 1/2 cups water, divided
- 1 1/2 tsps. black peppercorns
- 2/3 cup Grade B maple syrup
- 1/2 cup malt vinegar
- 1/2 cup all-purpose flour
- 5 cups turkey stock , heated to liquefy if gelled
- Equipment: kitchen string ;17- by 14-inch flameproof roasting pan with a flat rack; a 1-qt measuring cup; a fat separator (optional)

Direction

- For the turkey: Heat up the oven to 425 degrees Fahrenheit with the rack in its lowest position.

122

- Rinse the inside and outside of the turkey and pat dry. Place it on the rack in a roasting pan and sprinkle skin and cavities with 1 tsp. pepper and 2 tsps. salt. Fold skin of the neck under the body and tie together the drumsticks using kitchen string, then tuck the wings under the body.
- Add in 1 cup of water and roast the turkey for 1 hour without basting.
- For the glaze: Place the peppercorns into a small resealable bag or wrap them securely with a kitchen towel, then use a rolling pin or the bottom of a heavy pan to crack them. Move into a heavy small saucepan and add in the syrup, then cook on medium-low heat until it heats through. Take off the heat and allow to steep until you're about to glaze the turkey.
- To glaze turkey: Once the turkey has roasted for 1 hour, rotate the pan and add in 1 cup water. Roast for 45 more minutes without basting.
- Before the end of the 45 minutes, pour the syrup through a small sieve (fine-meshed) into small bowl, throwing away the peppercorns.
- Brush syrup all over the turkey and continue roasting (if pan bottom is totally dry, add leftover cup of water) for 15-20 minutes longer until an instant read thermometer reads 170 degrees Fahrenheit (test both fleshy part of thighs near the bone but not touching it). The total roasting time will be around 2 hours.
- Tilt the turkey carefully so the juices in the large cavity run in the roasting pan, then move the turkey onto a platter, setting the juices aside. Let the turkey sit without a cover for 30 minutes (thigh meat temperature should rise to 175 degrees Fahrenheit).
- For the gravy: Place the roasting pan onto 2 burners and add in vinegar to deglaze the pan by boiling it on high heat. Stir and scrap brown bits up, 2 minutes. Strain through a fine-mesh sieve into a measuring cup and let it sit until the fat rises to the surface. Skim and reserve the fat. If you are using a fat separator, strain the juices through the sieve into the separator and let sit until the fat rise to the

surfaces, 1-2 minutes. Pour juices from the separator carefully to a measuring cup and reserve fat.
- Heat up 6 tbsps. of the reserved fat (you can use butter as a substitute) into a medium heavy saucepan and whisk in the flour. Cook while whisking on medium heat, 5 minutes. Add in stock and pan juices in a speedy stream, constantly whisking to avoid lumps, then set to boil while whisking. Stir in any of the turkey juices from the platter and simmer briskly, whisking often, until the gravy thickens, around 10-15 minutes. Season with pepper and salt.

Nutrition Information

- Calories: 961
- Total Carbohydrate: 30 g
- Cholesterol: 410 mg
- Total Fat: 34 g
- Fiber: 0 g
- Protein: 127 g
- Sodium: 852 mg
- Saturated Fat: 9 g

186. Maple-pecan Pie

"An easy pie recipe."
Serving: Makes 8 servings

Ingredients

- 1 cup pure maple syrup
- 3/4 cup (packed) golden brown sugar
- 3 large eggs
- 1/4 cup sugar
- 3 tbsps. butter, melted
- 1 tbsp. all purpose flour
- 1 tsp. vanilla extract
- 1 9-inch frozen deep-dish pie crust
- 1 1/2 cups coarsely chopped pecans

Direction

- Preheat an oven to 350°F. In medium bowl, whisk first 7 ingredients to blend. On baking sheet, put unbaked crust; spread nuts on crust. Put filling over; bake for 1 hour till slightly puffed and filling is set. Put pie on rack; fully cool.

Nutrition Information

- Calories: 544
- Total Carbohydrate: 71 g
- Cholesterol: 81 mg
- Total Fat: 28 g
- Fiber: 3 g
- Protein: 5 g
- Sodium: 155 mg
- Saturated Fat: 7 g

187. Marbleized Root Vegetable Purée

"A veggie dish."
Serving: Serves 10

Ingredients

- 2 lbs. russet potatoes (about 3 large), peeled, cut into 2-inch pieces
- 8 oz. turnips (about 2 medium), peeled, cut into 2-inch pieces
- 8 oz. parsnips, peeled, cut into 1-inch pieces
- 1 medium pear (about 6 oz.), peeled, cored, cut into 1-inch pieces
- 1/2 cup whipping cream
- 8 tbsps. (1 stick) butter
- 1 1/2 lbs. carrots (about 6 large), peeled, cut into 1-inch pieces
- 1/8 tsp. ground nutmeg
- Additional ground nutmeg

Direction

- Set oven to 350° F and start preheating. Brush butter on a 2-qt. baking dish. In a big pot filled with boiling salted water, cook pear, parsnips, turnips and potatoes 20 minutes until very tender. Drain then bring back to the pot. Stir on low heat 1 minute until excess moisture has

evaporated. Put in 5 tbsps. butter and cream; mash until smooth. Season with pepper and salt.

- At the same time, in another big pot filled with boiling salted water, cook carrots 15 minutes until tender; drain. Remove to a processor. Put in 1/8 tsp. nutmeg and 2 tbsps. butter; puree until smooth. Season with pepper and salt.
- By 1/2 cupful, place potato puree and then carrot puree in the baking dish. Draw a knife through the purees for marbleizing. Melt 1 tbsp. butter and drizzle over the purees. Sprinkle extra nutmeg over top. Use foil to cover. (Can be prepared 1 day in advance. Keep chilled.) Bake the covered puree 35 minutes until heated through (if chilled, bake 45 minutes).

188. Martha's Potato Salad

Serving: Serves 8 to 10

Ingredients

- 8 medium-large boiling potatoes (about 3 1/4 lbs.)
- 1 cucumber
- 3 celery ribs
- 1 green bell pepper
- 1 small bunch radishes (about 8)
- 1 cup mayonnaise
- 2 tbsps. yellow (ballpark) mustard

Direction

- Place potatoes covered by 2-in. of salted cold water in a 5-qt. kettle and simmer for 30-35 minutes till just tender; drain potatoes in a colander. Fully cool. Peel potatoes; cut into 3/4-in. pieces. Put potatoes in a big bowl.
- Peel then seed cucumber; cut bell pepper, celery and cucumber into 1/4-in. dice. Slice radishes thinly; add diced veggies to potatoes, gently tossing. Whisk together mustard and mayonnaise in a small bowl; drizzle on salad. Toss salad gently till well combined; season with pepper and salt. You can make salad 1

day ahead, chilled, covered, Serve salad at cool room temperature or chilled.

Nutrition Information

- Calories: 321
- Total Carbohydrate: 27 g
- Cholesterol: 11 mg
- Total Fat: 23 g
- Fiber: 4 g
- Protein: 3 g
- Sodium: 234 mg
- Saturated Fat: 3 g

189. Mashed Potatoes With Crisp Ham

Serving: Makes 4 servings | Prep: 20m

Ingredients

- 2 lbs. boiling potatoes, peeled and cut into 1 1/2-inch pieces
- 2 tbsps. unsalted butter
- 1 tbsp. olive oil
- 1 cup chopped cooked ham (5 oz.)
- 3 scallions, chopped

Direction

- Cover potatoes in cold water in a 3-4-qt. saucepan; add 1/2 tsp. salt. Simmer for 15 minutes till tender.
- Meanwhile, melt oil and butter in medium heavy skillet on medium high heat; cook ham, occasionally mixing, for 5 minutes till brown. Mix in 1/4 tsp. pepper and scallions; cook for 2 minutes.
- Put 1 cup of potato cooking liquid aside. Drain potatoes; mash. Mix in ham mixture and enough cooking liquid to get desired consistency; season with pepper and salt.

Nutrition Information

- Calories: 361
- Total Carbohydrate: 43 g

- Cholesterol: 49 mg
- Total Fat: 15 g
- Fiber: 5 g
- Protein: 14 g
- Sodium: 605 mg
- Saturated Fat: 6 g

190. Mashed Yucca With Garlic

"Simple and tasty."
Serving: Serves 6

Ingredients

- 4 lb fresh yuca (also called cassava; preferably 2 inches in diameter) or 3 lb frozen
- 1 3/4 to 2 1/4 cups hot milk
- 2 garlic cloves, minced
- 1 tbsp. fresh lime juice
- 2 tsps. salt

Direction

- From fresh yuca, trim ends; peel leftover, removing pinkish layer under and all waxy brown skin.
- Cut yuca to 3-in. thick pieces.
- Boil yuca covered in 2-in. salted water for 50 minutes – 1 1/4 hours till beginning to fall apart and tender.
- Drain; put onto cutting board. Lengthwise halve hot yuca pieces carefully; remove thin woody cores. Put yuca, salt, juice, garlic and 1 3/4 cups milk in pot. Mash yuca coarsely, adding extra milk if desired; immediately serve.

Nutrition Information

- Calories: 536
- Total Carbohydrate: 120 g
- Cholesterol: 8 mg
- Total Fat: 3 g
- Fiber: 5 g
- Protein: 7 g
- Sodium: 853 mg

- Saturated Fat: 2 g

191. Melon With Feta, Red Onion, And Pine Nuts

Serving: Serves 8

Ingredients

- 1 tbsp. vegetable oil
- 2 red onions, sliced 1/4 inch thick
- 2 cantaloupes
- 1 honeydew melon
- 1/4 cup chopped fresh mint leaves
- 1 tbsp. fresh lime juice
- 1/2 cup crumbled feta cheese (about 4 oz.)
- 1/4 cup pine nuts, toasted

Direction

- Heat oil in a big skillet on medium heat till hot yet not smoking; cook onions till just soft, occasionally mixing. Take the skillet off heat; cool onions.
- Cut a slice from bottom and top of every melon with a sharp knife to explode the flesh; put on a cutting board, cut side down. Remove rind, cutting from top to bottom. Halve melons; discard the seeds. Cut 1 honeydew half and 1 cantaloupe half to 1-in. thick wedges; put onto a platter. Cut leftover lemon to 3/4-in. chunks; toss with pepper to taste, lime juice and mint in a bowl.
- Put melon mixture on melon wedges on a platter; top with onions, feta and pine nuts. Toss mixture to combine before serving.

Nutrition Information

- Calories: 187
- Total Carbohydrate: 27 g
- Cholesterol: 13 mg
- Total Fat: 8 g
- Fiber: 3 g
- Protein: 5 g
- Sodium: 177 mg

- Saturated Fat: 3 g

192. Meringue Hearts With Mint Ice Cream And Fudge Sauce

"So delicious."
Serving: Serves 6

Ingredients

- 6 tbsps. (3/4 stick) unsalted butter
- 1/4 cup dark corn syrup
- 5 oz. imported bittersweet chocolate (not unsweetened) or semisweet chocolate, chopped
- 1/4 cup powdered sugar, sifted
- 2 tbsps. whipping cream
- 4 large egg whites
- 1 cup sugar
- 2 pints vanilla ice cream, softened slightly
- 1/2 cup finely crushed hard peppermint candies
- 1/8 tsp. peppermint extract
- Powdered sugar
- Coarsely chopped hard peppermint candies

Direction

- Sauce: Melt corn syrup with butter in small heavy saucepan on medium low heat, occasionally mixing. Add cream, sugar and chocolate; whisk till sugar and chocolate melts. You can make it 1 week ahead, chilled, covered.
- Meringues: Preheat an oven to 225°F. Line foil on 2 baking sheets; butter foil. On foil-lined sheet, put 3 3/4-in. heart-shaped cookie cutter. Beat whites with electric mixer to soft peaks in big bowl. Add 1 cup sugar slowly; beat till shiny and stiff. Put 1/4 cup meringue in cookie cutter onto sheet. Evenly spread using back of spoon. Lift cookie cutter up; put on another part of foil-lined sheet. Repeat using leftover meringue, making 6 hearts of every sheet.

- Bake meringues for 1 hour till dry and crisp; cool meringues for 10 minutes on sheets. Peel off meringues from foil. You can make it 1 day ahead. Fully cool; keep airtight in room temperature.
- In medium bowl, mix extract, 1/2 cup of crushed peppermint candy and ice cream; cover. Freeze for 2 hours till nearly semi-firm.
- Put meringues on baking sheet, flat side up; freeze for 15 minutes. Put 1/2 cup ice cream on 1 meringue; put another meringue over, flat side up. To flatten, gently press, making sandwich. To even sides, run spatula around ice cream's sides. Freeze. Repeat with leftover ice cream and meringues. Cover; freeze for 1-6 hours.
- Mix sauce till warm on medium low heat. Sift powdered sugar over meringues, fully coating; put on plates. Put sauce around then sprinkled chopped candy on sauce.

Nutrition Information

- Calories: 687
- Total Carbohydrate: 96 g
- Cholesterol: 75 mg
- Total Fat: 34 g
- Fiber: 3 g
- Protein: 7 g
- Sodium: 136 mg
- Saturated Fat: 21 g

193. Mesclun Salad

"This salad is very tasty yet easy to make."
Serving: Makes 4 servings | Prep: 15m

Ingredients

- 1 tbsp. fresh lemon juice
- 1/2 tsp. Dijon mustard
- 1/4 tsp. sugar
- 2 tbsps. olive oil
- 5 oz. mesclun (8 cups)

Direction

- In a big bowl, combine 1/2 tsp. salt, sugar, mustard, and lemon juice until the sugar and salt dissolve, and then pour in a slow stream of oil, stirring until emulsified.
- Add greens to the dressing and mix to blend. Enjoy immediately.

Nutrition Information

- Calories: 73
- Total Carbohydrate: 3 g
- Total Fat: 7 g
- Fiber: 1 g
- Protein: 1 g
- Sodium: 27 mg
- Saturated Fat: 1 g

194. Meyer Lemon And Vanilla Bean Marmalade

Serving: Makes about 4 1/2 cups

Ingredients

- 1 1/4 lbs. Meyer lemons
- 5 cups water
- 5 1/2 cups (about) sugar
- 1 vanilla bean, split lengthwise
- Pinch of salt

Direction

- Lengthwise halve lemons working on big plate to get juice; crosswise cut very thinly. Discard seeds. To get 2 1/2 cups, pack enough lemons and juice. Put into big nonreactive pot then add 5 cups water; boil. Lower heat to medium; simmer for 10 minutes. Take off heat; stand overnight, uncovered.
- Get 5 1/2 cups lemon mixture then put into same pot; add even 5 1/2 cups sugar amount. From vanilla bean, scrape in seeds; add bean and pinch of salt. Boil, mixing till sugar dissolves. Attach a clip-on candy thermometer. Cook, maintaining active boil,

adjusting heat to avoid boiling over, occasionally mixing, for 30 minutes till temperature reads 230°F. Cool to room temperature. Put into jars. Cover; chill. You can make it 2 weeks ahead, kept refrigerated. Before serving, bring to room temperature.

Nutrition Information

- Calories: 444
- Total Carbohydrate: 115 g
- Total Fat: 0 g
- Fiber: 2 g
- Protein: 1 g
- Sodium: 36 mg
- Saturated Fat: 0 g

195. Michael Romano's Secret-ingredient Soup

"A satisfying soup. You may use red pepper flakes for Aleppo pepper if needed."
Serving: 4 to 6 servings

Ingredients

- 2 tbsps. olive oil
- 3/4 cup finely chopped onion
- 3/4 cup finely chopped peeled carrot
- 3/4 cup well-washed thinly sliced leeks
- 1 tsp. finely chopped garlic
- 1 1/2 tsps. kosher salt
- 1/4 tsp. freshly ground black pepper
- 1/4 tsp. Aleppo pepper or red pepper flakes
- 8 oz. Italian fennel sausage (sweet or hot), casings removed
- 2 tbsps. medium-grind cornmeal (polenta)
- 5 cups Chicken or Vegetable Stock
- 4 cups packed stemmed and coarsely chopped kale or chard leaves, or a combination
- Grated Parmigiano-Reggiano for serving

Direction

- Heat oil on medium heat in a big saucepan. Add Aleppo pepper, black pepper, salt, garlic,

leeks, carrot and onion; cook for 8-10 minutes till onion is translucent, mixing. Add sausage; cook for 5 minutes till not pink, breaking up with a wooden spoon to small pieces.
- Drain extra fat off; leave 2 tbsp. in pan. Mix in cornmeal; add stock, mixing. Boil. Lower heat; simmer for 30 minutes, covered, occasionally mixing.
- Mix in greens; cook till tender for 15 minutes.
- Put into bowls; garnish with grated parmigiano.

Nutrition Information

- Calories: 343
- Total Carbohydrate: 18 g
- Cholesterol: 43 mg
- Total Fat: 25 g
- Fiber: 4 g
- Protein: 12 g
- Sodium: 1141 mg
- Saturated Fat: 7 g

196. Milk-braised Pork With Lemon And Sage

"Braising the pork shoulder creates a fall-apart tender roast. Adding milk will result in a sauce that is richly infused with ricotta."
Serving: Serves 6–8 | Prep: 20m

Ingredients

- 2 tbsps. olive oil
- 1 (2–2 1/2-lb.) boneless pork shoulder (Boston butt)
- 1 tbsp. kosher salt
- 1 tsp. freshly ground black pepper
- 1 bunch sage
- 1 lemon, peeled
- 1 1/2 cups whole milk
- 1 large bunch Swiss chard, ribs and stems removed, torn into 3-inch pieces

Direction

- Set the oven to 250°F for preheating.
- Put oil in a large heavy pot or Dutch oven and heat it over medium-high until shimmering. Season salt and pepper all over the pork. Cook the pork for 12-15 minutes, flipping occasionally until all sides are browned. Pour any excess fat off the pot. Add the milk, sage, and lemon peel. Bring the mixture to a boil. Adjust the heat to medium-low. Cover the pot and place it inside the oven. Roast the pork for 3 1/2-4 hours until very tender.
- Place the meat in a serving platter, discarding the lemon peel. Toss the Swiss chard into the remaining sauce in the pot until wilted. Place the Swiss chard around the pork using the tongs. Top the pork and Swiss chard with the remaining sauce. Serve.

197. Mini Chicken Pot Pies With Bacon And Marjoram

"A very fun recipe."
Serving: Makes 4 servings

Ingredients

- 5 applewood-smoked bacon slices
- 1 1/2 cups chopped onion
- 12 oz. peeled whole baby carrots (about 2 1/2 cups)
- 1 8-oz. package trimmed haricots verts or other slender green beans, halved crosswise
- 4 tsps. chopped fresh marjoram
- 1 3/4 cups low-salt chicken broth
- 2/3 cup plus 1 tbsp. crème fraîche
- 3 cups coarsely shredded chicken from 1 small purchased roasted chicken (skin removed)
- 1 sheet frozen puff pastry (half of 17.3-oz. package), thawed

Direction

- Preheat an oven to 450°F. Cook bacon till crisp in big heavy skillet on medium heat. On paper towels, drain. Chop bacon. Put onion in

drippings in skillet; sauté for 8 minutes till golden and tender. Add next 3 ingredients; mix for 1 minute. Add broth; boil on high heat. Lower heat to medium high; boil for 8 minutes till some liquid reduces and veggies are nearly tender. Mix in bacon, chicken and 2/3 cup crème fraiche; simmer. Use pepper to season. Divide to 4 2-cup soufflé dishes.
- Onto work surface, unfold puff pastry; roll to 12-in. square. Cut to 4 even squares. Put filling in soufflé dishes with the pastry; fold down edges onto dish's rims. Brush leftover 1 tbsp. crème fraiche over crust (not edges). In middle of crusts, cut small X; use fork to pierce all over. Bake for 22 minutes till filling heats through and crusts are golden brown.

198. Mixed Vegetable Gratin

Serving: Serves 8

Ingredients

- 2 1/2 lbs. russet potatoes
- 3 large celery stalks, cut into 1/2-inch pieces
- 3 large carrots, peeled, cut into 1/2-inch pieces
- 1 large green bell pepper, cut into 1/2-inch pieces
- 2 tbsps. minced garlic
- 2 tbsps. chopped fresh basil or 2 tsps. dried, crumbled
- 2 tsps. chopped fresh rosemary or 1/2 tsp. dried, crumbled
- 1/4 cup (1/2 stick) butter
- 1 1/2 cups grated Monterey Jack or Fontina cheese (optional)

Direction

- Set the oven to 400 degrees F to preheat. In a big bowl, mix the first seven ingredients together, then pour butter over mixture and toss to coat well. Use pepper and salt to season. Move the vegetable mixture to a 13"x9"x2" glass baking dish. Use aluminum foil to cover and bake for 40 minutes. Take off foil and bake for about half an hour more while stirring sometimes, until vegetables are starting to brown and softened.

- Preheat broiler. Use cheese to sprinkle over the mixture and broil for about 4 minutes, until cheese starts to brown and melts.

Nutrition Information

- Calories: 185
- Total Carbohydrate: 31 g
- Cholesterol: 15 mg
- Total Fat: 6 g
- Fiber: 3 g
- Protein: 4 g
- Sodium: 47 mg
- Saturated Fat: 4 g

199. Molasses-and-spice Pumpkin Pie

"A fun filling recipe."
Serving: Makes one 9-inch pie

Ingredients

- 1 cup sugar
- 1 1/2 tsps. cornstarch
- 1 tsp. ground cinnamon
- 1/2 tsp. ground ginger
- 1/4 tsp. ground allspice
- 1/4 tsp. salt
- 1 15-oz. can pure pumpkin
- 2 large eggs
- 1/2 cup heavy whipping cream
- 1/2 cup whole milk
- 1 1/2 tbsps. mild-flavored (light) molasses
- 1 9-inch unbaked homemade or purchased pie crust

Direction

- Mix first 6 ingredients to blend in big bowl. Add molasses, milk, cream, eggs and pumpkin; whisk the filling to blend.
- Preheat an oven to 350°F. Put filling in crust; bake pie for 1 hour 5 minutes till slight puffed

around edges and set in center. Cool pie on rack.

Nutrition Information

- Calories: 3147
- Total Carbohydrate: 395 g
- Cholesterol: 744 mg
- Total Fat: 169 g
- Fiber: 18 g
- Protein: 36 g
- Sodium: 1828 mg
- Saturated Fat: 84 g

200. Molasses-baked Onions

"Rich and sweet onions great with baked ham, pork roast, or broiled chicken."
Serving: Makes 8 side-dish servings | Prep: 30m

Ingredients

- 4 large sweet onions such as Vidalia, Walla Walla, or Oso Sweet (3 to 4 lb total)
- 1 1/2 cups tomato juice (12 fluid oz.)
- 1 1/2 cups water
- 2 tbsps. unsalted butter
- 2 tbsps. molasses (regular or robust; not blackstrap)
- 1/2 tsp. salt, or to taste
- 8 bacon slices (1/2 lb.), halved crosswise

Direction

- Set the oven rack in center place and preheat the oven to 400°F.
- Remove skin and clip the onions, retaining root ends attach, then cut each in half lengthwise. In a 13×9×2-inch glass baking dish or another 2 1/2-quart shallow baking dish, lay in a single layer cut sides facing up.
- In a 2-quart heavy saucepan, boil salt, molasses, butter, water and tomato juice, mixing from time to time, then put on top of onions. Let the onions bake without a cover for 2 hours, basting with juices every 30 minutes, till soft.

- On top of every onion half, drape 2 pieces of bacon side by side and keep baking the onions for an hour longer, basting one time with juices midway through baking, till juices are thickened, bacon is browned and onions are extremely soft.

Nutrition Information

- Calories: 232
- Total Carbohydrate: 21 g
- Cholesterol: 26 mg
- Total Fat: 14 g
- Fiber: 2 g
- Protein: 6 g
- Sodium: 358 mg
- Saturated Fat: 6 g

201. Molten Chocolate Cakes With Mint Fudge Sauce

"Gooey and yummy!"
Serving: Makes 6

Ingredients

- 4 1/2 oz. bittersweet (not unsweetened) or semisweet chocolate, chopped
- 2 oz. unsweetened chocolate, chopped
- 1/3 cup hot water
- 1/4 cup light corn syrup
- 3/4 tsp. peppermint extract
- 5 oz. bittersweet (not unsweetened) or semisweet chocolate, chopped
- 10 tbsps. unsalted butter
- 3 large eggs
- 3 large egg yolks
- 1 1/2 cups powdered sugar
- 1/2 cup all purpose flour
- Vanilla ice cream

Direction

- Sauce: Mix both chocolates till melted on top of double boiler above barely simmering water. Add extract, corn syrup and 1/3 cup hot water; whisk till smooth. Take from above water; slightly cool. You can make it 2 days ahead, chilled, covered. Rewarm in saucepan on low heat, constantly mixing, before serving.
- Cakes: Preheat an oven to 450°F. Butter 6 custard cups/3/4-cup soufflé dishes. Mix butter and chocolate till melted in medium heavy saucepan on low heat; slightly cool. Whisk egg yolks and eggs to blend in big bowl. Whisk in sugar then flour and chocolate mixture; put batter in dishes, evenly dividing. You can make it 1 day ahead, chilled, covered.
- Bake cakes for 11 minutes or 14 minutes for refrigerated batter till sides are set yet middle is runny and soft; to loosen, run small knife around the cakes. Turn cakes onto plates immediately; put sauce around cakes then serve with ice cream.

Nutrition Information

- Calories: 704
- Total Carbohydrate: 81 g
- Cholesterol: 236 mg
- Total Fat: 42 g
- Fiber: 5 g
- Protein: 9 g
- Sodium: 60 mg
- Saturated Fat: 25 g

202. Moroccan Skirt Steak Salad With Chermoula

"A Moroccan inspired salad made form pomegranate seeds, feta, cucumbers and carrots, served with herbaceous chermoula sauce."
Serving: Serves 4 | Prep: 30m

Ingredients

- 1 lb. skirt steak, sliced crosswise into 5–6-inch-long pieces
- 1/2 tsp. kosher salt
- 1/4 tsp. freshly ground black pepper
- 1/2 cup Blender Chermoula Sauce
- Vegetable oil (for grill)

- 2 medium carrots, shaved into long thin ribbons
- 2 small Persian cucumbers, thinly sliced into rounds
- 6 cups baby arugula
- 1/4 tsp. kosher salt
- 1/4 tsp. freshly ground black pepper
- 1 cup (packed) mixed herb leaves, such as parsley, cilantro, and mint, divided
- 1/2 cup Blender Chermoula Sauce, divided
- 1/4 cup crumbled feta
- 1/4 cup pomegranate seeds

Direction

- To prepare, marinate and grill the steak: Put pepper and salt to season steak, then put it in a bow or big resealable bag. Put chermoula on and coat by tossing; let it sit for a minimum of 1 hour at room temperature.
- Set a grill pan on medium-high or a grill on medium-high heat. Oil the pan or grate lightly. Take out the steak from its marinade; get rid of the marinade. Grill the steak for 2 to 3 minutes on each side for medium-rare, until an inserted instant-read thermometer in the middle reads 125 degrees F. Move to a cutting board and let it sit for 10 minutes prior to slicing; slice against the grain.
- Assembling salad: In a big bowl, toss in the 1/4 cup chermoula sauce, 1/2 cup herbs, pepper, salt, arugula, cucumbers and carrots. Distribute the salad on four plates, put the steak on top and the leftover 1/2 cup herbs. Drizzle the leftover 1/4 cup chermoula sauce on top of the salad. Put pomegranate seeds and feta on top.
- You can marinate the steaks 10 hours in advance and let it chill in the bag. Prior to cooking, allow the steak to come to room temperature for a minimum of 1 hour.

Nutrition Information

- Calories: 537
- Total Carbohydrate: 13 g
- Cholesterol: 87 mg
- Total Fat: 42 g

- Fiber: 3 g
- Protein: 29 g
- Sodium: 866 mg
- Saturated Fat: 10 g

203. Moroccan-style Roast Chicken

Serving: Makes 4 servings

Ingredients

- 1/4 cup (1/2 stick) unsalted butter, melted
- 1/4 cup honey
- 1 tsp. ground cinnamon
- 1/4 tsp. turmeric
- 1 (4 3/4- to 5-lb.) whole chicken, rinsed, patted dry

Direction

- In bottom oven third, put rack; preheat it to 400°F. In small bowl, mix turmeric, cinnamon, honey and butter; season with pepper and salt. In small bowl, put 1/4 cup honey butter; put aside.
- On rack in a roasting pan, put chicken. Brush some leftover honey butter; sprinkle pepper and salt. Roast chicken for 1 hour 10 minutes till inserted thermometer in thickest thigh part reads 165-170°F; brush honey butter occasionally. If it browns too quickly, loosely cover in foil. Put on platter; serve it with reserved honey butter.

Nutrition Information

- Calories: 977
- Total Carbohydrate: 18 g
- Cholesterol: 312 mg
- Total Fat: 68 g
- Fiber: 0 g
- Protein: 70 g
- Sodium: 266 mg
- Saturated Fat: 23 g

204. Mushroom Consommé With Morels And Pastry "hats"

"You can use other dried exotic mushrooms for morels or omit then float a thin fresh white mushroom slice over soup before covering bowl with pastry."
Serving: Serves 6

Ingredients

- 2 lbs. fresh white mushrooms, chopped fine (preferably in a food processor)
- 2 onions, chopped
- 2 quarts cold water
- 1 tsp. salt
- 1 1/2 cups boiling water
- 3/4 oz. dried morels* (about 1 cup)
- 3/4 cup Sercial Madeira
- 2 tbsps. 1-inch pieces fresh chives
- a 17 1/4-oz. package frozen puff pastry sheets (2 pastry sheets), thawed
- an egg wash made by beating 1 large egg with 1 tsp. water
- *available at specialty foods shops and by mail order

Direction

- Mushroom consommé: Simmer consommé ingredients, uncovered, for 2 hours in a 6-qt. stockpot or kettle. Put consommé through rinsed and squeezed paper towel-lined big fine sieve into big saucepan, gently pressing on solids to get 5 cups consommé. Add water to get 5 cups if it isn't enough. Boil to reduce to 5 cups if it's too much. Use pepper and salt to season it.
- As consommé simmers, prep morels: Put boiling water on morels in a small bowl; stand till morels are soft for 20 minutes. Remove morels; put soaking liquid aside. Simmer morels in Madeira in small saucepan, covered, for 5 minutes. Put morel mixture in consommé. Let the kept soaking liquid settle; put into consommé slowly, leaving last 1 tbsp. with sediment in bowl. Simmer the consommé

for 3 minutes, covered; cool to room temperature. You can make consommé 2 days ahead, covered, chilled. Before continuing, bring it to room temperature.
- Preheat an oven to 400°F. Prep 9-10-oz. ovenproof ramekins that are 3 1/2-4-in. across top/6 12-oz. truffle soup bowls. Divide chives and consommé with morels to ramekins/bowls.
- Prep pastry hats: Roll 1 puff pastry sheet out to 12-in. square on lightly floured surface; use round cutter 3/4-in. bigger than bowl's diameter to cut 4 rounds out. Roll 2nd puff pastry sheet out; in same manner, cut 2 more rounds out. Brush extra flour from both rounds sides.
- Brush 1/2-in. wide egg wash border around pastry edges, 1 pastry round at 1 time; invert pastry rounds over ramekins/bowls, stretching 1/2-in. down side carefully, pressing to seal.
- Brush leftover egg wash on tops when all ramekins/bowls are covered with pastry. At this point, you can prep it 4 hours ahead, chilled. When coming straight from fridge into oven, pastry won't rise as high. Put ramekins/bowls onto big baking sheet; bake consommé in center of oven for 12-18 minutes till pastry hats are golden and puffed.

Nutrition Information

- Calories: 311
- Total Carbohydrate: 30 g
- Cholesterol: 31 mg
- Total Fat: 17 g
- Fiber: 3 g
- Protein: 10 g
- Sodium: 529 mg
- Saturated Fat: 4 g

205. Mussel And Carrot Soup

"Best created with fresh carrot juice."
Serving: Makes 6 servings

Ingredients

- 2 tbsps. olive oil
- 2 shallots, finely chopped (1/2 cup)
- 1/4 cup finely chopped peeled fresh ginger
- 4 garlic cloves, chopped
- 2 tsps. curry powder
- 1 cup dry white wine
- 2 (3-inch) fresh tarragon sprigs
- 3 lb mussels (8 dozen; preferably cultivated), scrubbed well and beards discarded
- 1 cup chicken stock or low-sodium chicken broth
- 3 cups fresh carrot juice
- 2 (8-oz) bottles clam juice
- 1/3 cup fresh lime juice
- 1 tbsp. sour cream

Direction

- Heat oil in a 6-qt. heavy pot on medium heat till hot yet not smoking; cook curry powder, garlic, ginger and shallots for 2 minutes till shallots are golden, mixing. Mix mussels, tarragon and wine in; cook till mussels just open wide, covered, frequently checking after 3 minutes, transferring opened mussels into a bowl. Discard any mussels that remain unopened after 6 minutes. Put clam juice, carrot juice and stock in a pot; simmer, occasionally mixing.
- Whisk lime juice into the sour cream in a small bowl. In a stream, add lime juice mixture to the soup, whisking till smooth; season with pepper and salt. Put mussels back in a pot; cook on low till just heated through, occasionally mixing; don't boil.

Nutrition Information

- Calories: 363
- Total Carbohydrate: 27 g
- Cholesterol: 66 mg
- Total Fat: 11 g
- Fiber: 2 g
- Protein: 35 g
- Sodium: 1293 mg
- Saturated Fat: 2 g

206. Mussels In Saffron And White Wine Broth

"A simple and tasty recipe."
Serving: Makes 8 servings | Prep: 25m

Ingredients

- 2 tsps. butter
- 3 garlic cloves, chopped
- 1 cup dry white wine
- 2 tbsps. half and half
- 2 1/2 tsps. saffron threads
- 1 cup clam juice
- 4 scallions, thinly sliced
- 3 tomatoes, seeded, and chopped
- 3 tbsps. lemon juice
- 8 lbs. mussels, scrubbed and debearded
- 2 1/2 tbsps. chives, chopped

Direction

- Melt butter in big pot and add garlic. Sauté for 1 minute till garlic is fragrant. Add saffron, half and half and wine; simmer for 5 minutes. Add clam juice, scallions, tomato, and lemon juice, scallions, tomato, and lemon juice; simmer for 5 minutes.
- Add mussels, then cover; steam for 5-7 minutes till they open. Shake pot to redistribute mussels, holding lid down with kitchen towel. Discard unopened mussels. Divide mussels to 8 bowls; evenly distribute broth to bowls; put fresh chives over each.
- Cleaning mussels: Under cold running water, hold mussel. Use brush with stiff bristles to scrub mussel thoroughly to remove mud, sand and grit from shell's exterior. From each mussel, especially non-farmed ones, they usually have dark, shaggy beard extending

from each shell. Remove them for cleaner appearance in final dish. Pull beard away from shell till taut after scrubbing a mussel; sharply pull beard down toward dark hinge. It will easily snap away. Do this before cooking because it kills the mussel.

Nutrition Information

- Calories: 441
- Total Carbohydrate: 21 g
- Cholesterol: 131 mg
- Total Fat: 12 g
- Fiber: 1 g
- Protein: 57 g
- Sodium: 1492 mg
- Saturated Fat: 3 g

207. My Cobb Salad: Iceberg, Tomato, Avocado, Bacon, And Blue Cheese

"An American classic salad recipe."
Serving: Serves 4

Ingredients

- 2 1/2 oz. smoked bacon, rind removed, cut into matchsticks (3/4 cup)
- 1 head iceberg lettuce, chopped (4 cups)
- 2 ripe heirloom tomatoes, cored, peeled, seeded, and chopped
- 1 large ripe avocado, halved, pitted, peeled, and cubed
- 4 oz. chilled blue cheese (preferably Roquefort), crumbled (1 cup)
- 4 small spring onions or scallions, white part only, trimmed, peeled, and cut into thin rounds
- Yogurt and Lemon Dressing
- Coarse, freshly ground black pepper

Direction

- Brown bacon for about 5 minutes on moderate heat until golden and crispy in a big, dry

skillet. Move the bacon onto a few paper towel layers to absorb the fat using a slotted spoon. Blot a few layers of paper towels onto the bacon to absorb any extra fat. Put aside.
- Mix spring onions, cheese, avocado, tomatoes, lettuce and bacon in a big and shallow bowl. Evenly and lightly coat the ingredients by mixing with just an enough amount of dressing. Add a generous amount of pepper to season, then serve.

Nutrition Information

- Calories: 354
- Total Carbohydrate: 15 g
- Cholesterol: 44 mg
- Total Fat: 28 g
- Fiber: 6 g
- Protein: 14 g
- Sodium: 546 mg
- Saturated Fat: 11 g

208. My Mother's Strawberry Jam

Serving: Makes about 3 1/2 cups

Ingredients

- 3 pints strawberries, hulled
- 1/2 cup sugar cubes (important to use sugar cubes; it's the best sugar for jam, according to my mother)

Direction

- Cook berries in heavy pan on low heat, mixing every 15 minutes, for 3 hours till jamlike in consistency. Add around 3/4 cup sugar in jam sweetener if desired; mix till melted. Put jam in jar; cool. Refrigerate. Keep refrigerate for 2 weeks only; it is fresh. Creates 3 1/2 cups.

Nutrition Information

- Calories: 182
- Total Carbohydrate: 46 g
- Total Fat: 1 g

- Fiber: 5 g
- Protein: 2 g
- Sodium: 3 mg
- Saturated Fat: 0 g

209. Nectarine Lime Curd Tart With A Brown-sugar Crust

"This recipe takes time."
Serving: Serves 4 generously

Ingredients

- 1 firm-ripe medium nectarine
- 5 large egg yolks
- 1/3 cup granulated sugar
- 2 tbsps. fresh lime
- 2 tbsps. unsalted
- 1/8 tsp. vanilla
- 3/4 stick (6 tbsps.) cold unsalted butter
- 1 cup all-purpose flour
- 1/3 cup packed dark brown sugar
- 3/4 tsp. salt
- 4 firm-ripe medium nectarines
- 1/3 cup peach jam

Direction

- To make the curd: Cut the nectarine in half and pit. Continue to cut the halves into pieces, then purée in a blender until smooth. Whisk the purée, vanilla, butter, lime juice, granulated sugar and yolks in a heavy saucepan. Over moderately low heat, cook the mixture for about 7 minutes, constantly whisking, until it just reaches a boil; then remove the pan immediately from the heat. Through a sieve, strain the curd into a bowl and let it cool, cover its surface with a buttered round of wax paper. Allow the curd to be chilled for up to 2 days (at least 2 hours).
- To make the crust: Set the oven at 375°F to preheat.
- Chop butter into pieces. Pulse flour, salt and brown sugar in a food processor until well blended. Put in the butter and continue to

blend until it begins to form a dough (the mixture should hold together once squeezed between fingers). Evenly press the dough up sides and into the bottom of a 13 1/2- by 4- by a 1-inch rectangular tart pan with a removable fluted rim. In the middle of the oven, bake the crust for 20 minutes, then allow to cool in the pan on a rack. The crust can be made 2 days in advance, covered and kept at room temperature in the pan.
- Cut the nectarines in half and pit. Keep cutting the halves into 1/4-inch-thick slices. Scoop the curd into the shell, smoothen the top, then decoratively place on top with the nectarine slices. Over low heat, heat jam in a small saucepan until hot. Through a sieve, pour the jam into a bowl and press hard on the solids. Brush the fruit lightly with the glaze. Cover loosely with plastic wrap, let the tart chill until ready to serve. The tart can be prepared 1 day in advance, covered and chilled.

Nutrition Information

- Calories: 624
- Total Carbohydrate: 97 g
- Cholesterol: 276 mg
- Total Fat: 24 g
- Fiber: 4 g
- Protein: 9 g
- Sodium: 463 mg
- Saturated Fat: 13 g

210. Octopus Salad

"This salad with octopus, parsley, celery, carrot plus lemon, and olive oil dressing is famous in Puglia."
Serving: Makes 8 (as part of antipasti) servings | Prep: 30m

Ingredients

- 2 lb. frozen octopus, thawed and rinsed
- 1/3 cup chopped flat-leaf parsley
- 3 garlic cloves, finely chopped

- 1 celery rib, halved lengthwise and thinly sliced crosswise
- 1 carrot, halved lengthwise and very thinly sliced crosswise
- 1/4 cup extra-virgin olive oil
- 1/4 cup fresh lemon juice
- 1/2 tsp. fine sea salt
- 1/4 tsp. dried oregano

Direction

- Cut and remove the octopus' head; slice the tentacles in 1-inch portion, then move to a heavy medium pot. Pour in enough water to cover the octopus; let it simmer for 45 minutes to an hour without cover until tender.
- Use a colander to drain and let the octopus cool down to room temperature; move to a bowl. Mix in the rest of the ingredients, more sea salt to taste, and half tsp. pepper.
- Set aside for half an hour to let the flavors blend.
- The salad can be made a day in advance without parsley; cover and chill. Mix in parsley then serve.

Nutrition Information

- Calories: 161
- Total Carbohydrate: 4 g
- Cholesterol: 54 mg
- Total Fat: 8 g
- Fiber: 0 g
- Protein: 17 g
- Sodium: 335 mg
- Saturated Fat: 1 g

211.Orange-glazed Carrot Ribbons

Serving: Makes 4 servings

Ingredients

- 2 lbs. large long carrots, peeled
- 2 cups orange juice
- 1 1/2 tsps. (packed) dark brown sugar

- 2 tbsps. (1/4 stick) butter
- 2 tsps. honey
- 1/4 tsp. balsamic vinegar
- Chopped chives

Direction

- Down the carrot's length, run vegetable peeler, shaving long ribbons off to get 8 cups ribbons. Cook for 2 minutes in big saucepan with boiling salted water. Drain; pat dry gently. You can make it 6 hours ahead. Cover then chill. Mix sugar and orange juice in big heavy skillet till sugar dissolves on medium high heat; boil for 5 minutes till reduced to a scant 1 cup. Add butter and carrots; simmer for 4 minutes till carrots absorb most of the orange syrup. Add vinegar and honey; gently mix. Season with pepper and salt. Put carrots into serving bowl; sprinkle chives.

212. Panettone

"This puffed dome of panettone bread has something abundantly festive. A delicious yeast dough is garnished with jewel-toned glacéed citron and golden raisins in this old-fashioned Italian holiday favorite."
Serving: Makes 2 loaves | Prep: 45m

Ingredients

- 1 cup golden raisins (5 oz)
- 1/2 cup sweet Marsala
- 1/2 cup warm milk (105–115°F)
- 2/3 cup plus 2 tsps. sugar
- 4 tsps. active dry yeast (from two 1/4-oz packages)
- 3 1/4 cups unbleached all-purpose flour
- 3 large eggs at room temperature for 30 minutes
- 1 large egg yolk
- 1 tbsp. finely grated fresh lemon zest
- 1 tbsp. fresh lemon juice
- 3/4 tsp. salt

- 1 stick (1/2 cup) unsalted butter, cut into 8 pieces and softened, plus additional for buttering cans
- 1 cup diced fine-quality candied citron (not a supermarket brand; 6 oz)
- 1 large egg yolk
- 1 tbsp. water
- a stand mixer fitted with paddle attachment; 2 (10- to 15-oz) clean coffee cans (paper or plastic labels removed); parchment paper

Direction

- Preparing the dough: In a small saucepan, simmer the raisins in Marsala for two minutes. Take out from the heat and allow to sit until cooled to lukewarm.
- In the meantime, in the bowl of a mixer, mix together 2 tsps. of sugar and warm milk. Drizzle yeast on top of the mixture and let to sit for about 5 minutes until foamy. (In case the yeast does not foam, get rid of the mixture and start over with new yeast.) Pour in 1/4 cup of flour and then beat at medium speed until blended. Add the remaining 2/3 cup of sugar, whole eggs, salt, lemon juice, yolk, and zest and then beat until incorporated. Decrease the speed to low, then stir in the remaining three cups of flour, half cup at a time. Raise the speed to medium-high, and then slowly beat in the butter, several pieces at a time. Continue beating for 4 to 6 minutes until the dough forms strands from paddle to bowl and becomes shiny. (The dough should be very soft and sticky.) Then drain the raisins and get rid of Marsala. Add to the dough together with candied citron and then combine at low speed until incorporated.
- Into a bowl that is lightly oiled, scrape the dough and then use plastic wrap to cover. Allow the dough to rise in a draft-free area at warm room temperature for about 2 to 3 hours until doubled in volume.
- As the dough is rising, butter the coffee cans generously and line with parchment paper on the bottom and side of each (You can use a rectangle for side and a round for the bottom).

- Use lightly floured hands to punch the dough down and then flip out on a surface that is lightly floured. Divide the dough in half and then spoon one half into each can and gently press to get rid of air bubbles. Use a lightly buttered plastic wrap to loosely cover the cans. Allow the dough rise in a draft-free area at warm room temperature for 2 to 3 hours until the dough reaches the top of the cans. (Alternatively, allow the dough to rise in the fridge for about 8 to 12 hours and then bring to lukewarm for about 3 to 4 hours prior to baking.)
- Baking the panettone: Place the oven rack in lower third of the oven and then preheat oven to 375 degrees F.
- Beat water and yolk together. Then use the egg wash to lightly rub the top of the dough. Bake for about 35 to 40 minutes until the bottoms make a hollow sound when tapped (first remove from cans) and the tops become deep golden brown. (Thump the bottoms of the inverted cans firmly to remove.) Place the loaves onto a rack and get rid of parchment. Let to cool to lukewarm.
- Note that Panettone tightly wrapped in plastic wrap and then foil can be kept frozen for three weeks.

213. Parsnip-leek Soup With Lump Crab

"These high-in-folate parsnips are slightly nutty and sweeter."
Serving: Makes 8 servings

Ingredients

- 1 lb. parsnips, peeled and cut into medium-size pieces
- 2 tbsps. olive oil (not extra-virgin)
- 1 1/2 cups (about 1 large) chopped leeks, white and light-green parts only
- 4 sprigs fresh thyme or lemon thyme, divided
- 1/4 cup dry white wine

- 3 cups low-sodium chicken or vegetable stock, divided
- 1/4 cup heavy cream (optional)
- 1 tsp. kosher or sea salt
- Juice of 1/2 lemon
- 2 tbsps. unsalted butter
- 1/4 lb. lump crabmeat

Direction

- Set the oven to 350°F. Toss the parsnips in a medium roasting pan with oil. Cover the pan with foil and roast the parsnips for 20 minutes. Add the leaves of 2 thyme sprigs and leeks. Toss them well until coated with oil. Splash them with wine. Cover the pan with the same foil and roast for 30 minutes, stirring occasionally until the vegetables are soft, discarding any burned bits. Boil 2 cups of stock and vegetables in a large pot. Lower the heat and simmer it for 10 minutes. Allow them to cool slightly. Blend the soup in a food processor using the low setting until the soup is smooth. Pour the blended soup back into the pot. If desired, add the cream. Simmer the soup very low, and then season it with black pepper and salt. Pour in the remaining one cup of stock until the desired thickness is reached. (The crabmeat must be able to sit on the top.) Just before serving, microwave the juice, leaves of 2 thyme sprigs, and butter in a bowl for 20 seconds until the butter has melted. Toss the crabmeat into the lemon-butter mixture. Distribute the soup among the 8 demitasse cups. Place 1 1/2 tsp. of crab on top of each soup. (You can roast the leeks and parsnips 1-2 days ahead. Just cover them so that they won't dry out, and then refrigerate until ready to serve the soup.)

214. Passion-fruit Gelée With Basil Cream

"A tasty recipe."
Serving: Makes 4 servings | Prep: 45m

Ingredients

- 1 3/4 tsps. unflavored gelatin (from a 1/4-oz envelope)
- 1/4 cup water
- 2 cups passion-fruit nectar (preferably Looza brand)
- 1/2 cup loosely packed fresh basil leaves
- 1/2 cup sugar
- 1 1/2 cups well-chilled heavy cream
- 1 tsp. unflavored gelatin (from another 1/4-oz envelope)
- 2 tbsps. water
- Garnish: 4 fresh basil leaves (optional)
- 1 empty egg carton; 4 (6- to 8-oz) slender clear glasses (not stemmed)

Direction

- Gelee: Sprinkle gelatin on water in small saucepan; stand to soften for 1 minute. Cook on low heat, mixing, for 1-2 minutes till gelatin dissolves. Take off heat; whisk in 1 tbsp. passion-fruit nectar at 1 time till gelatin mixture is cool. Whisk in leftover nectar.
- Put into metal bowl; put bowl into bigger bowl half full of cold water and ice. Stand, occasionally mixing, for 15-25 minutes till gelee has raw egg white consistency.
- Put egg carton into shallow baking pan; put glasses in cartons. Tilt glasses to 45° angle. Divide gelee to glasses. Put pan with glasses in fridge carefully; chill for 1 hour till gelee is set.
- When gelee sets, make cream: Pulse pinch of salt, sugar and basil till finely chopped in a food processor; put into bowl. Add cream, mixing till sugar just dissolves.
- Sprinkle gelatin on water in small saucepan; stand to soften for 1 minute. Cook on low heat, mixing, for 1-2 minutes till gelatin dissolves.

Take off heat; whisk in 1 tbsp. basil cream at 1 time till gelatin mixture is cool. Whisk in leftover cream. Through fine-mesh sieve, put into metal bowl. Press on solids hard; discard.

- Put bowl in bigger bowl half-full of cold water and ice; stand, occasionally mixing, for 15-25 minutes till cream has raw egg white consistency.
- Fill glass slowly with basil cream, holding 1 gelee glass at 45° angle, righting glass slowly as filed. In same manner, fill leftover glasses. Chill, covered, for 1 hour till set.
- You can chill gelees with cream for 2 days.

Nutrition Information

- Calories: 588
- Total Carbohydrate: 55 g
- Cholesterol: 285 mg
- Total Fat: 38 g
- Fiber: 12 g
- Protein: 11 g
- Sodium: 133 mg
- Saturated Fat: 22 g

215. Passion-fruit Meringues

"Varying this dessert into triangular, square, or round meringue to serve different occasions. We loved the look of passion-fruit seeds and sparkling, ruby-red pomegranate seeds (along with a bit of juice) as a garnish, but you could substitute fresh raspberries or sliced strawberries."
Serving: Serves 2

Ingredients

- 2 large egg whites
- 1/8 tsp. cream of tartar
- 1/2 cup sugar
- 4 passion fruits
- 1/3 cup well-chilled heavy cream
- 1 1/2 tsps. sugar
- 1 small pomegranate (optional)

Direction

- Prepare the meringue layers: Set an oven to 200°F and start preheating, coat a baking sheet with oil. Draw 6 hearts guided by a 3- or 4-inch heart-shaped cutter on a sheet of parchment paper. Flip the parchment and place onto the baking sheet.
- Whisk the egg whites together with a pinch salt and the cream of tartar in a large bowl using an electric mixer just until soft peaks are held. Whisk in gradually the sugar just until the meringue holds glossy and stiff peaks.
- Fill the meringue into a pastry bag evenly fitted with 1/2-inch plain pipe and tip on parchment hearts (You can use a small spatula to fill meringue in the parchment hearts).
- In the middle of the oven, bake the meringue layers until they become firm and crisp, or for 45 minutes (Extend the cooking time if the weather is humid). On the baking sheet in the turned-off oven, allow to cool the meringue layers then peel the parchment off carefully. You can keep the meringue layers arranged between the sheets of the parchment paper in an airtight container placed in a dry and cool place for up to a week.
- Prepare the filling: Divide 3 passion fruits in half and spoon out the pulp (with juice and seeds) to a sieve placed over a bowl. Press hard on the seeds and strain the pulp using the sieve, then discard the seeds. Whisk the cream in a bowl until soft peaks form, then fold in sugar and passion-fruit juice just until they are blended.
- Prepare garnish: Divide the remaining passion fruits in half, then take out seeds and save. Divide pomegranate in half. Bend the back rinds and remove some of the seeds from the membranes, save seeds and some juice.
- Top each of 2 plates with a meringue heart. Put whipped cream over the hearts, add pomegranate seeds and some of the saved passion-fruit to garnish. Put 1 more meringue heart atop each. You can prepare desserts 2 hours in advance, loosely covered and cooled.

Before serving, place the desserts to room temperature.

- Add some of the saved juice, pomegranate seeds, and additional passion-fruit to the desserts to decorate.

Nutrition Information

- Calories: 395
- Total Carbohydrate: 63 g
- Cholesterol: 54 mg
- Total Fat: 15 g
- Fiber: 4 g
- Protein: 5 g
- Sodium: 81 mg
- Saturated Fat: 9 g

216. Pasta With Chicken, Curly Endive, And Blue Cheese

"A perfect pasta!"
Serving: Makes 6 servings

Ingredients

- 1 lb. gnocchi-shaped pasta (such as cavatelli) or shell pasta
- 3 tbsps. olive oil
- 1 large red onion, halved, sliced crosswise
- 4 skinless boneless chicken breast halves, cut crosswise into 1/3- to 1/2-inch-thick slices
- 4 tsps. chopped fresh rosemary
- 1 head of curly endive, trimmed, very coarsely chopped (about 12 cups)
- 1 1/2 cups crumbled blue cheese (such as Maytag; about 9 oz.)
- 3/4 cup coarsely chopped toasted walnuts (optional)

Direction

- In a big pot with boiling salted water, cook pasta until tender yet still firm to the bite, mixing occasionally.
- At the same time, in a heavy, deep and big skillet on medium-high heat, heat oil. Put in

onion and sauté 4 minutes until lightly softened. Sprinkle chicken with pepper and salt; put into the skillet together with rosemary; sauté 4 minutes till chicken is mostly cooked through. Put in endive; toss 1 minutes until lightly wilted and chicken has been cooked through.

- Drain pasta, saving 3/4 cup of pasta cooking liquid. Bring pasta back to pot. Put in blue cheese, chicken mixture, enough pasta cooking liquid to moisten; toss to combine. Season with pepper and salt. Remove to a big bowl; if wanted, sprinkle with nuts.

217. Peach-raspberry Milk Shake

Serving: Makes about 4 cups, serving 2 to 4

Ingredients

- 1 cup picked-over raspberries plus additional for garnish
- 1/2 cup milk
- 1 pint vanilla ice cream, softened slightly
- 1 lb. (about 6 small) peaches, peeled, pitted, and chopped
- 2 tbsps. sugar, or to taste

Direction

- Puree milk and 1 cup raspberries in a blender; strain puree through coarse sieve into glass measure. Press on solids hard. Put into cleaned blender. Add sugar, peaches and ice cream; blend till thick yet smooth. Garnish with extra raspberries; serve.

Nutrition Information

- Calories: 448
- Total Carbohydrate: 68 g
- Cholesterol: 64 mg
- Total Fat: 17 g
- Fiber: 4 g
- Protein: 9 g
- Sodium: 132 mg
- Saturated Fat: 10 g

218. Peanut Butter Bread Pudding

Serving: Makes 4 large or 16 small servings

Ingredients

- 2 Pullman loaves or other sweet (not sour) bread, cut into 1-inch-wide slices (remove crust if desired)
- 4 1/2 cups whole milk
- 4 1/2 cups heavy cream
- 2 cups granulated white sugar
- 2 vanilla beans, split and scraped
- 15 egg yolks
- 4 cups creamy peanut butter
- 2 cups honey
- 3 cups high-quality strawberry jam

Direction

- Boil vanilla beans, sugar and milk in heavy pot; immediately turn off. Steep vanilla beans with milk for 30 minutes. Whisk yolks till smooth; tempter hot-milk mixture into them slowly, continuously mixing. Put cream into mix immediately; put in ice bath till cool.
- Mix honey and peanut butter till homogenous with standing mixer or by hand. Keep 1/2 cup of mix to heat and serve as sauce with pudding.
- Assembling pudding: Put sliced bread in 8x10-in. metal/Pyrex pan lined with parchment paper piece to cover pan's bottom. Spread 1/2 peanut butter mixture on top then 1 cup strawberry jam. Put extra bread layer over jam; repeat layers. Finish with bread's final layer; make sure pudding is completely together by pressing down firmly on bread's top. Put 8 cups custard as follows over pudding: use wooden skewer/knife to poke holes through pudding's top to make sure entire pudding gets saturated. Put 2 cups custard over; soak in for 10 minutes. Pour 2 cups more; soak in. Repeat process till you use all the custard. Sit in the fridge for several hours – overnight; this creates a uniform pudding, or in other words, all the pieces saturated equally.
- Baking pudding: Preheat an oven to 350°F when ready to bake; use foil piece that's lightly buttered to cover pudding. Put pudding in water bath so water reaches halfway up pan's sides. Bake for an hour; check to ensure pudding is set fully. A pressed finger in center of pudding should leave dry without any custard on it. Bake for 10 minutes longer then check again if not set. Remove foil; keep baking for 20 minutes longer so top has crunchy and lovely brown crust.
- Take out of oven and water bath; refrigerate till cool. Run sharp knife around pudding edges; put pan on top. Invert it quickly; cut to 8 slices. Invert them so crust is on the top.
- Serving pudding: Preheat an oven to 400°F before serving; put pudding pieces in oven for 5 minutes to warm. Directly put warmed pudding on plate drizzled with warmed strawberry jam and warm peanut butter mixture. Immediately serve; you can serve with just a dash of confectioners' sugar or dollop of whipped cream.

Nutrition Information

- Calories: 4886
- Total Carbohydrate: 579 g
- Cholesterol: 942 mg
- Total Fat: 260 g
- Fiber: 24 g
- Protein: 101 g
- Sodium: 1348 mg
- Saturated Fat: 100 g

219. Peanut Butter Sandwich Cookies, Aka "the Nora Ephron"

"Plan accordingly; you need to chill shaped cookie dough. Use same/similar brands of peanut butter like Skippy or Adams. Moist brown sugar from resealable plastic bags are better than the ones from boxes. Cut amount in half if using table salt instead of kosher salt."
Serving: Makes about 24 sandwich cookies (3 inches in diameter)

Ingredients

- electric Mixer, 1-oz. ice Cream scoop (optional but recommended for the most uniform cookie sandwiches)
- 1 1/2 cups (14 oz./400 grams) creamy peanut butter, such as Skippy
- 6 tbsps. (3/4 stick/3 oz./168 grams) unsalted butter, softened
- 2 tbsps. powdered sugar
- 2 tbsps. honey
- 1 tsp. kosher salt
- 1 1/2 cups (8 oz./227 grams) all purpose flour
- 1 tsp. baking soda
- 1/2 tsp. baking powder
- 1 2/3 cups (5 1/4 oz./99 grams) rolled oats, such as Quaker old fashioned
- 1/2 tsp. kosher salt
- 1 cup plus 2 tbsps. (2 sticks plus 2 tbsps./11 1/4 oz./320 grams) unsalted butter, softened
- 1/3 cup (3 1/2 oz./125 grams) crunchy natural peanut butter, such as Adams, well mixed
- 3/4 cup (5 1/4 oz./150 grams) granulated sugar
- 2/3 cup (5 1/4 oz./150 grams) packed brown sugar
- 2 large eggs at room temperature
- 1 tsp. pure vanilla extract

Direction

- Peanut butter filling: Use a whisk to mix all filling ingredients in bowl. Cover; chill till filling cookies.

- Peanut butter cookies: Sift together baking powder, baking soda and flour in a bowl; mix in salt and oats. Put aside dry ingredients.
- Mix cream, sugars, chunky peanut butter and butter on medium high speed for 3 minutes till pale and very fluffy, scraping mixing bowl down as needed, in an electric mixer's bowl with paddle attachment.
- Put mixer on medium low. One by one, add eggs; beat to incorporate each egg, scraping bowl down as needed; beat in vanilla extract. In 3-4 additions, add dry ingredients at low speed; mix just till combined. Don't over mix. Take bowl from mixer; use rubber spatula to scrape down bowl, going all the way to bottom of bowl to stir in dry ingredients well.
- Portion all cookies in 1-oz. scoops using an ice cream scoop or use 1 heaping tbsp. per cookie; put scoops onto parchment lined baking sheet to get 48 cookies. For chilling step, put all cookies close together; space to bake later. Chill scooped cookies for 2 hours or more.
- Bake cookies: Preheat oven to 375°F. Put 8 cookies on every parchment-lined baking sheet, evenly spaced apart and staggered. Don't flatten cookies; they'll flatten while baking. Put baking sheet in a separate baking sheet to double the pan; put into oven. Bake for 12 minutes, rotating pan halfway through cooking time, till evenly golden. Switch between racks if there's 2 double panned pans in oven at same time. Remove pan from oven; cool for 10 minutes on wire rack. Use a metal spatula to remove cookies; fully cool before filling cookies.
- Cookie sandwich: Flip 1 cookie flat side up; spread little less than 2 tsp. filling. You may slightly underfill to portion filling/underfill 1 tbsp. if you have 1-oz. scoop. Put another cookie over, flat side down, gently pressing; repeat till you make all cookies into sandwiches.

Nutrition Information

- Calories: 344
- Total Carbohydrate: 33 g

- Cholesterol: 46 mg
- Total Fat: 22 g
- Fiber: 2 g
- Protein: 7 g
- Sodium: 165 mg
- Saturated Fat: 9 g

220. Pear And Granola Whole Wheat Muffins

"Nourishing muffins, great for quick breakfast or snack."
Serving: Makes 10

Ingredients

- 3/4 cup pear nectar
- 2 large eggs
- 2 tbsps. vegetable oil
- 1 tbsp. fresh lemon juice
- 1 tsp. grated lemon peel
- 1 cup whole wheat flour
- 1 cup all purpose flour
- 2/3 cup (packed) golden brown sugar
- 1/2 cup low-fat granola
- 1 tbsp. baking powder
- 1/2 tsp. ground nutmeg
- 1/2 tsp. salt
- 1 1/4 cups finely chopped unpeeled pear (about 1 medium)

Direction

- Preheat the oven to 350°F. Line foil muffin papers on 10 muffin cups, 1/3-cup in size. In a big bowl, mix the initial 5 ingredients to incorporate. In medium size bowl, mix sugar and both flours till sugar lumps are gone. Stir in salt, nutmeg, baking powder and granola. Put in the pear; toss till coated. Mix to egg mixture the flour mixture barely to incorporate, batter will become thick. Distribute between prepped muffin cups, piling in the middle.
- Let muffins bake for 20 minutes till golden brown in color and inserted tester in the

middle gets out clean. Turn the muffins onto rack and cool down.

Nutrition Information

- Calories: 223
- Total Carbohydrate: 43 g
- Cholesterol: 37 mg
- Total Fat: 5 g
- Fiber: 3 g
- Protein: 5 g
- Sodium: 224 mg
- Saturated Fat: 1 g

221. Pecan And Goat Cheese Marbles

"So delicious!"
Serving: Makes 50 to 60 hors d'oeuvres | Prep: 40m

Ingredients

- 1 cup pecans (1/4 lb.)
- 1 tbsp. unsalted butter, melted
- 1/2 tsp. sugar
- 1 (11-oz.) log soft goat cheese
- 1 tsp. minced rosemary
- 1 tsp. coriander seeds, crushed with side of a large knife, then chopped
- About 50 to 60 large flat-leaf parsley leaves

Direction

- Preheat an oven with rack on upper third to 400°F.
- Toss 1/2 tsp. salt, sugar and butter with pecans; toast in 4-sided sheet pan for 8-10 minutes till shade darker and fragrant. Put onto plate; fully cool.
- Pulse pecans till finely chopped in a food processor; put into shallow wide bowl.
- Mix 1/2 tsp. pepper, coriander, rosemary and goat cheese till well combined. Shape tsps. of cheese mixture to marbles between palms; roll in pecans till coated. Briefly roll between your palms; put onto plate.

- Under each cheese marble, put a parsley leaf; use a wooden pick to spear together.
- You can make and coat cheese marbles with pecans 1 day ahead, chilled.
- You can spear cheese marbles 1 day ahead with parsley, chilled.

Nutrition Information

- Calories: 32
- Total Carbohydrate: 0 g
- Cholesterol: 3 mg
- Total Fat: 3 g
- Fiber: 0 g
- Protein: 1 g
- Sodium: 27 mg
- Saturated Fat: 1 g

222. Penne With Hazelnut Gremolata And Roasted Broccolini

"Such a tasty recipe."
Serving: Makes 2 servings

Ingredients

- 1/2 lb. broccolini, thick stalks cut in half lengthwise
- 3 tbsps. olive oil, divided
- 2 tbsps. hazelnuts, toasted, finely chopped
- 2 tbsps. finely chopped fresh Italian parsley
- 2 tsps. finely grated lemon peel
- 1 garlic clove, pressed
- 1/4 lb. penne (about scant 1 1/4 cups)

Direction

- Preheat an oven to 400°F. On big rimmed baking sheet, put broccolini. Drizzle 2 tbsp. oil; sprinkle pepper and salt. Toss; spread in an even layer.
- Roast broccolini, occasionally tossing, for 18 minutes till golden brown around edges and tender; cool. Coarsely chop. You can make it 4 hours ahead; stand in room temperature.

- In small bowl, mix garlic, finely grated lemon peel, chopped parsley and hazelnuts. You can make gremolata 2 hours ahead. Cover; refrigerate.
- Cook pasta, occasionally mixing, till tender yet firm to chew in a big saucepan with boiling salted water. Drain; put into saucepan. Add broccolini; toss to rewarm on medium heat. Put into medium bowl. Add leftover 1 tbsp. oil and gremolata; toss to evenly distribute. Season with pepper and salt to taste.

Nutrition Information

- Calories: 478
- Total Carbohydrate: 52 g
- Total Fat: 26 g
- Fiber: 6 g
- Protein: 12 g
- Sodium: 44 mg
- Saturated Fat: 3 g

223. Petits Pains Au Chocolat

"An easy to make tasty small pastries."
Serving: Makes 24

Ingredients

- 2 sheets frozen puff pastry (one 17.3-oz. package), thawed, each sheet cut into 12 squares
- 1 large egg beaten to blend with 1 tbsp. water (for glaze)
- 4 3.5-oz. bars imported bittersweet or milk chocolate, each cut into six 2x3/4-inch pieces
- Sugar

Direction

- To prepare: Line parchment paper on the baking tray. Use the egg glaze to brush the top of each puff pastry square. On the edge of each pastry square, put 1 chocolate piece, then roll up the dough tightly to enclose the chocolate. Redo the process with the leftover chocolate and pastry. On a baking tray, put the pastry rolls, seam side down. Do a head: This can be prepared 1 day in advance. Use plastic wrap to cover the pastries and let it chill in the fridge. Put cover and chill the leftover egg glaze in the fridge.

- Set an oven to preheat to 400 degrees F. Brush the leftover glaze on tops of the pastry rolls, then lightly sprinkle with sugar. Let it bake for about 15 minutes, until the pastries turn golden brown in color. Serve it at room temperature or warm.

Nutrition Information

- Calories: 206
- Total Carbohydrate: 20 g
- Cholesterol: 12 mg
- Total Fat: 13 g
- Fiber: 1 g
- Protein: 3 g
- Sodium: 67 mg
- Saturated Fat: 5 g

224. Pineapple, Arugula, Macadamia Nut

"This blend is super-perfect and green, invigorating and tasty. The alkalinizing crisp pineapple matches perfectly with the flavor of the arugula/rocket. Both macadamia nuts and chia seeds are nutritious, yummy and they are good for your health."
Serving: Makes about 3 cups/720 ml; serves 2

Ingredients

- 3/4 cup/180 ml filtered water
- 1 cup/240 ml fresh-pressed apple juice
- 1 1/2 cups/255 g chopped fresh pineapple, chilled
- 3/4 cup/20 g firmly packed arugula/rocket, tough stems removed
- 3/4 cup/20 g firmly packed fresh mint leaves
- 2 tbsp roughly chopped raw macadamia nuts
- 2 tbsp chia seeds or flax seeds
- Pinch of sea salt

Direction

- In a blender, mix the salt, chia seeds, macadamia nuts, mint, arugula/rocket, pineapple, apple juice and water together. Process them until smooth.

Nutrition Information

- Calories: 247
- Total Carbohydrate: 38 g
- Total Fat: 10 g
- Fiber: 8 g
- Protein: 4 g
- Sodium: 75 mg
- Saturated Fat: 1 g

225. Pineapple-glazed Chicken With Jalapeño Salsa

"Bright and spicy."
Serving: Makes 4 servings

Ingredients

- 1/4 cup pineapple juice
- 2 tbsps. (packed) brown sugar
- 1 tbsp. yellow mustard
- 3/4 cup 1/4-inch cubes fresh pineapple
- 3 tbsps. finely diced red bell pepper
- 3 tbsps. chopped fresh cilantro
- 1 1/2 tbsps. finely chopped red onion
- 1 1/2 tbsps. canned sliced jalapeño chiles, drained, coarsely chopped
- 4 boneless chicken breast halves with skin (1 3/4 lbs. total)

Direction

- Preheat an oven to 400°F. Boil mustard, brown sugar and pineapple juice in small saucepan, mixing to dissolve sugar; boil for 1 minute till glaze slightly thickens. Season with pepper and salt.
- In medium bowl, mix chiles, onion, cilantro, red pepper and pineapple; season with pepper and salt.

- Line foil on baking sheet. Put chicken on sheet; brush glaze. Bake for 15 minutes. Brush glaze; broil, closely watching to avoid burning, for 5 minutes till golden and cooked through. Rest for 5 minutes.
- Put salsa on chicken; serve.

226. Pink Cuts

"Try this eastern European inspired tea cakes and reminisce your childhood with every bite!"
Serving: Makes 20 small tea cakes | Prep: 1.5h

Ingredients

- Butter for greasing baking pan
- 1 cup minus 1/2 tbsp. cake flour (not self-rising)
- 1/4 tsp. salt
- 5 large eggs, separated
- 3/4 cup granulated sugar
- 1 tsp. pure vanilla extract
- Confectioners sugar for dusting
- 1 tbsp. cornstarch
- 1/2 cup whole milk
- 1 large egg yolk
- 3/4 stick (6 tbsps.) unsalted butter, softened
- 1/4 cup confectioners sugar
- 1 tsp. pure vanilla extract
- 1 rounded tbsp. red-currant jelly
- 4 to 5 tbsps. hot water
- 2 cups confectioners sugar, sifted
- 1/2 tsp. kirsch (optional)
- parchment paper; a clean kitchen towel (not terry cloth); an offset spatula

Direction

- To make the cake: Heat oven to 352 degrees F and place rack at the middle. Prepare a 17x12x1 inch baking pan by coating sides with butter and lining bottom using parchment paper. In a bowl, sieve salt, and flour.
- Set electric mixer into high speed and whisk egg whites into a big bowl until soft peaks form. Add in 1 tbsp. of granulated sugar at a time, whisking until mixture form glossy, stiff peaks for 3-4 minutes using a stand mixer and 4-6 minutes in a handheld mixer. Stir in vanilla and yolks; whisk the mixture for about 2 minutes until very thick.
- Sieve flour mixture in 3 batches over the egg mixture, gently but thoroughly folding in each batch. Transfer batter in the lined baking pan; spread equally.
- For 5-18 minutes, bake until the top of the cake is pale golden in color and when lightly pressed, it bounces back. Let cake in pan cool on the rack for 5 minutes. To loosen the cake, run the small knife around the edges. Dust lightly with confectioners; sugar the top of the cake. Turn over the pan into a kitchen towel. Take out the pan and peel off the parchment paper. For about 15 minutes, allow the cake to cool completely.
- While the cake is baking and cooling, start making the pastry cream. In a 1-quart heavy saucepan, beat milk and cornstarch together until turns smooth. On moderate heat, allow the mixture to boil, constantly stir, then boil, constantly stir for 1 minute. In a small bowl, gradually beat in the milk mixture into the egg yolk. Pour mixture into the saucepan. On moderate heat, cook the mixture, stirring constantly for 1 minute. Pour into a metal bowl. Place the metal bowl with mixture over a bigger bowl of ice and cold water. Let the pastry cream cool, mixing occasionally, to room temperature for 6-8 minutes.
- Set at medium speed the cleaned beaters and whisk vanilla, butter, and a 1/4 cup of confectioner sugar in a medium bowl until the mixture turns fluffy and pale for about 2 minutes. Beat in 1 tbsp. at a time the cooled pastry cream into the butter mixture until smooth.
- Cake assembling: Cut cake into lengthwise half. Place the half into the cutting board and add all the pastry cream; spread. Place remaining half on top.

Nutrition Information

- Calories: 143

- Total Carbohydrate: 21 g
- Cholesterol: 67 mg
- Total Fat: 6 g
- Fiber: 0 g
- Protein: 2 g
- Sodium: 51 mg
- Saturated Fat: 3 g

227. Pinto-bean Mole Chili

"A rich, meatless chili."
Serving: Makes 6 servings | Prep: 30m

Ingredients

- 2 medium dried ancho chiles, wiped clean
- 1 dried chipotle chile, wiped clean
- 1 tsp. cumin seeds, toasted and cooled
- 1 tsp. dried oregano, crumbled
- Rounded 1/8 tsp. cinnamon
- 2 medium onions, chopped
- 2 tbsps. olive oil
- 4 garlic cloves, finely chopped
- 3 medium zucchini and/or yellow squash, quartered lengthwise and cut into 1/2-inch pieces
- 3/4 lb. kale, stems and center ribs discarded and leaves coarsely chopped
- 1 tsp. grated orange zest
- 1/8 tsp. sugar
- 1 oz. unsweetened chocolate, finely chopped (3 tbsps.)
- 1 (14 1/2-oz.) can whole tomatoes in juice, drained, reserving juice, and chopped
- 1 1/4 cups water
- 3 (15-oz.) cans pinto beans, drained and rinsed
- Equipment: an electric coffee/spice grinder
- Accompaniments: rice; chopped cilantro; chopped scallions; sour cream

Direction

- Lengthwise slit chiles. Stem; seed. Heat a heavy dry medium skillet till hot on medium heat; toast chiles, opened flat, for 30 seconds till slightly changed in color and pliable, pressing with tongs, turning. Tear to small pieces.
- Pulse chiles and cumin seeds till finely ground in grinder; put into a small bowl. Mix in 1 1/2 tsp. salt, cinnamon and oregano.
- Cook onions in oil till soft in a big heavy pot on medium high heat, occasionally mixing. Add garlic; cook for 1 minute, mixing. Add chile mixture; cook for 30 seconds, mixing. Mix in kale and zucchini; cook for 5 minutes, covered. Add water, tomatoes with juice, chocolate, sugar and zest; simmer for 15 minutes till veggies are tender, occasionally mixing, uncovered.
- Mix in beans; simmer for 5 minutes. Use salt to season.
- If made 1-2 days ahead, it improves in flavor; chill till cool, uncovered, then cover.

228. Piquant Bell Peppers

"Quick and tasty."
Serving: Makes 8 servings | Prep: 20m

Ingredients

- 3 lbs. (about 7) bell peppers, a combination of red, yellow and/or orange
- 1/4 cup olive oil
- 1/2 cup red wine vinegar
- 2 tbsps. sugar

Direction

- Lengthwise cut peppers to 1/2-in. thick strips.
- Heat olive oil on medium heat in big heavy skillet. Add 1/2 tsp. salt and peppers; cook, mixing, for 10-15 minutes till wilted.
- Add 1/2 tsp. salt, sugar and vinegar; cook, occasionally mixing, for 10-15 minutes till most liquid evaporates leaving emulsified sauce and peppers are tender. Serve at room temperature/warm.
- You can make peppers 2 days ahead, kept chilled, covered; heat, covered, in 350°F oven before serving for 20 minutes or bring to room temperature.

Nutrition Information

- Calories: 155
- Total Carbohydrate: 23 g
- Total Fat: 7 g
- Fiber: 4 g
- Protein: 2 g
- Sodium: 1 mg
- Saturated Fat: 1 g

229. Pistachio Shortbread

"A yummy nutty shortbread recipe."
Serving: Makes 32 cookies

Ingredients

- 1 cup unsalted, shelled raw pistachios (about 4 1/2 oz.)
- 1 1/4 cups all-purpose flour
- 3/4 cup sugar
- 1/2 cup (1 stick) chilled unsalted butter, cut into 1/2" pieces
- 1 tsp. kosher salt
- 1/4 tsps. vanilla extract

Direction

- Pulse pistachios for 30 seconds till finely ground yet not paste in a food processor. Add vanilla, salt, butter, sugar and flour; pulse till it has a cornmeal-consistency. Drizzle in 2 tbsp. ice water as machine runs; don't overprocess, crumbly dough should form.
- Put dough on parchment paper sheet; pat to rectangle. Put another parchment sheet over; roll to 12x8-in. rectangle. Put dough on baking sheet (still in parchment paper); chill for 1 hour till firm.
- Put racks in lower and upper oven thirds; preheat it to 350°F. Remove top parchment paper sheet from dough; discard. Lengthwise cut dough to 8 even strips; crosswise cut each strip to quarters, making 32 rectangles. Put rectangles onto 2 parchment-lined baking sheets, 1-in. apart.

- Bake shortbread for 18-20 minutes, rotating sheets halfway through, till golden brown. Put onto wire racks; cool.
- You can make shortbread 5 days ahead; keep at room temperature, airtight.

Nutrition Information

- Calories: 84
- Total Carbohydrate: 10 g
- Cholesterol: 8 mg
- Total Fat: 5 g
- Fiber: 1 g
- Protein: 1 g
- Sodium: 40 mg
- Saturated Fat: 2 g

230. Pizza Margherita

"A good pizza shouldn't be overwhelmed with too much toppings. Even basic dough is enough to make a tasty grilled bread for the base. Form it like individual pizza then grill for two minutes per side on hot coals. After flipping, add olive oil, rosemary, oregano, thyme, and basil."
Serving: Makes 4 individual pizzas or 1 large pizza

Ingredients

- 3/4 cup warm (105-115°F) water
- 2 1/2 tsp (1 package) dry yeast
- 1 tsp honey
- 1 1/3 cups bread flour
- 1 cup semolina flour
- 1/4 tsp salt
- Vegetable oil for coating
- Cornmeal for sprinkling (optional)
- 1 Tbsp extra-virgin olive oil
- 1 Tbsp chopped fresh basil
- 1 tsp chopped fresh oregano
- 1 clove garlic, minced
- Freshly ground pepper
- 1 cup tomato purée
- 4 plum (Roma) tomatoes, sliced
- 4 1/4 oz part-skim mozzarella, thinly sliced
- 1/4 cup grated Parmesan

Direction

- In a big bowl, mix honey, yeast and water. Mix in enough bread flour until you have a batter with buttermilk consistency; cover. Store in a warm area for an hour until the top is puffy.
- Add salt, semolina flour, and the remaining bread flour. Knead by hand for 10mins or on medium speed in a stand mixer fitted with dough hook or by hand, 4 minutes with the mixer until the dough is elastic, springy, and smooth. Lightly massage oil all over the dough then put in a clean bowl; use cloth to cover. Store at room temperature for 1 1/2hrs until it rises and doubles in size.
- Press the dough down, sinking your fist into it until it deflates; leave it whole to make a big pizza or split equally into four parts for individual pizzas. Shape the dough into smooth ball(s) then cover; let it rise again for 45-60mins until it doubles in size.
- Preheat an oven to 450 degrees F. Grease a 16-in pizza pan or a big baking sheet lightly using vegetable oil or spread with cornmeal.
- Roll and stretch out the ball of doughs on a lightly floured surface evenly until a quarter inch thick. Stretch and spin simultaneously the dough to help in relax properly so it wouldn't spring back as you stretch it. You can do this on a flat surface or by tossing and spinning it in the air and catching it using the back of your hands. Avoid from making very thin patches or tearing the dough. Move the dough round to the prepared pan.
- To make the topping, combine pepper, garlic, oregano, basil and olive oil together to taste; evenly spread the mixture over the pizza dough. Evenly spread tomato purée then add mozzarella and sliced tomatoes on top; sprinkle with parmesan on top.
- Bake the individual pizza for 10-12mins or one large pizza for 20-30mins until the toppings are very hot and the dough is golden brown. Slice into wedges then serve right away or cool for 5-10mins then serve warm.

Nutrition Information

- Calories: 538
- Total Carbohydrate: 76 g
- Cholesterol: 24 mg
- Total Fat: 16 g
- Fiber: 6 g
- Protein: 23 g
- Sodium: 454 mg
- Saturated Fat: 5 g

231. Plum And Berry Summer Puddings

"A colorful treat; make this 1-2 days before serving."
Serving: Makes 6 servings

Ingredients

- 12 1/2-inch-thick egg bread slices
- 12 oz. red or purple plums (about 3 large), halved, pitted, each half cut into 6 slices
- 3/4 cup sugar
- 2 1/2-pint baskets raspberries (about 2 2/3 cups)
- 1 1/2-pint basket blueberries (about 1 1/3 cups)
- 1 tsp. fresh lemon juice
- Sweetened whipped cream

Direction

- Line plastic wrap on 6 3/4-cup custard cups; on all sides, leave 3-in. overhang. Cut 1 round out from each bread slice using 3-in. cookie cutter; put aside.
- Mix sugar and plums in medium heavy saucepan on medium low heat till syrup forms and sugar dissolves; simmer, mixing often, for 5 minutes till plums are translucent and tender. Add all berries; simmer, mixing occasionally, for 5 minutes till berries release the juices. Mix in lemon juice; cool it to room temperature.
- On bottom of every custard cup, put 2 cooked plum slices; put 2 tbsp. fruit mixture with

juices over plums then a bread round. Put leftover fruit mixture with juices, evenly dividing, over each. Put 1 bread round on each; to compact, press into fruit mixture. Use plastic-wrap overhang to tightly cover puddings. Put custard cups onto baking sheet and put another baking sheet over cups; to weight down, put a few food cans onto top baking sheet. Chill overnight. You can make it 2 days ahead, kept chilled.

- From tops of the custard cups, unfold plastic wrap; invert puddings onto the plates. Remove plastic wrap. Put whipped cream alongside; serve.

232. Plum-glazed Stuffed Shiitake Mushrooms

"You can use small portobellos for shiitakes."
Serving: Makes 40

Ingredients

- 40 small shiitake mushrooms (about 1 1/4 lbs.), stemmed
- 12 oz. bulk pork sausage
- 1/2 cup Chinese plum sauce
- 1 tbsp. oriental sesame oil
- 1/2 cup chopped fresh chives

Direction

- Put shiitake mushrooms on big rimmed baking sheet, stem side up; mound 1/2 tbsp. pork sausage on each. Mix plum sauce till melted in small heavy saucepan on medium heat; whisk in oil. Brush all plum sauce mixture on mushrooms. You can make it 1 day ahead, refrigerated, covered.
- Preheat an oven to 400°F. Bake mushrooms for 15 minutes till sausage cooks through. Put onto big platter; sprinkle chives.

Nutrition Information

- Calories: 39
- Total Carbohydrate: 3 g
- Cholesterol: 6 mg
- Total Fat: 3 g
- Fiber: 0 g
- Protein: 2 g
- Sodium: 85 mg
- Saturated Fat: 1 g

233. Plums With Prosciutto, Goat Cheese, Baby Arugula, And Champagne Vinegar

"A simple and wonderful recipe."
Serving: Makes 6 servings

Ingredients

- 8 oz. soft fresh goat cheese
- 3/4 tsp. ground black pepper
- 6 thin prosciutto slices
- 2 tsps. Champagne vinegar or white wine vinegar
- 1 tsp. minced shallot
- 1/2 tsp. Dijon mustard
- 1/2 tsp. honey
- 2 tbsps. extra-virgin olive oil
- 4 oz. baby arugula
- 6 sweet firm red plums (such as Burgundies or Satsumas), halved, pitted, cut into 1/4-inch-thick wedges
- 1 tsp. thinly sliced fresh mint (for garnish)

Direction

- Roll cheese to 10-in. long 1-in. thick log; sprinkle 3/4 tsp. pepper. Crosswise cut log to 6 even pieces; use prosciutto to wrap each piece.
- Whisk honey, mustard, shallot and vinegar in medium bowl; whisk oil in slowly. Season with pepper and salt. Add arugula; toss till coated. Divide prosciutto-wrapped goat cheese pieces and plums to plates; put dressed arugula next to it. Use mint to garnish.

Nutrition Information

- Calories: 193
- Total Carbohydrate: 9 g
- Cholesterol: 23 mg
- Total Fat: 13 g
- Fiber: 1 g
- Protein: 10 g
- Sodium: 386 mg
- Saturated Fat: 6 g

234. Poblano Corn Chowder With Shrimp

Serving: Makes 12 first-course or 6 main-course servings

Ingredients

- 4 tbsps. (1/2 stick) butter, room temperature
- 2 tbsps. all purpose flour
- 1 medium onion, coarsely chopped
- 3 celery stalks, coarsely chopped
- 2 large poblano chilies,* seeded, chopped
- 2 14 3/4- to 15-oz. cans cream-style corn
- 1 16-oz. package frozen corn kernels, thawed
- 2 14-oz. cans low-salt chicken broth
- 1 cup whipping cream
- 2 tsps. sugar
- 1/2 tsp. cayenne pepper
- 1 lb. uncooked shrimp, peeled, deveined, coarsely chopped
- 6 tbsps. chopped fresh cilantro

Direction

- Mix flour and 2 tbsp. butter to blend in small bowl; put aside.
- Chop celery and onion finely in processor. Melt 2 tbsp. butter on medium high heat in big pot. Add chilies and onion-celery mixture; sauté for 6 minutes till soft. Add creamed corn with next 5 ingredients; boil. Lower heat. Whisk in the flour-butter mixture; simmer to blend flavors for 15 minutes. Add 4 tbsp. cilantro and shrimp; simmer for 5 minutes till

shrimp cook through. Season with pepper and salt.
- Put chowder into bowls; sprinkle leftover 2 tbsp. cilantro.

Nutrition Information

- Calories: 248
- Total Carbohydrate: 28 g
- Cholesterol: 80 mg
- Total Fat: 12 g
- Fiber: 2 g
- Protein: 10 g
- Sodium: 436 mg
- Saturated Fat: 7 g

235. Poblano Potato Gratin

"Potato gratin made with forest-green poblano that gives it a fruity and mild heat."
Serving: Makes 8 (side dish) servings | Prep: 45m

Ingredients

- 1 1/2 lbs. fresh poblano chiles (about 5)
- 1 lb. onions, cut lengthwise into 1/4-inch strips
- 1 tbsp. vegetable oil
- 3 lbs. large Yukon Gold potatoes
- 1 1/2 cups heavy cream
- 3/4 cup whole milk
- Equipment: an adjustable-blade slicer

Direction

- Preparing to roast the chiles and make the rajas: On the racks of the gas burners, roast the chiles on their sides on high for about 10 minutes, flipping it using tongs, until the skins become blackened all over. Move to a bowl right away and allow it to stand for 10 minutes, tightly covered.
- Once the chiles are cool enough to touch, rub or peel off the skin. Slit the chiles lengthwise, take off the seed and stem, then devein. Slice it lengthwise into thin strips.

- In a 12-inch heavy frying pan, cook the onions with 1 tsp salt in oil on medium-low heat for about 8 minutes, stirring from time to time, until it turns golden. Mix in chiles and take out the rajas from heat. For the topping, set aside 1/2 cup of the rajas.
- Making the gratin: Set an oven to preheat to 400 degrees F and place the rack in the middle. Butter a 3-qt. shallow baking dish liberally.
- Take off the skin from the potatoes and use a slicer to slice it crosswise into 1/16-inch thick pieces. Move to a small heavy pot. Add 1 tsp salt, milk and cream, then bring just a boil on medium heat, stirring from time to time (the liquid will get thick). Mix in rajas, then evenly pour the mixture into the baking dish. Sprinkle the top with the reserved 1/2 cup of rajas.
- Let it bake for 45 minutes to 1 hour, until the potatoes become tender. Allow it to stand for 15 minutes prior to serving.
- Cook's notes: The chiles can be roasted, turning, for 8-10 minutes by broiling on a broiler pan and place it 2 inches from the heat source.
- The rajas can be prepared 3 days in advance and chilled in the fridge.
- The gratin can be prepared 1 day in advance and chilled in the fridge. Bring to room temperature and rewarm for about 30 minutes in a 350 degrees F oven with cover.

Nutrition Information

- Calories: 371
- Total Carbohydrate: 45 g
- Cholesterol: 63 mg
- Total Fat: 20 g
- Fiber: 6 g
- Protein: 7 g
- Sodium: 47 mg
- Saturated Fat: 11 g

236. Polenta Stack With Navy Bean Salad

"Healthy and tasty."
Serving: Makes 4 servings

Ingredients

- Vegetable oil cooking spray
- 2 cans (15.5 oz. each) navy beans, rinsed and drained
- 1 lb. plum tomatoes, chopped
- 1/2 cup basil, chopped, plus 15 leaves for garnish
- 10 oz. crumbled feta, divided
- 1 tube (18 oz.) prepared polenta, cut into 16 slices
- 1 lb. zucchini, cut into 1/4-inch slices
- 2 bottles (7 oz. each) roasted red peppers, drained

Direction

- Heat a grill. Fold 4 18-in. long foil pieces in half; unfold. Coat inside using cooking spray. Mix 5-oz. feta, chopped basil, tomatoes and beans in a bowl. Put 1/4 bean mixture in middle of 1 half of every foil piece. One packet at 1 time, put 4 polenta slices in overlapping circle on beans. Top with 1/4 leftover 5-oz. feta, 1/4 red peppers and 1/4 zucchini slices. To close, fold foil; to seal packets, crimp edges. Put on grill and close lid; cook for 10 minutes till packets are fully puffed. Cut foil carefully to open; garnish with basil leaves.

237. Polenta With Mushroom Ragout

"The polenta is served on soup plates and eaten using a spoon. Top this polenta with a mushroom stew that is incredibly delicious when combined with some varieties."
Serving: 4 as a first course or side dish, 2 as a main course

Ingredients

- 2 cups water

- 1/2 cup yellow cornmeal
- 1/4 tsp. salt
- 1/4 tsp. freshly ground black pepper
- 1 tbsp. unsalted butter
- 1 tbsp. peanut oil
- 1 small onion, chopped (1/2 cup)
- 5 oz. mushrooms (cultivated, wild, or a combination), trimmed, cleaned, and cut into 1/2-inch pieces (2 cups)
- 3 garlic cloves, crushed and finely chopped (2 tsps.)
- 4 plum tomatoes, halved, seeded, and cut into 1/2-inch pieces (1 1/4 cups)
- 2 small ears corn, husked and kernels cut off (1 cup)
- 1/2 cup homemade chicken stock or low-salt canned chicken broth
- 1/4 tsp. salt, or to taste
- 1/8 tsp. freshly ground black pepper
- 2 tbsps. chopped fresh chives

Direction

- For the polenta, boil water in a medium saucepan. Sprinkle its top with cornmeal while stirring it in with a whisk. Mix in salt and pepper. Boil the mixture. Adjust the heat to low. Cover the mixture with its lid to prevent it from splattering. Gently cook for 6-8 minutes, stirring for some time until it has a consistency of a creamy puree and the polenta is cooked. Cover and put it aside.
- For the ragout, put oil and butter in a large saucepan and heat the mixture until hot. Add onion to the hot mixture and cook for 30 seconds. Add the mushrooms and cook over high heat for 2 minutes until the liquid they released evaporated. Add the corn, garlic, salt, chicken stock, tomatoes, and pepper. Bring the mixture to a strong boil. Adjust the heat to medium. Cook it for 2-3 more minutes.
- Spoon the polenta into the middle of each four soup plates. Top each with the mushroom ragout. To serve, sprinkle each with chives.

Nutrition Information

- Calories: 185
- Total Carbohydrate: 27 g
- Cholesterol: 8 mg
- Total Fat: 7 g
- Fiber: 3 g
- Protein: 5 g
- Sodium: 428 mg
- Saturated Fat: 3 g

238. Pomegranate Caramel Ice-cream Sauce

"This can be prepared in less than 45 minutes. But take note that it also requires additional unattended time."
Serving: Makes about 2 cups

Ingredients

- 2 pomegranates
- 1/2 cup sugar
- 1/4 cup water
- 1 1/2 tbsps. arrowroot
- Accompaniment: Vanilla ice cream

Direction

- Cut the pomegranates in half. Use a manual citrus juicer to squeeze enough juice from the 2 halves, it should measure up to 2/3 cup. Make sure that you will press the sides against the center of the juicer and use your thumbs to press the whole seeds into the juicer.
- Use your hands to break the remaining 2 pomegranate halves in two. Bend the back rinds and remove the seeds from the membranes.
- Cook the sugar in a dry 1 1/2-qt heavy saucepan over moderately low heat, stirring the sugar slowly using a fork until pale golden and melted. The fork will help the sugar to melt evenly. Cook the caramel, swirling the pan and not stirring it until deep golden. Add the pomegranate juice (the caramel will harden and steam after adding). Cook over moderately low heat, stirring often until the caramel is dissolved. Mix water and arrowroot in a small bowl and add the mixture into the

caramel mixture. Cook the sauce, stirring often using the wooden spatula and scraping frequently the bottom of the pan until the mixture starts to thicken and boil. Let the sauce cool. Cover and chill the sauce for about 2 hours until cold. Add the pomegranate seeds into the sauce; stir. Take note that the sauce can be prepared 2 days ahead. Keep it covered and chilled.

- Spoon the sauce over the ice cream.

Nutrition Information

- Calories: 216
- Total Carbohydrate: 52 g
- Total Fat: 2 g
- Fiber: 6 g
- Protein: 2 g
- Sodium: 6 mg
- Saturated Fat: 0 g

239. Poppy Seed Pound Cake With Plum Pluot Compote

"A fun and tasty recipe."
Serving: Makes 8 servings | Prep: 25m

Ingredients

- 2 cups sifted cake flour (not self-rising; sift before measuring)
- 1/4 cup poppy seeds
- 3/4 tsp. baking powder
- 1/2 tsp. salt
- 1/2 vanilla bean
- 1 3/4 sticks unsalted butter, softened
- 1 1/2 cups sugar
- 3 large eggs, warmed in very warm water 10 minutes
- 1/2 cup half-and-half at room temperature 30 minutes
- 2 lbs. firm-ripe plums and pluots, peeled and cut into 1/2-inch wedges
- 3/4 cup sugar, or to taste
- 1 tsp. grated lemon zest , divided
- 1 tbsp. fresh lemon juice

- 1/2 tsp. grated nutmeg
- Accompaniment: lightly sweetened whipped creamAccompaniment: lightly sweetened whipped cream

Direction

- For lb. cake: Preheat an oven with rack in center to 350°F; butter then flour a 9x5-in. loaf pan.
- Whisk salt, baking powder, poppy seeds and flour.
- Use a paring knife tip to scrape seeds from vanilla bean into bowl. Add sugar and butter; use electric mixer to beat on medium high speed for 3 minutes till fluffy and pale. One by one, add eggs; beat well after each addition. At low speed, in 3 batches, add flour mixture, alternating with half-and-half, starting and ending with flour; mix just till incorporated.
- Put batter into loaf pan; smooth top.
- Bake for 1-1 1/4 hours till golden brown and an inserted wooden pick in middle exits with crumbs adhering. Cool for 30 minutes in pan. To loosen, run knife around the cake edge; invert cake onto a rack. Fully cool, right side up.
- For Compote: Mix lemon juice, 1/2 tsp. zest, 3/4 cup sugar and fruit in a heavy medium saucepan. Simmer for 30 minutes till liquid is slightly syrupy and fruit starts to fall apart, occasionally mixing. Take off heat; mix extra sugar (optional), nutmeg and leftover 1/2 tsp. zest in. Put into bowl; cool. Serve at room temperature or warm.
- You can bake lb. cake 3 days ahead; keep at room temperature in an airtight container.
- You can make compote 1 day ahead; chill.

Nutrition Information

- Calories: 643
- Total Carbohydrate: 98 g
- Cholesterol: 128 mg
- Total Fat: 26 g
- Fiber: 3 g
- Protein: 7 g
- Sodium: 217 mg

- Saturated Fat: 15 g

240. Pork Enchiladas Rojas

"Use Californian/New Mexico chiles for guajillo chiles and chipotle Chile in adobo for moritas if needed."
Serving: Serves 4

Ingredients

- 1 tsp. coriander seeds
- 2 tbsps. cumin seeds
- 14 guajillo chiles, seeds removed
- 4 ancho chiles, seeds removed
- 3 morita chiles
- 4 cups homemade chicken stock or low-sodium chicken broth
- 8 cloves garlic, peeled
- 2 tbsps. tomato paste
- 1 tsp. crushed Mexican or Italian oregano
- 1 tbsp. vegetable oil
- 1 lb. boneless pork shoulder (Boston butt), fat trimmed
- Kosher salt
- 2 bay leaves
- 1 cup vegetable oil
- 8 (6-inch) white corn tortillas
- 10 oz. queso fresco, crumbled, plus more for serving
- 1 avocado
- 2 tbsps. sour cream
- 1 tbsp. fresh lime juice
- Kosher salt
- 1/2 onion, sliced into thin rings
- Lime wedges, (for serving)
- A spice mill or mortar and pestle

Direction

- Filling and sauce: Toast coriander seeds in small skillet on medium head, swirling pan often, adding cumin seeds at final 30 seconds of cooking, for 2 minutes till fragrant. Cool; finely grind with mortar and pestle or in spice mill.

- Boil stock and morita, ancho and guajillo chiles in medium saucepan on medium high heat. Cover; take off heat. Sit to let chiles soften for 30 minutes.
- Put chile mixture into blender. Add oregano, tomato paste, garlic and toasted spices; puree for 2 minutes till smooth.
- Preheat an oven to 250°F. In medium heavy pot, heat oil on medium high heat. Season the pork with salt; cook, occasionally turning, for 10-12 minutes till all sides are brown. Pour extra oil off; add bay leaves and chile puree. Boil; cover. Put in oven; braise pork for 1 1/2-2 hours till meat easily shreds and is very tender. Use salt to season.
- From chile sauce, skim extra fat; discard bay leaves. Put pork in big bowl; slightly cool. Use 2 forks to shred. Stir 1/2 cup chile sauce into the pork; season with salt. Put aside leftover sauce.
- Assembly: Preheat an oven to 425°F. Heat oil till it immediately bubbles when tortilla edges touch surface in medium skillet on medium high heat. Fry tortillas, one by one, for 10 seconds per side till crisp and just start to brown yet somewhat pliable. Put onto paper towels; drain.
- Dip both sides of every tortilla to just coat in chile sauce; put on rimmed baking sheet. Down the length of 13x9-in. baking dish, spread 1 cup sauce. Put 1/4 cup of pork mixture across center of tortilla; fold 1 side on filling then roll tortilla up. Put in prepped baking dish, seam side down. Repeat with leftover tortillas and more sauce; enchiladas have to nestle against each other in the pan. Put leftover sauce and cheese over; bake for 15-20 minutes till cheese starts to brown and sauce is bubbly. Sit for 10 minutes.
- Meanwhile, puree 1/4 cup water, lime juice, sour cream and avocado, adding more water as needed to thin, till creamy and smooth in a food processor; season using salt.
- Put onion slices over enchiladas; drizzle avocado cream. To squeeze over, serve with lime wedges.

241. Pot Roast With Winter Root Vegetables

Serving: Makes 8 to 10 servings

Ingredients

- 2 tsps. chopped fresh thyme
- 2 tsps. Hungarian sweet paprika
- 2 tsps. coarse kosher salt
- 2 tsps. freshly ground black pepper
- 1 tsp. dry mustard
- 1 tsp. (packed) golden brown sugar
- 1 4-lb. boneless grass-fed beef chuck roast, tied
- 6 oz. slab bacon, cut crosswise into 1/4-inch-thick slices, then into 1x1/2-inch rectangles
- 2 cups dry red wine
- 1/2 cup low-salt chicken broth
- 2 large onions, thinly sliced
- 12 small shallots, peeled
- 12 garlic cloves, peeled
- 3 bay leaves
- 4 large carrots (about 1 lb.), peeled, cut into 1-inch pieces
- 3 medium parsnips (about 12 oz.), peeled, cut into 1-inch pieces
- 1 small celery root, peeled, cut into 1-inch cubes

Direction

- Preheat an oven to 350°F. Mix initial 6 ingredients in a small bowl; all over beef, rub spice blend.
- In a big heavy ovenproof pot, cook bacon on medium heat till lightly crisp and browned. Transfer bacon using a slotted spoon to paper towels; drain. Discard all but 2 tbsps. of drippings from the pot. Put heat to medium high; put beef in. Cook for 12 minutes total till all sides are browned. Put beef on plate. Put red wine in a pot; boil, scraping browned bits up. Boil for 5 minutes till reduced to 1/2 cup. Add bacon and broth; put beef over bacon. Scatter bay leaves, garlic, shallots and onions around beef.
- Cover pot; put in the oven. Roast for an hour. Flip beef; mix onions. Cover; roast, adding water if dry by 1/4 cupfuls, for 1 more hour. Put beef on a plate. Add celery, parsnips and carrots in pot; mix to coat. Put beef over vegetables; cover. Roast for 45 minutes till vegetables and beef are tender. Put beef on platter; spoon fat off sauce's surface. Season sauce with pepper and salt to taste. Put sauce on beef; serve.

Nutrition Information

- Calories: 532
- Total Carbohydrate: 31 g
- Cholesterol: 150 mg
- Total Fat: 20 g
- Fiber: 7 g
- Protein: 52 g
- Sodium: 838 mg
- Saturated Fat: 7 g

242. Potato And Kale Galette

"A fun potato cake."
Serving: Makes 8 to 10 servings | Prep: 45m

Ingredients

- 1 lb kale, tough stems and center ribs discarded
- 1 stick (1/2 cup) butter, 6 of the tbsps. melted and cooled
- 4 garlic cloves, finely chopped
- 3/4 tsp. salt
- 3/4 tsp. black pepper
- 2 lb russet (baking) potatoes (4 medium)
- a 12-inch heavy nonstick skillet; an adjustable-blade slicer

Direction

- Cook kale, uncovered, in 4-6-qt. pot with boiling salted water for 4-6 minute still just tender. Drain in colander; to stop cooking, rinse under cold water. Drain well and squeeze handfuls of kale to remove extra moisture; chop coarsely.

- Heat 2 tbsp. unmelted butter till foam subsides on medium high heat in skillet. Add garlic; cook, mixing occasionally, for 1 minute till golden. Add 1/4 tsp. pepper, 1/4 tsp. salt and kale; sauté, mixing, for 4 minutes till kale is tender. Put into bowl; clean the skillet.
- Peel potatoes; use slicer to crosswise slice thinly, 1/16-in. thick. Brush some melted butter on bottom of skillet generously, quickly to avoid potatoes from discoloring; cover, slightly overlapping, with 1/3 potato slices. Use some melted butter to dab potatoes.
- Spread 1/2 kale on potatoes; sprinkle 1/8 tsp. pepper and 1/8 tsp. salt.
- Use leftover 1/2 potato slices to cover; dab with butter. Put leftover kale over. Sprinkle 1/8 tsp. pepper and 1/8 tsp. salt. Top with leftover potatoes; sprinkle leftover 1/4 tsp. pepper and 1/4 tsp. salt.
- Brush melted butter on foil sheet; brush leftover butter on galette. Put foil on top, buttered side down; to weight galette, put 10-in. heavy skillet over foil.
- Cook galette on medium heat for 12-15 minutes till bottom is golden brown. Remove foil and top skillet. Slide galette onto baking sheet carefully, wearing oven mitts; invert skillet over. Invert galette, holding them together, back into skillet with browned side up. Cook, uncovered, on medium heat for 12-15 minutes till potatoes are tender and bottom is golden brown. Slide onto serving plate.
- You can make galette 6 hours ahead; cool, uncovered, then keep on baking sheet covered using foil in room temperature. Remove the foil; reheat in 425°F oven for 20 minutes till crisp and heated through.

"A low-fat entrée that uses ready-made wrappers for an easy one."
Serving: Makes 10 blintzes (5 servings)

Ingredients

- 1 tbsp. vegetable oil
- 1 1/4 lbs. onions (about 2 large), sliced
- Pinch of sugar
- 1 1/2 lbs. buttery potatoes (such as Yukon Gold) or russet potatoes, peeled, cut into 1-inch pieces
- 1/4 cup milk (do not use low-fat or nonfat)
- 10 7-inch square purchased egg roll wrappers, corners trimmed to make rounds
- 1 egg white
- 1 tbsp. vegetable oil
- Nonfat yogurt

Direction

- In big heavy skillet, heat the oil on moderately-high heat. Put in sugar and onions. Put skillet's cover and cook for 20 minutes, till onions are browned nicely, mixing often. Add pepper and salt to season.
- Meantime, on a rack of vegetable steamer, put the potatoes and let steam in pot with cover on top of boiling water, for 15 minutes, till tender. Turn potatoes onto a big bowl. Put in milk and crush till nearly smooth. Season with pepper and salt to taste. Stir in 1/2 of the onions. May be done a day in advance. Separately cover the rest of the onions and the potato filling and refrigerate. Reheat onions prior to serving.
- Lay on work surface with one egg roll wrapper. Brush egg white on edges. Place scant one third cup potato filling horizontally in 3-inches log barely below the middle. Fold the dough bottom on top of filling then the sides on top. Roll wrapper up to fully seal the filling. Redo with the rest of wrappers and filling.

- In big, heavy, nonstick skillet, heat half tbsp. vegetable oil on moderately-low heat. Put 1/2 of blintzes, seam side facing down, and fry for 10 minutes, till heated completely, crisp and golden brown on each of the 4 sides. Use paper towels to briefly drain the blintzes. Redo with the rest of the blintzes.
- Place blintzes on the plates. Put spoonful of leftover onions and dollop of yogurt on the side and serve right away.

244. Potato Gnocchi

"One of the great classic Italian dishes."
Serving: Makes 4 servings

Ingredients

- 3 lbs. russet or other starchy potatoes, peeled
- Kosher salt
- 1 1/2 cups all-purpose or "00" flour, plus more as needed
- 2 large eggs, plus 1 large egg yolk
- Freshly ground nutmeg
- 3/4 cup (1 1/2 sticks) unsalted butter
- 8 torn fresh sage leaves
- 3/4 cup grated Parmigiano-Reggiano cheese

Direction

- In a medium stock pot, put potatoes and pour in enough cold water to cover by approximately 2 inches. Put salt into the water and boil over moderately high heat. Let the potatoes cook for 12 to 14 minutes till fork-tender, time will vary on potatoes size. Drain the potatoes and allow them to dry in pot for about 3 minutes on low heat. Push potatoes through a potato ricer or food mill onto a slightly floured work area.
- Collect potatoes into a mound and create a well in the middle. Into the well, scatter 1/2 of flour and gently put in nutmeg, egg yolk and eggs. Combine the ingredients using hand till a soft dough creates. If needed, put in additional flour, a small amount at a time, till

dough consistency is smooth, evenly moistened.
- Dust the work surface lightly with flour and split dough into 6 or 8 pieces. Roll the pieces into an-inch-thick ropes and cut ropes into an-inch portions. To shape gnocchi, roll them on top of a fork, if wished. When done shaping, gnocchi can be stored in refrigerator, on a baking sheet dusted with flour and covered loosely, for up to 8 hours.
- Once ready to serve, boil a big pot of salted water. Put in gnocchi and mix several times to soak and separate them. Let it cook at a gentle boil for 2 to 3 minutes till gnocchi are soft and just starting to float. Darin the gnocchi well and serve along with a preferred cheese or sauce.
- To Brown Butter-Sage Sauce: melt 1 1/2 sticks or 3/4 cup of unsalted butter in a medium pot over medium-high heat along with 8 torn fresh leaves of sage. Cook for 2 to 3 minutes till butter is slightly browned and with smells nutty. In a serving dish, put gnocchi and scatter 3/4 cup of grated Parmigiano-Reggiano cheese on top. Top gnocchi with scoop of brown butter and jazz up with sage leaves.

245. Potatoes With Leeks And Gruyère

Serving: Serves 12

Ingredients

- 2 tbsps. (1/4 stick) butter
- 1 lb. leeks (white and pale green parts only), thinly sliced
- 1 8-oz. package cream cheese, room temperature
- 1 1/2 tsps. salt
- 1 tsp. ground black pepper
- 1/4 tsp. ground nutmeg
- 1 cup whole milk
- 3 large eggs

- 2 lbs. large white-skinned potatoes, peeled, shredded
- 3 cups grated Gruyère cheese (about 12 oz.)

Direction

- Preheat an oven to 350°F. Butter a 13x9x2-in. baking dish. Melt 2 tbsp. butter on medium heat in big skillet. Add leeks; sauté for 10 minutes till tender. Put into big bowl.
- In processor, blend nutmeg, pepper, salt and cream cheese. Add eggs and milk; process till just blended. Put in bowl with leeks. Add gruyre and potatoes; mix to blend. Put into prepped baking dish.
- Bake potatoes for 1 hour till top is brown and cooked through. You can make it 1 day ahead. Slightly cool. Cover; refrigerate. Rewarm, covered, for 25 minutes in 350°F oven.

Nutrition Information

- Calories: 311
- Total Carbohydrate: 21 g
- Cholesterol: 106 mg
- Total Fat: 20 g
- Fiber: 2 g
- Protein: 14 g
- Sodium: 456 mg
- Saturated Fat: 11 g

246. Prosciutto-wrapped Figs With Gorgonzola And Walnuts

"You can use dried black Mission figs for fresh figs; get ones that are moist and soft."
Serving: Makes 18

Ingredients

- 9 large fresh black Mission figs, stemmed, halved
- 18 1x5-inch thin strips prosciutto (about 3 oz.)
- 3 tbsps. Gorgonzola cheese
- 18 large walnut pieces, toasted

Direction

- Preheat a broiler. Use foil to cover big rimmed baking sheet. With 1 prosciutto strip, wrap each fig half; put on prepped sheet. Broil for 1 1/2 minutes till prosciutto slightly chars on edges. Flip figs; broil, closely watching to avoid burning, for 1 1/2 minutes. On top of each fig half, put 1/2 tsp. Gorgonzola. Put walnut piece on each top; serve at room temperature/warm.

Nutrition Information

- Calories: 107
- Total Carbohydrate: 19 g
- Cholesterol: 5 mg
- Total Fat: 3 g
- Fiber: 3 g
- Protein: 3 g
- Sodium: 139 mg
- Saturated Fat: 1 g

247. Pumpkin Cheesecake Pie With Cornmeal Crust

Serving: Makes 8 servings

Ingredients

- 3 tbsps. (or more) ice water
- 1 large egg yolk
- 1 1/3 cups all purpose flour
- 1/4 cup yellow cornmeal
- 1 tbsp. sugar
- 1/2 tsp. salt
- 1/2 cup (1 stick) chilled unsalted butter, cut into 1/2-inch pieces
- 6 oz. cream cheese, room temperature
- 1/2 cup sugar
- 1/2 cup (packed) golden brown sugar
- 2 large eggs
- 1 large egg yolk
- 1 cup canned pure pumpkin
- 3/4 cup half and half
- 1 tsp. ground cinnamon

- 1 tsp. ground nutmeg
- 1/2 tsp. grated lemon peel
- 1/2 tsp. ground ginger
- 1/4 tsp. salt

Direction

- Crust: Whisk egg yolk and 3 tbsp. ice water to blend in small bowl. In processor, mix salt, sugar, yellow cornmeal and all-purpose flour. Add chilled butter; process with on/off turns till it looks like coarse meal and drizzle egg yolk mixture on top; process till moist clumps form with on/off turns. If dough is dry, add extra ice water by teaspoonfuls. Gather dough to ball; flatten dough to disk. In plastic, wrap dough; refrigerate for 30 minutes. You can make it 1 day ahead, kept refrigerated.
- Put rack on bottom third of oven; preheat it to 350°F. Roll dough out to 12-in. round between 2 waxed paper sheets; remove top waxed paper sheet. Invert dough into 9-in. diameter glass pie dish, paper side up; remove the waxed paper from the dough. Decoratively crimp dough edges.
- Filling: Beat 6-oz. cream cheese with electric mixer till fluffy in a big bowl. Add 1/2 cup golden brown sugar and 1/2 cup sugar; beat till fluffy and light. One by one, beat in egg yolk and eggs; add leftover ingredients. Beat till blended well; put filling in prepped crust.
- Bake pie for 55 minutes till just set in middle and filling is slightly puffed. Put pie on rack; fully cool. Cover pie; refrigerate for 4 hours till cold. You can make it 1 day ahead, kept refrigerated. Serve pie while cold.

Nutrition Information

- Calories: 449
- Total Carbohydrate: 52 g
- Cholesterol: 155 mg
- Total Fat: 24 g
- Fiber: 2 g
- Protein: 7 g
- Sodium: 333 mg
- Saturated Fat: 14 g

248. Pumpkin Mousse Trifle

"A great recipe!"
Serving: Makes 4 servings

Ingredients

- Vegetable oil cooking spray
- 1 tbsp. pumpkin seeds
- 1 cup canned pumpkin
- 1/8 tsp. cinnamon
- Pinch of ground nutmeg
- Pinch of ground cloves
- 2 egg whites
- 1/2 cup plus 1 tbsp. sugar, divided
- 1/4 cup reduced-fat sour cream
- 8 store-bought shortbread cookies

Direction

- Heat an oven to 325°F. Use cooking spray to coat baking sheet. Evenly spread pumpkin seeds on sheet; bake for 25 minutes, mixing once, till golden. Mix cloves, nutmeg, cinnamon and pumpkin till smooth in bowl. Use electric mixer to whip egg whites till soft peaks form in 2nd bowl. Add 1/2 cup sugar; whip till stiff meringue peaks form. Fold pumpkin mixture gently into meringue till just combined. Mix leftover 1 tbsp. sugar and sour cream in 3rd bowl. Pulse cookies to fine crumbs in food processor. Divide then layer 1/2 shortbread crumbs and 1/2 pumpkin mousse in each of the 4 5-oz. glasses; repeat layers. Put 1 tbsp. sweetened sour cream then sprinkle pumpkin seeds over each; immediately serve.

249. Pumpkin-caramel Tart With Toasted-hazelnut Crust

"A fun recipe for thanksgiving."
Serving: 8 servings

Ingredients

- 1 1/4 cups skin-on hazelnuts
- 1 cup all-purpose flour
- 2 tbsps. granulated sugar
- 3/4 tsps. kosher salt
- 1/2 cup (1 stick) chilled unsalted butter, cut into pieces
- Pinch of cream of tartar
- 1 1/4 cups granulated sugar, divided
- 1 cup heavy cream
- 1 cup canned pumpkin purée
- 2 tbsps. light brown sugar
- 1 tbsp. all-purpose flour
- 1 1/2 tsps. finely grated peeled ginger
- 3/4 tsp. ground cinnamon
- 3/4 tsp. kosher salt
- 3 large eggs
- Whipped cream (for serving)
- A 9" springform pan

Direction

- Crust: Preheat an oven to 350°F. On rimmed baking sheet, toast hazelnuts, tossing once, for 8-10 minutes till slightly darkened and fragrant; cool. Rub hazelnuts together with kitchen towel to remove most skins; it's okay if there's some stubborn bits left.
- Pulse 3/4 cup hazelnuts, salt, sugar and flour till it has coarse meal consistency in a food processor; for filling, put leftover 1/2 cup hazelnuts aside. Put butter in dry ingredients; pulse till there's only few pea-sized butter pieces left.
- Put it into a big bowl then drizzle 3 tbsp. ice water; mix, adding around another splash of water if needed, to just bring dough together.
- Evenly press dough using your fingers 1 1/2- 2-in. up sides then into bottom of pan;

compact then smooth with glass/straight-sided, flat measuring cup; chill for 20 minutes.
- Bake crust for 15-20 minutes till golden yet not fully baked through. Put onto wire rack; cool for 10 minutes.
- Assembly and filling: Boil 2 tbsp. water, 1 cup granulated sugar and cream of tartar in medium saucepan on medium heat, mixing till sugar dissolves. Put heat on medium high heat; cook, occasionally swirling pan (don't mix), for 8-10 minutes till caramel gets deep amber color. Take off heat. Add cream carefully, constantly whisking; it'll vigorously bubble and be very hot; whisk till smooth. Slightly cool caramel in pot.
- Whisk salt, cinnamon, ginger, flour, brown sugar and pumpkin puree in a big bowl. Add eggs and caramel slowly, whisking till blended well; scrape filling into prepped crust.
- Bake tart, rotating it halfway through, for 30-35 minutes till center barely jiggles and filling sets around edges. Put onto wire rack; cool in pan.
- Meanwhile, chop reserved 1/2 cup of hazelnuts coarsely; cook in small skillet with 1 tbsp. water and leftover 1/4 cup sugar, constantly mixing, on medium heat till sugar evenly coats hazelnuts and caramelizes. Put caramelized hazelnuts onto parchment paper sheet; fully cool. Chop coarsely. Scatter caramelized hazelnuts on tart; serve with whipped cream.
- You can make tart without nuts 2 days ahead. Cover; chill. You can caramelize hazelnuts 2 days ahead; keep airtight in room temperature.

Nutrition Information

- Calories: 577
- Total Carbohydrate: 57 g
- Cholesterol: 141 mg
- Total Fat: 37 g
- Fiber: 4 g
- Protein: 8 g
- Sodium: 391 mg
- Saturated Fat: 16 g

250. Quick Tiramisu

""Try this tiramisu using store-bought ladyfingers that work very well.""
Serving: Makes 4 servings

Ingredients

- 15 ladyfingers
- 1 cup good strong coffee, freshly brewed
- 4 tbsps. sugar
- 1 lb. 2 oz. mascarpone
- 2 vanilla beans
- 1/2 cup vin santo or sweet sherry
- Zest and juice of 1 orange
- 3 1/2 oz. best-quality bittersweet chocolate (70 % cocoa solids)

Direction

- Arrange ladyfingers snugly in layers on top of each other in an 8-10 inches diameter dish or a medium deep bowl. Mix 2 tbsps. sugar to your coffee to sweeten it. Shower the coffee over the ladyfingers, ensuring the top layer is fully covered-you'll see the ladyfingers absorbing the coffee. While soaking, whisk the remaining sugar and mascarpone in a bowl.
- Cut the vanilla beans lengthwise and remove the seeds out into the bowl of mascarpone, leaving beans for making vanilla sugar if wished. Keep on stirring and while you do, shower in the sherry or vin santo. You should have a shiny consistency of the mixture to loosen. Add a little orange juice to loosen it if it turns too thick before you squeeze the rest of the juice over the ladyfingers. Smear the vanilla mascarpone over the ladyfingers and either make shavings using a peeler or a knife or grate all chocolate over it. Lightly dust a bit of finely grated orange zest and store in the fridge until you're ready to serve.

Nutrition Information

- Calories: 385
- Total Carbohydrate: 59 g
- Cholesterol: 99 mg
- Total Fat: 14 g
- Fiber: 3 g
- Protein: 6 g
- Sodium: 92 mg
- Saturated Fat: 7 g

251. Quinoa-mushroom Frittata With Fresh Herbs

"Healthy and yummy."
Serving: Serves 6

Ingredients

- 3/4 cup uncooked quinoa (or 1 1/2 cups cooked)
- 6 large pasture-raised eggs
- 1/2 cup grated Parmesan cheese
- 1/4 cup chopped fresh basil
- 2 tbsps. chopped fresh chives or tarragon
- 1 tsp. minced fresh thyme leaves
- 1/4 tsp. freshly ground black pepper
- 4 green onions or garlic scapes, thinly sliced
- 1 cup sliced mushrooms such as maitake, shiitake, or chanterelle, brushed clean and sliced
- Olive oil
- 1/4 cup assorted pitted olives, whole or chopped

Direction

- Follow package directions to cook quinoa; put aside.
- Whisk eggs in a big bowl; mix in mushrooms, garlic scapes/green onions, pepper, herbs, parmesan and quinoa.
- Use a thick olive oil layer to coat medium ovenproof skillet; put on medium high heat. Add egg mixture; sprinkle olives and cook without mixing for 2-3 minutes.
- Preheat broiler with rack in 2nd position from top; broil frittata for 3-4 minutes till eggs firm up in middle and top browns lightly.

- Remove frittata from oven; rest for 3 minutes. Use a spatula to loosen edges; cut to 6 wedges. Immediately serve.

252. Radish And Carrot Salad With Tuna And Capers

"A surprisingly tasty salad."
Serving: Serves 4 | Prep: 20m

Ingredients

- 1 bunch radishes (about 1/2 lb.)
- 2–3 medium carrots (about 1/2 lb.)
- 2 1/4 tsps. kosher salt, divided
- 2 tsps. fresh lemon juice
- 2 tsps. white wine or Champagne vinegar
- 3/4 tsp. Dijon mustard
- 1/4 tsp. freshly ground black pepper, plus more
- 2 tbsps. olive oil
- 1 1/2 tbsps. capers
- 4 oz. drained oil-packed canned flaked tuna (about 3/4 cup)
- 2 tbsps. parsley leaves

Direction

- Slice radishes into very thin rounds. Lengthwise peel carrots to thin, long slices with a vegetable peeler. Mix together 3 cups ice water and 2 tsp. salt in a medium bowl; soak carrots and radishes for 10 minutes. Drain; pat dry.
- Meanwhile, whisk the leftover 1/4 tsp. salt, pepper, mustard, vinegar and lemon juice till combined in a small bowl; in a slow stream, whisk in oil.
- Toss capers, carrots and radishes with just enough vinaigrette to coat in a big bowl; divide into 4 plates. Put parsley and tuna over; drizzle over the leftover vinaigrette. Top with several grinds of black pepper.

Nutrition Information

- Calories: 119

- Total Carbohydrate: 7 g
- Cholesterol: 10 mg
- Total Fat: 7 g
- Fiber: 3 g
- Protein: 7 g
- Sodium: 373 mg
- Saturated Fat: 1 g

253. Raspberry And Aperol Floats

"Easy and tasty."
Serving: Makes 4 servings

Ingredients

- 1 sprig thyme
- 1/4 cup sugar
- 1/4 cup (or more) Aperol
- 1 1/3 cups raspberries (about 6 oz.)
- 1 pint vanilla ice cream or gelato
- 2 12-oz. cans club soda

Direction

- Boil 1/4 cup water, sugar and thyme in a small saucepan, mixing till sugar dissolves. Take off heat; cover. Sit for 15 minutes. Discard thyme sprig; cool. Mix in 1/4 cup of Aperol.
- Divide raspberries and syrup to 4 tall glasses; gently muddle. Evenly dividing, add ice cream; top each off with club soda and, if desired, more Aperol.

Nutrition Information

- Calories: 220
- Total Carbohydrate: 34 g
- Cholesterol: 29 mg
- Total Fat: 8 g
- Fiber: 3 g
- Protein: 3 g
- Sodium: 90 mg
- Saturated Fat: 4 g

254. Raspberry Jam Tart With Almond Crumble

"An easy dessert."
Serving: Makes 8 servings | Prep: 15m

Ingredients

- 2 cups sliced natural almonds
- 2/3 cup sugar
- 1 1/4 sticks (1/2 cup plus 2 tbsps.) cold unsalted butter, cut into pieces
- 11/4 cups all-purpose flour
- 1 rounded 1/4 tsp. salt
- 2 tbsps. beaten egg
- 1 cup raspberry jam

Direction

- Preheat an oven to 400°F.
- Keep 1/4 cup almonds for topping in a bowl. Grind sugar and leftover 1 3/4 cups nuts finely in food processor.
- Add salt, flour and butter; process till it looks like sand. Put 1 cup flour mixture in reserved almonds. Put beaten egg in leftover flour mixture; pulse till it clumps together.
- From processor, put mixture in 9x1-in. round tart pan that has removable bottom; use floured fingers to press mixture up pan's sides and bottom of pan. Bake for 15 minutes in center of oven.
- Meanwhile, to loosen, mix raspberry jam. Rub the reserved almond mixture in the bowl between palms to make small clumps.
- Take tart shell from oven; spread jam on bottom. On jam, sprinkle almond mixture; bake tart for 15 minutes. Cool the tart in pan on the rack. Use a knife to loosen side of pan; remove it.
- You can make it 1 day ahead; before chilling, cool, covered. Before serving, bring to room temperature.

Nutrition Information

- Calories: 592
- Total Carbohydrate: 82 g
- Cholesterol: 39 mg
- Total Fat: 26 g
- Fiber: 4 g
- Protein: 10 g
- Sodium: 307 mg
- Saturated Fat: 10 g

255. Raspberry-hazelnut Galette

"A rustic tart recipe."
Serving: Makes 6 to 8 servings

Ingredients

- 3/4 cup raw hazelnuts, skin on
- 3/4 tsp. kosher salt
- 1 1/4 cups all-purpose flour plus more for work surface
- 1/2 cup (1 stick) chilled unsalted butter, cut into 1/2" pieces
- 1/4 cup sugar
- 2 large egg yolks
- 1 cup raspberry jam
- 1 tsp. finely grated lime zest
- 1 tbsp. fresh lime juice
- 1 large egg, beaten to blend
- 2 tbsps. raw sugar
- Hazelnut or vanilla ice cream (for serving; optional)

Direction

- Preheat an oven to 375°F. Process 1 1/4 cups flour, salt and hazelnuts till nuts are ground very finely in a food processor. Put into medium bowl; put aside.
- Process sugar and butter till smooth in food processor. Add egg yolks; pulse to just mix. Add reserved hazelnut mixture; pulse till just blended. Bring to ball and flatten to disk; wrap in plastic. Chill it for 2 hours. You can make dough 1 day ahead, kept chilled; stand for 15 minutes at room temperature before rolling it out.
- Mix lime juice, lime zest and jam to blend in small bowl; put aside.

- Roll dough out to 14-in. 1/8-in. thick round, dusting flour on dough as needed to avoid sticking on floured parchment paper sheet. Spread jam mixture on dough; leave 1 1/2-in. border. Brush border of dough with beaten egg. Fold dough's border on jam using parchment paper for aid, pinching together cracks in dough. Onto baking sheet, slide parchment paper with the galette. Brush beaten egg on top of dough; sprinkle raw sugar.
- Bake galette for 30-40 minutes, rotating halfway through, till crust gets deep golden brown. To release tart from jam that bubbles out, run a big offset spatula/knife between paper and tart. Fully cool on pan on wire rack. You can make galette 3 days ahead; keep at room temperature, loosely covered.
- Cut to wedges; if desired, serve with ice cream.

Nutrition Information

- Calories: 564
- Total Carbohydrate: 72 g
- Cholesterol: 133 mg
- Total Fat: 28 g
- Fiber: 3 g
- Protein: 8 g
- Sodium: 270 mg
- Saturated Fat: 11 g

256. Raspberry-yogurt Cake

"A special cake recipe."
Serving: Makes 10 to 12 servings

Ingredients

- 3 cups unbleached all purpose flour, divided
- 1 1/2 tsps. baking powder
- 1/4 tsp. salt
- 1 cup (2 sticks) unsalted butter, room temperature
- 1 3/4 cups sugar
- 2 tbsps. fresh orange juice
- 1 1/2 tsps. almond extract, divided
- 1 tsp. finely grated orange peel
- 3 large eggs, room temperature
- 1 cup plain low-fat yogurt
- 2 1/2 cups fresh raspberries (two 6-oz. containers)
- 1 cup powdered sugar
- 1 tbsp. (or more) water

Direction

- Preheat an oven to 350°F then butter a 12-cup Bundt pan. In medium bowl, whisk 1/4 tsp. salt, baking powder and 2 1/2 cups flour.
- Beat sugar and butter using electric mixer till creamy in big bowl; beat in orange peel, 1 tsp. almond extract and orange juice. One by one, add eggs; beat after each. Stir in yogurt.
- Put dry ingredients in batter; beat till just blended.
- In big bowl, toss raspberries and 1/2 cup flour; fold berry mixture into the batter. Put batter in prepped pan; smooth top.
- Bake cake for 1 hour 10 minutes till inserted wooden skewer near middle exits clean; cool for 30 minutes.
- Invert cake onto a plate; cool.
- You can make it 1 day ahead. Cover; stand in room temperature.
- In medium bowl, whisk 1/2 tsp. almond extract, 1 tbsp. water and powdered sugar; as needed, add 1/2 tsp. full more water for thick glaze. Drizzle on cake; stand till glaze sets.

Nutrition Information

- Calories: 540
- Total Carbohydrate: 82 g
- Cholesterol: 106 mg
- Total Fat: 21 g
- Fiber: 3 g
- Protein: 8 g
- Sodium: 155 mg
- Saturated Fat: 12 g

257. Red Rice Salad With Pecans, Fennel, And Herbs

"If needed, get short-grain brown rice for red rice."
Serving: 4 Servings

Ingredients

- 1 cup red rice
- 1 small fennel bulb, very thinly sliced
- 1/4 medium red onion, thinly sliced
- 3 tbsps. fresh lime juice, divided
- 2/3 cup pecans, divided
- 1/4 cup olive oil
- 1/2 cup cilantro leaves and finely chopped tender stems
- Kosher salt, freshly ground pepper
- Toasted pistachio oil or almond oil (for serving; optional)

Direction

- Follow package directions to cook rice. Spread out on rimmed baking sheet; cool.
- Meanwhile, toss 2 tbsp. lime juice and onion with fennel; sit, occasionally tossing, for 10-15 minutes till lime juice is nearly fully absorbed.
- Chop 1/3 cup pecans coarsely; chop leftover nuts finely. Cook in olive oil in small saucepan on medium low heat for 5-10 minutes till golden brown; cool.
- Put pecans and rice in fennel mixture with 1 tbsp. lime juice; toss to mix. Fold in cilantro gently; season with pepper and salt. If desired, drizzle pistachio oil; serve.
- You can chill rice salad without cilantro 1 day ahead; before serving, bring to room temperature.

Nutrition Information

- Calories: 425
- Total Carbohydrate: 43 g
- Total Fat: 27 g
- Fiber: 5 g
- Protein: 6 g
- Sodium: 330 mg
- Saturated Fat: 3 g

258. Redneck Mimosa

"A simple and tasty drink."
Serving: Serves 1.

Ingredients

- 1/2 pint golden lager or wheat beer
- 1/2 pint orange juice

Direction

- Use orange juice to fill pint glass halfway; to fill, add beer.

Nutrition Information

- Calories: 107
- Total Carbohydrate: 17 g
- Total Fat: 0 g
- Fiber: 0 g
- Protein: 1 g
- Sodium: 6 mg
- Saturated Fat: 0 g

259. Ribollita With Italian Sausage

"You can cook it 1 day ahead then reheat and serve the next day; add croutons last."
Serving: 6 Servings

Ingredients

- 2 cups coarsely torn day-old sourdough bread
- 3 tbsps. olive oil, plus more
- Kosher salt
- 1 lb. sweet Italian sausage, casings removed
- 1 cup dry white wine
- 1 medium onion, finely chopped
- 3 medium carrots, peeled, finely chopped
- 3 celery stalks, finely chopped
- 2 anchovy fillets packed in oil, drained, chopped
- 3 garlic cloves, thinly sliced
- 1 tsp. crushed red pepper flakes

- 1 bunch Tuscan kale, ribs removed, leaves torn into 2" pieces
- 1 15 oz. can whole peeled tomatoes, drained, finely chopped
- 1 15 oz. can cannellini (white kidney) beans, rinsed
- 8 cups low-sodium chicken broth
- 1 tbsp. red wine vinegar
- 4 oz. Parmesan, shaved

Direction

- Preheat an oven to 350°F. On rimmed baking sheet, toss 3 tbsp. oil and bread, squeezing to moisten then season with salt; toast, occasionally tossing, for 15-18 minutes till crunchy and golden brown. Cool.
- Mix wine and sausage till smooth with your hands in a medium bowl; cook, occasionally mixing, in a big saucepan on medium heat for 4 minutes till firm yet not brown.
- Add red pepper flakes, garlic, anchovies, celery, carrots and onion; cook, occasionally mixing, for 20-25 minutes till veggies are tender yet hold their shape. Add broth, beans, tomatoes and kale; boil. Lower heat; simmer, occasionally mixing, for 1 hour till flavors meld and kale has no resistance when bitten.
- Add 1/2 croutons and vinegar to soup before serving, mixing to break to smaller pieces. Divide leftover croutons to bowls; put soup over. Top with parmesan then drizzle extra oil; serve.

Nutrition Information

- Calories: 466
- Total Carbohydrate: 34 g
- Cholesterol: 37 mg
- Total Fat: 21 g
- Fiber: 7 g
- Protein: 33 g
- Sodium: 1644 mg
- Saturated Fat: 7 g

260. Rice Pudding

"Creamy and yummy!"
Serving: 6

Ingredients

- 1 cup cooked white rice
- 1 quart milk
- 1/2 cup white sugar
- 1/4 tsp. salt
- 2 eggs, beaten
- 1/2 tsp. vanilla extract
- 1 tsp. butter
- 1 pinch ground nutmeg

Direction

- Preheat an oven to 175°C/350°F; butter the 2-qt. baking dish.
- Scald milk in 2-qt. saucepan on medium heat; take off heat. Add salt, sugar and rice; mix well. Add eggs, butter and vanilla slowly; put it into 2-qt. baking dish. Sprinkle nutmeg; bake for 40 minutes. Mix pudding after 20 minutes.

Nutrition Information

- Calories: 212 calories;
- Total Carbohydrate: 32 g
- Cholesterol: 77 mg
- Total Fat: 5.7 g
- Protein: 8.2 g
- Sodium: 192 mg

261. Rice With Green Lentils, Raisins, And Dates

"A very delicious dish!"
Serving: Serves 4-6 | Prep: 35m

Ingredients

- 400 g/14 oz basmati rice
- 3 tbsps. salt
- 150 g/5 oz green lentils

- 100 g/3 1/2 oz raisins (or sultanas/golden raisins)
- 50 g/2 oz dates
- 1 medium onion
- 2 medium potatoes for the tahdig* (optional)
- Approximately 1 litre/1 1/4 pints water
- 150 g/5 oz butter
- 100 ml/3 1/2 fl oz vegetable oil
- 2 tsps. turmeric
- 4 tbsps. liquid saffron

Direction

- Wash rice; soak it for 2 hours.
- Thoroughly wash lentils; drain. Wash raisins; on kitchen paper, pat dry. Take pits/stones out of dates; chop to same size as raisins. Peel onion; finely chop.
- Wash, peel then thinly slice potatoes if using; to avoid discoloration, put into bowl with cold water.
- Put lentils and just under 1-pt./500-ml cold water into saucepan; don't add salt. Boil; cook on medium heat till lentils become al dente. Drain; put aside.
- Heat 2 tbsp. oil and 1-oz./30-g butter in a skillet/frying pan on medium heat; fry onion till golden.
- Lower heat. Add dates and raisins; mix. Add 1 tsp. turmeric and cooked lentils; to taste, add salt. Mix; put aside.
- Into heavy-based saucepan, put 14 fl-oz./400-ml water; boil. Drain rice; add with 1 tbsp. salt, 3 tbsp. oil and 2-oz/50-g butter to boiling water. Simmer, uncovered, for 10 minutes on medium heat till holes begin to appear on rice's surface and all water is absorbed.
- Tip rice into shallow dish. Instead of potato, make rice tahdig: Put 2 heaped tbsp. plain rice aside. Fold raisin and lentil mixture into rice gently. Add 3 tbsp. liquid saffron; as you mix, don't break grains.
- Drain then dry potato slices if using potatoes for tahdig. Put saucepan on heat. Add 2 tbsp. vegetable oil; put sliced potatoes to cover bottom of pan in 1 layer when it is sizzling. Or,

use few tbsp. cooked plain rice for potato slices or create another kind of tahdig.
- Put rice and lentil mixture over potato layer; keep rice away from pan's sides as much as possible and in pyramid shape. Dot leftover butter over rice. Wrap lid in clean tea towel; firmly put on pan. Steam on low heat (on gas flame with heat diffuser) for 50-60 minutes.
- When rice is done, dip bottom of pan in cold water/stand pan for few minutes in 2-in/5-cm cold water to release bottom layer. Serve rice in shallow dish, fluffing rice while spooning it out. Drizzle leftover liquid saffron on rice. Detach then break crisp layer of plain rice/potatoes from bottom of pan; serve on another plate.
- Serve: Accompany with plate of spring onions/scallions, radishes and fresh herbs and pickles or mango chutney.
- Tahdig: Crust forms in bottom of pan during steaming process that's called tahdig. Add different ingredients to adjust flavor and thickness. Before putting boiled rice into saucepan, heat mix of vegetable oil and butter in pan, enough to cover base of pan, on medium heat till sizzling. Use layer of your preferred ingredient to cover bottom of pan. Put rice on top carefully; steam.
- Add all polo ingredients you want to rice before starting tahdig process if making tahdig for polo.
- When serving, you may add butter to rice if rice looks dry; lentils absorb lots of oil.
- For tahdig, don't use rice mixed with the lentils; lentils become hard pellets in oil and dates and raisins will burn.

Nutrition Information

- Calories: 1107
- Total Carbohydrate: 138 g
- Cholesterol: 81 mg
- Total Fat: 55 g
- Fiber: 8 g
- Protein: 18 g
- Sodium: 1203 mg
- Saturated Fat: 21 g

262. Riesling-braised Sauerkraut And Apples

"Weinkraut Mit Äpfeln"
Serving: Makes 6 side-dish servings

Ingredients

- 4 cups drained sauerkraut from 2 lb. packages sauerkraut (not canned)
- 1 Granny Smith apple
- 1 McIntosh apple
- 3 tbsps. unsalted butter
- 1 cup finely chopped shallot (3 large)
- 1 cup finely chopped onion (1 medium)
- 1 (1/2-oz.) piece slab bacon, rind discarded
- 1 cup dry Riesling
- 1 cup chicken broth
- 2 tsps. minced fresh thyme
- 5 juniper berries *
- 1/2 Turkish or 1/4 California bay leaf
- 2 cups heavy cream (optional)
- 3 tbsps. apple schnapps (optional)
- 3/4 tsp. salt
- 1/4 tsp. black pepper

Direction

- Submerge the sauerkraut by 1 inch in a big bowl filled with cold water; allow it to soak for 5 minutes then use a colander to drain the soaked sauerkraut. Soak and drain the sauerkraut one more time, push on the sauerkraut it drains.
- Preheat the oven to 325°F.
- Remove the skin and the core of the apples and slice it to pieces that are 1/4 inch in thickness.
- In a 4- to 5-quart pot, put in the butter, shallot and onion and sauté the mixture over moderate heat setting for 8-10 minutes while stirring it until the onion and shallot become soft. Put in the juniper berries, wine, apples, bay leaf, broth, bacon and thyme and allow the mixture to simmer; add in the sauerkraut

and mix. Use an aluminum foil to cover the pot then put the lid on; put it in the middle layer of the preheated oven and let it cook for 1 to 1 1/2 hours until softened. Throw away the bay leaf.
- While the apples-and-sauerkraut mixture is cooking in the oven, in a 2-quart saucepan, let the schnapps and cream simmer for about 40 minutes until the mixture has reduced in volume to about 1 cup.
- Thoroughly mix the salt, pepper and cream mixture into the braised apples-and-sauerkraut mixture.

Nutrition Information

- Calories: 204
- Total Carbohydrate: 23 g
- Cholesterol: 20 mg
- Total Fat: 9 g
- Fiber: 6 g
- Protein: 4 g
- Sodium: 722 mg
- Saturated Fat: 5 g

263. Rigatoni With Cheese And Italian Sausage

"Double this recipe then prep it in 1 big baking dish if you want a family-style dinner. Use a purchased sauce or your preferred marinara recipe."
Serving: Makes 4 appetizer servings

Ingredients

- 1/2 lb. rigatoni
- 1/4 lb. spicy Italian sausage, casing removed
- 2 garlic cloves, thinly sliced
- 1 1/2 cups prepared marinara sauce
- 1/2 tsp. dried crushed red pepper
- 1/4 cup grated mozzarella cheese
- 2 tbsps. grated Parmesan cheese
- 1 tsp. chopped fresh Italian parsley
- Extra-virgin olive oil

Direction

- Cook rigatoni, occasionally mixing, till just tender yet firm to chew in a big pot with boiling salted water; drain pasta.
- Meanwhile, preheat a broiler. Cook sausage, frequently mixing, breaking up using back of wooden spoon, in a big heavy pot on medium high heat till not pink. Add garlic; sauté for 2 minutes till soft. Drain extra oil off; put pot on medium high heat. Mix in crushed red pepper, marinara sauce then pasta; season with pepper and salt to taste. Divide pasta to 4 1 1/4-cup custard cups/soufflé dishes. Sprinkle parmesan and mozzarella. Put in broiler for 1 1/2 minutes, closely watching to avoid burning, till cheese starts to brown and melts. Sprinkle parsley on rigatoni; drizzle olive oil. Serve.

Nutrition Information

- Calories: 434
- Total Carbohydrate: 51 g
- Cholesterol: 35 mg
- Total Fat: 18 g
- Fiber: 4 g
- Protein: 17 g
- Sodium: 773 mg
- Saturated Fat: 6 g

264. Roast Leg Of Lamb With Grilled Summer Beans And Anchovy-parsley Butter

"An amazing dish!"
Serving: Makes 8 to 10 servings | Prep: 1h

Ingredients

- 1 6 3/4-lb. bone-in leg of lamb, well trimmed
- 11 anchovy fillets; 8 halved, 3 whole
- 7 garlic cloves; 4 quartered, 3 whole
- 10 1/2 tbsps. olive oil, divided, plus additional (for brushing lamb)
- 1 1/2 cups (lightly packed) fresh Italian parsley leaves
- 2 1/4 tsps. finely grated lemon peel
- 6 tbsps. (3/4 stick) unsalted butter, room temperature
- Coarse kosher salt
- 2 1/2 lbs. summer beans (such as green, purple, and yellow wax beans)
- 1 1/2 tbsps. fresh lemon juice
- Grill basket for barbecue

Direction

- Create 16 1-in. deep slits all over the lamb with a small sharp knife; in each slit, push 1 garlic quarter and 1/2 anchovy. Put lamb onto small rack in middle of big rimmed baking sheet. Brush olive oil on lamb. Use plastic wrap to cover; chill overnight.
- In processor, blend 6 tbsp. olive oil, lemon peel, 3 whole garlic cloves, 3 whole anchovies and parsley to coarse paste. Add butter and blend till smooth. Season butter using freshly ground pepper and coarse salt. Put anchovy-parsley butter in small bowl. You can make it 1 day ahead. Cover then chill. Before using, bring to room temperature.
- Preheat an oven to 450°F. Roast the lamb for 30 minutes, uncovered. Lower heat to 325°F; roast the lamb for 1 hour till inserted thermometer in thickest part reads 135-140°F. Rest lamb for 30-45 minutes.
- Meanwhile, prep barbecue to medium high heat. Mix 3 tbsp. oil and beans in a big bowl. Sprinkle pepper and coarse salt; toss to coat.
- On barbecue, put grill basket. Spread beans out in basket; put bowl aside. Grill beans for 15-18 minutes till charred slightly, tossing often. Put beans in reserved bowl; toss with 1 1/2 tbsp. lemon juice and 1 1/2 tbsp. oil. Season with pepper and coarse salt.
- Put lamb on platter; serve with anchovy-parsley butter and grilled beans.

Nutrition Information

- Calories: 1726
- Total Carbohydrate: 12 g

- Cholesterol: 345 mg
- Total Fat: 155 g
- Fiber: 4 g
- Protein: 69 g
- Sodium: 1642 mg
- Saturated Fat: 77 g

265. Roasted Baby Potatoes With Capers And Rosemary

Serving: Makes 8 servings

Ingredients

- 3 lbs. assorted baby potatoes (such as red-skinned, White Rose, and baby purple), halved
- 1/4 cup extra-virgin olive oil
- 3 sprigs fresh rosemary, each broken into 4 pieces plus more for garnish
- 3 large garlic cloves, halved
- 1 1/2 tsps. coarse kosher salt
- 3 tbsps. drained capers

Direction

- Preheat an oven to 400°F. Put potatoes on big rimmed baking sheet in 1 layer. Drizzle oil. Sprinkle salt, garlic and rosemary pieces; toss to coat. Roast, mixing every 15 minutes, for 45 minutes total till potatoes are tender. Mix in capers; roast for 5 minutes till flavors blend. Season with pepper. Put into bowl; use rosemary sprigs to garnish.

Nutrition Information

- Calories: 194
- Total Carbohydrate: 30 g
- Total Fat: 7 g
- Fiber: 4 g
- Protein: 4 g
- Sodium: 423 mg
- Saturated Fat: 1 g

266. Roasted Beets With Dill

"An easy side dish."
Serving: Makes 6 servings

Ingredients

- 2 lbs. beets, trimmed (about 6 medium)
- 1/4 cup water
- 6 tbsps. (3/4 stick) unsalted butter
- 1/4 cup chopped fresh dill
- 1 tbsp. fresh lemon juice

Direction

- Preheat an oven to 400°F. Put 1/4 cup water and beets in a small roasting pan; tightly cover pan with foil. Bake for 1 hour till beets are tender when a knife pierces them; slightly cool. You can make it 1 day ahead. Cover; refrigerate. Peel the beets; cut to 1-in. pieces.
- Melt butter on medium heat in big heavy skillet; mix in lemon juice and dill. Add beets; toss for 5 minutes till heated through. Season with pepper and salt. Put into bowl; serve.

Nutrition Information

- Calories: 168
- Total Carbohydrate: 15 g
- Cholesterol: 31 mg
- Total Fat: 12 g
- Fiber: 4 g
- Protein: 3 g
- Sodium: 120 mg
- Saturated Fat: 7 g

267. Roasted Clams With Pancetta And Red Bell Pepper Coulis

"A lovely recipe."
Serving: Serves 4 as appetizers

Ingredients

- 1 large red bell pepper
- 1 tbsp. olive oil

- 1 tsp. dried oregano
- 1 garlic clove, peeled
- 24 littleneck clams, scrubbed
- 3 slices pancetta or bacon, cut into 24 pieces
- Lemon wedges

Direction

- Char bell pepper in broiler/above gas flame till all sides blacken. Enclose in paper bag; stand for 10 minutes. Peel then seed; chop bell pepper coarsely. Put in processor. Add garlic, oregano and oil; puree till smooth. Use pepper and salt to season coulis.
- Preheat an oven to 500°F. Line foil on big baking sheet; put clams on sheet. Bake for 6 minutes till clams open; discard unopened ones. Slightly cool. Remove top shells and discard; leave clam in half shells on the sheet.
- Preheat a broiler. Put 1 tsp. coulis then piece of pancetta over each clam; broil clams for 3 minutes till pancetta browns and coulis bubbles. Put onto platter and garnish with lemon; serve.

Nutrition Information

- Calories: 207
- Total Carbohydrate: 6 g
- Cholesterol: 40 mg
- Total Fat: 13 g
- Fiber: 1 g
- Protein: 16 g
- Sodium: 664 mg
- Saturated Fat: 3 g

268. Roasted Kabocha Squash With Cumin Salt

"A flavor-enhancing salt recipe."
Serving: Makes 4 servings

Ingredients

- 1 tsp. cumin seeds, toasted 1 minute in a dry skillet

- 1 bay leaf
- 1/4 tsp. smoked paprika (pimenton) or regular paprika
- 2 tsps. packed brown sugar
- 1 tsp. sea salt
- 1 kabocha squash (about 2 1/2 lbs.), partially peeled, seeded, cut into 1-inch chunks
- 1 tbsp. olive oil

Direction

- Heat an oven to 375°F. Briefly process paprika, bay leaf and cumin seeds in a clean coffee grinder/spice mill. Add salt and sugar; process to mix. Put aside. Toss oil with squash then cumin mixture then spread onto 2 baking sheets; roast for 25 minutes till tender.

269. Roasted Pork Chops With Hard Cider Jus

"A tasty porkchop recipe."
Serving: Makes 8 servings | Prep: 30m

Ingredients

- 8 (1-inch-thick) rib pork chops (4 lb total)
- 1 tsp. fine sea salt
- 1 1/4 tsps. black pepper
- 2 1/2 tbsps. unsalted butter
- 1 lb large shallots (8), bulbs separated if necessary and each bulb halved lengthwise
- 1 cup hard cider
- an instant-read thermometer

Direction

- Preheat an oven to 450°F.
- Pat dry porkchops; sprinkle pepper and sea salt on both sides. Heat 1 1/2 tbsp. butter till foam subsides in 12-in. heavy skillet on medium high heat. In 3 batches, brown chops, flipping once, for 6 minutes per batch; put into big 1-in. deep shallow baking pan with tongs.
- Put leftover 1 tbsp. butter and shallots in skillet; cook on medium heat, occasionally turning, for 6-8 minutes till tender and golden

brown. Add cider; boil, mixing, scraping brown bits up, for 3 minutes till reduced to 3/4 cup.

- Put sauce and shallots around chops; roast in lower oven third for 7-9 minutes till a horizontally inserted thermometer in middle of 1 chop without touching bone reads 150°F.
- Stand chops for 5 minutes, loosely covered with foil; as it stands, temperature rises to 155°F. Serve chops with sauce and shallots.

270. Roasted Potatoes With Cream Cheese And Sun-dried Tomato Filling

"You can make this in less than 1 hour."
Serving: Makes 12 hors d'oeuvres, serving 2

Ingredients

- a 1/2-lb. russet (baking) potato
- 1 tbsp. olive oil
- 3 tbsps. cream cheese, softened
- 2 tbsps. minced drained bottle sun-dried tomatoes in oil
- 1 tbsp. minced scallion greens

Direction

- From middle of potato, cut 12 1/4-in. thick rounds; discard ends. Use paper towels to pat dry; brush oil on both sides. Roast potato slices on baking sheet in upper third of preheated 500°F oven till bottoms are golden for 6 minutes. Flip slices; roast till bottoms are crisp and golden for 6 minutes. Cool till you can handle them.
- As potatoes roast, mix pepper and salt to taste, scallion, tomatoes and cream cheese in a bowl. Spread filling on 1/2 potato slices; top with leftover potato slices, pressing slices together to make sandwiches. Halve sandwiches.

Nutrition Information

- Calories: 572
- Total Carbohydrate: 57 g

- Cholesterol: 24 mg
- Total Fat: 39 g
- Fiber: 12 g
- Protein: 12 g
- Sodium: 549 mg
- Saturated Fat: 8 g

271. Roasted Red Peppers And Cherry Tomatoes With Ricotta

"A great salad for summer."
Serving: Serves 8

Ingredients

- 4 red bell peppers, halved, seeds and ribs removed
- 6 oil-packed anchovy fillets, finely chopped
- 4 garlic cloves, thinly sliced
- 1 cup basil leaves, divided
- Kosher salt, freshly ground pepper
- 2 tbsps. plus 1/3 cup olive oil
- 1 pint cherry tomatoes, halved
- 1/3 cup fresh ricotta
- 1/4 cup pitted small black and/or green olives
- Flaky sea salt

Direction

- Preheat an oven to 375°F. In a shallow baking dish, put bell peppers with skin side down; top with garlic and anchovies. Tear 1/4 cup of basil leaves on top; season with black pepper and kosher salt. Drizzle 2 tbsp. oil; bake for 35-45 minutes till peppers slightly char around edges and are tender yet hold their shape; cool.
- Meanwhile, blend leftover 1/3 cup oil and leftover 3/4 cup basil till smooth in a blender; season basil oil with black pepper and kosher salt.
- Put bell peppers onto platter; top with olives, ricotta, tomatoes and more basil. Drizzle basil oil; season with black pepper and sea salt.

Nutrition Information

- Calories: 168
- Total Carbohydrate: 6 g
- Cholesterol: 8 mg
- Total Fat: 15 g
- Fiber: 2 g
- Protein: 3 g
- Sodium: 319 mg
- Saturated Fat: 3 g

272. Roasted Savoy Cabbage With Raisins

Serving: Makes 4 servings | Prep: 20m

Ingredients

- 2 tbsps. golden raisins
- 1 large head Savoy cabbage (2 1/2 lbs.), quartered and cored
- 2 1/2 tbsps. peanut oil
- 3/4 tsp. kosher salt
- 1/4 tsp. black pepper
- 3 tbsps. unsalted butter
- 2 fresh thyme sprigs

Direction

- Put oven rack in center position; preheat the oven to 400°F.
- Soak raisins covered in very hot water for 30 minutes in small bowl; as it gets tepid, replace hot water 1-2 times.
- Tear cabbage to big pieces.
- Heat oil till hot yet not smoking in 12-in. heavy ovenproof skillet/pot on medium high heat. In 5 batches, add cabbage, adding some pepper and salt with every batch, mixing, adding next batch as last batch starts to wilt; some of cabbage will brown. Add thyme and butter; cook, frequently mixing, for 3 minutes till all cabbage wilts. Drain raisins; add to cabbage. Put skillet in oven; roast, mixing every 10 minutes, for 30-40 minutes till

cabbage is tender. Before serving, discard thyme sprigs.

Nutrition Information

- Calories: 243
- Total Carbohydrate: 21 g
- Cholesterol: 23 mg
- Total Fat: 17 g
- Fiber: 9 g
- Protein: 6 g
- Sodium: 434 mg
- Saturated Fat: 7 g

273. Roasted Squash With Date Relish And Pumpkin Seeds

"Use deglet noor or a different kind of firm date for this recipe."
Serving: Makes 8 to 10 servings

Ingredients

- 1/3 cup shelled raw pumpkin seeds (pepitas)
- 1 tsp. plus 3/4 cup extra-virgin olive oil, divided
- Kosher salt
- 4 lb. kabocha or acorn squash, each squash halved through root end, seeded
- 1 tbsp. fresh thyme leaves
- Freshly ground black pepper
- 1/4 cup (or more) fresh lemon juice
- 1/4 cup chopped flat-leaf parsley
- 1 bunch dandelion greens, tough ends trimmed (about 4 oz.)
- 1 cup Deglet Noor dates (about 3 1/2 oz.), pitted, thinly sliced lengthwise
- 2 oz. Parmesan, cut into 1/4" cubes (about 1/3 cup; optional)

Direction

- Put racks in lower and upper oven thirds; preheat to 375°F. Spread pumpkin seeds out in 1 layer on rimmed baking sheet; toast on top rack, mixing 1-2 times, for 7 minutes till aromatic, puffed and lightly browned. Toss pumpkin seeds with pinch of salt and 1 tsp. oil on sheet; cool on sheet. Put onto work surface; chop coarsely. You can prep pumpkin seeds 1 day ahead; keep at room temperature, airtight.

- Put oven temperature on 425°F. Put squash onto cutting board, cut side down. Remove peel carefully with a sharp knife. Lengthwise cut squash to 3/4-in. thick wedges. Put thyme, 1/4 cup oil and squash in a big bowl; season with pepper and salt. Toss to coat then divide squash, cut side down, in 1 layer to 2 big rimmed baking sheets.
- Roast squash, rotating the sheets halfway through, for 25-30 minutes till tender when fork pierces them; put aside.
- In a medium bowl, mix parsley, 1/4 cup lemon juice and leftover 1/2 cup oil; season dressing with extra lemon juice (optional), pepper and salt. Put dandelion greens in a big bowl; drizzle 1 tbsp. dressing. Season with pepper and salt; toss to coat. Add parmesan (optional) and dates to leftover dressing in bowl for the date relish.
- On a big platter, put dandelion greens; put warm squash over. Top with date relish; garnish with pumpkin seeds.

Nutrition Information

- Calories: 379
- Total Carbohydrate: 36 g
- Cholesterol: 5 mg
- Total Fat: 26 g
- Fiber: 5 g
- Protein: 7 g
- Sodium: 693 mg
- Saturated Fat: 5 g

"You can use basil for tarragon."
Serving: Makes 6 servings

Ingredients

- 6 cups halved hulled strawberries, patted dry (2 to 2 1/2 lbs.), plus 6 whole strawberries for garnish
- 12 sprigs fresh tarragon, divided
- 2 tbsps. plus 1/2 cup sugar
- 1/2 tsp. fresh lemon juice
- 1 cup crème fraîche
- 2 1/2 tbsps. cold water
- 2 tsps. unflavored gelatin
- 1 4-inch piece vanilla bean, split lengthwise
- 1/2 cup whipping cream

Direction

- Preheat an oven to 350°F. In 13x9x2-in. glass baking dish, mix 6 tarragon sprigs and 6 cups strawberries; sprinkle lemon juice and 2 tbsp. sugar. Toss till coated. Roast, uncovered, occasionally mixing, for 20 minutes till syrup forms and strawberries are soft. Cool for 30 minutes.
- Into medium bowl, strain strawberry mixture, pressing fruit to remove as much pulp as you can. Discard seeds in the strainer. Put 1 1/2 cups strawberry puree into another medium bowl; stir in crème fraiche. Keep leftover puree for another time.
- Sprinkle 2 1/2 tbsp. cold water in a small saucepan, sprinkle gelatin; stand for 15 minutes till gelatin softens.
- From vanilla bean halves, scrape seeds into separate small saucepan then add bean. Add leftover 1/2 cup sugar and cream; simmer on medium heat, mixing till sugar dissolves. Take off heat. Add gelatin mixture; mix to dissolve. Slightly cool. Mix gelatin-cream mixture into the strawberry cream. Strain into big measuring cup; divide to 6 3/4-cup small goblets/ramekins. Cover; chill for 6 hours – 1

day till panna cotta sets. Garnish with leftover tarragon sprigs and whole strawberries.

Nutrition Information

- Calories: 227
- Total Carbohydrate: 24 g
- Cholesterol: 42 mg
- Total Fat: 14 g
- Fiber: 0 g
- Protein: 3 g
- Sodium: 29 mg
- Saturated Fat: 8 g

275. Roquefort And Pear Strudel

"A satisfying recipe. Start 1 day ahead."
Serving: Makes 8 servings

Ingredients

- 2 cups all purpose flour plus additional for dusting
- 3/4 cup warm water (105°F to 115°F)
- 1/4 cup vegetable oil
- 1/2 tsp. salt
- 1 1/2 tsps. unsalted butter plus 1/4 cup (1/2 stick) unsalted butter, melted
- 1 1/2 lbs. firm but ripe Bosc pears, peeled, halved, cored, cut into 1/3-inch cubes (about 3 1/2 cups)
- 6 oz. Roquefort cheese, crumbled (about 1 1/3 cups)
- 1/2 cup chopped toasted pecans
- 1 tbsp. all purpose flour
- 1 1/2 tsps. fresh lemon juice
- 2 tbsps. sugar
- 2 tbsps. plain dried breadcrumbs

Direction

- Dough: Mix 1/2 tsp. salt, oil, 3/4 cup warm water and 2 cups flour for 3 minutes on medium speed (it will be sticky) in a stand mixer's big bowl with paddle attachment. Take strudel dough from bowl; halve. Shape each dough half to ball; in plastic, wrap each. For strudel, refrigerate a dough ball overnight; freeze 2nd dough ball for another time.
- Filling: In big heavy skillet, melt 1 1/2 tsp. butter on high heat. Add pears; sauté for 4 minutes till soft. Strain pear mixture; discard juice. Put pears, spacing apart, on rimmed baking sheet; fully cool. Put cooled pears into big bowl. You can make it 1 day ahead. Cover; chill.
- Add lemon juice, flour, pecans and cheese to pears; gently toss to mix.
- Put 36x24-in. clean cotton tablecloth/cotton cloth on big worksurface; to keep in place, secure all 4 of the corners to work surface using tape. Use flour to lightly dust cloth. Unwrap refrigerated strudel dough; put in middle of prepped cloth. Lightly sprinkle flour. Roll dough out as thinly without tearing as possible using rolling pin; as needed, lightly dust dough with flour to avoid sticking.
- Line parchment paper on rimmed baking sheet. Slide hands under middle of dough; pull with palms gently, not fingers, toward edges; don't stretch to thin rectangle or tear dough. Pull dough edges gently to make 34x18-in. rectangle with floured fingertips. Trim edges to make 33x17-in. rectangle using sharp knife. Lengthwise halve dough rectangle, making 2 33x8 1/2-in. rectangles. Lightly brush melted butter on each dough rectangle; evenly sprinkle 1 tbsp. dried breadcrumbs and 1 tbsp. sugar on each. Crosswise put filling, starting 1-in. from 1 dough short end, on each dough rectangle, leaving 1-in. plain border on both rectangle's long sides, in 1 1/2-in. wide log. Beginning at cloth edge nearest to filling, lift cloth edge, using cloth as aid; roll strudel dough up to start, not cloth, on filling, fully enclosing filling, making 2 strudels. Tuck in dough's short ends; to seal, pinch. Put strudels on prepped baking sheet; brush melted butter all over strudels. Chill for 1-6 hours.
- Put rack in bottom oven third; preheat to 375°F. Bake the strudels for 40 minutes till

golden brown; cool for 30 minutes on baking sheet.

- Crosswise cut strudels to 1-in. thick slices; serve at room temperature/warm.
- To get best texture, you need to create full dough batch even if you only use half; you can keep leftover dough airtight for 1 month in the freezer.

Nutrition Information

- Calories: 385
- Total Carbohydrate: 44 g
- Cholesterol: 21 mg
- Total Fat: 19 g
- Fiber: 4 g
- Protein: 9 g
- Sodium: 282 mg
- Saturated Fat: 5 g

---

276. Rotelle With Mushroom Sauce

"You can make this in under 1 hour."
Serving: Serves 4 to 6

Ingredients

- 1 onion, chopped fine
- 2 tbsps. unsalted butter
- 1 1/2 lbs. mushrooms, chopped fine
- 2 flat anchovy fillets, patted dry between paper towels and minced
- 2 tsp. Worcestershire sauce
- 1/4 cup heavy cream
- 1 tbsp. fresh lemon juice
- 1 lb. rotelle (corkscrew-shaped pasta)
- 1/2 cup minced fresh parsley leaves

Direction

- Cook onion in butter in heavy skillet on medium heat, mixing, till soft. Add mushrooms; cook, occasionally mixing, till mushrooms lightly brown and liquid given off by mushrooms evaporate for 15 minutes. Mix in lemon juice, cream, Worcestershire sauce

and anchovies; cook for 2 minutes. Season with pepper and salt.

- As mushrooms cooks, boil rotelle in kettle with boiling salted water till al dente; put 1/2 cup cooking water aside. Drain rotelle well. Put rotelle into big bowl. Add parsley and mushroom mixture; toss well, adding enough reserved cooking water so sauce thins to desired consistency.

Nutrition Information

- Calories: 583
- Total Carbohydrate: 95 g
- Cholesterol: 37 mg
- Total Fat: 14 g
- Fiber: 6 g
- Protein: 22 g
- Sodium: 129 mg
- Saturated Fat: 8 g

---

277. Rye Dinner Rolls With Crisp Tops

"Tender and yummy."
Serving: Makes 16 rolls | Prep: 45m

Ingredients

- 1 1/4 tsps. active dry yeast
- 1 scant cup warm water (105-115°F), divided
- 3/4 tsp. sugar
- 2 1/4 cups unbleached all-purpose flour plus more for kneading and dusting
- 1/3 cup light or dark rye flour
- 1 1/4 tsps. salt
- 1/4 cup unbleached all-purpose flour
- 2 tbsps. light or dark rye flour
- 1/8 tsp. salt
- 2 tbsps. water
- 1 tbsp. olive oil
- 1 large egg white

Direction

- Dough: Mix sugar, 1/4 cup warm water and yeast in a big bowl; stand for 5 minutes till foamy. Begin again with new yeast if it doesn't foam.
- Use a wooden spoon to mix leftover scant 3/4 cup water, salt and flours into yeast mixture to make a soft dough.
- Turn dough onto well-floured surface; with lightly floured hands, knead for 6-8 minutes till dough is smooth and elastic yet slightly sticky and supple. Shape dough to ball.
- Put dough in oiled big bowl; turn to coat. Use plastic wrap/kitchen towel (not terry cloth) to cover bowl; rise in draft-free place for 1-2 hours at warm room temperature till doubled.
- Rolls: Punch dough down; don't knead. Take out of bowl; like a letter, fold to thirds. Divide to 16 pieces; roll each piece to ball, putting onto parchment paper-lined baking sheet. Cover with towel/plastic wrap loosely; rise for 1 hour in a warm place till doubled.
- Brush some egg white lightly on each dough ball. Lay rye-crisp dough round, egg wash side up, over each roll gently; bake for 20 minutes till golden brown. Cool to room temperature/warm.
- As rolls rise, make rye-crisp tops: Mix salt and flours; mix in oil and water till dough forms. Turn dough onto lightly floured surface; knead 4-5 times. Divide to 16 very small pieces then roll each piece out to 2-in. round (doesn't have to be perfect) on lightly floured surface. Put on a parchment sheet in 1 layer.
- Beat pinch of salt and egg white; brush some of it lightly on rounds. Stand, uncovered, to slightly dry as rolls rise.
- Bake rolls and assemble: Preheat an oven with rack in center to 425°F.
- Brush some egg white on each dough ball lightly. Lay a rye-crisp dough round, egg wash side up, over each roll gently; bake rolls for 20 minutes till golden brown. Cool to room temperature/warm.
- You can shape dough to balls and let slowly rise, covered with plastic wrap well, chilled for 8-16 hours. As you make rye-crisp tops, bring to room temperature.
- Best the same day as baked; you can freeze, first fully cooled then wrapped well, for 1 month. Thaw; reheat on baking sheet in 350°F oven for 5-10 minutes till warmed through.

Nutrition Information

- Calories: 93
- Total Carbohydrate: 18 g
- Total Fat: 1 g
- Fiber: 1 g
- Protein: 3 g
- Sodium: 101 mg
- Saturated Fat: 0 g

278. S'mores Bars

"Can be made in less than 45 minutes."
Serving: Makes about 24 bars

Ingredients

- 2 cups graham cracker crumbs
- 1/3 cup sugar
- 1/4 tsp. salt
- 1 stick (1/2 cup) unsalted butter, melted
- 1 lb. milk chocolate
- 4 cups mini-marshmallows

Direction

- Preparation: In a bowl combine thoroughly the butter, the salt, the sugar, and the crumbs and, save 1 cup of the mixture, push the rest of the mixture into a 13 by 9 by 2 inches flameproof baking dish's bottom. In a preheated 350°F oven, bake the crust until it is golden, or for 12 minutes, and allow to cool on a rack in the dish. Melt the chocolate in a metal bowl place on top of a saucepan with barely simmering water, stir, evenly spread it over the crust, and sprinkle the marshmallows on top, lightly press them and the reserved crumb mixture. Under a preheated broiler, broil the dessert for 30 seconds about 2 inches away from the heat, or until marshmallows are golden, allow to cool thoroughly, and slice into squares.

279. Saffron Couscous With Fresh Peas And Chives

"This side dish is quite fascinating with peas and chives."
Serving: Makes 4 servings

Ingredients

- 1 (14 1/2-oz.) can low-salt chicken broth
- 1 1/2 cups shelled fresh peas or frozen peas
- 2 tbsps. (1/4 stick) butter
- Pinch of saffron threads
- 1 1/4 cups couscous
- 1/4 cup chopped fresh chives

Direction

- Preparation: Heat chicken broth to simmer in a medium saucepan. Add in peas and cook for about 2 minutes until softened. Place peas to bowl with a slotted spoon. Put in saffron threads and 2 tbsps. of butter to broth and heat to a boil. Take away from heat. Put in couscous; stir to combine. Cover tightly and allow to stand for about 5 minutes until liquid is absorbed and couscous softens. Use a fork to fluff the couscous. Lightly combine in peas and chives. Season with pepper and salt. Place couscous to a large bowl.

Nutrition Information

- Calories: 310
- Total Carbohydrate: 50 g
- Cholesterol: 15 mg
- Total Fat: 7 g
- Fiber: 5 g
- Protein: 12 g
- Sodium: 91 mg
- Saturated Fat: 4 g

280. Sage And Garlic Mashed Potatoes

Serving: Serves 6 to 8

Ingredients

- 1 large garlic clove, sliced
- 3 tbsps. olive oil
- 1 tbsp. fresh sage leaves, minced or 1 1/2 tsps. dried sage, crumbled
- olive oil for frying
- 12 whole fresh sage leaves
- coarse salt for sprinkling
- 4 russet (baking) potatoes (about 2 lbs.)
- 1 cup plain yogurt
- 1 tbsp. unsalted butter, softened

Direction

- Simmer garlic in oil till golden in a small saucepan. Mix in sage; take off the heat. Stand mixture for 15 minutes. Through a fine-sieve, drain oil into a small bowl; throw away solids.
- Fried sage leaves: Heat 1/8-in. oil in a small skillet on moderately high heat till hot but not smoking; 1 at a time, fry sage leaves till crisp for about 3 seconds, transferring to paper towels with a slotted spoon to drain. Sprinkle coarse salt on sage leaves.
- Peel then quarter potatoes. Cover potatoes by 1-in. salted cold water in a big saucepan; simmer for approximately 20 minutes till tender. Keep about 1/3 cup cooking liquid; drain potatoes.
- Preheat an oven to 350°F.
- Force potatoes while still warm through a medium food mill disk or ricer into a bowl; beat in pepper and salt to taste, seasoned oil, butter, yogurt and enough leftover liquid to get preferred consistency. Put into an ovenproof serving dish. You can make mashed potatoes 1 day ahead, covered, chilled.
- In oven, heat potatoes till heated through; put fried sage leaves on top.

Nutrition Information

- Calories: 462
- Total Carbohydrate: 24 g
- Cholesterol: 10 mg
- Total Fat: 40 g
- Fiber: 4 g
- Protein: 4 g
- Sodium: 505 mg
- Saturated Fat: 7 g

281. Sage Cloverleaf Rolls

Serving: Makes 12 rolls

Ingredients

- 2/3 cup milk
- 3/4 stick (6 tbsps.) unsalted butter
- 1 tbsp. sugar
- a 1/4-oz. package (2 1/2 tsps.) active dry yeast
- 1 large whole egg, beaten lightly
- 1 1/2 tsps. salt
- 2 1/2 to 3 cups all-purpose flour
- 1/4 cup minced fresh sage or 2 tbsps. crumbled dried
- an egg wash made by beating 1 large egg with 1 tbsp. water

Direction

- Mix sugar, 4 tbsps. butter and milk in saucepan, let mixture heat over medium-low heat, mixing from time to time, till a candy thermometer reads between 110°F to 115°F, and dissolve the yeast in it for 5 minutes, or till mixture is frothy. Mix in 2 1/2 cups flour, salt and whole egg, mixing till mixture creates a dough. Knead dough on a floured area, working in sufficient of leftover half cup of flour to create soft dough, work in sage, and knead the dough for an additional of 8 to 10 minutes, or till pliable and smooth. Shape dough into a round, turn it into buttered bowl, and roll it to cover with butter. Allow the dough to rise for an hour with plastic wrap as cover, in warm area, or till it is double in volume.
- Punch the dough down and split into 36 even portions. Shape the portions into balls, dunking the balls as formed into leftover 2 tbsp. of liquified butter, and place 3 balls in every of a dozen buttered one third-cup muffin tins. Allow rolls to rise for half an hour in warm area, or till they are double in bulk volume, brush egg wash on surfaces, ensure to not allow the egg to drip down sides, and in the center of a prepped 400 °F oven, let the rolls bake for 15 to 20 minutes, or till they turn golden. Rolls can be done a day ahead and wrap with foil and store at room temperature. Rewarm rolls for 15 minutes, with foil as wrap, in a prepped 350°F oven, or till hot.

Nutrition Information

- Calories: 190
- Total Carbohydrate: 25 g
- Cholesterol: 48 mg
- Total Fat: 8 g
- Fiber: 2 g
- Protein: 5 g
- Sodium: 144 mg
- Saturated Fat: 4 g

282. Salad With Canadian Bacon And Poached Eggs

Serving: Makes 4 servings | Prep: 20m

Ingredients

- 1 tsp. Dijon mustard
- 1/4 tsp. salt
- 2 tbsps. minced shallots
- 1 tbsp. finely chopped fresh flat-leaf parsley
- 5 1/2 tsps. red-wine vinegar
- 4 tbsps. extra-virgin olive oil
- 6 oz sliced Canadian bacon, cut into 1- by 1/4-inch pieces
- 1/2 tsp. black pepper
- 4 large eggs

- 6 cups torn frisée

Direction

- In a big bowl, whisk 4 1/2 tsp. vinegar, parsley, shallots, salt and mustard. In a slow stream, add 3 tbsp. oil, whisking till emulsified.
- In a 12-in. skillet, heat leftover tbsp. oil on high heat. Brown bacon with pepper for 1-2 minutes, mixing.
- Fill 1 1/2-in. water and 1 tsp. vinegar into a deep 10-in. skillet; simmer. In a cup, break 1 egg; slide into water. Repeat with leftover 3 eggs, evenly spacing them. At a bare simmer, poach for 2-3 minutes till yolks are runny yet whites are firm. Put eggs onto paper towels. Season with pepper and salt.
- Toss dressing with frisee. Put eggs and bacon on top; serve.
- The eggs won't be cooked fully, which can be a problem is salmonella is common in your area.

Nutrition Information

- Calories: 255
- Total Carbohydrate: 4 g
- Cholesterol: 206 mg
- Total Fat: 20 g
- Fiber: 2 g
- Protein: 16 g
- Sodium: 422 mg
- Saturated Fat: 4 g

283. Salade Verte Avec Croutes De Roquefort

"A great salad recipe."
Serving: Serves 6

Ingredients

- twelve 1/3-inch-thick diagonal slices of French or Italian bread
- 1/2 cup crumbled Roquefort (about 2 oz.), softened
- 2 tbsps. unsalted butter, softened
- 1 tbsp. Sherry vinegar or red-wine vinegar
- 1 tsp. Dijon-style mustard
- 1/4 cup extra-virgin olive oil
- 4 cups torn frisée (French or Italian curly chicory), rinsed and spun dry
- 4 cups torn arugula, rinsed well and spun dry

Direction

- Toasts: Bake bread slices in 1 layer on baking sheet in center of preheated 350°F oven till golden for 10-15 minutes. You can bake toasts 1 day ahead; keep in airtight container. Or, bake at same time as croutons for pea soup. Cream butter and Roquefort in a bowl; spread mixture on toasts.
- Salad: Whisk pepper and salt to taste, mustard and vinegar in a big bowl. In a stream, add oil, whisking; whisk dressing till emulsified. Add arugula and frisee; toss to coat greens in dressing well. Season salad with pepper then divide to 6 salad plates; on each plate, put 2 toasts.

Nutrition Information

- Calories: 1891
- Total Carbohydrate: 322 g
- Cholesterol: 19 mg
- Total Fat: 38 g
- Fiber: 18 g
- Protein: 59 g
- Sodium: 4116 mg
- Saturated Fat: 11 g

284. Salmon Hash With Horseradish-dill Cream

"A good way to use leftover potatoes or cooked salmon."
Serving: Serves 2

Ingredients

- 1 12-oz. salmon fillet (about 1 inch thick)
- 12 oz. small white potatoes
- 6 tbsps. chilled whipping cream
- 4 tbsps. prepared white horseradish
- 3 tbsps. chopped fresh dill
- 1/2 tsp. white wine vinegar
- 1/2 cup chopped green onions
- 2 tbsps. unsalted butter

Direction

- Preheat an oven to 350°F. Put salmon on baking sheet; season with pepper and salt. Bake for 18 minutes till just cooked through; put on plate. Chill till cold, covered. Flake salmon to 1/2-in. pieces. In pot with boiling salted water, cook potatoes for 10 minutes till just tender. Drain potatoes well; cool. Peel; dice.
- Whisk 2 tbsps. dill, 2 tbsps. horseradish and 5 tbsps. cream till very thick in small bowl. Whisk vinegar in. Season with pepper and salt to taste; chill.
- Mash 1 tbsp. dill, 2 tbsps. horseradish, 1 tbsp. cream and 3/4 cup of diced potatoes till nearly smooth in medium bowl. Mix leftover potatoes, onions and salmon in lightly. Season with pepper and salt. Melted butter in a heavy medium nonstick skillet on high heat; add hash then press to compact. Lower heat to medium. Cook for 10 minutes till bottom is crusty and brown. Flip hash in sections with a big spatula. Lightly press. Cook for 5 minutes till bottom is brown. Turn hash out on 2 plates then serve with the horseradish cream.

Nutrition Information

- Calories: 729
- Total Carbohydrate: 34 g
- Cholesterol: 174 mg
- Total Fat: 49 g
- Fiber: 6 g
- Protein: 40 g
- Sodium: 277 mg
- Saturated Fat: 21 g

285. Salmon With Potato Salad And Horseradish Yogurt

"You can use a bigger fish piece to easily double up the recipe."
Serving: 4 servings

Ingredients

- 1 1/2 lbs. small Yukon Gold potatoes, scrubbed, sliced 1/2-inch thick
- Kosher salt
- 1 1/2 lbs. skin-on salmon fillet
- 2 tbsps. olive oil
- Freshly ground black pepper
- 3/4 tsp. caraway seeds, coarsely chopped
- 1/4 cup olive oil
- 1 tbsp. white wine vinegar
- 3 scallions
- 1 tbsp. torn tarragon
- 1 tbsp. finely grated peeled horseradish (from about a 2-inch piece)
- 1 tsp. white wine vinegar
- Kosher salt
- 1 cup plain Greek yogurt
- 1 tbsp. olive oil
- Freshly ground black pepper
- Kosher salt, freshly ground pepper
- 1/2 cup vegetable oil
- 1/2 cup mixed tender herb sprigs (such as parsley, tarragon, and sage)
- 1 tbsp. cornstarch
- Flaky sea salt

Direction

- Salmon and potatoes: Preheat an oven to 250°F. Put potatoes in medium pot. Cover in water. Add a few big pinches of salt; boil. Lower heat. Simmer gently for 20-25 minutes till paring knife pierces potatoes easily.

- Meanwhile, put salmon in big baking dish; coat in oil. Season with pepper and salt on both sides. Put skin side down. Sprinkle caraway on. Bake for 25-30 minutes till a thin knife blade/cake tester inserted laterally in fillet meets no resistance. Fish should flake and be opaque throughout. While let potatoes and salmon bake, make horseradish yogurt and dressing.
- Dressing: Whisk vinegar and oil in a bowl large enough to hold potatoes. Whisk tarragon and 1/2 scallions into dressing. Put tarragon and leftover scallions for serving aside.
- Yogurt: In small bowl, mix big pinch of salt, vinegar and horseradish. Let sit for 5 minutes. Whisk oil and yogurt in. Season with pepper and salt.
- Assembly and herbs: When potatoes are done; drain. Add to bowl with the dressing. Toss till coated. Season with pepper and kosher salt.
- Heat oil in big saucepan on medium heat. In fine-mesh sieve, toss cornstarch and herbs. Add an herb leaf to test oil temperature. Oil should intensely sizzle, might spatter, and leaf should get dark on contact. In batches, fry herbs, 5 seconds per batch, till vibrant green and crisp. Use a slotted spoon to put on paper towels. Lightly season with kosher salt. You can skip this step and use chopped herbs alternatively.
- Dress salmon with sea salt and fried herbs. Redistribute dressing by tossing potatoes. Put tarragon, reserved scallions and sea salt on top. Serve salmon with horseradish yogurt and potatoes next to it.

286. Salt Cod In Tomato Garlic Confit

"Excellent salt cod in this irresistible dish."
Serving: Makes 12 servings (as part of tapas buffet) | Prep: 40m

Ingredients

- 1 lb. center-cut skinless boneless salt cod (bacalao), rinsed well and cut into 1 1/2-inch pieces
- 8 large garlic cloves, peeled
- 1/3 cup extra-virgin olive oil
- 4 (14-oz.) cans diced tomatoes, drained
- 1/4 tsp. sugar
- 6 tbsps. mayonnaise
- 1/4 cup crème fraîche
- 1 tbsp. water

Direction

- Soak and poach cod: in big bowl, submerge cod in 2-inch of cold water and refrigerate to soak, changing the water thrice a day, for a maximum of 3 days.
- Let cod drain and turn onto a 3-quarts saucepan, then put in 6 cups of water. Let come barely to a simmer and take off from heat. Cod will barely start to flake; prevent from boiling otherwise it will turn tough. Slowly turn cod onto a plate lined with paper towel using a slotted spatula to let drain. Cover in a moistened paper towel and refrigerate while preparing confit.
- Prepare confit and cook the fish: in a heavy 12-inches skillet on medium low heat, let garlic cook in oil for 10 to 15 minutes, flipping from time to time, till golden. Put in sugar and tomatoes and cook for 45 minutes to an hour, mixing often, till tomatoes cooked down into an extremely thick sauce and the oil separates.
- Crush garlic cloves to a sauce and put in to taste with pepper and salt. In one 3-quarts gratin dish or a different shallow flameproof

baking dish, scatter sauce and place fish on sauce.

- Preheat the broiler.
- Whip water, crème fraiche and mayonnaise together and spread on each fish piece. Let fish broil for 2 minutes, 5- to 6-inch away from heat barely till mayonnaise mixture is slightly browned.
- Notes: salt cod brands vary in the degree of saltiness: A less salty kind may require just a day of soaking, on the other hand other may need up to 3. To check it, just taste a little piece a day after; it has to be pleasantly salty and not overwhelming.
- Confit may be done 2 days in advance and cool with no cover, then refrigerate with cover. Reheat prior to using.

Nutrition Information

- Calories: 249
- Total Carbohydrate: 6 g
- Cholesterol: 63 mg
- Total Fat: 14 g
- Fiber: 3 g
- Protein: 25 g
- Sodium: 2714 mg
- Saturated Fat: 2 g

287. Salted-caramel Semifreddo With Hot Fudge

"So delicious!"
Serving: Makes 6 servings

Ingredients

- 1/2 cup heavy whipping cream
- 3 egg whites
- 6 tbsps. sugar, divided
- 3 tbsps. caramel sauce
- 1/4 tsp. salt
- 5 tbsps. half-and-half
- 2 oz. dark chocolate
- 2 tsps. light corn syrup

Direction

- Beat whipping cream for 2-3 minutes till soft peaks form in a bowl. Beat egg whites, adding 1 tbsp. sugar at a time, for 3-4 minutes till glossy and fluffy in a 2nd bowl. Mix salt and caramel sauce in microwave-safe bowl; nuke for 15-30 seconds till warm. Fold caramel sauce and whipped cream into egg white mixture slowly; cover. Freeze for 4-6 hours till solid. Heat corn syrup, chocolate and half and half in small saucepan on low heat, mixing, for 2-3 minutes till viscous and smooth. Divide hot fudge and semifreddo to 6 bowls.

288. Sauteed Green Beans With Coconut

"This dish is colorful and flavorful!"
Serving: Makes 4 servings | Prep: 20m

Ingredients

- 1/2 cup finely grated unsweetened coconut* (1 1/2 oz)
- 1/3 cup water
- 1 lb green beans, trimmed
- 3 tbsps. vegetable oil
- 2 tsps. black mustard seeds*
- 1 (1 1/2-inch) dried hot red chile, seeded and crumbled
- 1 Turkish bay leaf or 1/2 California
- 1/4 tsp. salt
- 1/4 tsp. black pepper

Direction

- In a bowl, stir water and coconut together. Allow to soak at the room temperature for 60 minutes or until the water is absorbed.
- In a 6-quart heavy pot, cook beans in the boiling salted water, with no cover, for 6-7 minutes or until crisp-tender. Place beans into colander placed in a bowl of cold water and ice to stop cooking. Drain well.
- In a 12-inch heavy pan, heat oil over moderately high heat until it's hot but not

smoking. Put in bay leaf, chile and mustard seeds. Sauté while stirring for one minute or until the mustard seeds create bursting sounds. Put in beans, mix until coated with oil. Put in coconut mixture. Cook while stirring for 2-3 minutes or until heated through. Get rid of the bay leaf. Add pepper and salt to season.

Nutrition Information

- Calories: 205
- Total Carbohydrate: 11 g
- Total Fat: 18 g
- Fiber: 5 g
- Protein: 3 g
- Sodium: 157 mg
- Saturated Fat: 7 g

289. Scallops With Spice Oil

"Quick and delicious."
Serving: Makes 2 servings | Prep: 20m

Ingredients

- 1 tsp. cumin seeds
- 1 tsp. paprika
- 1/4 tsp. crushed red pepper flakes
- 6 black peppercorns plus freshly ground for seasoning
- 1/2 tsp. kosher salt plus more
- 1/4 cup olive oil
- 2 garlic cloves, minced
- 1 tsp. finely grated lemon zest
- 1 tbsp. (or more) fresh lemon juice
- 1 1/2 tbsps. grapeseed or vegetable oil
- 8 large or 12 medium sea scallops, side muscle removed
- Kosher salt and freshly ground black pepper
- 2 cups mixed cilantro and flat-leaf parsley with tender stems
- Olive oil (for drizzling)
- 1 tbsp. fresh lemon juice
- A spice mill

Direction

- Spice oil: Grind 1/2 tsp. salt and initial 4 ingredients to fine powder in a spice mill. Put into small saucepan on medium low heat then add oil; cook for 2-3 minutes till oil starts to simmer. Scrape into small bowl; mix in lemon zest and garlic. Cool for 5 minutes; mix in 1 tbsp. lemon juice. Season with more juice (optional), pepper and salt. You can make it 1 week ahead. Cover then chill. Before using, rewarm.
- Scallops: Heat grapeseed oil till oil starts to smoke in big heavy skillet on high heat. Season scallops with pepper and salt; sear for 3 minutes till well browned. Flip; cook for 30 seconds till barely opaque in middle.
- Meanwhile, put herbs into medium bowl; drizzle lemon juice and olive oil. Season salad with pepper and salt to taste. Divide scallops to 2 plates; put 1 tbsp. spice oil on each plate. Keep leftover oil for another time. Garnish using salad.

290. Scrambled Eggs

"A great recipe!"

Ingredients

- Allow 2 medium eggs per person for an appetizer or light snack, or 3 medium eggs per person for a main course
- 3 tbsp (40g) butter

Direction

- Melt butter in heavy shallow pan on heat diffuser on low heat/in bain-marie. Into a bowl, break eggs; very lightly beat using fork. Tip into pan with hot, melted butter; mix.
- Cook on low heat, occasionally and gently mixing with a wooden spoon.
- It'll take 3-4 minutes to just make eggs set yet very creamy and 6 minutes if using bain-

marie. Cook for 2 more minutes if you want dryer, firmer scrambled eggs.

- Add 2 tbsp. heavy/light cream or a bit of butter when eggs are done as you desire; season with pepper and salt. Best served immediately.

291. Sea Bass With Spicy Roasted Bell Pepper Sauce

"I also used this sauce as a pasta sauce, on garlic toast and a dip. It's based on romesco, a Spanish sauce."
Serving: 4 servings

Ingredients

- 1 1/2 lbs. red bell peppers
- 1/2 cup almonds, toasted
- 6 tbsps. olive oil
- 2 tbsps. red wine vinegar
- 1 1/2 tbsps. tomato paste
- 1/4 tsp. cayenne pepper
- 4 6- to 7-oz. sea bass fillets

Direction

- Char bell peppers under broiler/on gas flame until all sides are blackened. Cool for 10 minutes in a closed paper bag. Peel then seed peppers. Put in a processor. Add cayenne pepper, tomato paste, vinegar, 4 tbsp. olive oil and almonds. Process until peppers are nearly smooth and almonds are ground finely. Season with pepper and salt.
- In skillet, heat 2 tbsp. oil on medium high heat. Sprinkle pepper and salt on fish. Put fish in the skillet. Sauté for 5 minutes per side just until center is opaque. Put fish on plates. Top with sauce. Serve alongside remaining sauce.

Nutrition Information

- Calories: 521
- Total Carbohydrate: 15 g
- Cholesterol: 76 mg
- Total Fat: 33 g
- Fiber: 6 g

- Protein: 40 g
- Sodium: 181 mg
- Saturated Fat: 4 g

292. Seafood-stuffed Cabbage

"To make these look really nice, use savoy cabbage and trim cabbage leaves to lie flat. Right after blanching leaves, lay each leaf onto cutting board, rib side up; slice off thick center rib."
Serving: Serves 8

Ingredients

- 2 tbsps. butter
- 2 tbsps. flour
- 1 shallot, chopped
- Leaves from 1 sprig fresh thyme, chopped
- 1 pinch cayenne pepper
- 2 cups seafood broth
- 1/2 cup white wine
- Salt
- Freshly ground black pepper
- 2 tbsps. olive oil
- 1 onion, diced
- 1 bell pepper, diced
- 2 cloves garlic, minced
- 1 lb. small Louisiana or American wild shrimp, peeled, deveined, and chopped
- 2 eggs, lightly beaten
- 1 1/2 cups diced fresh bread
- 1/2 cup milk
- 2 dashes Tabasco
- 1 pinch celery salt
- 1 lb. jumbo lump crabmeat
- 1 head Savoy cabbage, leaves separated

Direction

- Preheat an oven to 325°. Sauce: Melt butter till it starts to bubble in cast iron pot on medium heat. Add flour; briskly whisk till incorporated thoroughly. Let bubble for 1 minute; don't darken. Add cayenne, thyme and shallot; whisk while mixing in wine and seafood broth. Simmer sauce; cook till it nicely thickens. Season with pepper and salt. Put sauce into bowl; refrigerate.

- Cabbage: Heat olive oil on medium heat in a skillet. Add garlic, bell pepper and onions; sweat till soft. Put into big mixing bowl; mix in celery salt, tabasco, milk, bread, eggs and shrimp. Fold in crabmeat carefully, keeping lumps intact. Cool seafood filling as you blanch cabbage leaves.
- Boil a big pot with salted water. To cool leaves as blanched, prep a big bowl with ice water nearby. One by one, add cabbage leaves to boiling water; blanch for 30 seconds. Put in ice water; remove from water quickly. Flat on towels, drain.
- Put 2 tbsp. seafood mixture in middle of every cabbage leave; roll up like a burrito. Put seafood sauce on bottom of cleaned cast iron pot; put each cabbage roll carefully and snugly together on sauce, seam side down; should have enough space so it can rise halfway up roll's sides. Bake for 20-25 minutes, covered.

Nutrition Information

- Calories: 229
- Total Carbohydrate: 13 g
- Cholesterol: 176 mg
- Total Fat: 9 g
- Fiber: 2 g
- Protein: 22 g
- Sodium: 722 mg
- Saturated Fat: 3 g

293. Seared Scallions With Poached Eggs

"A good method of steaming eggs in the microwave."
Serving: Makes 2 servings | Prep: 5m

Ingredients

- 2 bunches scallions
- 3 tbsps. extra-virgin olive oil, divided
- 1 tsp. fresh lemon juice
- Kosher salt and freshly ground black pepper

- 2 large eggs

Direction

- Dice a whole scallion, place into a bowl and mix in lemon juice and 2 tbsps. oil. Add salt and pepper to taste and set aside the scallion sauce. On a plate, place the leftover scallions. Pour the remaining oil on them and rotate the plate to spread the oil over it. Add salt and pepper to taste. Place a large cast-iron grill pan or skillet over medium heat. Heat scallions for about 5 minutes, turn them occasionally, until they become slightly charred and soft. Portion the scallions between plates.
- Into each of the two 8-oz. microwave-safe coffee cups, pour 1/2 cup of water. Break one egg into each one, making sure it sinks completely. Use a saucer to seal each cup. Heat 1 egg in a microwave for 1 minute on high power, ensure the white part of the egg is fairly hard and the yolk is runny. Please note that the time it takes to cook depends on the microwave. Transfer the egg to the top of one of the scallion servings using a slotted spoon. Dress with half of the scallion sauce. Repeat this with the remaining sauce and egg; serve.

294. Shrimp And Scallion Pancakes

"These savory pancakes are dotted with veggies and meat or seafood and are common side dish in Korea. To make them classic, you can chop these pancakes into small pieces to be easily picked with chopsticks and enjoyed in few bites."
Serving: Makes 8 (first course) servings | Prep: 45m

Ingredients

- 2 garlic cloves
- 3/4 cup water
- 2 large eggs, beaten
- 1 tbsp. Asian sesame oil
- 3/4 cup all-purpose flour
- 1 bunch scallions, cut into thin matchsticks

- 1/2 red bell pepper, cut into thin matchsticks
- 1/2 lb. medium shrimp, peeled and halved lengthwise
- 1/4 cup vegetable oil, divided
- Accompaniment: soy-pickled jalapeños including liquid

Direction

- Preheat an oven to 200°F. Assemble the rack in a four-sided sheet pan and place in the oven. Then mince and mash the garlic together with 3/4 tsp. of salt. Whisk with sesame oil, eggs, and water. Whisk in the flour until the resulting mix is smooth. Mix in shrimp, bell pepper and scallions.
- Over medium-high heat, heat one tbsp. of oil in a 12-inch nonstick skillet until it's hot. Mix the batter, and cook the pancakes in batches of four for 3 to 5 minutes per batch (two tbsps. each along with some veggies and one or two pieces of shrimp), pushing down lightly using a big spatula in order to flatten and distribute the veggies evenly, flip once, until cooked through and golden. Then drain with paper towels, and transfer onto a rack in oven to keep them warm. Pour oil into the skillet in between the batches as need be.
- You can keep the pancakes warm up to 1 hour.

Nutrition Information

- Calories: 166
- Total Carbohydrate: 11 g
- Cholesterol: 82 mg
- Total Fat: 10 g
- Fiber: 1 g
- Protein: 7 g
- Sodium: 182 mg
- Saturated Fat: 1 g

295. Shrimp Soup With Pasilla Chiles

"Soup made with a chile puree, epazote leaves, and tortilla."
Serving: Makes 4 servings

Ingredients

- 5 pasilla chiles, seeded, deveined, halved
- 4 tbsps. olive oil
- 6 1/2 cups water
- 5 medium tomatillos, husked
- 1 garlic clove
- 1/2 small white onion, chopped
- 1 lb. uncooked medium shrimp, peeled, shells reserved
- 1 6-inch-diameter corn tortilla
- 10 epazote leaves
- 8 lime wedges

Direction

- Cut 4 halves of chiles into fine strips. Place a small skillet over high heat and heat 1 tbsp. of oil. Add the chile strips and fry for 10 seconds until crisp. Drain and reserve the strips for garnish. In a medium skillet over medium-high heat, toast the rest of the chile halves for 1 minute. Transfer the chile to a bowl of cold water and soak for 30 minutes. Drain, then rinse the chile halves with cold water.
- Add 1 1/2 cups of water in a small saucepan and bring to a boil. Add tomatillos and boil for 15 minutes, or until softened. Drain. Puree garlic, tomatillos, and the soaked chiles in a blender. In a large saucepan over medium-high heat, heat 3 tbsps. of oil. Add onion and sauté for 2 minutes, or until translucent. Add the chile puree and stir for 5 minutes over medium heat, or until the puree slightly thickens.
- Fill a large pot with 5 cups of water and bring to a boil. Add shrimp shells to the pot and boil for 10 minutes. Strain the shrimp broth into the chile puree. Directly atop a burner, toast the tortilla for 4 minutes, or until blackened in spots and crisp. Add the tortilla to the chile

puree then add epazote leaves. Simmer for 15 minutes over medium heat, or until tortilla has softened. Puree the soup in a blender until texture smoothens, working in batches. Return the soup into the saucepan and add salt to season. Bring to a boil. Add the shrimp and simmer for 3 minutes, or until just cooked through. Ladle the soup into bowls and garnish each serving with the fried chile strips. Serve with lime wedges.

296. Skillet-roasted Chicken With Farro And Herb Pistou

"A fantastic chicken recipe."
Serving: Makes 2-4 servings

Ingredients

- 1/3 cup extra-virgin olive oil plus more for drizzling
- 3 tbsps. chopped fresh chives, divided
- 2 tbsps. chopped fresh thyme
- 1 tbsp. chopped fresh chervil
- 1 tbsp. chopped flat-leaf parsley
- 1 tbsp. chopped fresh tarragon
- 2 garlic cloves, finely chopped
- 1 tsp. finely grated lemon zest
- 1/2 tsp. freshly ground black pepper
- 1 2 1/2-3-lb. chicken, halved, backbone removed
- 2 1/2 tsps. kosher salt
- 2 tbsps. vegetable oil
- Farro with Acorn Squash and Kale
- Herb Pistou
- 1 lemon, halved

Direction

- In a medium bowl, whisk 1 tbsp. chives, 1/3 cup olive oil and next 7 ingredients; divide marinate to 2 gallon sized resealable plastic freezer bags. Use 2 1/2 tsp. salt to season chicken; in each bag, put 1 chicken half. Seal bags; release extra air. Chill overnight.

- Put bags in a big pot, side by side; to cover by 2-in., add cold water. Heat water till an instant-read thermometer reads 150°F on medium heat. Turn heat off; cover. Poach chicken for about 50 minutes. Put bags into big bowl with ice water for 15 minutes to cool. Take chicken from bags and pat dry.
- Preheat an oven to 450°F. Heat the vegetable oil on high heat in a big cast iron skillet. Add chicken halves with chicken sitting against pan's sides, skin side down; cook, occasionally moving chicken to evenly cook, till skin browns all over. Flip chicken; put skillet in oven. Roast for 15 minutes till an instant-read thermometer in thickest thigh part reads 165°F. Rest for 10 minutes.
- Serve: Divide farro with kale and acorn squash to plates; put chicken over farro. Drizzle around farro with 1/4 cup herb pistou. Drizzle 1 tsp. extra-virgin olive oil on each plate then squeeze lemon halves on chicken. Sprinkle 2 tbsp. chives.

Nutrition Information

- Calories: 1402
- Total Carbohydrate: 12 g
- Cholesterol: 318 mg
- Total Fat: 115 g
- Fiber: 5 g
- Protein: 81 g
- Sodium: 1701 mg
- Saturated Fat: 24 g

297. Slow-roasted Tomato Crostini

"A lovely winter plum tomato recipe!"
Serving: Makes 6 servings | Prep: 20m

Ingredients

- 6 medium plum tomatoes (1 lb), halved lengthwise
- 2 tbsps. extra-virgin olive oil plus additional for brushing
- 7 garlic cloves, unpeeled

- 12 1/2-inch-thick slices baguette or Italian bread (about 2 1/2 inches wide)
- 1 to 2 tbsps. finely sliced fresh mint
- 4 Kalamata or other brine-cured black olives, pitted and chopped

Direction

- Preheat an oven to 350°F.
- Put tomatoes in shallow baking dish big enough to hold all in 1 layer, cut sides up. Drizzle 2 tbsp. oil; season with pepper and salt. Scatter garlic around tomatoes; roast in center of oven for 1 hour till skins wrinkle and tomatoes are tender. Cool. Put tomatoes onto platter; keep oil and garlic in baking dish.
- Put bread slices onto baking sheet as tomato cools; lightly brush extra oil on both sides. Bake in center of oven for 15-18 minutes till golden.
- Peel roasted garlic cloves; mash with juices and oil from baking dish to a paste. Spread paste on toasts; put tomato half on each toast, cut side up.
- Serve crostini with olives and mint on top.
- You can prep garlic paste and tomatoes 1 day ahead, covered, chilled; before proceeding, bring to room temperature.
- You can bake toasts 1 day ahead; keep at room temperature in airtight container.
- Heat assembled crostini before serving if you make components ahead in 350°F oven.

Nutrition Information

- Calories: 165
- Total Carbohydrate: 23 g
- Total Fat: 6 g
- Fiber: 2 g
- Protein: 4 g
- Sodium: 255 mg
- Saturated Fat: 1 g

298. Smoked Salmon And Basil Rolls With Crème Fraîche

Serving: Makes 8 first-course servings

Ingredients

- 12 4x2 1/2-inch slices smoked salmon
- 3/4 cup (about) crème fraîche or sour cream
- 3/4 cup chopped fresh basil
- 12 large fresh basil leaves

Direction

- On work surface, add 1 salmon slice. Use 2 tbsps. of crème fraiche to spread over salmon. Use 2 tsps. of chopped basil to sprinkle on top. Dust with pepper. Roll salmon slice up from 1 short end to enclose the filling. Use 1 tsp. of crème fraiche to spread onto roll top; use 1 tsp. of chopped basil to sprinkle. Slice the roll into 5 pieces crosswise (keep the sliced roll together). Continue with the remaining chopped basil, crème fraiche and salmon. (This can be prepared 6 hours before serving. Place salmon rolls onto plate and chill with cover.) On platter, add basil leaves. Arrange 1 sliced salmon roll on top of each basil leaf with a small spatula, fanning slightly.

Nutrition Information

- Calories: 91
- Total Carbohydrate: 1 g
- Cholesterol: 21 mg
- Total Fat: 6 g
- Fiber: 0 g
- Protein: 8 g
- Sodium: 296 mg
- Saturated Fat: 3 g

299. Sorrel-onion Tart

"A pleasing recipe."
Serving: Makes one 9-inch tart

Ingredients

- 1 recipe Tart Dough
- 4 tbsps. butter, in all
- 1 large red onion, thinly sliced
- 1/2 tsp. salt
- 4 to 8 oz. sorrel leaves
- 2 large eggs
- 1 cup heavy cream
- 2 oz. Gruyère cheese, grated
- Pepper

Direction

- Prep tart dough and partially prebake it; put aside.
- Melt 3 tbsp. butter in wide pan; add salt and onion. Cover pan; slowly stew for 10 minutes till onion is fully soft. Occasionally check and mix.
- As onions cook, cut stems off sorrel leaves; slice leaves roughly. Melt leftover 1 tbsp. butter in a pan. By big handfuls, add sorrel; it'll quickly cook down to nearly nothing. Cook on low heat for 3-4 minutes till they are grayish-green color and wilt.
- Whisk cream and eggs; mix in 1/2 cheese, sorrel and onion. Taste for salt; season using freshly ground black pepper.
- Preheat an oven to 375°F. Distribute leftover cheese on crust; put filling over. Bake in middle of oven for 35-40 minutes till custard is well colored and set. Serve while hot.

Nutrition Information

- Calories: 2367
- Total Carbohydrate: 153 g
- Cholesterol: 883 mg
- Total Fat: 171 g
- Fiber: 15 g
- Protein: 61 g
- Sodium: 2332 mg
- Saturated Fat: 100 g

300. Spaghetti With Garlic And Cumin

"An intriguing dish."
Serving: Makes 4 to 6 first-course servings

Ingredients

- 1/2 cup olive oil
- 1/2 cup chopped fresh Italian parsley
- 3 large garlic cloves, minced
- 1 tbsp. ground cumin
- 1/2 tsp. dried crushed red pepper
- 12 oz. spaghetti
- Freshly grated Parmesan cheese

Direction

- In small bowl, mix first 5 ingredients; put aside. Cook spaghetti, occasionally mixing, in big pot with boiling salted water till just tender yet firm to chew. Drain spaghetti; put 3/4 cup cooking liquid aside. Put pasta in pot then add oil mixture; toss on medium heat for 1 minute to coat. If dry, add reserved cooking liquid by around 1/4 cupfuls. Season with pepper and salt. Sprinkle parmesan cheese; serve.

301. Spaghetti With Red Clam Sauce

"Break out your usual red-checkered tablecloth once you make this briny, spicy and excellently balanced variation of the Italian-American staple at home."
Serving: Makes 4 to 6 servings | Prep: 20m

Ingredients

- 1/3 cup olive oil
- 3 large garlic cloves, chopped
- 1/2 tsp. dried hot red-pepper flakes

- 1 (28- to 32-oz.) can whole tomatoes in juice, coarsely chopped, reserving juice
- 2 tsps. sugar
- 1 lb. spaghetti
- 3 dozen hard-shelled clams such as littlenecks

Direction

- Pour the oil in a 12-14-inch hefty skillet set over medium heat. Heat the oil until it shimmers; drop the garlic with red-pepper flakes, cooking them while stirring for 1 to 2 minutes until it turns pale golden. Drop the tomatoes with its juices, 1/2 tsp. salt and sugar then simmer briskly without any cover. Stir the mixture from time to time for about 7-10 minutes until the consistency turns thick.
- Fill a pasta pot of salted water and allow to boil (place about 3 tbsps. of salt for each 6 quarts of water) Place the spaghetti and let it cook until al dente.
- Meanwhile, drop the clams (in shells) in the sauce mixture and cook while covered. Shake the skillet from time to time for about 6 to 10 minutes until each clams open wide (dispose any clams that remain unopened after 10 minutes). Place the clams (still in shells) as cooked on a big shallow bowl. If the sauce ended up too watery, let it boil for about 2 minutes until slightly thickened.
- Drain the spaghetti. Place the clams back to the sauce and add the pasta. Toss them well.

302. Speculaas Tart With Almond Filling

"To make cookies for topping, use 2-in. gingerbread-man cutter."
Serving: Makes 12 to 16 servings

Ingredients

- 2 3/4 cups all purpose flour
- 2 tsps. ground cinnamon
- 1 tsp. ground ginger
- 1/2 tsp. salt
- 1/2 tsp. baking powder
- 1/4 tsp. ground nutmeg
- 1 cup (2 sticks) unsalted butter, room temperature
- 1 cup (packed) dark brown sugar
- 1 large egg
- 1 1/2 cups blanched slivered almonds (about 6 oz.)
- 3/4 cup sugar
- 1/4 cup (1/2 stick) unsalted butter, room temperature
- 1 large egg
- 2 tsps. grated lemon peel
- 2 tsps. fresh lemon juice
- 1 tsp. vanilla extract
- 3/4 tsp. almond extract
- Powdered sugar
- Apricot preserves

Direction

- Dough: Into medium bowl, sift first 6 ingredients. Beat sugar and butter till blended using electric mixer; beat in egg. Add the flour mixture; beat till moist clumps form. Bring dough to ball; divide to 2 pieces, 1 slightly bigger than other. Flatten dough to disks; wrap. Chill for 2 hours. You can make it 2 days ahead, kept chilled. Slightly soften before rolling.
- Filling: Blend initial 8 ingredients till nuts are finely chopped in processor; put into small bowl. Cover and chill for 2 hours – 2 days.
- Preheat an oven to 325°F. Butter a 9-in. diameter springform pan. Roll bigger dough piece out to 13-in. round on lightly floured surface. Put in pan; gently press up sides and on bottom, pressing tears together. In dough, spread filling. Trim dough sides to 1/2-in. over filling level; fold dough in on filling.
- Roll 2nd dough disk out to 12-13-in. round on lightly floured surface. Cut 9-in. diameter dough round out using cake pan's bottom for aid. Slide dough round on a plate; freeze to firm for 5 minutes. For cookies, reserve dough scraps. On tart, put chilled dough round; press to seal edges and adhere.

- Bake tart for 50 minutes till crust is brown. Remove springform pan's sides; fully cool tart on pan bottom and maintain the oven temperature.
- Line parchment paper on 2 baking sheets. Roll dough scraps out to scant 1/4-in. thick on lightly floured surface. Cut out cookies with 2-in. gingerbread-man cutter. Put cutouts on prepped sheets; repeat with all dough.
- Bake cookies for 8 minutes till golden; cool them on sheets. You can make cookies and tart ahead; cover. Keep for 1 day at room temperature/refrigerate for 3 days.
- Sift powdered sugar on top of tart. On back of a cookie, put small preserves dab; put at tart's top edge. Repeat with extra cookies, making border around tart. Put tart on platter; stand for 1 hour at room temperature.

Nutrition Information

- Calories: 426
- Total Carbohydrate: 49 g
- Cholesterol: 70 mg
- Total Fat: 24 g
- Fiber: 2 g
- Protein: 6 g
- Sodium: 116 mg
- Saturated Fat: 11 g

303. Spiced Cucumbers And Coconut Milk

"So delicious."
Serving: Makes about 4 cups

Ingredients

- 1 tbsp. vegetable oil
- 2 cups 1/4"-thick slices peeled lemon cucumber or any other cucumber.
- Kosher salt
- Freshly ground black pepper
- 2 peeled, seeded, coarsely chopped small tomatoes
- 4 thinly sliced scallions
- 2 thinly sliced red thai chiles (with seeds)
- 1 smashed garlic clove
- 1/2 cup unsweetened coconut milk
- 1 1/2 tsp. honey
- 1/4 cup fresh cilantro leaves
- Fresh lime juice

Direction

- Heat vegetable oil on medium heat in a medium saucepan. Add peeled lemon cucumber slices/other cucumber; sauté for 1 minute till starting to soften. Season with freshly ground black pepper and kosher salt. Add smashed garlic clove, sliced red Thai chiles including seeds, sliced scallions and chopped small tomatoes; sauté for 2-3 minutes till veggies are soft. Add honey and unsweetened coconut milk; simmer for 2-3 minutes till veggies cook through. Mix in squeeze of the fresh lime juice and fresh cilantro leaves; season with pepper and salt. If desired, serve with rice.

Nutrition Information

- Calories: 131
- Total Carbohydrate: 11 g
- Total Fat: 10 g
- Fiber: 2 g
- Protein: 2 g
- Sodium: 455 mg
- Saturated Fat: 6 g

304. Spiced Matzo-stuffed Chicken Breasts

"A fun recipe!"
Serving: Makes 6 servings | Prep: 40m

Ingredients

- 1 large onion, chopped
- 1 red bell pepper, chopped
- 6 tbsps. olive oil, divided
- 2 garlic cloves, chopped

- 4 cups packaged matzo farfel (small pieces of matzo)
- 1/2 cup shelled pistachios, chopped
- 1/2 cup golden raisins
- 1/3 cup chopped flat-leaf parsley
- 2 large eggs
- 1 3/4 cups reduced-sodium chicken broth, divided
- 2 tsps. ground coriander
- 1 tsp. hot paprika or 1/2 tsp. cayenne
- 3/4 tsp. ground cinnamon
- 1/2 tsp. ground allspice
- 1/4 tsp. ground cloves
- 6 boneless chicken breast halves with skin (about 3 lbs.)
- 1/2 cup dry white wine
- 1 tsp. potato starch

Direction

- Preheat an oven with racks in lower and upper thirds to 425°F.
- Cook bell pepper and onion in 3 tbsp. oil in 12-in. heavy skillet on medium heat, occasionally mixing, for 15 minutes till golden and soft. Add garlic; cook for 2 minutes, frequently mixing.
- Rinse matzo farfel under warm running water in a colander till soft for 30-60 seconds as onion mixture cooks; drain, gently press to remove extra water.
- Take onion mixture off heat; mix in 1/2 tsp. pepper, 3/4 tsp. salt, parsley, raisins, pistachios and farfel. Whisk 3/4 cup broth and eggs; mix into the farfel mixture.
- Put 1 1/2 cups stuffing aside; put leftover into 1 1/2-qt. generously oiled shallow baking pan.
- In lower oven third, bake stuffing in dish for 30 minutes till golden and set.
- Mix 1/2 tsp. pepper, 1 tsp. salt and spices in a big bowl as stuffing bakes.
- Horizontally insert paring knife into center of thicker end of every breast half, pausing 1-in. from opposing end; open incision using your finger to make 1-in. wide pocket. In each pocket, pack 3 tbsp. stuffing. Pat dry chicken then add to spices, tossing till coated.
- Across 2 burners, straddle big flameproof roasting pan. Add leftover 3 tbsp. oil; heat till it shimmers on medium high heat. Sear chicken with skin side down for 5 minutes till skin is deep golden. Flip chicken; roast in upper oven third for 16-20 minutes till it cooks through.
- Put chicken onto platter. Across 2 burners, straddle roasting pan. Add wine; boil to deglaze, mixing, scraping brown bits up, for 1 minute. Mix in 3/4 cup broth. Whisk potato starch and leftover 1/4 cup broth; whisk into sauce. Cook, whisking, for 2 minutes till slightly thick. Through fine-mesh sieve, strain sauce into measuring cup; stand for 1-2 minutes till fat rises to top. Skim off fat; discard. Or use the fat separator. Use salt to season sauce.

Nutrition Information

- Calories: 524
- Total Carbohydrate: 37 g
- Cholesterol: 139 mg
- Total Fat: 29 g
- Fiber: 4 g
- Protein: 28 g
- Sodium: 253 mg
- Saturated Fat: 6 g

305. Spiced Plum Pie

Serving: Makes 8 servings

Ingredients

- 2 Tender Pie Crust dough disks
- 3 tbsps. plus 1 cup sugar
- 1 3/4 tsps. ground cinnamon, divided
- 2 tbsps. cornstarch
- 2 tsps. (packed) finely grated orange peel
- 3/4 tsp. ground cardamom
- 1/4 tsp. ground nutmeg
- 1/8 tsp. ground cloves
- 1/4 tsp. salt
- 1/2 vanilla bean, split lengthwise

- 2 1/2 lbs. plums, halved, pitted, each half cut into 4 wedges
- 2 tbsps. whipping cream

Direction

- On floured area, unroll a pie crust disk into 13 half-inch circle. Turn onto glass pie dish, 9-inch in size. Clip hanging over to an-inch. Chill the crust while making filling.
- In the middle of oven, place the rack; preheat the oven to 375°F. In base of oven, position baking sheet lined with foil to capture any spills. In small bowl, combine 1/4 tsp. of cinnamon and 3 tbsps. of sugar; reserve. In big bowl, beat next 6 ingredients, 1 1/2 tsps. cinnamon and a cup sugar. Scoop in vanilla bean seeds. Put plums and coat by tossing. Into the crust, scoop the filling, piling partially in middle.
- On floured area, unroll another pie crust disk into 13 half-inch circle. Lay crust on the filling; clip hanging over to an-inch. Pinch together edges of bottom and top crust. Fold the edges beneath; flute. In middle of top crust, cut 4 2-inch lengthy cuts with sharp knife for vent. Brush cream on crust but do not include the edges. Scatter reserved cinnamon sugar on top of crust.
- Let pie bake for half an hour. Loosely tent the pie in foil to avoid excessive browning. Keep baking for an hour more till filling bubbles thickly along the cuts. Cool fully on rack.

Nutrition Information

- Calories: 357
- Total Carbohydrate: 77 g
- Cholesterol: 4 mg
- Total Fat: 4 g
- Fiber: 4 g
- Protein: 6 g
- Sodium: 424 mg
- Saturated Fat: 1 g

306. Spiced Pumpkin Muffins

Serving: Makes 15

Ingredients

- Nonstick vegetable oil spray
- 1 cup all purpose flour
- 1/2 cup whole wheat flour
- 1/3 cup sugar
- 1/4 cup (packed) golden brown sugar
- 2 1/2 tsps. baking powder
- 1 tsp. ground cinnamon
- 1/4 tsp. ground cloves
- 1/2 tsp. salt
- 1/3 cup shelled pumpkin seeds (pepitas), lightly toasted
- 1/3 cup coarsely chopped walnuts, lightly toasted
- 1 1/4 cups canned pure pumpkin
- 1 cup whole milk
- 2 large eggs
- 6 tbsps. (3/4 stick) unsalted butter, melted
- 2 tsps. grated peeled fresh ginger

Direction

- Preheat an oven to 375°F. Spray nonstick spray on 15 2/3-cup capacity standard muffin cups. Whisk salt, spices, baking powder, both sugars and both flours to blend in big bowl; mix in 1/2 walnuts and 1/2 pumpkin seeds. Whisk ginger, melted butter, eggs, milk and pumpkin to blend in medium bowl. Add to dry ingredients; mix till just incorporated. Don't overmix.
- In each cup, put 1/4 cup batter; sprinkle leftover walnuts and pumpkin seeds. Bake for 25 minutes till inserted tester in middle exits clean and muffins are golden. Flip muffins onto rack; cool. You can make it 1 day ahead; keep muffins airtight in room temperature.

Nutrition Information

- Calories: 185
- Total Carbohydrate: 21 g
- Cholesterol: 39 mg

- Total Fat: 10 g
- Fiber: 2 g
- Protein: 4 g
- Sodium: 158 mg
- Saturated Fat: 4 g

307. Spicy Gingerbread Thins

Serving: Makes about 120 cookies

Ingredients

- 2 3/4 cups all-purpose flour
- 1 1/2 tsps. freshly ground black pepper
- 1 tsp. ground ginger
- 1/2 tsp. baking soda
- 1/2 tsp. salt
- 1/2 tsp. ground cinnamon
- 1/4 tsp. ground cloves
- 1/4 tsp. freshly grated nutmeg
- 1/2 cup unsulfured molasses
- 3 tbsps. strong brewed coffee at room temperature
- 1 stick (1/2 cup) unsalted butter, softened
- 1/2 cup packed dark brown sugar
- 1 tbsp. finely grated peeled fresh gingerroot
- Parchment paper for lining baking sheets

Direction

- Sift together the nutmeg, cloves, cinnamon, salt, baking soda, ground ginger, pepper and flour in a bowl. Mix together the coffee and molasses in a small bowl. Beat the brown sugar and butter together in a bowl with an electric mixer on medium speed, until it becomes creamy and light. Beat in the gingerroot in a mixer on low speed. Beat in the flour mixture alternately with the molasses mixture and start and end with the flour mixture. Split the dough to three. Shape each third to a ball and flatten it into disks. Let the disks chill for a minimum of 4 hours to a maximum of 3 days and separately wrap in plastic wrap.

- Set an oven to preheat to 350 degrees F and use parchment paper to line the 2 big baking trays. Break egg-size pieces from one disk (keep the leftover 2 disks chilled) and smear every piece once in a forward motion using the heel of your hand. Gather the pieces together and smear the dough several times to bring it together. Redo the process with the leftover 2 disks.

- Roll out 1/3 of the dough on a work surface that's lightly floured to 22x 8-inch rectangle (approximately 1/8-inch thick). Ensure that the dough doesn't stick to the surface (to lift the dough, use pastry scraper. If sticking, sprinkle extra flour on the surface). Cut out the shapes using 3 1/2-inch candy cane cutter or 2-inch gingerbread man cutter, then move to the baking trays using a spatula and lay it out approximately half an inch apart.

- Let the cookies bake in batches for 6-8 minutes in the lower third of the oven or until it becomes crisp. Don't allow the cookies to get too dark. Move the cookies to the racks to let it cool using a spatula. Make more cookie using the leftover 2/3 of dough and scraps in the same method. You can keep the cookies for 1 week at room temperature and stored in airtight containers.

Nutrition Information

- Calories: 25
- Total Carbohydrate: 4 g
- Cholesterol: 2 mg
- Total Fat: 1 g
- Fiber: 0 g
- Protein: 0 g
- Sodium: 15 mg
- Saturated Fat: 0 g

308. Spicy Lemon And Paprika Aïoli

"A lovely aioli."
Serving: Makes about 1 3/4 cups

Ingredients

- 1 1/2 cups mayonnaise
- 1/4 cup fresh lemon juice
- 6 large garlic cloves, minced
- 1 1/2 tbsps. tomato paste
- 1 1/2 tsps. hot smoked Spanish paprika (Pimentón de la Vera)* or 1 1/4 tsps. Hungarian sweet paprika and 1/4 tsp. cayenne pepper

Direction

- Whisk all ingredients to blend in small bowl; season aioli with pepper and salt to taste. You can make it 1 day ahead. Cover; refrigerate.

Nutrition Information

- Calories: 311
- Total Carbohydrate: 3 g
- Cholesterol: 17 mg
- Total Fat: 33 g
- Fiber: 0 g
- Protein: 0 g
- Sodium: 275 mg
- Saturated Fat: 5 g

309. Spicy Turkey Burgers

"Tired of boring turkey burgers? Spice it up with a wonderful blend of exotic spices and herbs. Over toasted and crisp bun with spiced mayonnaise and choice of fixings."
Serving: 8 | Prep: 20m | Ready in: 40m

Ingredients

- 2 lbs. lean ground turkey
- 2 tbsps. minced garlic
- 1 tsp. minced fresh ginger root
- 2 fresh green chile peppers, diced
- 1 medium red onion, diced
- 1/2 cup fresh cilantro, finely chopped
- 1 tsp. salt
- 1/4 cup low sodium soy sauce
- 1 tbsp. freshly ground black pepper
- 3 tbsps. paprika
- 1 tbsp. ground dry mustard
- 1 tbsp. ground cumin
- 1 dash Worcestershire sauce

Direction

- Set the grill on high heat. Combine ground turkey, ginger, garlic, red onion, cilantro, chili peppers, soy sauce, salt, paprika, black pepper, cumin, mustard and the Worcestershire sauce in a big bowl. Mix well and divide into 8 patties. Brush the grill lightly with oil and cook the turkey burgers until well done. Five to ten minutes each side.

Nutrition Information

- Calories: 204 calories;
- Total Carbohydrate: 6.4 g
- Cholesterol: 84 mg
- Total Fat: 9.6 g
- Protein: 24.4 g
- Sodium: 626 mg

310. Spinach With Bamboo Shoots

Serving: Makes 4 servings

Ingredients

- 1 lb. fresh spinach
- 1/2 cup peanut, vegetable, or corn oil
- 1/4 cup finely shredded bamboo shoots
- 1 1/2 tsps. salt
- 2 tsps. sugar

Direction

- 1. Thoroughly rinse the spinach leaves in cold running water then drain well.

- 2. Heat the skillet or wok with oil. Cook the bamboo shoots in hot oil on medium-high heat while continuously stirring for about 45 seconds.
- 3. Put in the spinach and cook and stir until the spinach is wilted.
- 4. Put in sugar and salt to taste and cook and stir the vegetable mixture for about 1 1/2 to 2 minutes more.
- 5. Put the stir-fried vegetables on a hot platter excluding the excess liquid.

Nutrition Information

- Calories: 282
- Total Carbohydrate: 7 g
- Total Fat: 28 g
- Fiber: 3 g
- Protein: 3 g
- Sodium: 354 mg
- Saturated Fat: 4 g

311.Stage Planks

"These molasses cookies are a bit spicy and usually topped with pink or white icing."
Serving: 16 cookies

Ingredients

- 3-3 1/2 cups all-purpose flour
- 1 tbsp. ground ginger
- 1 tsp. cinnamon
- 1/2 tsp. ground cloves
- 1 tsp. baking soda
- 1 cup buttermilk
- 1/4 tsp. salt
- 3/4 cup molasses
- 1/4 cup sugar
- 6 tbsps. unsalted butter, softened

Direction

- Set the oven to 375 degrees Fahrenheit. Use parchment paper to line two cookie sheets and put aside. Sift together salt, baking soda, cloves, cinnamon, ginger, and 3 cups of flour in a medium bowl, then put aside. In a standing mixer bowl, add butter, sugar, and molasses, then mix on a medium-high speed until the color lightens, around 2 minutes. Setting the mixer on a low speed, alternate buttermilk and flour with the butter mixture. Turn the speed up to a medium and mix for 30 seconds. The dough should be stiff enough for you to roll out. If not, mix in flour, up to 1/2 cup, to get the right consistency.
- Roll the dough on a floured hard surface into a 10x16 inch rectangle. Horizontally slice down the middle, then at 2-inch intervals vertically to make 16 cookies. Place the pieces individually onto the prepared cookie sheets, minimum an inch apart. Bake until the tops become firm, around 15 minutes. Take out of the oven and completely cool in the pans.

Nutrition Information

- Calories: 196
- Total Carbohydrate: 35 g
- Cholesterol: 12 mg
- Total Fat: 5 g
- Fiber: 1 g
- Protein: 3 g
- Sodium: 151 mg
- Saturated Fat: 3 g

312. Steak Fajitas With Fresh Lime

"Best with guacamole on the side."
Serving: Makes 4 servings

Ingredients

- 2 12-oz. skirt steaks, each halved
- 3 tbsps. fresh lime juice, divided
- 1 large onion, halved lengthwise, thinly sliced
- 4 large garlic cloves, pressed
- 1 1/2 tbsps. hot chili sauce (such as sriracha)*
- 1 tbsp. ground cumin
- 1 tsp. finely grated lime peel
- 2 tbsps. olive oil

- 12 cherry tomatoes
- 1/3 cup thinly sliced fresh basil
- *Available in the Asian foods section of many supermarkets and at Asian markets.

Direction

- Warm corn/flour tortillas; put steaks in glass 13x9x2-in. baking dish. Sprinkle pepper and salt. Mix 2 tbsp. lime juice then following 5 ingredients in medium bowl; put onion mixture on steaks. Turn to evenly coat; marinade for 10 minutes.
- In big nonstick skillet, heat oil on high heat then add steaks with onion mixture and cook steaks for 1 minute per side. Add basil and tomatoes; cook steaks for 3 minutes for medium rare to desired doneness, occasionally turning. Sprinkle 1 tbsp. lime juice on mixture. Cook to blend flavors for 1 minute. Put steaks on work surface. On slight diagonal, cut across grain to 1/2-in. thick strips; put fajitas in bowl then serve with tortillas.

Nutrition Information

- Calories: 428
- Total Carbohydrate: 9 g
- Cholesterol: 109 mg
- Total Fat: 29 g
- Fiber: 2 g
- Protein: 35 g
- Sodium: 257 mg
- Saturated Fat: 9 g

313. Steamed Clams With Cilantro And Red Pepper

"A tasty recipe."
Serving: Makes 6 servings

Ingredients

- 5 tbsps. unsalted butter
- 1 1/2 cups thinly sliced green onions
- 1 1/4 cups chopped fresh cilantro

- 2 cups sake or dry vermouth
- 4 garlic cloves, pressed
- 1 tsp. Worcestershire sauce
- 1/2 tsp. dried crushed red pepper
- 4 dozen littleneck clams, scrubbed

Direction

- Melt 4 tbsp. butter on medium heat in big pot. Add green onions; cook for 3 minutes. Add 1 cup of chopped fresh cilantro with next 4 ingredients. Put heat on high; boil. Add clams and cover pot; cook, shaking pot often, for 7 minutes till clams open. Put clams in 6 soup bowls using slotted spoon; discard unopened clams. Boil leftover liquid on high heat for 1 minute till slightly thick. Whisk in leftover 1 tbsp. butter; season with pepper and salt. Put sauce on clams. Sprinkle leftover 1/4 cup chopped cilantro; serve.

Nutrition Information

- Calories: 263
- Total Carbohydrate: 9 g
- Cholesterol: 60 mg
- Total Fat: 11 g
- Fiber: 1 g
- Protein: 18 g
- Sodium: 718 mg
- Saturated Fat: 6 g

314. Steamed Jasmine Rice

"Jasmine rice came from Southeast Asia. The long grains of this rice softens and become nutty in flavor once cooked. They also smell really good when cooked."
Serving: Makes 8 servings | Prep: 5m

Ingredients

- 3 cups jasmine rice
- 3 1/2 cups water

Direction

- In a medium-sized bowl, wash rice in 3 or 4 replacements of cold water until the water is really clear, drain the rice using a sieve in each water replacement. Use a sieve to drain the rinsed rice for 5 minutes.
- In a heavy medium-sized pot, put in let the water and the rinsed rice com to a boil. Adjust the heat to the lowest heat setting and let the rice cook while covered tightly for about 15 minutes until the rice has absorbed the water and has already softened. Remove the pot away from the heat and allow it to stand for 10 minutes with cover. Use a fork to fluff up the cooked rice.

Nutrition Information

- Calories: 253
- Total Carbohydrate: 55 g
- Total Fat: 0 g
- Fiber: 1 g
- Protein: 5 g
- Sodium: 8 mg
- Saturated Fat: 0 g

315. Strawberry Panachee

"You can use any cookies."
Serving: Makes 4 servings

Ingredients

- 2 1/2 cups ripe strawberries
- 1/4 cup jam (raspberry, currant, or strawberry are good)
- 4 shortbread cookies
- 1/3 cup crème fraîche or sour cream, plus additional for garnish
- 4 sprigs mint or basil

Direction

- Cut off top and bottom of every berry to get 1 1/4 cups. Slice middle of berries; put aside. Push bottoms and tops of berry and jam through food mill/process in mini food processor till pureed. Mix sliced berries into puree; use plastic wrap to cover. Refrigerate till needed.
- Put cookies into plastic bag at serving time; coarsely crush using rolling pin. Divide crumbs to 4 goblets or bowls. Put 1/2 berry mixture over cookies; to loosen it, mix crème fraiche/sour cream then put over berries. Put leftover berry mixture over; garnish every dessert with mint sprig. If desired, pass with some sour cream/crème fraiche.

Nutrition Information

- Calories: 148
- Total Carbohydrate: 29 g
- Total Fat: 3 g
- Fiber: 2 g
- Protein: 1 g
- Sodium: 50 mg
- Saturated Fat: 1 g

316. Strawberry Prosecco Soup

Serving: Makes about 4 cups | Prep: 10m

Ingredients

- strawberries with Prosecco, tarragon, salt, and 2 tbsps. sugar
- Purée mixture in a blender until smooth, then set aside 1 cup purée. Blend remaining mixture with yogurt and sugar to taste. Serve soup drizzled with reserved purée.

Direction

- Preparation

317. Strawberry Rhubarb Napoleons

"You can use any metal cooling rack for a wire mesh one. You'll have to bake this in batches if your rack is small and can't cover pastry all in one go."
Serving: Serves 6

Ingredients

- 1 lb. rhubarb, cut into 1/4-inch-thick slices (about 3 cups)
- 1/2 cup firmly packed light brown sugar
- 1/4 tsp. cinnamon
- 1 1/2 tsps. fresh lemon juice
- 1 pint strawberries
- 1 sheet frozen puff pastry (about 1/2 lb.), thawed
- Garnish: confectioners' sugar
- Accompaniment: Lemon Cream

Direction

- Filling: Simmer all filling ingredients but strawberries in a heavy saucepan on low heat, occasionally mixing, till rhubarb falls apart and is soft for 10-15 minutes. Put it into bowl; fully cool. Hull strawberries; cut to 1/4-in. thick slices to get 2 cups. Put strawberries in rhubarb mixture, tossing till well combined. You can make filling 1 day ahead, covered, chilled. Before assembling napoleons, bring filling down to room temperature.
- Preheat an oven to 375°F.
- Roll pastry to 14x10-in. 1/8-in. thick rectangle on lightly floured surface; cut pastry to 4 14x2 1/2-in. strips. One by one, create 3 4-in. long parallelograms per strip, with long side facing you to get 12 parallelograms total. Discard end scraps. Invert 2 baking sheets; put 6 parallelograms on each in 1 layer; freeze pastry till firm for 15 minutes.
- Take 1 baking sheet from the freezer; invert metal cooling rack directly on pastry to fully cover parallelograms. The cooling rack will weigh down the pastry to make decorative pattern. Bake pastry with the cooling rack in center of oven for 10-15 minutes till cooked through and golden brown. Remove rack from pastry carefully; put pastry onto another rack. Fully cool. In same manner, bake leftover pastry. You can make these 4 days ahead; keep at room temperature in airtight container.
- Napoleon assembly: Put 6 parallelograms on dessert plates, design sides up; put 1/2 cup filling over each. Put leftover 6 parallelograms over filling, design sides up; sprinkle confectioners' sugar.
- Serve lemon cream with napoleons.

Nutrition Information

- Calories: 313
- Total Carbohydrate: 43 g
- Total Fat: 15 g
- Fiber: 3 g
- Protein: 4 g
- Sodium: 103 mg
- Saturated Fat: 4 g

318. Summer Minestrone With Pesto

"A fun soup recipe."
Serving: Makes 6 servings

Ingredients

- 3 tbsps. olive oil
- 1 medium onion, chopped
- 6 cups low-salt chicken broth
- 2 carrots, peeled, cut into 1/2-inch-thick rounds
- 2 celery stalks, cut into 1/2-inch pieces
- 4 small red-skinned potatoes, quartered
- 1/2 lb. green beans, trimmed, cut into 1-inch pieces
- 3 small zucchini, halved lengthwise, cut into 1/2-inch pieces
- 1 15-oz. can cannellini (white kidney beans), drained
- 2 tomatoes, peeled, crushed

- 2 cups fresh spinach leaves, chopped
- 6 tbsps. Classic Pesto
- Freshly grated Parmesan cheese

Direction

- Heat olive oil on medium heat in big heavy pot. Add onion; sauté for 4 minutes till soft. Add broth with next 7 ingredients. Put heat on high; boil soup. Lower heat to medium low; cover pot partially. Simmer for 10 minutes till potatoes are tender. Mix in spinach; simmer for 3 minutes. Season soup with pepper and salt to taste. Put soup in 6 bowls; use 1 tbsp. pesto to garnish each. Serve, separately passing cheese.

Nutrition Information

- Calories: 482
- Total Carbohydrate: 50 g
- Cholesterol: 5 mg
- Total Fat: 26 g
- Fiber: 10 g
- Protein: 17 g
- Sodium: 661 mg
- Saturated Fat: 5 g

319. Summer Succotash Pasta Salad

Serving: 4 Servings | Prep: 15m

Ingredients

- 1/2 lb. cooked bowtie pasta
- 1/2 cup halved cherry tomatoes
- 1/2 cup fresh or frozen, defrosted, corn kernels
- 1/2 cup fresh or frozen, defrosted, green peas
- 1/4 cup pitted black olives, sliced
- 1/4 cup grated parmesan cheese
- 1/4 cup extra virgin olive oil
- 2 tbsps. freshly squeezed lemon juice
- 1 tsp. salt

Direction

- Mix parmesan cheese, olives, peas, corn, cherry tomatoes and cooked pasta in a big bowl.
- Whisk salt, lemon juice and olive oil in a small bowl.
- Put dressing on pasta; toss to mix.

Nutrition Information

- Calories: 288
- Total Carbohydrate: 27 g
- Cholesterol: 5 mg
- Total Fat: 17 g
- Fiber: 3 g
- Protein: 8 g
- Sodium: 347 mg
- Saturated Fat: 3 g

320. Super Seed Sprinkle

"Great to add to things like grilled veggies, rice dishes, yogurt and salads."
Serving: Makes 8 servings

Ingredients

- 1/4 cup raw shelled pumpkin seeds
- 2 tbsps. sesame seeds
- 1 tbsp. fennel, aniseed, caraway, or cumin seeds
- 1 tbsp. pure maple syrup
- 1/4 cup hemp seeds
- 2 tbsps. chia seeds
- Kosher salt

Direction

- Toast pumpkin seeds, tossing often, in dry medium skillet on medium low heat for 2 minutes till golden. Add fennel and sesame seeds; toast for 2 minutes, tossing often, till golden brown.
- Stir in syrup; cook for 1 minute, tossing often, till glossy clumps form. Take off heat; mix in

chia and hemp seeds. Season with salt. Put onto parchment-lined baking sheet; cool.

321. Sweet Corn Ice Cream

"A lovely summer recipe."
Serving: 10 | Ready in: 4h

Ingredients

- 1½ tsps. unflavored gelatin
- 1 tbsp. water
- 2 cups corn kernels (see Tip)
- 2 cups low-fat milk
- 1 14-oz. can nonfat sweetened condensed milk
- 3 large egg yolks
- 1 cup buttermilk

Direction

- In small bowl, sprinkle gelatin on water; stand, mixing 1-2 times, while making ice cream's base.
- Heat milk and corn till steaming in a big saucepan on medium heat. Whisk egg yolks and condensed milk till combined in a big bowl. Put hot corn and milk into egg yolk mixture slowly, whisking till blended. Put it into pan; cook on medium heat, mixing with wooden spoon, for 3-5 minutes till back of spoon gets coated lightly. Don't boil.
- Take off heat; puree custard with immersion blender. Or, put custard into blender; puree till smooth. Be careful, it is hot. Strain custard through fine mesh sieve into big clean bowl; to extract liquid, press on solids. Discard the solids. Whisk gelatin into custard till melted; whisk in buttermilk. Put into fridge; chill for 2 1/2 hours – 1 day.
- Whisk ice cream mixture; put into an ice cream maker's canister. Follow manufacturer's instructions to freeze. Put ice cream into freezer before serving to firm up if needed.

Nutrition Information

- Calories: 185 calories;
- Total Carbohydrate: 34 g
- Cholesterol: 64 mg
- Total Fat: 2 g
- Fiber: 1 g
- Protein: 8 g
- Sodium: 116 mg
- Sugar: 30 g
- Saturated Fat: 1 g

322. Sweet Potato And Poblano Salad With Honey And Rosemary

Serving: Makes 8 servings

Ingredients

- 2 tbsps. honey
- 1 1/2 tbsps. white wine vinegar
- 1 tbsp. chopped fresh rosemary
- 1 tbsp. minced shallot (about 1 small)
- 2 tsps. Dijon mustard
- Dash of Worcestershire sauce
- 1/4 cup olive oil
- 2 1/2 lbs. red-skinned sweet potatoes (yams), peeled, quartered lengthwise
- Canola oil or vegetable oil (for brushing)
- 2 fresh poblano chiles (about 8 oz. total),* seeded, diced
- 1/4 cup green onions, thinly sliced diagonally (about 2)
- 1/4 cup chopped fresh Italian parsley

Direction

- In small bowl, whisk initial 6 ingredients; whisk in olive oil slowly. Season with pepper and salt to taste.
- Cook sweet potatoes for 6 minutes till just barely tender in a big saucepan with boiling salted water. Drain; to cool, run under cold water. Cover; chill for 1 hour – 1 day.
- Preheat barbecue to high heat. Brush canola oil on potato wedges; sprinkle pepper and salt. Grill potatoes for 2 minutes per side till grill

marks appear. On work surface, put potatoes; crosswise cut to 1-in. pieces. Put parsley, green onions, poblanos and potatoes in big bowl. Drizzle dressing; toss to coat. Season with pepper and salt to taste; serve at room temperature/warm. You can make it 1 day ahead. Cover; chill. Before serving, bring to room temperature.

- Don't overcook potatoes; they'll fall apart when you toss it in salad.

323. Sweet Potato Pancake Stack

Serving: Serves 4 | Prep: 15m

Ingredients

- 1 cup white whole wheat flour
- 2 tsps. baking powder
- 1/2 tsp. ground cinnamon
- 1/4 tsp. ground nutmeg
- 1/2 tsp. salt
- 1 large egg
- 1 1/4 cups milk
- 1 tbsp. brown sugar
- 1 tbsp. vegetable oil
- 1 cup sweet potato puree

Direction

- Whisk salt, nutmeg, cinnamon, baking powder and flour together in a bowl.
- Whisk leftover ingredients in another bowl.
- Add dry ingredients to wet ingredients slowly; mix just till combined.
- Heat a griddle/big skillet on medium heat; coat with oil/butter lightly.
- Put 1 tbsp. pancake mixture on griddle, create as many pancakes that can fit; cook for 2 minutes.
- Flip pancakes; cook for 1 minute more.

Nutrition Information

- Calories: 237
- Total Carbohydrate: 35 g
- Cholesterol: 54 mg

- Total Fat: 8 g
- Fiber: 4 g
- Protein: 8 g
- Sodium: 373 mg
- Saturated Fat: 2 g

324. Sweet Potatoes With Bourbon And Maple

"The complex syrup for this roasted potato recipe was inspired by Southern redeye gravy."
Serving: Makes 8 to 10 servings

Ingredients

- 1 1/2 cups strong hot coffee
- 9 tbsps. pure maple syrup
- 3 tbsps. (packed) dark brown sugar
- 1/2 tsps. instant espresso powder
- 1/3 cup bourbon
- 9 tbsps. unsalted butter, divided
- Kosher salt and freshly ground black pepper
- 5 lbs. red-skinned sweet potatoes (about 8 medium), peeled, cut into 2 1/2"-3" pieces
- 3 tbsps. olive oil
- 1/2 cup chopped smoked almonds (or toasted almonds)

Direction

- In a medium saucepan, stir together espresso powder, sugar, maple syrup, and coffee over medium-high heat until the sugar dissolves. Bring mixture to boil and cook for 6 - 7 minutes, until thick and reduced by half.
- Remove from heat and add 2 tbsps. butter and bourbon. Reduce the heat to medium and let simmer for 40 - 45 minutes, until the sauce reduces to about 3/4 cup. It should be able to coat a spoon but not sticky, it will thicken more as it cools. Season to taste with salt and pepper.
- (You can make this sauce 2 days ahead, covered and chilled. Just rewarm before serving.)

- Arrange some racks into the upper and lower thirds of an oven and preheat to 425 degrees F. In a small saucepan, melt remaining 7 tbsps. butter then pour into a large bowl. Add oil and sweet potatoes, seasoning with salt and pepper. Divide the mixture among 2 large rimmed baking sheets and roast for 30 - 35 minutes until potatoes are tender, crisp around the edges, and are starting to turn golden brown. Be sure to turn the potatoes often and rotate the sheets halfway through. (You can roast potatoes 4 hours ahead, letting it stand in room temperature. Rewarm before using.)
- Transfer the roasted potatoes onto a serving platter and drizzle with the warm sauce. Sprinkle over with almonds and serve with the remaining sauce on the side.

Nutrition Information

- Calories: 560
- Total Carbohydrate: 80 g
- Cholesterol: 34 mg
- Total Fat: 23 g
- Fiber: 10 g
- Protein: 7 g
- Sodium: 922 mg
- Saturated Fat: 9 g

325. Sweet-and-sour Sauerkraut

Serving: Makes 10 servings

Ingredients

- 1 large onion, halved lengthwise and thinly sliced crosswise (2 cups)
- 2 large garlic cloves, finely chopped
- 3 tbsps. vegetable oil
- 1 tsp. cumin seeds, toasted
- 10 whole allspice, crushed
- 1 (28-oz.) can whole tomatoes in juice
- 1/2 cup packed dark brown sugar
- 1 1/2 tsps. salt
- 1/4 tsp. black pepper

- 3 lb. packaged sauerkraut, rinsed well and drained

Direction

- Cook garlic and onion in oil in 3 1/2-4-qt. heavy saucepan on medium low heat, occasionally mixing (mix more frequently towards end of cooking) for 30 minutes till golden brown. Put heat on medium. Add allspice and cumin; cook for 30 seconds, mixing. Add pepper, salt, brown sugar and tomatoes with juice; simmer, occasionally mixing, breaking tomatoes up, for 10 minutes. Mix in sauerkraut; boil. Lower heat; simmer, covered partially, occasionally mixing, for 30 minutes till most liquid is absorbed.

Nutrition Information

- Calories: 139
- Total Carbohydrate: 25 g
- Total Fat: 5 g
- Fiber: 7 g
- Protein: 2 g
- Sodium: 997 mg
- Saturated Fat: 0 g

326. Tequila Shrimp

"An excellent and simple recipe to serve over pasta."
Serving: 6 | Prep: 10m | Ready in: 20m

Ingredients

- 2 tbsps. unsalted butter
- 4 cloves garlic, chopped
- 1 1/2 lbs. large shrimp - peeled and deveined
- 1/2 cup tequila
- 1/2 cup chopped fresh cilantro
- salt and pepper to taste

Direction

- In a big skillet, melt butter over medium heat. Sauté garlic till light brown. Place and cook shrimp in the pan for 3 minutes.

- Add in tequila and season with pepper, salt and cilantro. Cook for 2 minutes longer.

Nutrition Information

- Calories: 205 calories;
- Total Carbohydrate: 1.7 g
- Cholesterol: 157 mg
- Total Fat: 7.9 g
- Protein: 19.8 g
- Sodium: 174 mg

327. The Long Hello

"You'll surely feel the festivities with this a little effervescent punch recipe with a pretty ice mold."
Serving: Makes 16 servings

Ingredients

- 1 3/4 cups Calvados or other apple brandy
- 1 cup St-Germain (elderflower liqueur)
- 10 dashes bitters, preferably Fee Brothers Whiskey Barrel Aged Bitters or Angostura
- 1 750-milliliter bottle Champagne, chilled
- Freshly grated nutmeg
- One 12-cup Bundt or tube pan; 1 punch bowl

Direction

- Fill a ring mold with apples and pears and keep it in the freezer. Note: You may make the ring mold 1 week in advance. Cover the ring mold and store it in the freezer to let it stay frozen.
- In a punch bowl, combine the bitters, Calvados, 1 cup of water and St-Germain together. Put in the prepared ice ring followed by the Champagne. Use a ladle to fill the glasses with the prepared punch mixture; grate the nutmeg directly on top of each filled glass.

328. Tiramisu Affogato

Serving: Makes 6 servings

Ingredients

- 3/4 cup chilled heavy cream
- 1 tbsp. sugar
- 1 pint vanilla ice cream
- 1 pint coffee ice cream
- 9 savoiardi (Italian crisp ladyfingers), coarsely crumbled
- 1 1/4 cups freshly brewed espresso (10 oz.) or 1 1/4 cups boiling water and 3 tbsps. instant-espresso powder
- A small piece bittersweet chocolate

Direction

- Beat sugar and cream together until stiff peaks form.
- Split coffee and vanilla ice creams between glasses; add ladyfingers on top. Top with hot espresso and a blob of whipped cream. Top with grated chocolate.

Nutrition Information

- Calories: 361
- Total Carbohydrate: 35 g
- Cholesterol: 116 mg
- Total Fat: 23 g
- Fiber: 1 g
- Protein: 6 g
- Sodium: 113 mg
- Saturated Fat: 14 g

329. Tomato Salad

"This side dish calls for Plum tomatoes."
Serving: Serves 6

Ingredients

- 6 large plum tomatoes, each cut into 4 wedges

- 3 tbsps. extra-virgin olive oil
- 1 tbsp. balsamic vinegar

Direction

- In big bowl, put the tomatoes. In small bowl, mix vinegar and oil to incorporate. Add pepper and salt to season the dressing. Put on top of tomatoes and softly toss till coated.

Nutrition Information

- Calories: 76
- Total Carbohydrate: 3 g
- Total Fat: 7 g
- Fiber: 1 g
- Protein: 1 g
- Sodium: 5 mg
- Saturated Fat: 1 g

330. Tomato Terrine

"An elegant terrine."
Serving: Makes 8 servings

Ingredients

- 2 carrots, chopped
- 1 leek, thinly sliced
- 1 celery stalk, chopped
- 1 shallot, halved
- 1 garlic clove
- 10 flat-leaf parsley sprigs
- 10 black peppercorns
- 3 fresh bay leaves (or 1 dried)
- 6 lbs. large firm ripe tomatoes (a mix of colors but of similar size), peeled
- 1 tsp. kosher salt plus more for seasoning
- 1 1/2 tbsps. unflavored gelatin
- 1/4 cup thinly sliced chives plus more
- 2 tsps. red wine vinegar
- Nonstick vegetable oil spray
- Extra-virgin olive oil
- Sea salt
- You will need two 8x4 1/2" loaf pans

Direction

- Boil first 8 ingredients with 3 cups water in a big saucepan. Lower heat to medium; simmer for 15 minutes till stock is 1 1/2 cups. Above big measuring cup, put a fine-mesh strainer; strain stock. Discard solids. Cover and keep hot.
- Over another measuring cup, put fine-mesh strainer. Cut every peeled tomato to 4 wedges. Put wedges on work surface, cut side up. Cut pulp and seeds away from tomato; put into strainer. Put filleted tomatoes on double paper towels layer; drain. Sprinkle 1 tsp. kosher salt. Use more paper towels to pat tomatoes; stand for about 30 minutes.
- To get 1/2 cup tomato juice, press on seeds. Sprinkle gelatin on juice; stand to soften for 10 minutes. Add to hot stock; vigorously whisk to dissolve gelatin. Mix in kosher salt to taste, vinegar and 1/4 cup chives.
- Spray nonstick spray on 1 loaf pan. Line with plastic wrap; leave 3-in. overhang on every side. To remove wrinkles, smooth plastic. Put 1/2 cup stock in pan; chill for 40 minutes till set. Put 1 tomato layer in pan, gently pressing down; drizzle 2 tbsp. stock mixture. Repeat layers with leftover stock and tomatoes. Add leftover stock to fill pan. Use plastic wrap to cover terrine; put onto small rimmed baking sheet.
- Put 2nd loaf pan over terrine; put 2-3 small canned goods over pan to weigh down terrine. Some liquid mixture on bottom pan might spill out. Chill terrine for 6 hours till set. You can make it 2 days ahead, kept chilled.
- Uncover terrine and invert onto platter; remove plastic wrap and pan. Cut terrine; put onto plates. Drizzle oil; sprinkle sea salt and chives.

Nutrition Information

- Calories: 201
- Total Carbohydrate: 22 g
- Total Fat: 12 g
- Fiber: 6 g
- Protein: 6 g

- Sodium: 937 mg
- Saturated Fat: 1 g

331. Tomato-and-fennel-stuffed Salmon With Basil Sauce

"A gorgeous recipe."
Serving: Makes 8 to 10 servings | Prep: 45m

Ingredients

- 2 lbs. plum tomatoes, halved lengthwise
- 1/4 cup plus 1 tbsp. extra-virgin olive oil
- 1 3/4 tsps. salt
- 1 tsp. black pepper
- 2 tsps. herbes de Provence
- 2 large fennel bulbs (sometimes labeled "anise"; 2 lbs.), stalks cut off and discarded
- 1 (8-lb.) whole salmon (preferably wild coho), cleaned, butterflied, and boned, leaving head and tail intact
- 1/4 cup dry white wine
- 10 saffron threads
- 1/4 tsp. hot water
- 1 cup mayonnaise
- 1/2 cup loosely packed fresh basil leaves
- 1/4 cup extra-virgin olive oil
- 1 tbsp. Dijon mustard
- 1 large garlic clove
- 1 1/2 tsps. finely grated fresh orange zest
- 1/2 tsp. salt
- 1/4 tsp. black pepper
- an adjustable-blade slicer; heavy-duty foil

Direction

- Fish: In lower third and middle of oven, put oven racks; preheat the oven to 400°F.
- Toss 1 tsp. herbes de Provence, 1/4 tsp. pepper, 1 tsp. salt, 1 tbsp. oil and tomatoes in a bowl; put tomatoes in shallow baking pan, cut sides up. Put bowl aside; don't wipe it clean.
- Lengthwise quarter fennel; with slicer, cut to 1/8-in. thick. Toss fennel with leftover 1 tsp. herbes de Provence, 1/4 tsp. pepper, 1/2 tsp.
- salt and 1 tsp. oil in reserved bowl; spread out in 17x12-in. shallow heavy baking pan.
- Roast fennel in the lower oven third then tomatoes in center of oven, mixing fennel halfway through roasting, for 40-50 minutes till tomatoes lightly brown on edges (yet still juicy) and juices accumulate on bottom of pan and fennel starts to caramelize.
- Remove from oven. Press on tomatoes gently to get 2 tbsp. juice (leave in pan) if there aren't tomato juices in pan. Put oven temperature on 450°F.
- Line heavy-duty foil on 17x12-in. shallow baking pan; use 1 tbsp. oil to coat foil. Diagonally put salmon in roasting pan; open fish. Sprinkle leftover 1/2 tsp. pepper and 3/4 tsp. salt inside of fish. Coat with 1 tbsp. oil. Evenly put roasted tomatoes inside fish (with tail and head attached) on bottom half, reserving the juices in pan for the sauce. Put roasted fennel over tomatoes; put wine on veggies. Like a book, close fish to enclose stuffing; it won't be covered fully. Use several wooden picks to secure opening. Rub leftover 1 tbsp. oil to rub top of fish. Put baseball-size foil ball under head then golf ball-size foil ball under tail if tail and head hang over pan's edge to prop those up so juices go into pan. Tail and head will slightly curve upward.
- Roast salmon in center of oven for 25 minutes till just cooked through; the thickest part will get opaque.
- As fish roasts, make sauce: Mix hot water and saffron in a small cup; stand for 1 minute. Blend 2 tbsp. reserved tomato juices, leftover sauce ingredients and saffron mixture till smooth in blender. Put into bowl; chill till needed, covered.
- Serve: Onto platter, slice whole fish while on foil. Slightly lift fish's head with a wide/long spatula to remove foil; push foil toward center of fish. Lower the head end back onto the platter; in same manner, lift tail end to fully and gently remove foil. Serve fish with sauce alongside.
- Ask a fishmonger to bone and butterfly the salmon.

- You can make roasted veggies and sauce 2 days ahead, covered, chilled; before using, bring veggies to room temperature.

Nutrition Information

- Calories: 1330
- Total Carbohydrate: 11 g
- Cholesterol: 261 mg
- Total Fat: 99 g
- Fiber: 4 g
- Protein: 95 g
- Sodium: 1154 mg
- Saturated Fat: 19 g

332. Torta Sbrisolona

"So tasty!"
Serving: Makes one 10-inch cookie

Ingredients

- 1 3/4 sticks (14 tbsps.) unsalted butter, room temperature, plus more for the pan
- 1 3/4 cups all-purpose flour
- 1 1/2 cups (about 5 oz.) blanched almonds, finely ground
- 3/4 cups sugar
- 1/4 tsp. salt
- 1 1/2 tsps. pure vanilla extract

Direction

- Preheat an oven to 350°F. Butter the 10-in. springform pan; put aside. Whisk vanilla, salt, sugar, flour and ground almonds in a big bowl; use a pastry blender to cut in butter till there's no dry crumbs and are fully incorporated. Squeeze mixture to make pea-size to 1-in. clumps.
- Press 3/4 mixture gently in prepped pan; evenly sprinkle leftover crumbs. Bake for 25 minutes till cookie starts to be golden. Lower oven temperature to 300°F; bake for 10 minutes till fairly dry and golden brown. Put pan onto wire rack; fully cool. Remove pan sides to unmold; cookies keep, wrapped in

aluminum foil well, for 3 days at room temperature.

Nutrition Information

- Calories: 3656
- Total Carbohydrate: 344 g
- Cholesterol: 427 mg
- Total Fat: 238 g
- Fiber: 20 g
- Protein: 55 g
- Sodium: 637 mg
- Saturated Fat: 108 g

333. Tozzetti

"A yummy cookie recipe."
Serving: Makes 28

Ingredients

- 1 tbsp. baking powder
- 1/4 tsp. kosher salt
- 1 3/4 cups all-purpose flour plus more for work surface
- 3/4 cup sugar
- 1/4 cup (1/2 stick) unsalted butter, room temperature
- 2 large eggs
- 1 1/4 cups blanched almonds

Direction

- Preheat an oven to 325°. In medium bowl, whisk 1 3/4 cups flour, salt and baking powder; put aside. Beat butter and sugar with electric mixer at medium high for 2 minutes till creamy in medium bowl. One by one, add eggs, beating to blend between the additions, scraping bowl's sides occasionally, till combined. Put speed on low then add dry ingredients; mix to just blend. Fold in the almonds.
- Put dough on lightly floured work surface; knead 2 times to just bring together. Shape to 14-in. long, 1-in. thick and 2-in. wide log; put log onto parchment lined baking sheet.

- Bake for 25-30 minutes till starting to brown, cracked in spots and puffed. Put baking sheet onto wire rack; cool log.
- Diagonally slice log to 1/2-in. thick with serrated knife; put slices on same sheet and bake for 15-20 minutes till golden brown. Flip; bake for 5-10 minutes till other side gets golden brown. Put baking sheet on wire rack; cool.
- You can make tozzetti 1 week ahead; keep airtight in room temperature.

Nutrition Information

- Calories: 107
- Total Carbohydrate: 13 g
- Cholesterol: 18 mg
- Total Fat: 5 g
- Fiber: 1 g
- Protein: 3 g
- Sodium: 60 mg
- Saturated Fat: 1 g

334. Tropical Fruit Smoothie

"A tropical fruit smoothie."
Serving: 2 | Prep: 5m | Ready in: 5m

Ingredients

- 1 mango, peeled and seeded
- 1 papaya, peeled and seeded
- 1/2 cup fresh strawberries
- 1/3 cup orange juice
- 5 cubes ice

Direction

- In an electric blender, put ice cubes, orange juice, strawberries, papaya and mango. Blend till the mixture is smooth.

Nutrition Information

- Calories: 129 calories;
- Total Carbohydrate: 32.5 g
- Cholesterol: 0 mg

- Total Fat: 0.6 g
- Protein: 1.5 g
- Sodium: 7 mg

335. Truffle-scented Roast Turkey With Shallots And Chestnuts

"1 day before roasting, prep truffle butter then rub it on turkey."
Serving: Makes 12 servings

Ingredients

- 2 1-inch-diameter black truffles from jar*
- 6 tbsps. (3/4 stick) butter, room temperature
- 1 16-lb. turkey, neck reserved
- 8 large fresh thyme sprigs
- 4 large fresh parsley sprigs
- 6 bay leaves
- 12 large shallots (about 1 1/2 lbs.), peeled, cut in half
- 3 cups (or more) canned low-salt chicken broth
- 1/2 cup Cognac or brandy
- 3 tbsps. all purpose flour
- 3 7.4-oz. jars whole roasted peeled chestnuts*
- 2 tbsps. chopped fresh parsley

Direction

- Chop 1 1/2 truffles coarsely; put in processor. Add butter and process for 1 minute till truffles are finely chopped and well blended. Season truffle butter with pepper and salt. Slice leftover 1/2 truffle thinly. Cover; chill.
- Inside and out, rinse turkey; use paper towels to pat dry. Sprinkle pepper and salt in main cavity. Slide hand between breast meat and skin to loosen skin carefully, starting at neck end. Rub 1 tbsp. truffle butter at a time on breast meat under the skin then rub leftover truffle butter on your hands all over the outside of the turkey. Put turkey on small rack in big roasting pan. Tie 3 bay leaves, 2 parsley sprigs and 4 thyme sprigs together using kitchen string; repeat with leftover 3 bay leaves, 2 parsley sprigs and 4 thyme sprigs.

Put 1 herb bouquet in neck cavity then 1 in turkey's main cavity. To hold shape, loosely tie legs together. Use plastic wrap to cover turkey; chill overnight.

- Preheat an oven to 375°F. Tuck the turkey wings under. Around turkey in pan, put turkey neck and shallots. Sprinkle pepper and salt on neck, shallots and turkey. Roast for 1 hour 15 minutes till shallots and turkey are golden brown; mix shallots gently. Put 1 cup broth on turkey; roast for 30 minutes. Put 1 cup broth on turkey. Loosely cover turkey legs and breast with foil; roast, basting with pan drippings every 30 minutes then adding 1 dup extra broth in pan after 45 minutes, for 1 hour 15 minutes till inserted instant-read thermometer in thickest thigh part reads 175°F. Stand for 30 minutes; turkey's internal temperature will raise by 5-10°. Put shallots in bowl using slotted spoon; throw turkey neck.
- Into 4-cup measuring cup, put pan juices. Put fat from surface of pan juices off; keep 6 tbsp. fat. Throw leftover fat. To get 3 cups, add chicken broth to the pan juices. Put cognac in roasting pan; put on low heat. Boil, scraping browned bits up. Add into pan juices. Melt 2 tbsp. reserved turkey fat on medium low heat in big heavy saucepan. Add flour; mix for 1 minute. Whisk in pan juices slowly. Boil, whisking occasionally, for 5 minutes till sauce very slightly thickens; it'll be thin. Mix the reserved 1/2 sliced truffle into the gravy; season with pepper and salt. To keep warm, cover.
- Melt 4 tbsp. fat on medium high heat in big heavy skillet. Add chestnuts; sauté for 5 minutes till heated through. Add chopped parsley and roasted shallots; sauté for 4 minutes till heated through. Season with pepper and salt. Use chestnut-shallot mixture to surround turkey; serve with gravy.

Nutrition Information

- Calories: 848
- Total Carbohydrate: 36 g
- Cholesterol: 324 mg
- Total Fat: 31 g

- Fiber: 3 g
- Protein: 97 g
- Sodium: 508 mg
- Saturated Fat: 10 g

336. Tsatsiki

"A tasty recipe."
Serving: Makes about 1 cup | Prep: 10m

Ingredients

- 1/2 medium cucumber, peeled, seeded, and diced
- 1 garlic clove
- 2 tbsps. olive oil
- 1 cup plain yogurt (preferably goat's or sheep's milk)
- pita wedges or chips

Direction

- Toss 1/4 tsp. each pepper and salt with cucumber in a colander; drain for 15 minutes.
- Meanwhile, mince and mash 1/4 tsp. salt and garlic to paste; whisk with 1/4 tsp. pepper, yogurt and olive oil.
- Use your hands to squeeze out extra water from cucumbers; mix cucumbers into yogurt mixture then season with salt.

337. Tuna, White Bean, And Red Onion Salad

"A light tuna salad."
Serving: Makes 4 servings

Ingredients

- 4 cups cooked white beans (see Cannellini Beans with Garlic and Sage), drained, chilled
- 1 1/2 6-oz. cans tuna packed in olive oil, drained, broken into chunks
- 1 small red onion, very thinly sliced (about 1 1/2 cups)

- 1/4 cup extra-virgin olive oil

Direction

- In a big bowl, put onion, tuna and beans; drizzle oil. Gently toss to mix. Season with generous freshly ground black pepper amount then salt.

---

338. Tunisian Briks (brek)

"So tasty!"
Serving: Makes 8 servings

Ingredients

- 2 tbsps. unsalted butter
- 2 medium onions, peeled and finely chopped
- 2 5-oz. cans tuna, drained and flaked
- 1 tbsp. capers, drained, rinsed, mashed
- 3 tbsps. grated Parmesan cheese
- 3 tbsps. flat-leaf parsley, chopped
- Kosher salt and freshly ground black pepper
- 2 cups olive oil, for frying
- 8 (6-inch) prepared egg roll wrappers
- 1 egg white, lightly beaten with 1 tsp. of water
- 8 large eggs
- 1 lemon, cut into 8 wedges, for serving

Direction

- Filling: Melt butter in medium skillet on medium heat. Add onions; cook, occasionally mixing, for 10 minutes till tender. Put into medium mixing bowl; cool.
- Add parsley, cheese, capers and tuna to onions; season to taste with pepper and salt. Stir to mix; put aside.
- Assembly: Add around 1 1/2-in. oil, to reach up sides of pan, in high-sided, wide skillet on medium high heat; for frying, heat oil to 350°F.
- Spread egg roll wrappers out quickly on work surface; brush egg white on edges. Put rounded 2-3 tbsp. filling just off center on every wrapper. Press well into center of filling using a spoon. Break an egg on each filling portion, catching into well.

- Fold every egg roll over carefully to make a triangle, keeping egg inside the well. To seal closed, press edges together. Fold every rim over itself, around 1/2-in, to make a sturdier pocket; to seal, press.
- Slide briks into hot oil gently in batches; spoon hot oil on dough that isn't submerge. Fry, gently flipping as needed, for 3-4 minutes till briks are crispy and golden brown. Drain cooked brisk on cooling rack above sheet pan as others finish cooking then serve warm with lemon wedges.

Nutrition Information

- Calories: 448
- Total Carbohydrate: 22 g
- Cholesterol: 211 mg
- Total Fat: 32 g
- Fiber: 1 g
- Protein: 18 g
- Sodium: 419 mg
- Saturated Fat: 7 g

---

339. Turkey Meatballs With Sage And Cranberries

"A tasty turkey dish."
Serving: Makes 8 servings (about 56 one-inch mini-meatballs)

Ingredients

- 1/3 cup pine nuts
- 1 lb. ground lean turkey
- 1 large egg, beaten
- 1 cup fresh whole-wheat breadcrumbs, soaked in 1 oz. skim milk
- 1/2 cup finely chopped onion
- 1/3 cup packed Swiss chard, spinach or arugula, finely chopped
- 1/3 cup dried cranberries, chopped
- 2 tbsps. grated Parmesan
- 1 1/2 tbsps. finely chopped fresh sage
- 3/4 tsp. kosher or sea salt
- 1/4 tsp. ground marjoram

- 1/4 tsp. black pepper
- Parchment paper
- 1 tbsp. olive oil
- 10 oz. store-bought cranberry chutney (optional)

Direction

- Heat a small pan on medium heat then add pine nuts; mix for a few minutes till light brown and aromatic. Mix all ingredients in a bowl, from turkey through pepper; don't overmix. Cover; chill to keep help meatballs hold their shape while cooking for at least 2 1/2 hours. Heat an oven to 400°. Line parchment paper on a cookie sheet; brush oil on paper. Roll meat to 1-in. balls; put, 1/2-in. apart, on a baking sheet. Bake for 10-15 minutes till internal temperature is 165°, balls bounces back to touch and brown. Remove then rest. Serve warm and (optional) with chutney. You can make savory bites 48 hours ahead, keep in the fridge, covered; reheat for 15 minutes at 250°F.

340. Turkey Meatloaf With Mushrooms And Herbs

Serving: Makes 4 servings plus leftovers

Ingredients

- 2 tbsps. extra-virgin olive oil plus additional for brushing
- 2 cups 1/3-inch cubes crustless day-old pain rustique
- 1 cup low-salt chicken broth
- 8 oz. sliced button mushrooms
- 2 large eggs, lightly beaten
- 1/4 cup minced shallots
- 2 tbsps. chopped fresh Italian parsley
- 1 tbsp. chopped fresh thyme
- 2 tsps. coarse kosher salt
- 1/2 tsp. ground black pepper
- 1 lb. ground turkey (15% fat)
- 1 lb. ground turkey breast

Direction

- Preheat an oven to 350°F. Brush olive oil on 8 1/2x4 1/2x2 1/3-in. loaf pan.
- Toss broth and bread in big bowl; stand for 10 minutes till bread softens and absorbs broth. Mix in 2 tbsp. oil, pepper, coarse salt, thyme, parsley, shallots, eggs and mushrooms.
- Add turkey; mix till just blended. Put in pan, mounding in middle; bake for 1 hour 25 minutes till an inserted thermometer in middle reads 170°F. Before serving, rest for 15 minutes.

341. Turkischer

"A great coffee recipe."
Serving: Serves 6.

Ingredients

- 4 oz. dark- or Vienna-roast coffee beans
- 6 tbsps. sugar

Direction

- Grind coffee beans till fine like flour in a coffee grinder. Boil 2 cups water, sugar and 4 tbsp. ground coffee in a small heavy saucepan/copper Turkey coffee pot on high heat. Take off heat; mix well. Put pot on heat; boil again. Take off heat; let grounds settle. Repeat boiling and settling process twice more. Cover pot; stand for 2 minutes. Add 1/3 cup of cold water; let coffee settle for a minute. Into demitasse cups, put coffee.

Nutrition Information

- Calories: 147
- Total Carbohydrate: 38 g
- Total Fat: 0 g
- Protein: 0 g
- Sodium: 2 mg
- Saturated Fat: 0 g

342. Tuscan Salmon With Rosemary Orzo

"Healthy and tasty."
Serving: Makes 4 servings

Ingredients

- 6 oz. orzo
- 2 tsp. olive oil
- 1 1/2 cups chopped onion, divided
- 1 tbsp. chopped fresh rosemary
- 4 salmon fillets (5 oz. each), skin on
- 1/4 cup plus 1 tbsp. chopped fresh basil
- 1/4 tsp. salt
- 1/8 tsp. black pepper
- 2 cloves garlic, chopped
- 1 pint grape tomatoes, halved
- 1/4 cup pitted kalamata olives, sliced
- 2 tbsps. chopped fresh parsley

Direction

- Follow package to cook orzo till al dente. Heat oil on medium heat in a big nonstick skillet. Cook rosemary and 1/2 cup onion for 9 minutes till onion softens. Mix orzo in bowl. Season salmon using pepper, salt and 1 tbsp. basil. Heat same skillet on medium high heat then cook salmon, flesh side down, for 5 minutes per side till golden. Put aside. Add leftover 1 cup onion and garlic; cook for 2 minutes till soft. Add olives and tomatoes; cook for 3 minutes till tomatoes break up. Take off heat; mix in leftover 1/4 cup basil and parsley. Season with pepper and salt. Serve fish on orzo; put tomato mixture on top.

343. Twice-baked Goat Cheese Souffles

"A fun soufflé recipe."
Serving: Makes 8

Ingredients

- 1 3/4 cups whole milk
- 3/4 cup coarsely chopped onion
- 2 whole cloves
- 1/8 tsp. ground nutmeg
- 6 tbsps. (3/4 stick) butter
- 9 tbsps. all purpose flour
- 1/4 tsp. dry mustard
- 2 cups crumbled soft fresh goat cheese (such as Montrachet; about 9 oz.)
- 6 large egg yolks
- 1 1/4 tsps. salt
- 3/4 tsp. ground black pepper
- 8 large egg whites
- 1 cup whipping cream

Direction

- Boil nutmeg, cloves, onion and milk in medium heavy saucepan on medium heat; take off heat. Cover; stand for 30 minutes. Strain.
- Preheat an oven to 350°F. Butter 8 1 1/4-cup soufflé dishes. In big heavy saucepan, melt 6 tbsp. butter on medium heat. Add dry mustard and flour; whisk for 2 minutes; whisk in strained milk slowly. Boil, constantly whisking, for 2 minutes till smooth and very thick. Put soufflé base into big bowl. Add 1 1/2 cups of cheese slowly, whisking till smooth and melted. Add pepper, 1 tsp. salt and yolks; whisk till smooth. Cool it to lukewarm.
- Beat leftover 1/4 tsp. salt and egg whites till stiff yet not dry in another big bowl; fold beaten whites gently in 3 additions into cheese mixture.
- Evenly divide batter to prepped soufflé dishes; put dishes in 17x12-in. heavy roasting pan. To

reach halfway up dish's sides, put hot water into pan; bake for 20 minutes till soufflés just firm to touch on the top and are puffed. Put pan onto rack; cool soufflés fully in water. You can prep it 2 hours ahead; stand in room temperature.

- Preheat an oven to 425°F. Butter big heavy baking sheet. To loosen, cut around soufflé's sides using small knife. Invert every soufflé onto spatula; slide soufflés, evenly spacing, onto prepped sheet. Sprinkle 1/2 cup cheese; bake for 10 minutes till soufflés are puffed.
- Meanwhile, boil cream in small heavy saucepan; take off heat. Season with pepper and salt.
- Put soufflés onto plates using spatula; put seasoned cream around soufflés. Serve hot.

Nutrition Information

- Calories: 412
- Total Carbohydrate: 12 g
- Cholesterol: 220 mg
- Total Fat: 33 g
- Fiber: 1 g
- Protein: 17 g
- Sodium: 486 mg
- Saturated Fat: 20 g

344. Two-bean Turkey Chili

"Perfect for family gatherings, this flavorful chili just has a dash of heat in it. Serve with whole-grain rolls, sprinkled grated carrots and tossed green salad on the side."
Serving: Serves 10

Ingredients

- 4 cups cooked pinto beans (see tips)
- 1 tbsp oil
- 2 onions, finely chopped
- 2 stalks celery, thinly sliced
- 6 cloves garlic, minced
- 1 tbsp ground cumin (see tips)
- 2 tsp dried oregano
- 1/2 tsp cracked black peppercorns
- Zest of 1 lime
- 2 tbsp fine cornmeal
- 1 cup chicken or turkey broth
- 1 can (28 oz/796 mL) tomatoes with juice, coarsely chopped
- 2 lbs skinless boneless turkey breast, cut into 1/2-inch (1 cm) cubes (see tips)
- 2 cups frozen sliced green beans
- 1 tbsp New Mexico or ancho chile powder, dissolved in 2 tbsp (30 mL) lime juice
- 1 green bell pepper, diced
- 1 red bell pepper, diced
- 1 can (4 1/2 oz or 127 mL) diced mild green chiles
- 1 jalapeño pepper or chipotle pepper in adobo sauce, diced, optional
- Medium to large (3 1/2 to 6 quart) slow cooker

Direction

- Set a pan over medium heat and pour in oil. Toss in celery and onions and sauté for 5 minutes, stirring often, until celery is tender. Add garlic and stir-fry for another 1 minute. Mix in peppercorns, oregano, cumin and lime zest and cook for 1 minute while stirring frequently. Add cornmeal and blend well to coat then pour in broth and continue to cook while stirring until mixture starts to boil, about 1 minute. Mix in tomatoes, with its juice, and cook until it boils again. You can prepare all this step beforehand and refrigerate, covered, for up to 2 days. Continue with the rest of the steps when you're ready to cook.
- Transfer mixture to a stoneware slow cooker. Add the pinto beans, green beans and turkey and, keeping the pot covered, cook over low heat for 6 hours then or on high heat for 3 hours, until mixture is bubbling and turkey has become soft. Toss in green and red bell peppers, mild green chiles, jalapeno peppers (optional), and chile powder solution. Put the pot cover and cook on high heat until bell peppers are soft, about 30 minutes.
- If you're just cooking half of this recipe, just use a small slow cooker, about 2 to 3 1/2 quart in size.

- To intensify the cumin seeds' flavor, toast and stir the seeds in a dry pan over medium heat for about 3 minutes or until fragrant. Transfer toasted seeds to a spice grinder or mortar and crush.
- To make this chili, you'll require about 3 cups or 750 mL of cubed turkey breast (use leftover turkey if on hand). Use 3 cups or 750 mL of shredded cooked turkey with bell peppers added along.
- If you'd like the chili to be spicy, add the jalapeño pepper and if you prefer the sauce to have a smoky flavor, add chipotle in the adobo sauce.
- For this much of beans, use 2 cans (14 to 19 oz or 398 to 540 mL) pinto beans or cook 2 cups, equivalent to 500 mL, dried beans. Drain water from the beans and rinse.

Nutrition Information

- Calories: 485
- Total Carbohydrate: 61 g
- Cholesterol: 60 mg
- Total Fat: 10 g
- Fiber: 16 g
- Protein: 39 g
- Sodium: 223 mg
- Saturated Fat: 2 g

345. Upside-down Blood Orange–polenta Cake

"Use 4 navel oranges for blood oranges; depending on size, slice to 5-6 rounds."
Serving: 8 servings

Ingredients

- Nonstick vegetable oil spray
- 3/4 cup (packed) light brown sugar
- 3/4 cup (1 1/2 sticks) unsalted butter, room temperature, divided
- 6 blood oranges, peel and white pith removed, each sliced into 4 rounds, seeds removed
- 1 1/2 cups all-purpose flour
- 3 tbsps. polenta (not quick-cooking)
- 1 1/2 tsps. kosher salt
- 1 1/2 tsps. baking powder
- 1/2 tsp. baking soda
- 1 cup granulated sugar
- 1 vanilla bean, split lengthwise
- 4 large eggs, room temperature
- 3/4 cup buttermilk, room temperature
- Lemon omani (dried black limes), green cardamom pods, and softly whipped cream (for serving; optional)
- A 9" springform pan

Direction

- Preheat an oven to 350°F. Use nonstick spray to coat pan; put onto foil-lined rimmed baking sheet. In small saucepan, cook 2 tbsp. water, 1/4 cup butter and brown sugar on medium heat, mixing, till it is smooth and sugar dissolves. Boil; cook without mixing till slightly thick for 2 minutes. Put caramel in prepped pan; rest for 5 minutes till set.
- Put orange slices in 1 layer on caramel in concentric circles; begin with bigger slices around outside then smaller ones as you move towards center. Cut leftover citrus up to fill in gaps.
- In a medium bowl, whisk baking soda, baking powder, salt, polenta and flour. In a big bowl, put leftover 1/2 cup butter and granulated sugar. Scrape in vanilla seeds; for another use, save pod. Beat for 4 minutes till fluffy and light with electric mixer at high speed. One by one, add eggs; beat between additions to blend; beat for 3 minutes till it is very fluffy.
- Put mixer speed on low. Alternating with buttermilk with 2 additions, add dry ingredients in 3 batches, starting then finishing with dry ingredients; mix till batter is just smooth. Scrape batter in prepped pan; don't disturb orange slices. Use an offset spatula to smooth surface.
- Bake cake for 50-65 minutes till an inserted tester in middle exits clean and golden brown. Put pan on wire rack; cool cake for 10 minutes. To loosen, run knife around cake's edges;

unmold. Invert the cake onto rack; remove bottom of pan carefully. Fully cool.

- Grate cardamom pods and lemon omani finely on cake; if desired, and whipped cream. Serve whipped cream alongside cake.

Nutrition Information

- Calories: 549
- Total Carbohydrate: 79 g
- Cholesterol: 140 mg
- Total Fat: 24 g
- Fiber: 3 g
- Protein: 8 g
- Sodium: 570 mg
- Saturated Fat: 12 g

346. Vanilla-maple French Toast With Warm Berry Preserves

Serving: Makes 6 servings

Ingredients

- 9 eggs
- 2 1/4 cups whole or reduced-fat (2%) milk
- 1/3 cup maple syrup
- 1/4 cup sugar
- 1 1/2 tsps. vanilla
- 3/4 tsp. salt
- 12 3/4-inch-thick slices French bread
- 1/4 cup (1/2 stick) butter, melted
- Warm maple syrup
- Warm Berry Preserves

Direction

- In medium bowl, beat the eggs to mix. Slowly beat in milk. Put in salt, vanilla, sugar and 1/3 cup maple syrup; beat to incorporate. Distribute custard among 2 glass baking dishes, 13x9x2-inch in size. In dishes, set the bread in 1 layer. Allow to submerge for 10 minutes. Flip over, put cover, and chill overnight.

- Over moderate heat, heat big griddle or heavy big skillet. In batches, grease the griddle with some butter. Put in submerged bread; allow to cook for 4 minutes till brown on bottom. Flip the French toast over; let cook for 4 minutes till bottoms are brown. Put to plates. Serve along with Warm Berry Preserves and more syrup.

347. Walnut And Almond Cake With Orange Syrup

"Delicious and fun!"
Serving: Makes 18 servings

Ingredients

- 2 2/3 cups sugar
- 1 cup water
- 1 1/2 tbsps. grated orange peel
- 3 cups walnuts (about 12 oz.)
- 3 cups almonds (about 12 oz.)
- 16zwieback rusks, broken coarsely, or 1 cup ground graham crackers
- 3/4 tsp. ground cinnamon
- 12 large eggs, separated
- 1/2 tsp. vanilla extract
- 1/2 tsp. salt

Direction

- Preheat an oven to 350°F. Butter then flour 13x9x2-in. metal baking pan. Boil 1/2 tbsp. orange peel, 1 cup water and 1 cup sugar in small heavy saucepan, mixing often; boil for 2 minute. Refrigerate, uncovered, syrup.
- Finely grind 1/3 cup sugar, cinnamon, zwieback and all nuts in processor. Beat leftover 1 tbsp. orange peel, 1/3 cup sugar, vanilla and egg yolks using electric mixer for 4 minutes till very thick in big bowl. Beat salt and white using clean beaters to soft peaks in another big bowl. Add 1 cup sugar slowly; beat till stiff yet not dry. Fold whites into the yolk mixture; fold in nut mixture. Put batter in prepped pan.

- Bake cake for 50 minutes till inserted tester in middle exits clean. Put cool syrup on hot cake; fully cool. Cover; stand for 1 day. Cut to diamonds/squares.

Nutrition Information

- Calories: 450
- Total Carbohydrate: 46 g
- Cholesterol: 124 mg
- Total Fat: 26 g
- Fiber: 4 g
- Protein: 12 g
- Sodium: 170 mg
- Saturated Fat: 3 g

348. Warm Chicken Sandwiches With Mushrooms, Spinach And Cheese

"You can chill the sandwiches 1 day ahead (refrigerate spinach and chicken before assembling)."
Serving: Makes 4 servings

Ingredients

- 4 ciabatta rolls, halved horizontally
- 3 tbsps. extra-virgin olive oil, divided, plus more for drizzling
- Whole grain mustard
- 8 oz. Fontina cheese, shredded, divided
- 12 oz. sliced white mushrooms
- 2 tbsps. chopped shallots
- 3 garlic cloves, pressed
- 2 cups shredded roast chicken
- 1 5-oz. bag baby spinach

Direction

- To prepare: Preheat an oven to 400°F. Pull some bread from ciabatta rolls to form slightly hollow centers. Sprinkle olive oil onto ciabatta rolls. Smear whole grain mustard onto the roll bottoms. Drizzle half of Fontina cheese onto roll bottoms.

- Over medium-high heat, heat two tbsps. of oil in a large skillet, add mushrooms and then sauté for 4 minutes. Add pressed garlic and chopped shallots and then sauté for three minutes. Put in chicken and sauté for two minutes until heated through. Place onto a plate. Put one tbsp. of oil into the skillet. Put in spinach and then sauté for two minutes. Season with pepper and salt to taste. Then drain. Ladle the chicken mixture, then the spinach atop the roll bottoms. Add the remaining cheese on top. Place roll tops to cover. Tightly encase each sandwich with foil. Bake the sandwiches for about 20 minutes until the cheese melts.

Nutrition Information

- Calories: 823
- Total Carbohydrate: 63 g
- Cholesterol: 118 mg
- Total Fat: 39 g
- Fiber: 7 g
- Protein: 41 g
- Sodium: 1135 mg
- Saturated Fat: 15 g

349. Warm Onion-potato Gratin

"You can make this 8 hours ahead."
Serving: 4 servings

Ingredients

- 1 cup (packed) grated Gruy&ère cheese (about 4 oz.)
- 8 tbsps. (packed) freshly grated Parmesan cheese (about 2 oz.)
- 2/3 cup whipping cream
- 1 1/2 lbs. Yukon Gold potatoes, peeled, cut into 1/4-inch-thick slices
- 3/4 lb. onions, thinly sliced

Direction

- Cover sliced onions and Yukon Gold potatoes with enough water in a big heavy saucepan;

boil water. Lower heat. Simmer for 3 minutes till potatoes are nearly tender. Drain onion-potato mixture well.

- Put 1/2 onion-potato mixture in 11x7-in. glass baking dish; sprinkle pepper and salt. Sprinkle 1/3 cup Gruyere cheese on it then 2 tbsp. parmesan cheese; put leftover onion-potato mixture on cheeses. Top with cream; sprinkle pepper, salt then leftover 6 tbsp. parmesan cheese and 2/3 cup gruyere cheese. You can prep 8 hours ahead. Cover; refrigerate. Preheat an oven to 400°F; bake gratin for 25 minutes, uncovered, till cream thickens. Remove from oven and preheat broiler; broil gratin for 2 minutes till top is golden.

Nutrition Information

- Calories: 452
- Total Carbohydrate: 40 g
- Cholesterol: 83 mg
- Total Fat: 26 g
- Fiber: 5 g
- Protein: 17 g
- Sodium: 405 mg
- Saturated Fat: 16 g

350. Watermelon Gazpacho

"It's a great way to begin your hot-weather meal."
Serving: 6

Ingredients

- 2 cups 1/4-inch-diced watermelon
- 2 cups orange juice
- 2 tbsps. extra-virgin olive oil
- 1 seedless cucumber, cut into 1/4-inch dice
- 1 small yellow bell pepper, seeded and cut into 1/4-inch dice
- 1 small onion, cut into 1/4-inch dice
- 2 medium garlic cloves, minced
- 1 small jalapeno pepper, seeded and minced (optional)
- 3 tbsps. fresh lime juice
- 2 tbsps. chopped fresh parsley, basil or cilantro

- Salt and freshly ground black pepper

Direction

- In a food processor or blender, process together oil, orange juice and 1/2 cup of watermelon until pureed. Remove to a moderate-size bowl together with leftover ingredients. Use pepper and salt to season to taste, then chill until serving. You can make a few hours ahead of the serving time.

Nutrition Information

- Calories: 110 calories;
- Total Carbohydrate: 16.4 g
- Cholesterol: 0 mg
- Total Fat: 4.8 g
- Protein: 1.8 g
- Sodium: 3 mg

351. Watermelon Gazpacho With Feta Crema

"An incredibly juicy watermelon to taste."
Serving: 6 servings

Ingredients

- 1 lb. seedless watermelon, rind removed, coarsely chopped (about 3 cups)
- 1 large beefsteak tomato, coarsely chopped
- 1 English hothouse cucumber, peeled, coarsely chopped
- 1 jalapeño, seeds removed, sliced
- 2 tbsps. olive oil
- 2 tbsps. Sherry vinegar or red wine vinegar
- Kosher salt, freshly ground pepper
- 1/4 cup almonds
- 2 oz. feta, preferably French sheep's milk, crumbled (about 1/2 cup)
- 1/4 cup sour cream
- 3 tbsps. whole milk
- 3/4 lb. seedless watermelon, rind removed, cut into 1/2" pieces (about 2 cups)

- 1/2 English hothouse cucumber, peeled, cut into 1/2" pieces
- Olive oil (for serving)
- Flaky sea salt (such as Maldon)
- Freshly ground black pepper

Direction

- To prepare gazpacho: In a blender, purée vinegar, oil, jalapeño, cucumber, tomato, and watermelon until they are smooth.
- Place the gazpacho into a large bowl; flavor with pepper and kosher salt. Before serving, put a cover and let chill for no less than an hour.
- You can make Gazpacho a day in advance. Keep it chilled.
- For crema and assembly: Set an oven to 350 degrees and start preheating. On a rimmed baking sheet, toast the almonds and toss from time to time for 8-10 minutes until golden brown. You can apply this step alternatively in a dry small skillet on medium heat. Allow the almonds to cool, then chop them coarsely.
- In a small bowl, mash the feta into sour cream until smooth mostly, then beat in milk.
- Distribute cucumber and watermelon between bowls, then pour over with gazpacho. Add almonds and crema on top, sprinkle with oil, then flavor with pepper and sea salt.
- You can prepare crema a day in advance. Put a cover and let chill.

Nutrition Information

- Calories: 179
- Total Carbohydrate: 18 g
- Cholesterol: 11 mg
- Total Fat: 11 g
- Fiber: 2 g
- Protein: 5 g
- Sodium: 676 mg
- Saturated Fat: 3 g

352. Watermelon Popsicles

"You can find popsicle molds at some department stores and drugstores."
Serving: Makes about 8 1/4-cup popsicles

Ingredients

- 2 1/2 cups seeded diced watermelon
- 1/2 cup fresh raspberries or frozen unsweetened, thawed
- 6 tbsps. sugar
- 1 tbsp. plus 2 tsps. fresh lemon juice
- 1 tbsp. crème de cassis (black currant-flavored liqueur) or light corn syrup

Direction

- In a blender, mix all the ingredients; then purée until they are smooth. Filter into a 2-cup glass measuring cup, forcing on solids to release as much liquid from the solids as you can. Distribute purée among Popsicle molds evenly. Freeze purée overnight. You can prepare a week in advance. Keep them frozen.

Nutrition Information

- Calories: 61
- Total Carbohydrate: 15 g
- Total Fat: 0 g
- Fiber: 1 g
- Protein: 0 g
- Sodium: 1 mg
- Saturated Fat: 0 g

353. Whisky Caramel Sauce

"This whiskey caramel sauce is really a tasty embellishment for our favorite Bomboloni, fruit or ice cream."
Serving: Makes about 1 cup | Prep: 5m

Ingredients

- 1 cup granulated sugar
- 1/3 cup Scotch whisky
- 3 tbsps. unsalted butter, softened

- Pinch of salt

Direction

- In a dry 2-quart heavy saucepan, cook sugar on medium heat, undisturbed until it starts to melt.
- Keep on cooking while using a fork to stir sometimes, until sugar is melted into a deep golden caramel.
- Take away from heat and gently add in salt, butter and Scotch (caramel will harden and steam vigorously). Cook on medium low heat while stirring, until caramel is dissolved.
- Let the sauce cool to warm. Sauce can be prepared 3 days ahead while covered and chilled.

Nutrition Information

- Calories: 625
- Total Carbohydrate: 100 g
- Cholesterol: 46 mg
- Total Fat: 17 g
- Protein: 0 g
- Sodium: 149 mg
- Saturated Fat: 11 g

354. White Balsamic Custard Tart With Fresh Berry Topping

Serving: Makes 8 servings

Ingredients

- 1 1/4 cups all purpose flour
- 3 tbsps. sugar
- 1/4 tsp. salt
- 1/2 cup (1 stick) chilled unsalted butter, cut into 1/2-inch cubes
- 1 large egg yolk
- 1 tbsp. whipping cream
- 1/2 cup whipping cream
- 2 tbsps. cornstarch
- 2 large eggs
- 4 large egg yolks
- 1 tsp. vanilla extract
- 1/2 cup white balsamic vinegar
- 3/4 cup water
- 3/4 cup sugar
- 1/4 cup (1/2 stick) unsalted butter
- 2 large strawberries, hulled, sliced
- 2 1/2-pint containers blueberries
- 1 1/2-pint container raspberries

Direction

- Crust: blend salt, sugar and flour for 5 seconds in processor. Add butter; blend with on/off turns till you make coarse meal. Add cream and egg yolk; blend till moist clumps form with on/off turns. Bring dough to ball. Evenly press dough in 9-in. diameter tart pan that has removable bottom; use fork to pierce dough all over. Chill for 1 hour.
- Preheat an oven to 375°F. Bake the crust for 22 minutes till golden; if crust bubbles, press with back of fork. Cool.
- Filling: Mix cornstarch and cream till cornstarch dissolves in medium bowl. Add vanilla, egg yolks and eggs; whisk to blend.
- In medium heavy saucepan, boil vinegar for 3 minutes till reduced to 1/4 cup. Add butter, sugar and 3/4 cup water; mix till butter melts. Boil. Whisk vinegar mixture slowly into egg mixture; put into pan. Whisk for 1 minute till custard boils and thickens. Strain into bowl then cool. Spread custard in prepped crust. Cover; chill tart for 3 hours – 1 day.
- Topping: Put strawberry slices in middle of tart in star pattern; put raspberries in star pattern then surround with blueberries. Loosely cover; chill till serving. You can make it 6 hours ahead.

Nutrition Information

- Calories: 523
- Total Carbohydrate: 65 g
- Cholesterol: 226 mg
- Total Fat: 27 g
- Fiber: 7 g
- Protein: 7 g
- Sodium: 111 mg

- Saturated Fat: 16 g

355. White Beans With Anchovies

"Simple and tasty."
Serving: Makes 6 to 8 servings

Ingredients

- 1 lb. dried Great Northern beans
- 7 cups water
- 2 small bay leaves
- 1/2 tsp. salt
- 1/2 tsp. ground black pepper
- 1/4 cup extra-virgin olive oil
- 1/4 cup Sherry wine vinegar
- 1 2-oz. can anchovy fillets, drained, cut into 1/2-inch pieces
- 2 tbsps. chopped fresh parsley

Direction

- Cover dried great northern beans by 3-in. cold water in a big pot; boil for 2 minutes. Take off heat. Cover beans; stand for 1 hour. Drain. Put beans in same pot. Add bay leaves and 7 cups water; boil. Lower heat to medium low and simmer for 30 minutes. Put pepper and salt in beans; simmer for 30 minutes till beans are tender. Drain well. Put beans into big bowl.
- In small bowl, whisk sherry wine vinegar and olive oil. Add chopped fresh parsley, anchovy fillets and vinaigrette to warm beans; gently toss to blend. Season with pepper and salt. Put on plates; serve at room temperature/warm.

Nutrition Information

- Calories: 189
- Total Carbohydrate: 16 g
- Cholesterol: 8 mg
- Total Fat: 10 g
- Fiber: 4 g
- Protein: 8 g
- Sodium: 832 mg
- Saturated Fat: 2 g

356. White Chocolate Cheesecake With Cinnamon And Lemon

"Bake this 1 day before serving."
Serving: Makes 8-10 servings

Ingredients

- 1 cup whole almonds, toasted
- 3/4 cup ground crisp lemon-flavored cookies (about 2 1/2 oz.)
- 3 tbsps. sugar
- 1 tsp. grated lemon peel
- 1/4 cup (1/2 stick) unsalted butter, melted
- 3 oz. good-quality white chocolate (such as Lindt or Baker's), chopped
- 2 8-oz. packages cream cheese, room temperature
- 1 1/4 cups sugar
- 1 cup sour cream, room temperature
- 1/4 cup fresh lemon juice
- 2 tsps. finely grated lemon peel
- 2 tsps. vanilla extract
- 1 1/2 tsps. ground cinnamon
- 5 large eggs
- 4 oz. good-quality white chocolate (such as Lindt or Baker's), chopped
- 1/4 cup whipping cream
- 2 tsps. (packed) grated lemon peel
- 1/3 cup sliced almonds, toasted
- White chocolate curls

Direction

- Crust: Put rack in middle of oven; preheat it to 325°F. Use 2 foil layers to wrap outside of 9-in. diameter springform pan that has 2 3/4-in. high sides. Grind lemon peel, sugar, cookies and 1/2 cup almonds finely in processor. Add 1/2 cup almonds and butter; process till moist clumps form and nuts are chopped. Press it on bottom of pan, not sides; bake for 20 minutes till crust is golden. Cook. Maintain the oven temperature.

- Filling: Mix white chocolate till chocolate melts on top of double boiler above simmering water; cool, occasionally mixing, to lukewarm.
- Beat sugar and cream cheese using electric mixer till smooth in big bowl; beat in juice and sour cream slowly then cinnamon, vanilla, peel and melted chocolate. One by one, beat in eggs.
- Put filling in crust; bake for 1 hour 15 minutes till center is just set and cheesecake edges crack and puff. Remove from oven. Around cake's sides to loosen, run small knife; remove foil. Chill overnight, uncovered.
- Topping: Mix cream and white chocolate on top of double boiler above simmering water till chocolate melts then whisk in the grated lemon peel. Cool it to room temperature.
- From cake, release pan sides; put cake on platter. Put topping on middle of cake; evenly spread. Leave 1/2-in. border around cake's edge. Use white chocolate curls and sliced almonds to garnish; chill till topping is cold. You can make it 1 day ahead, kept chilled, covered.

Nutrition Information

- Calories: 815
- Total Carbohydrate: 65 g
- Cholesterol: 229 mg
- Total Fat: 57 g
- Fiber: 3 g
- Protein: 15 g
- Sodium: 322 mg
- Saturated Fat: 27 g

357. Whole Wheat Cinnamon Sticky Buns

"Use milk and butter substitutes to make this vegan."
Serving: Makes 1 1/2 dozen

Ingredients

- 1/4 cup unsalted butter or nonhydrogenated butter substitute
- 1 cup amber agave nectar
- 2 tbsps. ground cinnamon
- 3 tbsps. sprouted whole wheat flour or whole wheat pastry flour
- 1 cup walnuts, lightly toasted and finely ground in a food processor
- 3/4 cup raisins, soaked in 1 cup boiling water for 10 minutes and drained well
- 1 large baking potato, peeled
- 1 tbsp. active dry yeast
- 1/2 cup warm water
- 1/4 cup plus 2 tbsps. light agave nectar
- 1/2 cup 1 percent low-fat milk or unsweetened soy milk
- 3 tbsps. unsalted butter or nonhydrogenated butter substitute, melted
- 1 tsp. sea salt
- 4 to 5 cups sprouted whole wheat flour or whole wheat pastry flour
- Extra melted butter or butter substitute, for brushing
- 2 tbsps. unsalted butter or nonhydrogenated butter substitute, at room temperature
- 2 1/2 tbsps. unsweetened apple juice
- 1/2 cup nonfat dry milk or unsweetened soy milk powder
- 1/2 cup light agave nectar
- 1/2 tsp. vanilla extract
- 1/8 tsp. almond extract

Direction

- Filling: Use an electric mixer to cream agave nectar and butter for 2 minutes till smooth in a big bowl. Add flour and cinnamon; mix well. Mix in raisins and walnuts; refrigerate for 2 hours to firm it.
- Dough: Cook potato in boiling water till soft for 25-30 minutes. Drain; reserve 3/4 cup starchy water. Mash reserved water and potato till smooth. Put aside; cool it to room temperature.
- Pulse 2 tbsp. agave nectar, warm water and yeast a few times to melt yeast in a food processor; sit till foamy for 10 minutes. Add salt, melted butter, leftover 1/4 cup agave nectar, milk and cooled mashed potato; pulse

to mix a few times. Little by little, add flour, pulsing to blend till soft dough forms. Put dough on lightly floured surface; knead by hand gently till elastic and smooth for 1 minute. Put kneaded dough in lightly oiled bowl; rest it for 20 minutes. Punch dough down; turn into bowl to coat in oil. Use plastic wrap to cover bowl; to rise, put in draft-free place. Rise dough for 1 hour till doubled in bulk.

- Prep glaze as dough rises: Blend all glaze ingredients for 1 minute till smooth in a food processor; refrigerate till needed. It'll slightly thicken when chilled.
- Sticky buns: Line parchment paper on 2 rectangular jellyroll pans; spray canola oil spray lightly. Punch dough down gently. Roll out to make 18x20-in. rectangle on lightly floured work surface; it'll be sticky. Spread filling mixture on dough; on all sides, leave 1-in. border. Roll up dough carefully from long side to make a long log. Cut log into 18 even pieces. Put slices on prepped pan with roll's edges touched together lightly. Before starting next, fill 1 pan entirely so most rolls snuggly fit together. Brush melted butter on tops; cover with damp kitchen cloth. Put in a draft-free warm area. Let rolls rise till doubled in size for 40-45 minutes.
- Preheat an oven to 375°F.
- Bake till lightly golden for 25 minutes when rolls rise fully; cool rolls for 10-15 minutes on pans. Drizzle glaze. Gently pull apart then serve warm.
- Keep leftover rolls refrigerated; before serving, reheat for 10 minutes in 350°F oven.

Nutrition Information

- Calories: 340
- Total Carbohydrate: 61 g
- Cholesterol: 22 mg
- Total Fat: 10 g
- Fiber: 6 g
- Protein: 7 g
- Sodium: 125 mg
- Saturated Fat: 5 g

358. Whole-egg Molasses Buttercream

"Halve the recipe to make cupcakes."
Serving: Makes 6 cups | Prep: 25m

Ingredients

- 6 large eggs, room temperature
- 1 1/2 cups sugar
- 1/2 tsp. salt
- 3 cups (6 sticks) unsalted butter, room temperature and very soft
- 1 tsp. vanilla extract
- 4 tbsps. plus 1 tsp. molasses

Direction

- Put 1 cup water to right below a simmer in a medium saucepan on medium low heat; mix salt, sugar and eggs in a stand mixer bowl using handheld whisk. Put bowl over saucepan without touching water; cook egg mixture till an instant-read thermometer reads 160°F, slightly thickened and lightened in color, constantly whisking. Take off heat; beat with stand mixer with whisk attachment at medium speed for 10 minutes till tripled in volume and fully cooled. 1-2 tbsp. at a time, add butter; beat well after each till incorporated fully. Add molasses and vanilla; beat till just combined on medium low speed.
- You can make and refrigerate buttercream up to 5 days ahead or freeze for up to 1 month. Using refrigerated buttercream; sit at room temperature for 2 hours minimum till soft; beat with stand mixer with paddle attachment till smooth at medium speed. 1 tsp. at a time, beat in a little amount of water if texture isn't smooth. Defrost: Put buttercream from freezer into fridge to thaw overnight. Follow instructions to use refrigerated buttercream.

Nutrition Information

- Calories: 306

- Total Carbohydrate: 17 g
- Cholesterol: 117 mg
- Total Fat: 26 g
- Protein: 2 g
- Sodium: 77 mg
- Saturated Fat: 16 g

359. World Peace Cookies

"Intense and rich."
Serving: Makes about 36 | Prep: 25m

Ingredients

- 1 1/4 cups all purpose flour
- 1/3 cup natural unsweetened cocoa powder
- 1/2 tsp. baking soda
- 11 tbsps. (1 stick plus 3 tbsps.) unsalted butter, room temperature
- 2/3 cup (packed) golden brown sugar
- 1/4 cup sugar
- 1 tsp. vanilla extract
- 1/4 tsp. fine sea salt
- 5 oz. extra-bittersweet chocolate (do not exceed 85% cacao), chopped (no pieces bigger than 1/3 inch)

Direction

- Into medium bowl, sift baking soda, cocoa and flour. Beat butter using electric mixer till smooth yet not fluffy in big bowl. Add sea salt, vanilla and both sugars; beat for 2 minutes till fluffy. Add flour mixture; beat till just blended (it might be crumbly). Add the chopped chocolate; mix to just distribute. Lightly knead in bowl to make ball if dough won't come together. Halve dough. On plastic wrap sheet, put each half. Shape each to 1 1/2-in. diameter log; in plastic, wrap each. Chill for 3 hours till firm. You can make it 3 days ahead, kept chilled.
- Preheat an oven to 325°F. Line parchment paper on 2 baking sheets. Crosswise cut logs to 1/2-in. thick rounds using thin sharp knife. Put on prepped sheets, 1-in. apart; bake 1 sheet at 1 time for 11-12 minutes till cookies look dry (won't be golden at edges or firm). Put on rack; cool. You can make it 1 day ahead; keep airtight in room temperature.

Nutrition Information

- Calories: 89
- Total Carbohydrate: 12 g
- Cholesterol: 9 mg
- Total Fat: 5 g
- Fiber: 1 g
- Protein: 1 g
- Sodium: 36 mg
- Saturated Fat: 3 g

360. Yellow Salad With Citrus-date Vinaigrette

"Simple and tasty."
Serving: Makes 3/4 cup vinaigrette

Ingredients

- 2 Medjool dates, pitted
- 1/4 cup olive oil
- 2 tbsps. fresh lemon juice
- 2 tbsps. fresh orange juice
- 1 tbsp. whole grain Dijon mustard
- 1/2 tsp. ground cumin
- Kosher salt, freshly ground pepper
- Mixed yellow and orange raw fruits and vegetables (such as corn, Sun Gold tomatoes, golden beets, apricots, clementines, and pineapple), halved, sliced, and/or cut into wedges

Direction

- Process cumin, mustard, orange juice, lemon juice, oil and dates till smooth in a food processor. Use water to thin vinaigrette to pourable consistency then season with pepper and salt.

- Serve: Put some vinaigrette into shallow bowl; put preferred veggies and fruits over. Season with pepper and salt.
- You can make vinaigrette 2 days ahead. Cover; chill.

361. Yukon Gold And Sweet Potato Gratin

Serving: Makes 12 servings

Ingredients

- 6 tbsps. (3/4 stick) butter, room temperature, divided
- 2 1/4 lbs. Yukon Gold potatoes, rinsed
- 1 1/2 lbs. red-skinned sweet potatoes (yams), peeled
- 2 cups whole milk
- 1 garlic clove, pressed
- 1 tbsp. kosher salt
- 2 tsps. fresh thyme leaves
- 1 tsp. ground black pepper
- 1/8 tsp. ground nutmeg
- 1 cup whipping cream

Direction

- Preheat an oven to 400°F. Use 2 tbsp. butter to coat 13x9x2-in. glass baking dish. Slice all potatoes thinly; put in prepped dish. Boil milk with next 5 ingredients in medium saucepan; put on potatoes. Use 2 tbsp. butter to dot; use foil to cover. Bake for 50 minutes till milk is nearly absorbed and potatoes are tender.
- Boil cream in saucepan. Uncover potatoes; put cream over. Use 2 tbsp. butter to dot; bake, uncovered, for 25 minutes till top gets golden brown in spots. Slightly cool.

Nutrition Information

- Calories: 249
- Total Carbohydrate: 29 g
- Cholesterol: 41 mg
- Total Fat: 13 g
- Fiber: 4 g

- Protein: 4 g
- Sodium: 488 mg
- Saturated Fat: 8 g

362. Yukon Gold Garlic Mash

"Reheat the potatoes for 1-2 minutes."
Serving: Makes 4 to 6 servings

Ingredients

- 2 lbs. small Yukon gold potatoes
- 1 1/4 to 1 1/2 cups milk
- 4 tbsps. unsalted butter, cut up
- 2 large cloves of garlic, grated
- Salt and black pepper, to taste
- 1 tbsp. finely snipped fresh chives

Direction

- Boil a pot of water.
- Wash potatoes; halve. Put into boiling water; cook for 25 minutes till very tender. Drain. Put into pot; shake for 10 seconds on low heat to dry out. Remove then discard skins when cool.
- Mash potatoes in bowl. Warm grated garlic, butter and milk in a small saucepan on low heat; mix into potatoes till smooth. Use pepper and salt to season; mix in chives. Immediately serve.

363. Zucchini Noodles With Anchovy Butter

Serving: Serves 6

Ingredients

- 4 tbsps. (1/2 stick) unsalted butter
- 6 oil-packed anchovy fillets
- 2-3 large zucchini, thinly sliced into noodle-like ribbons with a vegetable peeler or mandoline (about 6 cups)
- 1/2 cup grated Parmesan
- 1 tsp. crushed red pepper flakes

Direction

- Melt butter on medium heat in small saucepan. Add anchovies; cook, using wooden spoon to break up, for 5 minutes till melted.
- Put anchovy butter, red pepper flakes, parmesan and zucchini ribbons in a big serving bowl; immediately serve.

Nutrition Information

- Calories: 137
- Total Carbohydrate: 5 g
- Cholesterol: 30 mg
- Total Fat: 11 g
- Fiber: 1 g
- Protein: 6 g
- Sodium: 288 mg
- Saturated Fat: 7 g

364. Zucchini With Cilantro And Cream

"A delicious recipe."
Serving: Makes 4 servings

Ingredients

- 2 tbsps. (1/4 stick) butter
- 2 large garlic cloves, minced
- 1 3/4 lbs. zucchini, trimmed, cut into 1/3-inch-thick rounds
- 4 tbsps. chopped fresh cilantro
- 1/3 cup whipping cream

Direction

- Melt butter on medium heat in big heavy skillet. Add garlic; sauté for 10 seconds. Add 2 tbsp. cilantro and zucchini; sauté for 5 minutes till zucchini is crisp-tender. Add cream; simmer for 1 minute till juices slightly thicken. Season with pepper and salt; sprinkle 2 tbsp. cilantro.

Nutrition Information

- Calories: 147
- Total Carbohydrate: 8 g
- Cholesterol: 37 mg
- Total Fat: 13 g
- Fiber: 2 g
- Protein: 3 g
- Sodium: 25 mg
- Saturated Fat: 8 g

365. Zuni Roast Chicken With Bread Salad

"You need to salt the bread 24 hours ahead."
Serving: 2 to 4 servings

Ingredients

- One small chicken, 2 3/4 to 3 1/2 lbs.
- 4 tender sprigs fresh thyme, marjoram, rosemary, or sage, about 1/2 inch long
- Salt
- About 1/4 tsps. freshly cracked black pepper
- A little water
- Generous 8 oz. slightly stale open-crumbed, chewy, peasant-style bread (not sourdough)
- 6 to 8 tbsps. mild-tasting olive oil
- 1 1/2 tbsps. Champagne vinegar or white wine vinegar
- Salt and freshly cracked black pepper
- 1 tbsp. dried currants
- 1 tsp. red wine vinegar, or as needed
- 1 tbsp. warm water
- 2 tbsps. pine nuts
- 2 to 3 garlic cloves, slivered
- 1/4 cup slivered scallions (about 4 scallions), including a little of the green part
- 2 tbsps. lightly salted chicken stock or lightly salted water
- A few handfuls of arugula, frisée, or red mustard greens, carefully washed and dried

Direction

- Seasoning chicken: 1-3 days prior serving or 2 days ahead for 3 1/4-3 1/2-lb. chickens. Remove lump of fat inside chicken; discard. Rinse chicken; inside and out, pat very dry. Be sure to make sure it is very dry.
- Slide a finger under skin of every breast, creating 2 small pockets, approaching from end of cavity. Gently loosen a skin pocket on outside of thickest section of every thigh using tip of a finger. Shove herb sprig into all 4 pockets using a finger.
- Liberally season chicken all over with pepper and salt; per lb. of chicken, I use 3/4 tsp. sea salt. Season thick sections a bit more heavily than wings and skinny ankles. Sprinkle little salt on backbone and inside cavity; don't need to season inside. Twist then tuck wing tips behind shoulders. Loosely cover; refrigerate.
- A few hours ahead maximum, begin bread salad: Preheat broiler. Cut bread to a few big chunks. Carve off most of side and top crust and all bottom crust (reserve side and top crusts for croutons in soups or salads). Brush olive oil all over bread; very briefly broil to lightly color surface and crisp. Flip bread chunks; crisp other side. Trim badly charred tips off. Tear chunks to a mix of irregular 2-3-in. wads, fat crumbs and bite-sized bits to get 4 cups.
- Mix pepper and salt to taste, white wine vinegar/champagne and 1/4 cup olive oil. In wide salad bowl, toss torn bread with 1/4 cup tart vinaigrette; bread will be dressed unevenly. Taste a saturated piece; add little pepper and salt if bland then toss again. Moisten currants with warm water/red wine vinegar in a small bowl; put aside.
- Salad assembly and roast chicken: Preheat an oven to 475°F. You might need to adjust heat as low as 450°F or high as 500°F while roasting chicken to properly brown; it depending on accuracy, efficiency and size of oven. Start temperature the next time you roast chicken if so. If your oven has a convection function, use it for initial 30 minutes to enhance browning; reduce total cooking time by 5-10 minutes.
- Choose shallow flameproof roasting pan/dish barely bigger than chicken or get a 10-in. skillet with all-metal handle. Preheat pan on medium heat. Wipe chicken dry; put it into pan, breast side up. It should sizzle. Put in middle of oven; it should brown and sizzle within 20 minutes. Progressively raise temperature if it doesn't till it does. Skin should blister yet if fat smokes or chicken starts to chare, lower temperature by 25°. Flip bird after 30 minutes; drying bird and preheating pan should avoid skin from sticking. Roast it for 10-20 minutes, varies on size; flip back to recrisp breast skin for 5-10 minutes. It'll be 45-60 minutes in total for oven time.
- As chicken roasts, put pine nuts into small baking dish; put in hot oven to just warm through for 1-2 minutes. Add to bowl with bread.
- In a small skillet, put spoonful of olive oil; add scallions and garlic. Cook on medium low heat, constantly mixing, till soft. Don't let color. Scrape into bread; fold to mix. Drain plumped currants; fold in. Dribble lightly salted water/chicken stock on salad; fold. Taste a few bread pieces; a dryish one and fairly saturated one. Add few drops of vinegar, pepper and/or salt then toss well if bland. Pile bread salad into 1-qt. baking dish. Tent with foil; put aside salad bowl. After you flip chicken the last time, put salad in oven.
- Finish then serve bread salad and chicken: Remove chicken from oven; turn heat off. Leave bread salad for around 5 minutes to keep warming. Lift chicken from roasting pan; put onto plate. Pour clear fat off from roasting pan carefully; leave lean drippings behind. Put 1 tbsp. water into hot pan; swirl. Slash stretched skin between breasts and thighs of chicken; to drain juice into drippings, tilt bird and plate above roasting pan. Put chicken in warm spot like a stovetop; leave to rest while finishing bread salad. As meat cools, it gets more uniformly succulent and tender.

- Put platter in oven for 1-2 minutes to warm. Tilt roasting pan; skim last of fat. Put on medium low heat then add other juice collected under chicken; simmer. Mix and scrape to soften hard golden drippings. Taste; juices should be very flavorful.
- Tip bread salad into salad bowl; it'll be a mix of crispy pieces, crisp outside and moist inside pieces, moist pieces, soft pieces and steamy-hot pieces. Drizzle then toss with spoonful of pan juices. Add greens and drizzle of vinaigrette; fold well. Taste.
- Cut chicken to pieces; spread bread salad onto warm platter. Nestle chicken into salad.

Nutrition Information

- Calories: 1863
- Total Carbohydrate: 69 g
- Cholesterol: 362 mg
- Total Fat: 129 g
- Fiber: 5 g
- Protein: 105 g
- Sodium: 2231 mg
- Saturated Fat: 28 g

Index

Black pepper, 12–13, 16–17, 29–30, 32–33, 36, 38, 40, 44, 55, 59–60, 70–75, 86–88,

96–98, 108, 110, 113, 118, 128, 131–132, 135, 151, 154, 157, 159, 163–164, 170, 173–175,

181, 183, 185–188, 190, 192, 194, 197–198, 205–206, 209, 213–215, 220–221, 223, 227–228

Blackberry, 3, 15, 26, 78

Blood orange, 3, 8, 27, 217

Blueberry, 3–5, 25, 28–29, 81, 86, 116, 150, 222

Brandy, 51, 54, 67, 84–85, 105–106, 207, 211

Bread, 3–4, 6, 8, 13, 19–22, 24, 30–31, 43–44, 64–67, 72, 74, 87–88, 93, 108, 110, 119, 137,

142, 149–151, 167–168, 182, 187–188, 191, 214, 218–219, 228–230

Breadcrumbs, 19, 22–23, 30, 93, 108, 177, 213

Brioche, 64–65

Brisket, 4, 86–87

Broccoli, 3, 5, 33, 93

Broth, 6, 13, 23, 25, 31–32, 45–46, 66, 73, 75, 89, 98, 107, 117–118, 129, 134, 152, 154,

156–157, 168, 170, 180, 187, 189, 195, 202–203, 211–212, 214, 216

Brown rice, 167

Brown sugar, 3, 17–18, 20–21, 35, 48–49, 53, 58, 84–86, 96, 104, 123, 136–137,

143–144, 146, 157, 160–162, 173, 193, 196–197, 202, 205–206, 217, 226

Brussels sprouts, 3, 33, 36

Buckwheat, 3, 28

Buckwheat flour, 28

Buns, 8, 224–225

Burger, 7, 198

Butter, 3–4, 6–8, 12–21, 23, 25, 27–32, 34–35, 37–38, 40–41, 43–46, 50–53, 56–57, 59–69,

72–77, 79, 81–85, 89–93, 96, 98, 100, 102, 104–107, 109, 111–112, 114–126, 129–132, 134,

136–139, 142–144, 147, 149, 152–155, 157–162, 165–166, 168–173, 175, 177–183, 186–187,

192–193, 196–197, 199–200, 205–206, 210–211, 213, 215–218, 221–228

Buttermilk, 3, 5, 38, 45, 56, 86, 92, 103–104, 111, 116, 150, 199, 204, 217

Butternut squash, 3, 39, 62

C

Cabbage, 5, 7, 22–23, 103–104, 107, 175, 187–188

Cake, 4–6, 8, 15–16, 51, 54–55, 57, 60–61, 65, 68, 82–83, 85, 90, 92, 104–105, 112,

114–115, 121, 131, 147, 155, 157, 166, 184, 193, 217–219, 224

Calvados, 4, 51, 207

Cannellini beans, 73

Capers, 6–7, 164, 172, 213

Caramel, 3–4, 6–8, 14, 36–37, 49, 52–53, 61, 84–85, 154–155, 162, 185, 217, 221–222

Caraway seeds, 66, 183

Cardamom, 58, 195, 217–218

Carrot, 3, 6, 13, 22–23, 39, 43, 56, 66, 74, 86–87, 107, 110, 119, 124, 128–129, 131–132,

134, 136–137, 157, 164, 167–168, 202, 208, 216

Cashew, 4, 13, 53–54, 62

Cassava, 125

P

Conclusion

Thank you again for downloading this book!

I hope you enjoyed reading about my book!

If you enjoyed this book, please take the time to share your thoughts and post a review on Amazon. It'd be greatly appreciated!

Write me an honest review about the book – I truly value your opinion and thoughts and I will incorporate them into my next book, which is already underway.

Thank you!

If you have any questions, **feel free to contact at:** _mshealthy@mrandmscooking.com_

Ms. Healthy

www.MrandMsCooking.com

Printed in Great Britain
by Amazon

63272834R00140